THE SUN AND THE MOON

THE
SUN AND THE
MOON

*The Remarkable
True Account of Hoaxers,
Showmen, Dueling Journalists,
and Lunar Man-Bats
in Nineteenth-Century
New York*

MATTHEW GOODMAN

BASIC
BOOKS

A Member of the Perseus Books Group
New York

Copyright © 2008 by Matthew Goodman
Published by Basic Books,
A Member of the Perseus Books Group

Books published by Basic Books are available at special discounts for bulk
purchases in the United States by corporations, institutions, and other
organizations. For more information, please contact the Special Markets
Department at the Perseus Books Group, 2300 Chestnut Street, Suite 200,
Philadelphia, PA 19103, or call (800) 810-4145, ext. 5000, or e-mail
special.markets@perseusbooks.com.

Designed by Brent Wilcox

Library of Congress Cataloging-in-Publication Data
Goodman, Matthew.
    The Sun and the moon : the remarkable true account of hoaxers,
showmen, dueling journalists, and lunar man-bats in nineteenth-century New
York / Matthew Goodman.
        p.   cm.
    Includes bibliographical references and index.
    ISBN 978-0-465-00257-3 (alk. paper)
    1. Moon—Miscellanea.   2. Fraud in science—New York (State)—
New York—History—19th century.   3. Journalism—Corrupt practices.
4. Day, Benjamin Henry, 1810–1889.   5. Sun (New York, N.Y. : 1833)
6. New York (N.Y.)—History—19th century.   I. Title.
QB581.9.G66 2008
974.7'103—dc22

                                                        2008023617

10 9 8 7 6 5 4 3 2 1

For my mother and father,
lifelong New Yorkers

Is there any thing as extravagant as the imaginations of men's brains?

An Essay on Human Understanding

CONTENTS

The Man on the Moon

A PENNY A PAPER: that was the basic equation. It was a penny a paper that brought the boys out this August morning before sunrise, as it did every morning, rousing them from the old crates and battered tin kettles and hogsheads still smelling of ale, from under staircases and above steam gratings and inside the backs of open wagons, out from New York's hidden places. Four or five hours of sleep, cramped and anxious, the sort of night that could make even a thirteen-year-old feel ragged. Blinking in the yellow flicker of the oil lamps, the boys brushed traces of coal ash and wood shavings from their trousers, stretched and groaned and tried to remember the night before. Papers sold during the day had given them pennies for the night, the coppers they tossed down for butter cakes in the cellar room at Butter-cake Dick's—only three cents bought a satisfyingly crisp, hot biscuit filled with butter, and a cup of coffee besides—where they could sit together at the scarred cherry tables and talk about the shows they had seen that evening, laughing and shoving, from the pits of the Olympic or the Chatham or the Broadway. Afterward, in ones and twos, they would wander out again in search of a place to sleep, ideally secluded and safe from any bored, drunken watchman looking to roust them for a bit of fun, or from a footpad who would turn their pockets out for the pennies.

Drowsily the boys navigated the crooked Dutch lanes that wound up from the Battery, where the high stone countinghouses crowded the sidewalks, and where even now the new Merchants' Exchange was rising on Wall Street, its white marble columns glowing pale in the dawn; they spilled out onto the great avenue, Broadway, its trim brick houses and expensive French shops brilliantly illuminated by gas lamps. From all over the city they came to the corner of Spruce and Nassau streets, converging on the offices of the *Sun,* where they gathered to await that morning's papers. For nearly two years newsboys had hawked the *Sun* on the streets of the city, haunting its steamboat landings, marketplaces, busy corners, all the places where crowds congregated—especially the crowds with clothing a bit more faded and frayed, those New Yorkers who had never before thought of themselves as newspaper readers. It was a new kind of selling for a new kind of newspaper.

At the *Sun*'s side door the clerk collected their money and handed them down their bundles. The newsboys paid sixty-seven cents for a hundred papers, which left a profit of thirty-three cents if they could sell them all. They had to pay in cash, up front, and they weren't allowed to return unsold papers (Mr. Day, the publisher of the *Sun,* had instituted that policy after he discovered that some of the boys were renting out papers to readers and then returning them to the *Sun* office, carefully refolded, for a refund at the end of the day), so they had to be careful about how many papers they chose to buy each morning. Thus the more careful boys made sure first to open a copy to page two, where the main news of the day was to be found, and scan it for a headline that could be yelled out on a street corner, one dramatic enough to make a passerby pause amid the noise and chaos of an outdoor market or ship landing. Murders were best, though their appeal depended on where the body had been found. The city's lower wards were serviceable, the upper ones less so, and the Sixth, the poorest and most turbulent ward of all—the "bloody Sixth," as it would later come to be known—meant to keep moving on down the page. Fires were excellent, shipwrecks would suffice, and scandals among the upper classes, although relatively infrequent, could be stretched out for days before readers lost interest and again ignored the newsboys' cries.

This particular morning—August 21, 1835—looked especially profitable. The first item, a brief reprint about astronomy taken from a paper in Scotland, was no good at all, but it was followed in quick succession by paragraphs headlined "Fires" (there had been three of them, the best at a brewery in the Five Points), "Coroner's Office" (an Englishman had accidentally walked off the dock at Broad Street and drowned), and "A Narrow Escape from Death" (the navy frigate *Constitution* had nearly collided with a steamboat that had several of the ship's officers aboard). But none had as much sales potential as the story that led the second column, prefaced by the lines "How sharper than a serpent's tooth it is / To have a graceless child." (Mr. Locke, recently brought on as editor of the *Sun,* seemed to have an affection for Shakespeare.) This story, which took up nearly the whole column, related the misfortunes of a prosperous gentleman from one of the state's western counties, who had recently come to New York in search of his daughter. The girl had stolen $300 and a valuable gold watch from her parents and run away to the city with a young man. The couple had been spotted by a friend of the man's in a Greenwich Street boardinghouse, where they had apparently been posing as husband and wife. Mr. Locke was known to be one of the city's finest paragraphists, and he had been sure to note up front that the older man searching for the girl wasn't her actual father: "The daughter, it is true, was the offspring of an indiscretion of her mother before she was married, and long prior to her first acquaintance with her present husband; but the knowledge of her mother's early imprudence, and the sad lesson its results, and the mortification and misery which followed in its train, were so eminently calculated to instil, appears not only to have been wholly lost upon her unhappy girl, but rather to have inflamed than allayed the unfortunate viciousness of her disposition, and to have hurried her on to, it is most probable, the consummation of her own early and utter ruin." The girl and her beau had still not been found, which promised further updates, and the boys purchased their papers that morning confident of their sale.

Years later, having long since gone on to other trades, the newsboys would recall this as the day they had, without even knowing it, come into a fortune. Because for the next few weeks—at least for those boys who didn't throw away their coins on cards or dice or lottery tickets—they had been able to bypass Butter-cake Dick's and eat at any of the dozens of oyster cellars around town. Not until summer had ended was it legal to eat oysters in New York, and so for the next week they made do with clam and crab, but on the first of September, with the papers still selling in dazzling numbers, they tucked into oysters each night, slurped them icy from their shells, then ordered them boiled, fried, steamed, stewed, tossed into omelettes, and simmered in soups, and when they grew tired of oysters they ate shad; and better yet, after eating their fill they only had to walk upstairs, not back onto the street, because they now had coins enough in their pockets to rent a real bed for the night.

And all this unexpected good fortune had come not from the brewery fire or the young runaway, or indeed from any of the unhappiness that typically brought improved sales. Rather, it had been that astronomical item out of Scotland, which in the coming weeks would develop into the most spectacular series of their careers, as the *Sun*'s newly purchased steam-powered presses labored around the clock to meet the public's demand. All of it had arisen from that single sentence, prefaced by the simple headline "Celestial Discoveries":

> The Edinburgh Courant says—"We have just learnt from an eminent publisher in this city that Sir John Herschel, at the Cape of Good Hope, has made some astronomical discoveries of the most wonderful description, by means of an immense telescope of an entirely new principle."

THE *Sun*'s astronomical series appeared at the end of an uncomfortable August. For nearly the whole month a hot, heavy dome of air had lain upon New York, materializing in the morning and evening into a peculiar thick fog of a sort no one could remember having seen before. The weather, the *Commercial Advertiser* remarked, was "fitful and cheerless," and had "scarce deigned to smile upon us." Men and women alike wore only white for their evening promenades around the Battery (including, for men, the low-crowned, broad-brimmed white hats that had come so much into vogue), seeking out the cool breezes that still drifted across the bay and brought a faint but bracing scent of the ocean. What shade the city offered— a store awning, an alley between buildings, the poplars lining Broadway— was no match for a heat that seemed to emanate from the air itself.

Even the occasional afternoon thunderstorm brought little relief. The vehicles crowding the city's streets—coaches, omnibuses, carriages, carts—were pulled by horses, thousands of them, and their manure piled up along the curbsides in great heaps that the summer rain dissolved into malodorous brown rivers that splashed even the most careful pedestrian. Pigs roamed wild ("ugly brutes," Charles Dickens called them after his visit to New York, comparing their brown backs to the lids of old horsehair trunks), and while they were efficient enough scavengers of the garbage that otherwise would have rotted in the streets, they inevitably added their own contributions to those of the horses.

Still, though no one much liked to discuss the fact, it was undeniable that the most upsetting of the waste fouling New York's streets was, in origin, neither equine nor porcine but human. The city was booming with new arrivals; New York had long ago surpassed Boston as the most populous city in the United States, and it would shortly surpass Mexico City as the most populous in North America. Incredibly, the city was now home to more than a quarter-million people. New York's size was a source of real pride among the city's residents, but it also created numerous problems, not least among them what to do with all of the waste that the population daily produced. For temporary storage, the city depended on what were called privy vaults, holding tubs dug beneath outhouses. City regulations required the privies to be large, deep, and well constructed, but many of them had not been built to code, and even the ones that had been could not meet the demands made on them by an increasingly numerous and crowded citizenry. Often the privies backed up and overflowed, their contents seeping up from the ground, like nightmarish hot springs, into yards and streets.

Home and shop owners were supposed to regularly sweep the sidewalk in front of their property, depositing accumulated dirt and garbage in the middle of the street, but this was a regulation residents rarely followed; nor, when they did, was the garbage often collected. New York, the largest and most vibrant city in the Union, lived with the constant reek of putrefaction. Even—especially—on the warmest days, shop doors were kept always shut, so as not to admit the smell from outside. "A person coming into the city from the pure air of the country," noted one New Yorker, "is compelled to hold his breath, or make use of some perfume, to break off the disagreeable smell arising from the streets."

It felt that month as if the summer would never end, although by the second week of August dispatches were already coming in telling of sharp frosts in Buffalo and parts of Connecticut. This was especially good news for Buffalo, where the cholera had appeared earlier in the summer; similarly distressing reports had arrived from several of the mid-Southern states, and all through the hot months New York's residents nervously monitored the weather, looking for the unusual conditions—pale and silvery skies, strong winds in the upper atmosphere, rounded cumulus clouds—that seemed to many to have presaged the afflictions of 1832: the "cholera year," as it would always be remembered by those who had lived through it. In just two months the disease had killed 3,513 New Yorkers; all that summer the sky above the city had been filled with the oily, acrid smoke of clothes and bedding being burned in the houses of the dead.

Those ominous weather patterns had not yet been spotted, but some unfortunates had been struck down in Buffalo, and until the cold weather arrived few New Yorkers could feel entirely confident that the disease would not hop aboard any of a thousand steamboats and make its way down the Erie Canal; thanks to the new canal, the trip would take little more than a week.

The cholera had managed to find New York the previous summer as well, although the toll proved not nearly as great as before, with deaths numbering in hundreds rather than thousands. In 1834 the more immediate concern had been not disease but riot: time and again that year armed troops had to be called out to protect New Yorkers from each other. In the cold April rains that accompanied the city's first direct mayoral election, roving bands of Democrats and Whigs fought in the streets with clubs, hurling paving stones and brickbats plucked from nearby construction sites. Each side raged against the other: to Democrats, Whig politicians were hired lackeys of the city's bankers and aristocrats, while Whigs denounced Democrats as ignorant roughs and "damned Irishmen" unworthy of political power. On the third day of violence, several hundred Whig supporters looted the gun shops of Broadway, then stormed the state arsenal and began arming themselves with swords and muskets. News of the attack quickly reached the ranks of the Democrats, and soon the arsenal was surrounded by a restless, angry crowd twenty thousand strong. Rumors circulated that the mayor was dead (he had been bloodied in an early skirmish), but he soon arrived at the arsenal, declared New York to be in a state of insurrection, and managed finally to restore order by calling out twelve hundred infantry and cavalry troops who marched down Broadway with bayonets and sabers drawn.

Sailors rioted downtown on Water Street, stonecutters uptown in Washington Square. A storekeeper on Chatham Street accused a woman of stealing a pair of shoes; a crowd gathered to defend her, and within an hour two hundred people lay injured. Every crowd, it seemed, had the makings of a mob. The worst violence came during three nights in July, when rioters, inflamed by lurid stories in some of the city's merchant newspapers, attacked the homes, stores, and churches of blacks and abolitionists. (The abolitionists, it was rumored, were adopting black children; the abolitionists were asking their own daughters to marry Negroes; one abolitionist minister had even declared that Christ was a colored man.) For hours they roamed the streets in defiance of the local watchmen, smashing windows, ransacking houses, and hauling furniture outside to be burned. By the final night, when the rioters targeted the poor, racially mixed area of Five Points, the violence had escalated to a disturbing level of organization. During the afternoon, word passed through the neighborhood that, come nightfall, white families should light candles and stand by their windows, so that, in a grim burlesque of Exodus, they might be identified and their houses passed over.

Summers had proven perilous of late, and in the sweltering August of 1835 the city was stalked by the memories of its recent dead and wounded. Menace swirled in the air like the persistent fog, thickening as darkness neared. Feelings were running high against local abolitionists (or "amalgamators," as they were routinely called in the merchant papers, since the term "miscegenation" had not attained wide use). On August 21, a group of New York's leading citizens gathered to plan a mass meeting in the park by City Hall as a way of demonstrating—especially to the city's trading partners in the South—that New York would no longer tolerate abolitionist attempts to divide the Union by interfering with the rights of the slaveholding states. When the meeting was held on August 27, the mayor himself called it to order. By that time new, more sinister rumors were blooming everywhere. Heavy rewards had already been posted in several Southern cities for the capture of Arthur Tappan, a wealthy dry-goods merchant and New York's most well-known abolitionist. Tappan had long been receiving threatening letters as a matter of course, but with the sense of danger intensifying, the mayor of Brooklyn, where Tappan lived, ordered nightly patrols of the streets around his house. Another prominent abolitionist, Elizur Wright, had reportedly barricaded his own doors and windows with planks an inch thick. The abolitionist Lydia Maria Child wrote to a friend from her home in Brooklyn, "I have not ventured into the city . . . so great is the excitement here. 'Tis like the times of the French Revolution, when no man dared to trust his neighbors."

In such times, it was no surprise that New Yorkers sought diversion, and the city's impresarios were happy to provide it. There were magicians, declaimers, piano forte players, Italian opera singers. Uptown on Prince Street, Niblo's Garden, the most fashionable of New York's nightspots, had vocal and theatrical performances, and, between acts, fireworks. Shakespeare, melodrama, and light comedy could be found at the city's

Looking south on lower Broadway in the year 1834. Trinity Church is in the background.
(Courtesy of the New York Public Library.)

many theaters, premier among them the Bowery Theater, the first American playhouse to have its stage illuminated by gas lights. By the end of September the Bowery would be presenting a new comic extravaganza, *Moonshine, or Lunar Discoveries,* inspired by the series of astronomical articles now being introduced in the *Sun.* Across from St. Paul's Church, the City Saloon featured the local artist Henry Hanington's peristrephic diorama "The Deluge," an ingenious pairing of art and mechanical effects that transported the audience from the creation of the world through the Great Flood and the salvation by Noah's ark. Within weeks Hanington's most popular attraction would be "Lunar Discoveries," carefully painted renderings of the moon's waters, woods, and wildlife stretching across more than one thousand feet of canvas.

At night, Broadway gave itself over to spectacle. The low, grave hymns that seeped through the doors of Trinity Church and St. Paul's in the mornings gave way to the high-pitched calls of the ticket takers, beckoning the crowds that surged along the boulevard. In just a few blocks, New Yorkers could sample what seemed to be all the exotica the world had to offer: stuffed birds and reptiles, tropical fish, fossils, shells, corals, minerals, wax figures, Egyptian mummies, Indian utensils, Indian dresses, and sometimes the Indians themselves. Peale's Museum, across from City Hall, was now featuring a "living ourang outang, or wild man of the woods" named Joe; the creature—as the newspaper advertisements did not fail to mention—had been wrenched from his mother's breast ("which required considerable violence") after she had been shot by hunters near the River Gabon in West Africa. Appearing with Joe was a fourteen-foot-long anaconda from Bengal that every Monday noon was fed a living chicken; to the surprise of its handlers, on June 30 the snake had swallowed a woolen blanket whole. Around the corner, Scudder's American Museum was exhibiting the "living Ai, or Sloth," which captivated audiences with its woebegone expression and apparently indomitable apathy. The more compelling attractions, though, were always the human ones, such as Emily and Margaret Martin, known theatrically as the Canadian Dwarfs, who were playing a limited engagement at Scudder's. One of the Martin sisters was said to measure just twenty-two inches from the ground; the other, though slightly taller, could converse with onlookers in both English and French.

Even that, however, could not compare with the attraction on view that summer in the Diorama Room upstairs at Niblo's. Her name was Joice Heth, and she had been born a slave in Virginia—reportedly in the year 1674, which made her 161 years old at the time of the exhibition. More extraordinary still, Joice Heth claimed to have been George Washington's nursemaid, and though blind and toothless and paralyzed on one side, she regaled her audiences with anecdotes of her young charge, whom she called "my dear little George." Day after day the *Sun* and the city's other newspapers brought fresh reports of "the old one," as she quickly came to be known around town. Her wizened appearance was compared to an Egyptian mummy, a bird of prey, and the shank end of a piece of smoked beef. "The dear old lady," editorialized the *Spirit of the Times,* "after carrying on a desperate flirtation with Death, has finally jilted him." That summer the city was flooded with handbills, pamphlets, and posters illustrated with Joice Heth's portrait, and the newspapers regularly received large advertisements, all of this publicity having been organized by her new promoter, who was already displaying a flair for the uses of the public press.

The promoter was only twenty-five years old, but he had already been a grocery clerk, general-store proprietor, lottery agent, bartender, owner of a porter house, and newspaper publisher. As a newspaperman, he had been sued for libel three times, and he once spent sixty days in jail for accusing a minister of usury. Although he had already made—and squandered—a good deal of money, none of his occupations had yet been able to satisfy what he liked to call his "organ of acquisitiveness." As he would write twenty years later in his autobiography, "My disposition is, and ever was, of a speculative character." Like thousands of other young men of the time, he had come to New York with a wife and child to seek his fortune. Each morning he read the "Wants" column in the *Sun,* hoping to find something that might suit him. He answered numerous advertisements, made his way up the narrow stairways of countless shabby buildings, but each time he discovered that the prospect was not as bright as had been claimed. Then one day in late July 1835, a former business associate offered to let him purchase the contract of an old black woman for one thousand dollars. Immediately he understood that he had at last discovered his true vocation: he was a kind of sorcerer, making desire appear out of thin air.

His name was Phineas Taylor Barnum, and in the summer of 1835, Joice Heth had shown him the future.

THAT summer in New York, one of the most highly anticipated attractions was celestial. After an interval of seventy-six years Halley's Comet was due to arrive soon, and its reappearance was being awaited with great excitement as well as national pride, as this was the first time the comet would ever streak through the skies over the United States of America. By August some enterprising businessmen had placed a telescope in the park by City Hall and were charging six cents a viewing for those hoping to catch a glimpse of the famous comet—although, from his observatory in South Africa, the British astronomer Sir John Herschel had predicted that it would not be seen until September at the earliest.

In New York attention was turning skyward, to the heavens and, without aid of telescope, to the balloonists—aeronauts, as they were then known—who were lately thrilling large crowds with their ascents into the upper atmosphere. Some three hundred miles to the south, in Richmond, Edgar Allan Poe had just published a story entitled "Hans Phaall—A Tale" that described a balloon journey to the moon made by a Dutch bellows mender. The story was loaded with scientific detail, much of it taken directly from John Herschel's *Treatise on Astronomy,* which had been published to great acclaim in the United States a year earlier. "Hans Phaall" was lengthy (it occupied fifteen of the *Southern Literary Messenger*'s densely type-covered pages), but its narration of Hans's arrival on the moon fulfilled only half of Poe's original conception of the story. The second part, which he had not yet started, was meant to describe the lunar scenery encountered by his hero. Poe, who had been fascinated by astronomy since his boyhood, had high hopes for this endeavor, but in September, when he read the *Celestial Discoveries* series in the *Sun,* he abandoned his plans for good. The articles, he believed, had stolen his idea and, worse, had supplanted it. "Having read the Moon story to an end and found it anticipative of all the main points of my 'Hans Phaall,'" he would write years later, "I suffered the latter to remain unfinished."

"Suffered" was the proper term: Edgar Allan Poe was nothing if not prideful, and being trumped by the *Sun* was a wound from which he would never fully recover. Nine years later, when he settled in New York in 1844, Poe's first order of business was to place his own scientific hoax in the pages of the *Sun,* one modeled on the moon stories of 1835. Two years after that (only three years before his death), in his series of written portraits of thirty-eight New York writers entitled *The Literati of New York City,* Poe would allot the greatest space not to such well-known authors such as Fitz-Greene Halleck or N. P. Willis, or even to his own recent love interest, Frances S. Osgood, but rather to the author of the moon stories, an enigmatic Englishman named Richard Adams Locke.

In August 1835, Richard Adams Locke was a thirty-five-year-old itinerant journalist who just two months earlier had been hired as the editor of the *Sun.* Born into a prosperous family in the southwest of England, Locke had arrived in the city (like P. T. Barnum, accompanied by his wife and infant daughter) in 1832 looking for newspaper work. In the succeeding three years, Locke had become known in journalistic circles as a clever, versatile writer, as comfortable handling crime stories as he was literary reviews, possessed of a formidable intellect and a good deal more sophistication than the average New York newspaperman. Not so well known was that Richard Adams Locke had left England because of his political radicalism, and that his background and education were not exactly as he liked to claim. Nor was it known—at least for several crucial days at the end of August 1835—that he was the man behind the *Sun* series that reported how intelligent life had been discovered on the moon.

Locke was the author of the eleven-thousand-word account (which the *Sun* attributed to the *Supplement to the Edinburgh Journal of Science*) revealing the remarkable lunar discoveries made by Sir John Herschel from his observatory at the Cape of Good Hope, including lakes, waterfalls, forests, beavers that walked on their hind legs, and unicorns. The crowning touch was the discovery of four-foot-tall "man-bats"—Vespertilio-homo, as Herschel was said to have named them—apparently rational beings who conversed, constructed temples, and fornicated in public (though the articles remained decorously mum about these particulars). The *Sun*'s articles would seem to defy credulity, but such was Locke's erudition—and the sheer bravura of his enterprise—that public opinion on their veracity was sharply divided, with, by all accounts, a significant majority of New Yorkers leaning toward belief.

Whether or not they took the stories to be true, everyone in New York wanted to read them. Edgar Allan Poe deemed the series "decidedly the greatest *hit* in the way of *sensation*—of merely popular sensation—ever made by any similar fiction either in America or in Europe." Echoing Poe, P. T. Barnum declared, "The sensation created by this immense imposture, not only throughout the United States, but in every part of the civilized world, and the consummate ability with which it was written, will render it interesting so long as our language shall endure." No other newspaper story of the age was as broadly circulated as Locke's moon series. A pamphlet containing the complete series sold twenty thousand copies in its first week, an exhausting but highly lucrative one for the *Sun*'s newsboys. The articles were reprinted in many of New York's competing newspapers, and later, in newspapers across the country. Illustrated editions were published in Great Britain, Italy, Germany, France. By the time the series had run its course, the *Sun* had become the most widely read newspaper in the world.

The Moon Hoax (as it came to be known) was among the most sensational stories of the age, but it also had a greater resonance, for Locke's time and for ours. It tells a story about the moment New York first came to see itself as not just one city among many, but as the leading city in the United States, and indeed one of the world's great cities. New York was also a city divided against itself, by class, by ethnicity, and by social conflicts over deeply contentious issues such as slavery. In that crucible a new kind of newspaper was born, one that was not merely an organ of the commercial elites, but rather a mass-market medium—politically independent, designed to be read by the average person, and featuring exactly the sort of reporting that continues to mark most newspaper journalism today: crime, scandal, sports, entertainment. It was a revolution in journalism, one that started in New York in the mid-1830s and then spread to cities across America, creating a nation of newspaper readers.

Richard Adams Locke's moon series was also a profound though little-known battle in the ongoing struggle in America between science and theology. Too often the pursuit of science has been inhibited by the power of religious authority, free inquiry forced to conform to the dictates of established belief. As Locke himself would write years later, "*theological and devotional* encroachments upon the legitimate province of science" will, if unopposed, "bind in the chains of sectarian faith and conventional dogmatism, inquiries into matters of fact that should be free as the mountain air and unchartered as the light of heaven." That age-old conflict too was bound up in Locke's fanciful stories of lunar unicorns and man-bats.

Needless to say, Richard Adams Locke could hardly have imagined all this when he sat down at his desk in the summer of 1835 and began to write. Nor could he have foreseen the impact that the series would have on his own life. Even though he would go on to edit two other major daily newspapers, including one that he founded, Richard Adams Locke would always be known as "the man on the moon." His life was forever defined by those weeks in the summer of 1835, when the largest part of the nation's largest city came to believe that the moon was inhabited, and that this most ancient of questions—whether we are alone in the universe—had finally been laid to rest. The moon series would be his singular distinction, but it was, in his mind, a mistake. Richard Adams Locke had produced the most successful hoax in the history of American journalism, and yet he had not intended it as a hoax at all.

Part One

THE SUN

CHAPTER 1

Benjamin Day's
Whistling Boy

THE ROOM IN WHICH journalistic history would be made measured twelve by sixteen feet, on the ground floor of a trim three-story brick factory building at the north end of William Street. It was Monday, September 2, 1833, and the young printer Benjamin Day had stood for hours at his composing table, working as the late-summer light bloomed orange and then dwindled to gray. He was setting advertisements that would run in the first issue of the newspaper he had named the *Sun:* notices for steamship passages to Albany and Hartford, for a writing academy and a piano forte warehouse, from employers seeking cooks and grocery clerks, insurance companies informing the public of attractive new rates for fire risks. In fact Day had not yet received a cent from these businesses, nor did they even know that the advertisements would appear in the *Sun;* he was simply copying ads that had already run in the city's six-penny papers. None of the firms would complain about the free publicity, he knew, and the advertisements would lend the *Sun* the prosperous appearance of a real newspaper.

The room was crowded with stacks of paper he had purchased at a discount from his brother-in-law, Moses Yale Beach, who owned a paper mill up the Hudson in Saugerties. His printing press, an awkward assemblage of cranks and levers, waited in the center of the room. At full speed, the press would throw off two hundred impressions in an hour as it printed one thousand copies of the newspaper—Day's ambitious plan for the first issue. With one impression for the front and back pages and another for pages two and three on the inside, the job would require at least ten hours of printing.

A boy whose name has been forgotten served as Day's printer's devil, mixing ink and fetching paper; a journeyman printer remembered only as Parmlee helped Day feed and crank the press. The three worked through Monday night into the next morning. Outside, the leisurely clop of the carriage horses gave way to silence, broken only by an occasional rumble from night carts racing over the cobblestones. The press whispered and clicked, as steady and rhythmic as the threshing of a loom. The small room was suffused with the smell of sweat and burning candle wax and the ripe-pineapple scent of printer's ink.

Before dawn Day went out and bought a copy of New York's largest morning newspaper, the *Courier and Enquirer*. Back at the office, he clipped and rewrote several of the news items and set them into type alongside the pieces he had already written. When pages two and three had been finished, he and Parmlee hand-fed the sheets back into the press to print the reverse sides. At some point one of them might have noticed that Day, in his exhaustion, had misset the date below the masthead as 1832 instead of 1833, but it was too late now to change it.

By noon the last of the pages had been printed and folded. Bleary with lack of sleep, blinking against the bright light of the day, Day and his assistants carried the papers out of his office and into the city.

To a modern reader, a six-penny newspaper from Benjamin Day's time would look very strange and unwelcoming: large pages divided into columns as long and narrow as stovepipes, and made nearly as black by row after row of minuscule type. The print was broken only by small woodcuts illustrating advertisements for steamboats and ladies' corsets and houses to let. Photographs, of course, were still decades away. Perhaps most strangely, news stories appeared not on the front page but inside, on page two. Headlines generally ran in the same size type as the text of the stories and consisted of a few words set off as italicized or capitalized print:

Coroners Inquest.—The body of a miserable looking man, apparently aged about 34 years, was found yesterday in Baker's wharf, near Catharine market. The deceased was attired in a coarse blue jacket, yellow vest, and a black striped fustian pantaloons.

All of the papers were only four pages long. It was a convenient format for publishers, as one sheet printed on both sides and folded over made a tidy four-page newspaper, of which little more than a page consisted of original news content. The front page was taken up by advertisements, which were supplemented by transcripts of speeches, serialized fiction, and, occasionally, special features (most of the papers would reprint the *Sun's* moon series on their front page). The back page was likewise given over to ads, printed in small type and usually only an inch or two long, much like today's classifieds. The advertisements paint a vivid portrait of upper-class life in nineteenth-century New York: houses and hotels and country residences for sale and lease, racehorses at auction, silk just arrived from Paris and linen from London, pearl needle cases, cravats made in India and Italy and Germany, coal from Pennsylvania, and sperm oil from Nantucket, as well as a parade of tonics, lotions, ointments, syrups, and elixirs, almost every one named after the doctor who discovered it ("Dr. Root's Celebrated Ointment," "Dr. Church's Antispasmodic Elixir"), and furnishing a certain cure for seemingly every human ailment, including convulsions, falling fits, the salt rheum, fever and ague, baldness, long-standing gleets (otherwise known as gonorrhea), involuntary emissions, irregular menses, gout, asthma, nervousness, impurities of the blood, and—if the complaint was of a less readily identifiable nature—general weakness.

Page three featured commercial matters, including inventories of the latest ship clearances, bank note tables, and sales by auction. Only on the second page would a reader find actual news, most of the stories no longer than a couple of paragraphs, mixed in with items that were actually editorials though not labeled as such. (By the 1830s most of the daily newspapers were no longer owned and operated by political parties, as they had been earlier in the century, but they still identified themselves as Whig or Democrat. This was just good business sense, because the party in power distributed lucrative printing contracts to friendly presses.) The papers had few local reporters on staff, and their city coverage tended toward dramatic events like fires or riots, or unfortunate ones like break-ins at the better residences or reports of crude gestures made by young dandies at the city's respectable ladies. Far more space was given to news from around the country, the items usually taken directly from newspapers in other cities, and to international news clipped from the foreign papers brought in by oceangoing packet ships. For a New York newspaper editor, it was said, the most important tools of the trade were not pen and paper but a pair of scissors and a paste pot.

Unlike today's editors, who generally oversee writing done by others, the editor of the 1830s wrote most of the original content that appeared in a newspaper. He also introduced the material reprinted from foreign newspapers, selected letters from readers for publication, and often replied to the letters as well. The editor was the public face of the newspaper, his name often the only one that appeared on a masthead. Editors advised readers about what politicians to vote for, what shows to see, what books to read, even what foods to eat. A newspaper's fortunes rose and fell on the personality of its editor, and in a crowded field—there were eleven daily newspapers in New York, seven published in the morning and four in the evening—success seems to have required from the editor an unusual level of personal confidence, one not easily distinguishable from pure egotism; a pride that ran into arrogance; and a competitiveness that verged on combativeness. It was not uncommon for rival editors to come to blows when they passed each other on the street, so deep was their personal animosity. Three times in a matter of weeks in 1836 James Watson Webb, the editor of the *Courier and Enquirer,* caned the editor of the *Herald,* James Gordon Bennett, as retribution for critical editorials, the third attack so vicious that Bennett afterward kept a set of loaded pistols in his office. Even the renowned poet William Cullen Bryant, longtime editor of the *Evening Post,* once horsewhipped a fellow editor in front of the American Hotel on Broadway after an exchange of editorial insults; his target, William Leete Stone of the *Commercial Advertiser,* fought back with a bamboo cane that shattered on impact, revealing inside it a long, slender steel sword.

In 1833 the most widely read of the city's newspapers was Webb's *Courier and Enquirer,* with a circulation of some 4,500. Among the evening papers, Bryant's *Evening Post* was the largest, with 3,000 readers, followed by the *Evening Star* at 2,500 and the *Commercial Advertiser* at 2,100. New York's eleven daily newspapers had a combined circulation of only 26,500—this in a city with a population of more than a quarter million, with tens of thousands more living in Brooklyn and nearby towns. For all the intensity of their rivalry, the newspapers were actually competing for a very thin slice of the city: those few New Yorkers who could afford to read them. Newspapers cost six cents per copy, and though copies could be bought at a newspaper's offices, publishers discouraged individual sales (they believed that advertisers preferred the guaranteed readership that came from long-term subscriptions) by offering a comparatively lower price for a year's subscription, ten dollars. This was still a great deal of money, about as much as a skilled artisan might expect to earn for a week's work. But these papers were not intended for skilled artisans, much less anyone lower on the economic scale. They were intended instead—to use the phrase then coming into vogue—for the upper crust, an emphasis that was reflected in their news coverage, which leaned heavily on international news (vitally important to merchants, since any sort of disruption around the world could dramatically affect the markets for import or export), political and economic news from Washington, currency conversion tables, and other matters of interest to the mercantile readership.

The merchant papers were all produced within a few blocks of each other in lower New York, from Wall Street running up William and Nassau streets, and their coverage of the city extended little farther than that. Thanks to the editors' zeal in appropriating the foreign papers, their readers could learn about a new prince installed in Greece or the launch of a new packet ship in Liverpool; thanks to their Washington correspondents, they could learn about the latest debate over the central bank or the passage of a new tariff on cotton or iron; or, thanks to the free exchange with other newspapers around the country, about an Indian battle that had been fought near St. Louis or a record steamship time that had been set in Charleston. But little was ever heard of the doings in nearby Corlear's Hook or Chatham Square or the Bowery. So closely focused on each other, the editors were blind to the changes that were rapidly overwhelming their city.

As the world's goods now flowed through New York Harbor, so too the world's people flowed through the city's streets. In the 1830s a visitor from Boston remarked with some wonder at the "English, German, French, and Spanish, which, with the addition of Italian, you may hear almost any day, in Broadway, at the hours when it is most frequented"; a local resident marveled at how New York had become a kind of "human patch-work," its inhabitants "the natives, and the descendants of the natives, of every nation, and kindred, and tongue on the face of the earth." The new arrivals were coming from everywhere, from around the country and around the world, and were doing so in unprecedented numbers; between 1821 and 1835 the population of each of New York's wards at least tripled. Taking advantage of this massive increase in population, the city's landlords were realizing that large buildings could be cheaply divided into much smaller units, each of which would provide rental income while requiring little maintenance. Packing families into these cramped quarters, they were creating the first of the tenant houses that would soon acquire a far more notorious name—tenements. Just a dozen blocks from the newspaper district, to the west of Chatham Square, a lake known as the Collect had been filled in and houses built on its unstable earth; by the beginning of the 1830s the area was known as the Five Points, and had declined into the most squalid of the city's neighborhoods, fouled by the run-off from the nearby slaughterhouses, glue factories, and turpentine distilleries, where the poorest of black and white lived packed together in rickety wooden structures with leaky roofs and walls roughly patched with handbills, eating from sawed-off barrel tops and sleeping on mattresses filled with straw. Outside, groups of boys were forming themselves into gangs with jaunty, aggressive names like the Plug Uglies, Dead Rabbits, Roach Guards, Buckoos, Hookers, Swamp Angels, and, for the most venerable gang of them all, the name that a century later the movies would make iconic—the Bowery Boys. Irish immigrants, both Catholic and Protestant, were arriving in New York by the thousands, in flight from oppression and destitution, and before long they would make up the most powerful political force in the city. Black New Yorkers, only recently assured of their freedom—slavery was not officially abolished in the state until 1827—were often left to do the jobs disdained by their fellow citizens. They worked as domestics, launderers, cooks, chimney sweeps, ragpickers, and, having been excluded from the occupation of regular carting, as "necessary tubmen," collecting and hauling the city's shit (as excrement was popularly known even then) under darkness of night. Yet even in these mean jobs they were increasingly being displaced by the new Irish immigrants, setting off a racial conflict that was fierce and durable and all the more bitter for bringing such meager rewards.

The orange sellers plying their trade in front of St. Paul's Chapel, the hot-corn girls and the basket men and the knife grinders sending their cries through the streets, the clerks and bookkeepers, grocers and tavern keepers, stevedores and draymen, the hackney drivers, the pawnbrokers and secondhand clothes men on Chatham Street, the cabinetmakers on Greenwich Street, the dyers and tanners and bone boilers in the uptown slaughterhouses, the cutters and stitchers turning out ready-made clothing in the huge new textile factories; the blacksmiths, carpenters, caulkers, and riggers building ships along the docks; the fat collectors and the candle lighters, the butchers with their top hats and bloody smocks—these were the city's bone and sinew, the people who kept it moving forward, and who, barring great misdeed or misfortune, never found their way into the papers.

In 1833 Benjamin Day was twenty-three years old, and he had been in New York for three years. He grew up in West Springfield in the southwestern part of Massachusetts near the Connecticut border, where at the age of fourteen he had left school to serve an apprenticeship at a new weekly newspaper, the *Springfield Republican.* By the age of twenty he was a first-class printer and had set his sights on the rapidly expanding metropolis to the south.

Not until 1868 would Horatio Alger send his Ragged Dick wandering the streets of New York, but real-life urban rags-to-riches tales were already making their way into the countryside, and nowhere more so than in New England, from which scores of entrepreneurially minded Yankees had lit out for the city and made fortunes in trade and manufacturing. Benjamin Day, however, came to New York not to get rich but simply to save enough money to support a family, with perhaps enough left over for the occasional brandy and cigar. A photograph taken in his first prosperous days shows a round-cheeked young man, his eyes peering suspiciously at the camera and his mouth set into a thin hard line, a few whiskers peeking out beneath his chin; he looks distinctly uncomfortable in a bowtie and ill-fitting top hat, like a teenager forced to dress up for a graduation picture. Day was never particularly interested in the trappings of wealth, most of which he considered foppish. Even as an old man, when he could afford otherwise, he walked rather than rode (he enjoyed walking, he explained), and when his favorite armchair needed new springs or one of his house's cuckoo clocks was running slow, he fixed it himself with a cherished old set of carpenter's tools.

"He was self-sufficient, he was firm and solid by nature, a man made of granite," his grandson Clarence would write. He could be aloof and was often irascible, though he was kind to family and a few close friends, and to those who had managed to win his favor; his *New York Times* obituary noted that he "was exceedingly charitable and concealed a very warm heart behind a brusque address." He had no time or patience for the glad-handing and drawing-room nicety that was the publisher's stock in trade, but unlike many of the men who had started their own newspapers he was genuinely interested in hearing what other people thought, although he rarely asked a direct question. Instead, he would toss out a few quiet remarks, seemingly offhand but in fact carefully calculated, and then observe the effects they produced. Benjamin Day was not an especially reflective man, except as the reflection touched on business. He was eminently practical, proud of his common-school education and suspicious of the merits said to be bestowed by higher learning. He was by trade a printer, and by chance an editor, but by nature he was always a businessman.

After arriving in New York in 1829 Day drifted among the merchant papers, working as a fill-in compositor, living frugally, saving whatever he could toward the purchase of types and a printing press of his own. Early the following year, in what turned out to be a pivotal decision, he joined the staff of the *Daily Sentinel,* a radical paper being started by several printers from the *Courier and Enquirer.* Compared to the men who ran the other newspapers in town—and to those he would later hire to write for the *Sun,* including Richard Adams Locke—Day was not very politically minded. He was distrustful of ideologies of any kind, but he had a strong feel for labor, having himself spent years composing by the light of a candle, working antiquated presses until his hands were blistered and his back was as stiff as iron. (Under his leadership the *Sun* would be a fierce advocate of higher wages and shorter working hours, and of the nascent labor movement in general. In early 1834, for instance, the paper gave extensive coverage to a strike by hundreds of Lowell mill girls, even reprinting the full text of their manifesto, *Union Is Power.*) There had been other radical newspapers in New York before, all of them directed at the city's artisan class, but the *Daily Sentinel* was different because it was also produced by artisans. Its six directors—Benjamin Day among them— described themselves in the first issue as "all practical printers . . . [who] have, in common with their fellow laborers in every branch of industry, participated largely in the distress which pervades the producing classes of this community." The *Daily Sentinel* took on all the working-class issues of the day but struggled to find a readership, in large part because a year's subscription cost eight dollars—an improvement on the ten dollars charged by the merchant newspapers but still far beyond the means of most of the working people the directors hoped to reach. After just two months, a frustrated Day went back to work as a compositor for the merchant papers.

In September 1831 Day married his cousin Eveline Shepard, a school-teacher who was in her way just as strong-willed as he, though tender-hearted where he was gruff. (In later years Eveline would open up several bedrooms in their house to needy old women, a decision Day put up with silently.) The following July Eveline gave birth to a son, Henry. For the first months of Henry's life Ben and Eveline lived in terror of the cholera epidemic that raged around them, horse-drawn carts bearing coffins arriving at houses up and down the block; they tried not to dwell on the most chilling sight of all, the tiny coffins built for children. The family survived the cholera, but the epidemic and its aftermath cut drastically into the business of the print shop Day had finally managed to open. In May 1833, anticipating another baby, the Days moved several blocks south from Chestnut Street to larger quarters on Duane Street at the lower edge of the working-class Fifth Ward, just a few blocks from the Five Points and all its miseries. As the months passed and business didn't improve, Day increasingly felt the pressure of family responsibilities bearing down on him, as hard and heavy as the platen of his little-used press, imprinting a single word: *ruin*. Some print jobs were still coming in, and he could find occasional extra work as a compositor for some of the newspapers, but he needed something regular, something steady; ideally, it would be something that would also help him publicize the quality of his print business.

As he stood for hours at the printing press in his tiny ground-floor shop, his mind kept returning to an idea proposed by a friend of his named Dave Ramsay, with whom he had worked as a compositor for the *Journal of Commerce*. Ramsay's idea was to publish a new kind of newspaper, meant not for merchants or politicians but for working people like them. All of the papers in town cost six cents, too much for most New Yorkers; this paper, though, would cost only one cent. At the time, Ben Day had laughed down the idea with the other compositors—how can you make any money selling newspapers for a penny?—but now he began to wonder if it could actually work.

Still, as Day must have been aware, a cheap paper had been tried earlier that year in New York, and the results were hardly encouraging. It had been the notion of a young man named Horatio Sheppard, a student at the nearby Eldridge Street Medical School. Walking to class each morning, Sheppard crossed the raucous Chatham Street marketplace, where the street vendors offered everything for just one cent. He noted to himself how cheerfully people parted with a penny, how little difference there seemed to be between having a penny and having no money at all. Buying something for a penny was, in their minds, almost like getting it for free. Though he was studying to be a doctor, Sheppard had long been interested in the print trades, and over time he became convinced that it was possible to profitably sell a newspaper, too, for only a penny. For a year and a half, whenever he had time away from class, he made the rounds of the city's printing offices, talking up his idea to anyone he could buttonhole. But he could not convince a single person of the practicality of his idea, until he met a foreman for one of the merchant papers named Francis Story. Story had been looking for the opportunity to start his own printing business and he agreed to go in on the plan, provided that Dr. Sheppard (he had by now received his medical degree) also bring on a printer friend of his, a moon-faced country boy named Horace Greeley.

Greeley had come to New York from Vermont less than two years earlier, dressed in ill-fitting homespun clothes and, like a character from a Grimm tale, carrying all his belongings in a bandana slung over his shoulder. But he was already an expert printer and had a reputation for remarkable intelligence (it was said that he had read the Bible through by the time he was five years old), and his unprepossessing appearance hid a restless ambition, one that eventually carried him to the editorship of the *New York Tribune,* where he would become one of the most celebrated of all the city's editors and in 1872 the presidential candidate of both the Democratic and Liberal Republican parties. Greeley found Sheppard's idea appealing, but he prided himself on his New England practicality and agreed to serve as the paper's master printer on the condition that it be sold for two cents rather than one. Sheppard was dumbfounded by Greeley's demand. The whole appeal of the enterprise lay in its cheapness—the difference between one cent and two, he insisted, was all the difference in the world—but Greeley was not to be dissuaded. Despairing of any alternative to partnership with these men, Sheppard saw no choice but to relent.

Pooling what little capital they had, they took a small office on Liberty Street, at the corner of Nassau. Their selling plan was one that had already met with success in London: boys would hawk the papers on the street. It was decided that the new paper would commence with the new year, and on January 1, 1833, the first issue of the *Morning Post* hit New York, along with the worst snowstorm in recent memory. The snow whirled across the city, whitening dark cloaks and frock coats, making great drifts on the streets and muffling the cries of the shivering newsboys. All the New

Yorkers who could stay at home did, and few of those who ventured outside cared to rummage around in their pockets to find two pennies for a newspaper they didn't know. Still, despite the terrible conditions the boys managed to sell several hundred copies of the paper each day, and through the first week Sheppard met his expenses, if just barely. By the second week, however, he was deferring payment to his printers, and by the third week Greeley and Story decided to close up shop. By that time Sheppard had prevailed on his partners to lower the price to a penny, and the rise in sales during those last two days convinced him that the paper would have been a success if only he insisted on his original formula: a penny a paper. But by that point it was too late. For Horatio Sheppard there was nothing left to do but put up his shingle: he opened a medical office on Eldridge Street and was never heard from again in the newspaper business.

As a member of New York's small fraternity of journeymen printers, Day had undoubtedly heard about the failure of Sheppard's *Morning Post,* and whenever he broached the subject to his friends they laughed and reminded him of the problems a penny paper would present: how many copies would have to be printed and sold each day, how much advertising would have to be brought in? And what sort of firm, they wanted to know, would advertise in a paper intended for readers who couldn't afford to buy a real paper? Day understood all this, but he had already proven himself to be good with money (unlike them, he had saved enough to start his own shop), and he thought he had figured out a way around some of the problems.

Though his stint at the *Daily Sentinel* had proven a failure, Day prided himself on always learning from experience, and that one had taught him some valuable lessons. The printers who founded the *Sentinel* had learned their trade on the merchant papers, and for all of their radicalism they were still in thrall to an old way of thinking about a newspaper. Like Horatio Sheppard, Day had come to understand that there was magic in the idea of a newspaper that could be had for only one cent: a "penny paper." For a year's subscription he would charge not ten or even eight dollars, but only three dollars, well within the range of most potential readers— and those subscriptions would be paid in advance, so he wouldn't have to spend endless hours chasing down subscribers who were behind on their accounts, the way the other newspapers did. In addition to cutting the price of the paper, he would cut the size of its pages as well. The newspaper pages of the time measured about three feet long by two feet wide, or fully four feet across when the paper was opened (because of their size, the papers were known around town as the "blanket sheets"). The format was perfectly convenient for merchant readers, who could spread out the pages on the table of a private library or on the desk of a counting house, but for Day's readers the pages would have to be much smaller. Not only would smaller pages be less intimidating to an eye not used to reading a newspaper, but a paper of that size could be held comfortably in the hands and then, if necessary, simply rolled up and carried in a pocket, to be finished later.

For a man with so little direct experience in selling, Benjamin Day had an unusually keen sense of the marketplace. By this point he had worked as a compositor for several of the six-penny papers, the *Evening Post,* the *Journal of Commerce,* the *Courier and Enquirer,* the *Mercantile Advertiser,* and like the rest of the men in the composing room he had felt the little chill that passed through when the editor entered in his finery, issuing orders. He recognized how great the distance really was between the Fifth Ward and the newspaper district, because he walked it each day. The city's editors knew little about most New Yorkers, and likely never even conceived of them as readers, but Day, who lived among them, knew that as a group they were strikingly literate. They had Bibles and devotional tracts for their religious needs; they had, for diversion, adventure stories and gallows confessions and broadsheet ballads. The more politically minded among them had broadsides and pamphlets. They had all kinds of printed matter. What they didn't have, yet, was a daily newspaper.

On that September day in 1833, any potential reader could see in an instant that Benjamin Day's new paper was dramatically different from the others being published around town. For one thing, its pages measured only eight by eleven inches, or about the size of a sheet of letter paper. And there on the front page—just below the *Sun* nameplate emblazoned with the American eagle holding shield and arrows—was that captivating phrase: PRICE ONE PENNY.

Inside, Day had made page two the news page, following newspaper tradition, though owing to its unusually small size, the page was printed in three columns rather than the six or even seven found in the blanket sheets. Most of the second column was taken up by reports from the police office, with Day's brief but colorful descriptions of recently heard cases, which included an assault ("John Evans, brought up for exercising the muscles of his right arm by pounding John Nixon on the head with his fist"); an attempt to pass counterfeit money to a boy selling oysters; a man who turned over a table of pies, peaches, and pickled lobsters near Fulton Market; and a woman arrested for attacking her husband, even though the man, having succeeded in calming "his tyrannical rib" (as Day described the wife), had decided to drop the charges. One of the lengthier reports even included a bit of dialect:

> Wm. Scott, from Centre Market, brought up for assaulting Charlotte Gray, a young woman with whom he lived. The magistrate, learning that they never were married, offered the prisoner a discharge, on condition that he would marry the injured girl, who was very willing to withdraw the complaint on such terms. Mr. Scott cast a sheep's eye towards the girl, and then looking out of the window, gave the bridewell a melancholy survey: he then gave the girl another look, and was hesitating as to which he should choose—a wife or a prison. The Justice insisted on an immediate answer. At length he concluded that he "might as well marry the critter," and they left the office apparently satisfied.

Day also included on the page short items more typical of the six-penny papers, such as news of the arrival in the city of the celebrated balloonist Charles Durant, a dinner given for the postmaster general in Nashville, and the continuing expansion of New York's economy. He devoted more space to a Dickensian account of an orphan boy from a local almshouse who had been taken in by a family on Pearl Street. On the first day in his new home, the boy told his foster mother about the only friend he had ever had, "old dusty Bob, the rag-man, died last week"—Bob, as it turns out, had once given the boy a piece of gingerbread. Considerable attention was given to a story copied from the *Courier and Enquirer* about the suicide of a young man in Boston who had taken laudanum "in a fit of temporary derangement occasioned by an affair of the heart in which his happiness was deeply involved." The items Day had taken from out-of-town papers were almost entirely occupied with murder: "a most outrageous and cold-blooded murder" perpetrated in Columbus, Ohio; a man in Pennsylvania on trial for the murder of his wife; an expatriate American family in South America murdered by a gang of slaves; in Hartford, a sighting on a steamboat of the notorious Ephraim K. Avery, the Methodist minister recently acquitted of the murder of a young woman.

Benjamin Day wasn't a graceful writer, but he had an eye for a compelling story, and the news page he put together on September 3, 1833, was unlike anything New York had ever seen before. As city journalism, it was—in both meanings of the word—sensational. Gone were the merchant papers' lengthy perorations on tariffs or trade policy, month-old reports from Gibraltar and Buenos Aires, and clever ripostes to jabs by rival editors, replaced by stories that were brief (the small page contained fully twenty-seven items), often amusing, and strongly seasoned with sex, romance, intrigue, violence, death—the types of stories Benjamin Day figured most New Yorkers wanted to read about.

The difference was evident on the front page. Not for Day any long-winded speeches from an editor's favored politicians; instead, he offered a humorous tale, presented almost entirely in dialogue, about a dueling Irish captain. The more notable item, though, was a smaller one, fitted in at the bottom-right corner:

A Whistler.—A boy in Vermont, accustomed to working alone, was so prone to whistling, that as soon as he was by himself, he unconsciously commenced. When asleep, the muscles of his mouth, chest, and lungs were so completely concatenated in the association, he whistled with astonishing shrillness. A pale countenance, loss of appetite, and almost total prostration of strength, convinced his mother it would end in death, if not speedily overcome, which was accomplished by placing him in the society of another boy, who had orders to give him a blow as soon as he began to whistle.

Was there really such a boy? Day hadn't placed the story on page two, which was reserved for news, but in a more ambiguous spot, on the front page, where newspapers occasionally ran works of fiction. Those pieces, however, were clearly labeled as fiction. This item was formatted like a news story, although it lacked the sort of identifying details that would be expected of one.

In its description of a country boy performing a routine act in an exaggerated way, "A Whistler" resembles a form of story just then becoming popular in the American West—the tall tale. But it is perhaps more suggestive of what the great showman P. T. Barnum, himself about to arrive in New York, liked to call a "humbug," a fanciful display of some sort, entertaining enough to "suddenly arrest public attention," as he put it, and possessing just enough verisimilitude to make it seem at least possibly genuine. New Yorkers, as it turned out, loved humbugs. They happily handed over their money for the privilege of being amused by them, and seemed never to tire of debating their veracity. P. T. Barnum would grow rich and famous on the strength of his humbugs, while the *Sun,* which placed on the front page of its first issue the story of a Vermont boy who whistled even in his sleep, would win untold readers with a series of articles announcing the discovery of unicorns and man-bats on the moon.

AFTER several hours of hawking their papers, Day and his two assistants counted up their pennies. All told, they had more than three dollars: over three hundred papers sold. Despite the encouraging start, Day could hardly have felt elated. It was Tuesday afternoon, he hadn't slept since Sunday, and it was already time to begin work on the next day's edition. He trudged back toward William Street, carrying the unsold papers, as New York careened around him. He needed help: help in writing the paper, and help in getting the papers sold. The answer to the first problem would arrive within the week; the answer to the second arrived even earlier and, like the *Sun* itself, would change the landscape of the city forever.

CHAPTER 2

The News of the City

THE NOTICE APPEARED in the very next issue of the *Sun,* on September 4, 1833—an innocuous-seeming four lines buried on page three. It was overshadowed by a pair of much larger theatrical advertisements, the more notable of them publicizing the new comedy at the Park Theater, *Rip Van Winkle,* that featured the dramatist himself, Mr. James Henry Hackett (coming off a celebrated run as Falstaff), in the title role. Benjamin Day had likely copied the theatrical advertisements from the six-penny papers, along with the help-wanted notices he placed directly underneath, from employers seeking cooks, nurses, and chambermaids. But there was one among them that clearly hadn't been taken from elsewhere, two sentences that an exhausted Benjamin Day must have composed with a commingled sense of hope and desperation:

TO THE UNEMPLOYED.—A number of steady men can find employment by vending this paper. A liberal discount is allowed to those who buy to sell again.

Day was expecting unemployed men to respond to his appeal, but the following morning a ten-year-old boy named Bernard Flaherty walked into the *Sun*'s office and announced that he was there for the job. He was new to the city, he explained, a recent arrival from Cork, in the south of Ireland. Day was taken aback by the sight of this ragged boy standing before him, but he had always been a great exponent of hard work and personal initiative; and perhaps he also recalled how he had worked as an apprentice printer when he was only a few years older than Bernard Flaherty and living in circumstances far less dire. He couldn't see the harm in giving the boy a chance, so he gave him a hundred papers and told him to go out and sell all he could. He would pay two dollars a week, Day said, and there was a bonus in it for him if he managed to sell more than a hundred papers in a day.

Bernard Flaherty proved to be unusually adept at the street patter that would come to be known as "hollering," seemed to understand instinctively how to charm a crowd into handing over their pennies (years later, under the stage name Barney Williams, he would become famous as an Irish-dialect comedian in plays such as *The Emerald Ring* and *The Connie Soogah*). He sold the hundred papers and more, and in the coming weeks he would be joined by several other boys, their piping voices crying out each morning the exclamatory headlines that Benjamin Day was learning sold best: *Double Distilled Villainy! Cursed Effects of Drunkenness! Awful Occurrence! Infamous Affair!*

For at least a century the scrappy, sharp-talking newsboy in his baggy trousers and soft cap, the urchin with a heart of gold, would be an iconic part of the city's life, beloved as an emblem of pluck and hustle and shrewdness, qualities on which New Yorkers prided themselves; but like all icons this was an idea made more of wish than fact, bearing little resemblance to the actual lives of the newsboys, which were as hard as the sidewalks that too often served as their bed, as unforgiving as the winter nights in which they huddled together in coal bins and sand boxes and ash heaps, warmed only by the closeness of their own bodies. Within a few years, when the newspapers that had now grown large and prosperous— at least in part on the boys' labor—began to purchase expensive steam-powered printing presses for their underground press rooms, the boys slept on the gratings outside the newspaper offices, enveloping themselves in the steam rising up from the machines that ran through the night to print the papers they would sell on awakening. When they could they slept in the lobbies of the newspaper offices, though often they were rousted by printers who poured water on them as they slept, a technique that had proven effective in scattering rats.

Some of the boys died quickly, of exposure, and others slowly, of consumption. Like Bernard Flaherty, many of them had been born in Ireland and come to America as outcasts, and many had no parents, or had parents whose only communication was through curses and blows, and either they had been thrown out or they had left by choice, preferring to make the streets of the city their home. Some of them, by the time they began selling papers, no longer even remembered their own names, although this proved less an obstacle than might be imagined, as the boys mostly dispensed with their given names, replacing them with ones they bestowed on each other: Sniffey, Pickle-nose, Fat Jack, Professor, Carrots, Dodge-me-John, Tickle-me-foot, Lozenges, Blood-sucker, The Ghost. Few had much schooling, but now during the day they learned arithmetic (eventually Benjamin Day worked out an arrangement in which he charged them sixty-seven cents cash for a hundred papers, or seventy-five cents on credit), while at night they learned English drama, shouting "Hi-hi-hi!" from the pits of the theaters, elbowing each other to stay awake, eating peanuts and then tossing the shells at the actors they didn't like. In time they developed their own dialect and traditions and codes of conduct, the prevailing one being the code of the wild, under which smaller newsboys were regularly plundered by larger ones, the littlest of them—some as young as five years old—being as weak and vulnerable as the baby fish that gave them their nickname: small fry.

For generations, countless boys thus kept themselves alive, and some of them—those who were especially enterprising or especially charming or especially violent—even managed to become rich. Mark Maguire, famed as "The King of the Newsboys," started out in life peddling the *Sun,* having only enough pennies to purchase two or three copies at a time. He built up his business little by little until eventually he started making deals with publishers to buy newspapers at a bulk discount and then subcontracted the selling to others, making a profit on each boy's sales. By the time he was twenty-five (still nearly as short and chubby as he had been when he was a newsboy) he had a wife and children and lived in a large house and drove a fast horse, and was said to control the fortunes of no fewer than five hundred newsboys.

Up to this time the city's newspaper editors had considered it ungentlemanly to seek out readers—a newspaper, after all, was not a molasses cake or a piece of fruit, to be hawked on the street by ragamuffins—and took pride in the fact that their readerships had been achieved without solicitation. But the success of the *Sun,* which by the end of the year was selling in the thousands, led the other daily papers to hire their own newsboys, transforming the newspaper business in the city, and the city itself. Newspapers had been forever removed from the cloister of plush drawing rooms and ornate countinghouses, and now could be found all over, in the wharves on the west side and the warehouses on the east, and the sounds of commerce that rose up each morning from the city streets always included high-pitched cries recounting what had happened there the day before.

DURING the first week of the *Sun*'s publication in early September 1833, Benjamin Day received another visitor looking for a job. The young man standing before him, George Washington Wisner, had the wavy dark hair, strong jaw, and coal-black eyes of a theatrical leading man, though Day could perceive an intelligence in those eyes, along with a cockiness and a certain hardness as well, the result of half a dozen years of difficult living on his own; and perhaps Day, who prided himself on his discernment of others, also detected in the young man's spare frame, in a certain hesitation of breath or movement, the fragile constitution that would compel him to leave the *Sun* only twenty months later, and to which he would eventually succumb, in a frontier town in Michigan, at the age of thirty-seven.

George Wisner was twenty-one years old, just two years younger than Benjamin Day, and although the two men had significant political differences (Wisner was more radical, particularly on the slavery question), they also had much in common. Like Day, Wisner was a printer by trade, moving to New York at the age of nineteen to seek his fortune. He came from the small town of Auburn in western New York, where he, like Day, had received a common-school education; at the age of fifteen Wisner had also left school to apprentice as a printer at a local newspaper. And like Day and so many other young men from the country, Wisner had come to New York looking for work in the burgeoning print trades. By 1833 he was working for a Nassau Street newspaper, the *New-York Evangelist*. The work, however, could not have been as steady as he would have liked, because the *Evangelist* was a weekly rather than a daily paper, and in September Wisner appeared at the *Sun* office on William Street looking for a job.

It was a fortuitous moment for Wisner to arrive, as Day was just seeking someone to work as his police court reporter. The *Sun*'s police reports had already proven highly popular with readers, and he was eager to continue them, but he had a problem. The police court went into session at four in the morning, to process more efficiently those whom the watchmen had rounded up the previous night, and Day couldn't attend the court sessions and do everything else that was required to bring out the *Sun* each day. He needed someone who was industrious, trustworthy, ready to get up before dawn to do his reporting, and, not incidentally, was willing to do it on the cheap. Wisner was young and single (and therefore inexpensive), and he was enthusiastic, and he came highly recommended by the foreman of the *Evangelist,* James G. Wilson, whom Day so respected that six years later he would ask him to be his partner on a new literary magazine called *Brother Jonathan.* Day offered Wisner four dollars a week to write the police column and in the afternoons help out with writing or composing, and though the sum would barely keep him housed and fed Wisner quickly agreed to the deal.

No New York newspaper had ever had a police court reporter on staff before. The *Courier and Enquirer* and one or two of the other papers occasionally ran police reports, but only on especially slow days, when none of the foreign or national papers had arrived and the editor was desperate to fill the news columns. And even this modest outlay of space had been met with furious criticism from rival papers, who assailed the reports as inappropriate for the pages of a respectable newspaper. "It is a fashion which does not meet with our approbation, on the score of either propriety or taste," declared the *Evening Post.* "To say nothing of the absolute indecency of some of the cases which are allowed occasionally to creep into print, we deem it of little benefit to the cause of morals thus to familiarize the community, and especially the younger parts of it, to the details of misdemeanor and crime." ("Besides," the *Post* added pragmatically, "it suggests to the novice in vice all the means of becoming expert in its devices.")

The *Sun,* on the other hand, reveled in the police court reports, which appeared without fail and eventually filled as much as a third of the entire news page. Every morning George Wisner rose at three and made his way through the dimly lit streets of Lower Manhattan to the long yellow police court building behind City Hall, settling himself into a corner of the noisy, crowded courtroom with his paper and pencil to await the call of the morning's cases.

William Smith, alias Fitz, "got drunk by drinking too much." The magistrate informed him that this was the way in which people always got drunk, and admonished him to lead a sober life in the future; after which he was discharged.

John Votey, of Reed street, was charged with getting drunk, and assaulting his father and mother. John was a mischievous boy of about

38—his father was 93, and his mother who appeared as complainant, was 88. John was in the constant habit of getting drunk and abusing his parents—yet the mother couldn't find it in her heart to have him sent to prison. The old lady was so overcome with the fatigue of getting to the police so early in the morning, that she fainted. One of the officers supported her in his arms until she recovered, and, taking the arm of her drunken, disgraceful son, she left the office in tears.

Mr. and Mrs. Townsend made their appearance this morning to settle their connubial disputes after the manner the law has prescribed. It appeared on investigation, that Mrs. Townsend asked her husband yesterday for a two shilling piece to buy some brandy "to wash the children's heads"; that the husband not believing that his lady would allow the spiritous liquid to go as high as the head, without saluting it with her lips, refused to grant the request; a quarrel ensued, and Mr. Townsend was driven out of the house by the infuriated dame. Last evening, when Mr. T. returned from his work to get his supper, he found his wife in an unmentionable condition, and upon his upbraiding her, she took up the tongs and smote him over the head. Mr. T. then knocked her down. They were both committed.

Susan Burke—a lady vagrant—hadn't any home for 3 months. The magistrate said it was time she had one, and gave her one for 6 months.

Passing through the courtroom each morning was a dismal parade of drunkards and wife beaters, con men and petty thieves, prostitutes and their johns. But Wisner could also see love, fear, anger, jealousy, greed, sometimes even tenderness and generosity, and while it is an overstatement to call him "the Balzac of the daybreak court," as he was called by a historian of the *Sun*, he did display a novelist's eye for the telling detail, the ability to limn a character in a few short strokes. His police reports were filled with the distinctive voices of the Five Points and its environs, by turns argumentative, wheedling, rueful, furious, mocking of themselves and those around them. Many of the cases he dispensed with in a single brisk sentence ("George McCarthy was charged with stealing a stove from 491 Pearl street. Committed."). Most he granted a couple of sentences, but sometimes, when the material seemed especially inviting, Wisner presented his readers little set pieces, complete with dialogue and stage directions:

Hugh Kelly, was charged with attempting to pass bills of a broken bank, knowing them to be such. Mr. Kelly was a man of about 40—bald head—long face—and had on a neat gray quaker coat.

> MAG.—What's your occupation, Kelly?
> PRIS.—(quite angry) My occupation!! I'm a *merchant*, Sir.
> M.—What do you deal in?
> P.—Goods, to be sure, and what does your honor suppose I'd be after dealing in?
> M.—Where's your store?
> P.—(Rather bothered) Why—its—its—what's that you say?
> M.—Where's your store?
> P.—O, your honor, I meant I was a *travelling* merchant.
> M.—Ah, you're a pedler, then—where are you from?
> P.—I have the misfortune to have come from Ireland.
> M.—Then you call it a misfortune to be an Irishman?
> P.—I do, your honor,—If ever the Almighty erred it was when he made my native country—my own swate Ireland. (Laughter.)
> M.—Stop Sir, we don't allow blasphemy here.
> P.—(Seating himself very coolly) Very good,

Nothing like this had ever appeared in an American newspaper. Wisner's police reports were at once scary and amusing and titillating, a daily glimpse into a world previously hidden from the public's gaze. New Yorkers were riveted by the spectacle; the police office column instantly became the most popular feature of the paper.

George Wisner was proving immensely valuable to Benjamin Day, and within weeks the two men had struck a new deal: Wisner would continue to receive four dollars a week, but he and Day would now split the *Sun*'s profits, with Wisner's share being applied toward a half ownership of the paper. By the end of October the *Sun*'s masthead read: "Published daily, at 222 William Street, by Benjamin H. Day and George W. Wisner." Day had originally conceived of the *Sun* primarily as a means of publicizing his printing business, and he was always more interested in the business side of the paper than in the actual writing of it. Though he retained the title of senior editor, he increasingly devoted his attention to production, advertising, and circulation, and after winning the printing contract for the nearby American Museum (the large collection of oddities that would later be acquired by P. T. Barnum) he left the editorial duties almost entirely to Wisner.

By the beginning of 1834 George Wisner was the de facto editor of the *Sun,* and the paper increasingly reflected his brand of radical politics, which included—highly unusual in a New York newspaper editor—strong sympathy for the city's abolition movement, a small but impassioned band of reformers comprising mostly middle-class blacks and whites led by two wealthy silk merchants, the brothers Arthur and Lewis Tappan. One *Sun* article, for instance, reported gleefully that the anniversary dinner of the New-York Colonization Society (a group encouraging the migration of free American blacks to Africa—a pet cause of the editors of the *Courier and Enquirer* and the *Commercial Advertiser*) had collected only $238, while the previous day's benefit for the American Anti-Slavery Society had garnered ten times that amount. In another story, reporting the arrest of a runaway slave by one of the city's marshals, the *Sun* acknowledged that while the officer had performed his duty as required by law, "We believe the day is not far distant when the clanking of slavery's chains will be heard no more—and America stand before the world practicing, as well as preaching, the glorious doctrine that *all* men are created free and equal."

In one especially striking item, Wisner reported the story of a Missouri slave driver who had purchased a young black woman married to another slave. The woman had been given ten minutes to prepare her departure and was not permitted to see her husband, although she did manage to send word to him that she was gone. Hearing the news, the husband was "absolutely stunned with the most unexpected blow" and thought to follow the slave driver into town to say good-bye, but this idea caused him greater anguish than he could bear. When he was asked what he intended to do, the slave replied, "I will tell master to sell me to the driver, and go with my poor wife; my days will not be long on earth, and I hope this will shorten them."

It was unusual enough that George Wisner recognized a slave's capacity for full human emotion—but actually to print the slave's words as he bewailed the injustice of his lot was, for a New York newspaperman, extraordinary. Wisner, though, did not end there. Having recounted the story of the sundered couple, he went on to challenge his readers directly:

Suppose, reader, the scales were turned. Suppose a negro should seize a white woman, force her away from her husband, carry her to a city of blacks, and sell her to some purse-proud, sooty African, as a slave—perhaps a paramour—what would be your feeling, at thus beholding the tenderest and holiest ties of human nature trampled upon?

It was a highly daring stance for a newspaper to take in New York, perhaps the most pro-Southern of Northern cities, with an economy highly dependent on the cotton trade. Nor would the story endear the *Sun* to its readers, many of whom were Irish immigrants engaged in a fierce economic struggle with American-born blacks. But that didn't seem to matter; week after week the *Sun*'s readership continued to grow. By November 1833, an editorial proudly reported a daily circulation of more than two thousand. "Its success," the *Sun* pronounced of itself, "is now beyond question."

No longer did Benjamin Day have to copy advertisements or clip news stories from rival papers. Advertising was now coming in steadily, the police reports were a sensation, and Wisner had branched out into book reviews and other features. The paper had also begun running a serial on its front page, *The Life of Davy Crockett;* Day was sure that the frontiersman's already legendary exploits in hunting bears and wrestling wildcats would appeal to his readers. The *Sun* had even begun occasionally to print illustrations alongside its articles. The very first one, a large woodcut stretching across two columns, was captioned "Herschel's Forty-Feet Telescope." It depicted the large reflecting telescope that had belonged to the late British astronomer Sir William Herschel, the discoverer of Uranus and the father of Sir John Herschel, who that very year had set sail with his own telescopes for the Cape of Good Hope—where, the *Sun* would later report, he made the most remarkable lunar discoveries.

In December 1833, with circulation approaching four thousand, nearly as great as that of the mighty *Courier and Enquirer,* Benjamin Day bought a new double-cylinder printing press; it was able to produce about one thousand impressions an hour, five times the capacity of his earlier one. With the new press turning out so many papers each day, Day realized that he needed help with production, and he hired the journeyman printers Willoughby Lynde and William J. Stanley to work for the *Sun* as compositors and pressmen.

Lynde and Stanley were old friends of Day's from his time at the *Daily Sentinel.* They had likely agreed to take the jobs because they felt more comfortable working for a friend than for any of the aristocratic six-penny editors, but in fact the opposite turned out to be the case: they were still trying to survive on a printer's salary of nine dollars a week, while their old friend Ben Day was earning profits that, in the early days of 1834, seemed potentially limitless. (By January, Wisner's share of the *Sun*'s profits had already purchased him a half ownership of the paper.) Before, Day had stood beside them in the composing room, just another itinerant printer with, as the saying went, itching feet and a parched throat, but now he was an editor himself, giving them orders in his gruff, no-nonsense manner, his attention largely taken up by the advertisers and subscribers who brought in the money. Lynde and Stanley must have envied Day's newfound success and resented taking instructions from a former colleague. They must also have regretted not listening more closely to his ideas about a penny paper when they had the chance, because only a few months after Day hired them, Lynde and Stanley left the *Sun* to start a penny paper of their own.

The new paper was to be called the *New York Transcript,* and another printer, Billings Hayward, would join them as co-owner. As the paper's editor they chose Asa Greene, a local bookseller and the author of several satirical novels. The *Sun* had shown the *Transcript*'s owners that a penny paper could not succeed without a police court reporter, and for that position they hired William H. Attree, a printer at a local type foundry, paying him the munificent salary of three dollars a week. (A recent English immigrant, Attree was, by every account, abrasive and mean-spirited, prone to confrontations, and not overly concerned with the accuracy of his news reports. The normally even-tempered Horace Greeley characterized him as "a shrewd, active and unprincipled penny-a-liner," while Isaac Clark Pray, a New York journalist of midcentury, observed that Attree was "facile with his pen" and "indifferent . . . to the feelings of the poor creatures left to its mercy." Attree's general character was perhaps most cogently captured in the nickname by which he was widely known around town: "Oily Attree.")

In March 1834 the *Transcript* began publication and proved to be a surprisingly potent rival. Attree's police columns, while coarser in tone, were otherwise strikingly similar to Wisner's (from the heading "Police Office" to the device of presenting certain cases in dramatic form), and thus helped negate an advantage the *Sun* would otherwise have had. The *Transcript* gave extensive coverage to prizefights and horse races, something the *Sun* had not emphasized, which won the paper a following among the city's sports fans; its printer owners had also chosen well in Asa Greene, who brought a winningly light touch to the paper's columns, with a special flair for amusing descriptions of city life. By the end of 1834 the *Transcript* was fast catching up to the *Sun* in total circulation and was even outselling it in the towns outside the city.

Benjamin Day, however, was not to be outdone. At the start of 1835 he bought yet another printing press for the *Sun,* this one a state-of-the-art Napier. He also increased the size of the *Sun's* pages to eleven by eighteen inches. (The new paper was costing him four-fifths of a cent per sheet, nearly as much as the price of the newspaper itself, but he hoped to make up the difference with the additional advertising the larger pages would allow.) The *Sun's* expanded news page offered each day a richly flavored salmagundi, in which a forceful call for the abolition of imprisonment for debt, an investigation into reports of new cholera cases, and a critique of urban renewal plans ("of all the improvements recently introduced, there is not one that does not favor the *rich,* to the inconvenience of the *poor*") might be mixed together with accounts of comically weaving drunkards and a local pig with a face like a human being's. In the spring, Wisner took the *Sun's* readers on a tour of the Five Points, offering them "a thorough examination of those haunts of iniquity which have become so infamously celebrated," its cellar lodgings and tipling houses and brothels with names like the Diving Bell and the Yankee Kitchen and Squeeze Gut Alley. For only a penny the *Sun's* readers were, from the safety of their own homes, allowed entry into "seats of vice, hot beds of debauchery, wretchedness, and poverty, such as few eyes have witnessed." It was a sensational story, done in classic *Sun* style: equal parts crusade and carnival.

A more fanciful story reported how a doctor in the city had successfully extracted a large black snake, more than four feet in length, that had been living for some months in a sailor's stomach. (The sailor claimed that he had drunk from a spring in Jamaica, at the bottom of which he later noticed several tiny hair snakes wriggling.) The ingenious physician had coaxed the snake out of the sailor's mouth with a bowl of warm milk—the face of the man had then "assumed a dark and ghastly appearance"—at which point the snake was immediately seized and killed. The snake story created quite a stir in the city, and in subsequent weeks the *Sun* published several follow-up items about the "singular operation." The *Courier and Enquirer* and the *Journal of Commerce* denounced the story as a hoax, but Day, whose first issue of the *Sun* had featured a boy who whistled while he slept, knew that his readers would enjoy debating its truthfulness and appreciate its entertainment value. For his part, Wisner preferred to see the story as an allegory: the black snake of slavery, swallowed small but now grown large and dangerous, might be coaxed into unwariness with milk (of human kindness), but this was only a halfway measure, and it then had to be seized and destroyed by violence.

Benjamin Day allowed Wisner to print his political views, but he also understood that his readers wanted to be entertained as well as edified. Even more, they wanted to find out about the life that was going on all around them. The best newspaper, he believed, served as a kind of omnium-gatherum that welcomed (as the *Sun* itemized in an article called "What Is a Newspaper?") "bombastic panegyrics, jests, anecdotes, deaths, marriages, conundrums, enigmas, puns, poetry, acrostics and advertisements of every shade and color, and form, from grave to gay, from lively to severe." News was not just the high doings of important persons, but rather the "shreds and patches" of everyday life, a daily record of the city in all its mottled and disorderly splendor.

Best of all, Day knew, were the crime stories (they were the ones that most fully engaged the attention of his readers), and in the spring of 1835 an especially promising crime story was developing in a town north of the city. For some years New Yorkers had been acquainted with a man named Robert Matthews, a carpenter from upstate who had grown his hair and beard long and rechristened himself Matthias the Prophet. Dressed in a green frock coat lined with pink silk, carrying a sword and preaching a furious gospel, Matthias had managed to win himself a small following among some of the city's prominent residents, a handful of whom gave him money and houses in exchange for his promise of eternal abundance in heaven. Matthias's disciples lived together in a farmhouse near the town of Sing Sing, up the Hudson, where they grew their own food, ate and bathed communally, and listened to his hours-long tirades against the human devils who would one day incur the wrath of the Lord, among them clergymen, doctors, disobedient women, and men who wore spectacles. Eventually dark stories began to spread about sexual escapades in the farmhouse, and when one of the disciples, a merchant named Elijah Pierson, fell sick and died and Matthias (known to the authorities as Robert Matthews) was arrested and charged with poisoning him, all of the ingredients—murder, madness, apostasy, depravity—were in place for what would become one of the most bizarre and sensational trials New York had ever seen, and for the *Sun,* a potential bonanza.

Ever since the arrest, the *Sun* had been devoting extensive coverage to the case, examining it from every possible angle, including a report from a phrenologist who claimed to have analyzed Matthews's cranial developments from across the courtroom during his arraignment ("Amativeness, large; Philoprogenitiveness, moderately large; Destructiveness moderately full; Combativeness rather small," etc.). There was no chance that Benjamin Day would miss out on the opportunity to bring the trial of Matthias the Prophet to his readers; unfortunately, the trial was being held in White Plains, well north of the city. Wisner was tied up with his daily police reports and Day, who was not a polished writer, didn't think he could render the events of the trial in all their lurid glory. In the end, he decided that he would travel up to White Plains; if necessary he would cover the trial himself, but he would much prefer to find someone who could do it for him. All of the newspapers in town, even the staid mercantile papers, had been reporting on the case in the months leading up to the trial, but to Day's mind the most colorful and lucidly written coverage had come from the writer for the *Courier and Enquirer.* Perhaps, he thought, he might offer the *Courier*'s man a little money to write for the *Sun* on the side. The articles would all be unsigned anyway, and surely the paper's editor, the redoubtable James Watson Webb, was not paying his reporter so well that he could afford to turn down extra money.

Inside the crowded courtroom, Day asked a spectator to point out the reporter from the *Courier and Enquirer.* He was directed to a man of middling stature, with a prominent forehead, crossed eyes, and pockmarked cheeks. Day introduced himself as the editor of the *Sun.* Was he the reporter from the *Courier?*

He was, the man replied. His name, he said, was Richard Adams Locke.

At the time of the Matthias trial Richard Adams Locke had not yet grown the beard he wears in the only known image of him, a portrait made by the New York engraver Augustus Robin. The engraving is undated, but Locke is now a man deep into his middle years, and has turned out for the sitting in his finest dress. His silk bowtie shines in the light; his collar is starched and high, and a thin triangle of white shirt peeks out beneath a black vest and topcoat. His nose is Roman, strong and sharp and aquiline at the bridge; little half-moons of age and worry wax under his

The only known image of Richard Adams Locke, in an undated
portrait made by the New York engraver Augustus Robin.
(Courtesy of the Library of Congress.)

eyes, which gaze sternly toward the horizon. The mouth is a thin, straight line. Locke's hair is still dark, but has now receded behind a great broad brow, one much admired by Edgar Allan Poe. "The forehead is truly beautiful in its intellectuality," Poe observed in his 1846 *Literati of New York City* essay about Locke. "I am acquainted with no person possessing so fine a forehead as Mr. Locke." His beard is modest and well trimmed, not as luxuriant as the ones favored by some of his journalistic contemporaries, but even so Locke surely hoped it might hide some of the scarring that pitted his face, remnants of the smallpox he had suffered as a boy in England. Some scars are visible on the cheeks and forehead, but Augustus Robin has clearly downplayed them in his engraving; moreover, the artist has positioned his subject in three-quarter profile, to minimize the effect of a severe case of strabismus—another unfortunate vestige of smallpox—in which not just one but both of Locke's eyes were permanently crossed.

It is a handsome engraving, the sort that any customer would have wanted to leave to his descendants, and to posterity. Yet it does not capture the man that Richard Adams Locke actually was, and not simply because of the engraver's generous attentions. The subject of this portrait is by all appearances a man of means, but at the time of his retirement at the age of sixty-one, having lived in New York for nearly three decades, Locke still did not own his own home and had accumulated a personal estate estimated at only one thousand dollars. The grim set of his mouth belies the memory of a man known around town for his fine sense of humor, who was a popular drinking companion among the journalists who regularly gathered after work for steaks at Windust's restaurant or drinks at the bar of the American Hotel. A winning congeniality was among the chief characteristics Locke's colleagues remembered; another was his modesty. In an age when a titanic ego seemed to be a job requirement for a New York newspaper editor, Richard Adams Locke shunned publicity. He spoke little of himself, and even less about the life he had left behind. When he did, however, he proved to be a distinctly unreliable narrator. So the history of Richard Adams Locke that has come down through the years bears a certain resemblance to the moon story itself: some of the details are genuine enough, but others are inventions of Locke's own, and it is not always an easy matter to tell them apart.

CHAPTER 3

Bearer of the
Falcon Crest

Richard Adams Locke made his name as newspaper fabulist, but his inventions were hardly confined to tales of life on the moon. They encompassed, as well, the stories of his family background, his education, even the location of his birth.

Parish records show that Locke was born on September 22, 1800, in East Brent, a village in the southwestern English county of Somerset. He was *not* born in New York City, which was the version of events that in later years he regularly told to census inspectors and officials of the New York Custom House, the institution that provided him a desperately needed salary for the final two decades of his work life, when he was no longer able to function as a journalist. Unfortunately, the New York story has been repeated in several reference works; even the introduction to the 1852 republication of the moon series, entitled *The Celebrated "Moon Story," Its Origins and Incidents,* claims, confusingly, that Locke was "of English parentage and education, but American birth." (The introduction was written by William Griggs, a friend of Locke's, who likely maintained the cover story to protect Locke's employment.)

Richard Adams Locke's branch of the family had lived in Somerset for centuries, as far back as records were kept. According to an eighteenth-century Locke family historian, himself a resident of East Brent, "The Locke family in this neighborhood consider themselves as descended from a very ancient house." It was an eminent line, with its own coat of arms, colored blue and gold, displaying an escutcheon of three indorsed falcons below a crest of another falcon bearing a padlock in its beak. The family's forebears included numerous ministers, sheriffs, merchants, army officers, and one very eminent philosopher. Richard Adams Locke was related to John Locke, although he was not, as he sometimes claimed, a direct descendant: his great-great-great-grandfather Lewis (who managed to father thirty-five children by four wives) was the philosopher's uncle.

Richard Adams Locke's grandfather—also named Richard Locke—was by all accounts a remarkable man, as shrewd as he was intelligent, possessed of keen powers of observation, boundless energy, and an indomitable will. Born into a farm family in Burnham, at the age of eighteen he became a land surveyor, a trade that he would pursue for nearly fifty years and eventually pass on to his son. Richard Locke, however, was not content to measure and assess the land; he was far more interested in improving it. Over the course of his life he almost single-handedly revolutionized farming in Somerset by developing innovative agricultural techniques and advocating land reform, in which formerly common fields were enclosed and the acreage allotted to individual farmers. He was a highly regarded writer as well, who published two major histories of Somerset, *The Western Rebellion* and *The Customs of the Manor of Taunton;* at his death he left three other manuscripts still unpublished, the most important being *A Survey of Somerset,* a massive undertaking (published posthumously) in which he scrupulously recorded the entire geography of the county, enumerated on the title page as "the Hundreds, Cities, Towns, Parishes, Tithings, Manors, Villages, Hamlets, Gentlemen's Seats, Capital Farms, Decayed Vills, Forests, Hills, Rivers, Bridges, Sites of Abbies, and old Encampments." Any profits from the book's publication, Locke noted in the manuscript, were to go to the Burnham Society, a religious debating society that he founded in 1772 and for which he was the main benefactor. He always viewed his writing much as he had his work for land reform: as motivated by social benefit rather than private gain. "I never published a pamphlet which I conceived would be written by another hand," he wrote proudly in his *Survey of Somerset,* adding, "I have never enriched myself by printing to the value of sixpence."

Still, Richard Locke was a man of vast ambitions, personal as well as communal, and what he avowed about printing did not necessarily obtain for other business matters. At eighteen he made his first purchase of land, a twenty-acre farm owned in absentia by the Lord Mayor of London, and for the rest of his life he accumulated parcels in small, steady increments;

by the time of his grandson's birth in 1800 he owned 146 acres, making him one of Burnham's wealthiest landowners, and he lived in the manor house of Highbridge, a small seaside village within Burnham.

This illustrious Locke lived to the age of sixty-nine (he outlived all three of his wives), leaving behind him four children, two books and innumerable shorter writings, and a permanently altered landscape. (At least one contemporary historian has cited him as "perhaps Burnham's most distinguished native inhabitant.") He had appointed his son Richard as his executor, and to him he left the bulk of his estate. Otherwise, not much is known of the younger Richard. The only written mention of him comes in a letter in a 1792 issue of *Gentleman's Magazine,* a passing reference to "the ingenious Mr. Richard Locke, of Magdalen-hall, Oxford," the Locke family having now risen into the educational elite of British society. At Oxford he studied theology, though rather than become a minister he followed his father into the surveying business. He also lived in a house that had been left to him by his father, called Mill Batch Farm, in the nearby village of East Brent. In all ways, it seems, he followed the course his father had set, none more striking than in his choice of wife: Anne Adams, the daughter of his father's third wife—his stepsister.

RICHARD and Anne Locke had two sons, the elder of whom carried both of his parents' names: Richard Adams Locke. He was the third of the Locke children, following Anne and Mary, and preceding the twins Emma and Jane, Christopher (who died in infancy), and Cecilia. Richard Adams Locke was born at the opening of the nineteenth century, but the landscape of his childhood might well have been recognizable to a resident born in the Middle Ages: lush fields dotted with long, low farmhouses built of stone dug from the nearby hills; cider houses with cool, dark cellars full of apples; graceful stone windmills standing atop the hillsides, their black canvas sails turning the intricate machinery that ground wheat into flour and beans into meal, operated by millers who dressed as they always had, in long white smocks, with red kerchiefs tied around their necks. East Brent was a modest farming village, just a narrow outcropping of thatch and stone with a few shops, towering above them the high, square white steeple of the Anglican church. There the days passed slowly, the essential rhythms still more attuned to the sun than the clock. For the children of East Brent there were games of leapfrog and prisoner's base, or hopscotch on a court drawn into the dirt with sticks, just six successive rectangles with the word *London* scrawled at the end, an ancient tradition that had surely lost its original meaning, the city as the endpoint of Roman armies on the Great North Road, now replaced with the vague notion of London as a far-off, desirable destination. English weather being what it is, though, more often the play was confined to the house, with spinning tops and cups and balls, games of draughts and dominoes, and for a bookish boy like Richard, hours on end spent reading, mostly tales of moral instruction but, when he could find them, exciting stories of voyages to distant lands, like *Robinson Crusoe* or *Gulliver's Travels*—fantastical tales, though all of them related as absolutely true. When he grew a bit older he could have made the steep climb to the top of Brent Knoll, the highest hill in the area, a good place to sit and read poetry or just gaze down at the countryside, that neat green patchwork of fields and hedges: a landscape attractive and familiar to him, but surely, even then, feeling uncomfortably small, like a hand-me-down garment worn too long.

Looking around from the top of the knoll, Richard Adams Locke would have seen no fewer than seven windmills at work, including one windmill to the north that belonged to his own family. That windmill had been in operation at Mill Batch Farm for well over a century; it was likely worked by a tenant miller living in one of the farm's outbuildings, who paid rent to the Locke family. This would have been just one of Richard Locke's sources of income; there were enough of these to enable him to be called, in the phrase of the day, a man of independent means. By this time he had become a surveyor, after the example of his father, although how much actual surveying he did is not clear. Nor do we know much about the relationship between father and son, although the son's later political activities might help illuminate that, as, perhaps, does another detail from the self-told story of Richard Adams Locke. In his introduction to *The Celebrated "Moon Story," Its Origins and Incidents,* William Griggs mentions that Richard Locke "served in Canada in the Corps of Royal Engineers and subsequently in other regiments throughout the Peninsular war, until the battle of Waterloo," surely information that he got from Richard Adams Locke himself. Though no specific dates are provided, the term of military service would have been fairly lengthy, starting sometime before 1808, when Britain entered the Peninsular War, and lasting at least until 1815, the year of the battle of Waterloo. It also means that Richard Locke would have been trained as an officer, as the Corps of Royal Engineers was an officer-only rank until 1856. Yet a search conducted by the National Archives of the United Kingdom, examining all available indexes of army officers, found no record of a Richard Locke serving in the Royal Engineers at any time from the mid-eighteenth to the mid-nineteenth century, in Canada or anywhere else; nor is there a record of his having served as an officer in any other regiment. So this would seem to be a story of Richard Adams Locke's own concoction—one in which, during a substantial portion of his childhood, his father was not present at all.

Richard Adams Locke's early schooling was conducted by his mother, as was typical among the landed families of that time and place, but by the time he was ten his father had hired him a private tutor; even at that age he had a powerfully descriptive writing style, and with his keen intelligence and seemingly bottomless capacity for knowledge he was already showing signs of becoming a genuine scholar. (Around the village it was often said that he had inherited his grandfather's genius.) The logical next step would have been for Richard Adams Locke to continue his education at one of England's citadels of higher learning, either Oxford or Cambridge. According to the conventional Locke story, he chose Cambridge; it is a detail that is repeated again and again in the historical citations of Richard Adams Locke, from the briefest entries in dictionaries of American writers to the more substantial accounts in Frank O'Brien's history of the *Sun* and William Griggs's introduction to the "*Moon Story*" volume. (According to Griggs's account, Locke "graduated for the Established Church, without taking orders," a story that concisely recapitulates his father's experience at Oxford.) The sole basis for this claim, however, would seem to be Locke's own word: there is no record of Richard Adams Locke ever having attended the University of Cambridge.

The *Alumni Cantabrigienses,* Cambridge's own authoritative, multivolume register, lists "all known students, graduates and holders of office at the University of Cambridge, from the earliest times to 1900." Nine Lockes are included in the volume covering the years 1752 to 1900, but Richard Adams Locke is not among them. (His father does appear in the Oxford equivalent, *Alumni Oxonienses.*) The absence is striking; if Locke's story were true, he would surely be listed there. He would have been included in the *Alumni Cantabrigienses* even if he never earned a degree from Cambridge; indeed, he would be listed even if he had attended a single lecture. To be named in the *Alumni Cantabrigienses* a student had only to matriculate—register for the university. Any student who had failed to matriculate would not have been permitted to take classes at Cambridge, much less graduate.

Richard Adams Locke did not, in fact, attend the University of Cambridge. He did not follow his father into a gentleman's education, before a life spent managing the family estate. The pressure to do so must have been enormous. He was, after all, a Locke of Somerset, a bearer of the falcon crest; even more powerfully, he was a *Richard* Locke, the fourth man in a row to carry that name, and he was his father's only son. Always there was the memory of his grandfather, who had risen from tradesman to lord of the manor, impressing himself on the landscape as deeply and permanently as the fences that now crisscrossed the hillsides, dividing one man's land from another's. Richard Adams Locke surely felt the weight of the generations bearing down on him, and it would not have been much of a surprise if he had finally relented and gone off to university for a time, and then come back home to stay.

But he didn't. Instead, he broke away, in pursuit of a different life. Lockes had lived in East Brent for countless generations, but for him it would be only the starting point. Now, as in one of his childhood games of hopscotch, he set out for London.

RICHARD Adams Locke's sojourn in London is not well chronicled, but it does offer one intriguing detail, the name of the political journal he is said to have written for: the *Republican*. From that brief and obscure period of his life, it is one of the few shards that have survived; still, it is a highly instructive one because it associates him with the cause of British republicanism, the noble effort to transform Great Britain's discriminatory political system by such measures as universal manhood suffrage, annual elections, and the secret ballot. Not only does his republicanism comport with much of what is known about Richard Adams Locke, but it also provides insight into the choices he would later make, including writing his moon series for the *Sun*. For that act can be understood only in the light of his radical politics, which, unfortunately, have always been downplayed in the subsequent retellings of the story.

According to William Griggs, Locke's work for the *Republican* constituted an "unsuccessful effort to indoctrinate the British people with the principles of American democracy." Frank O'Brien wrote essentially the same thing in his history of the *Sun*, although he chose the phrase "theories of American democracy." While these bland readings of Locke's early journalism would have been more palatable to American readers of, respectively, the 1850s and 1920s, they do not convey just how daring, and how dangerous, it was to be a Republican in Great Britain in the early nineteenth century—a time of intense social and political turmoil, when the British government passed an act that prohibited holding a public meeting of more than fifty people without the prior consent of a magistrate, and another that made it a crime to publish material that was seen as encouraging Britons to hate their government.

Many of the British Republicans of the 1820s were, as Griggs and O'Brien indicated, enamored of America; but the new nation served less as a working model than as a source of political inspiration, a symbolic alternative to the existing system, much as the Soviet Union did for many radicals of the following century. Apart from the institution of slavery, strongly condemned by Republicans, America was viewed as a bastion of religious tolerance and civil liberty; perhaps more than anything, it was revered as a society born of rebellion, in which an army of poor farmers had ousted the mighty British Crown, the very government against which the Republicans themselves were struggling. To support greater enfranchisement in Great Britain—not to mention a more equitable system of taxation, another important Republican cause—was to ally oneself with the working class against the aristocrats whom Republicans regularly denounced as useless and corrupt. Republicanism turned Lockean (that is, John Lockean) political philosophy on its head, arguing that *lack* of property, not possession of it, was the foundation of personal virtue, as it encouraged what Republican writer T. J. Wooler called "courage and firmness" rather than submission to the existing system of inequality.

The Republicans found their expression in cheaply printed newspapers and pamphlets, on placards and broadsheets posted on walls, and even on the walls themselves, in graffiti. (As one unsympathetic observer of the time described London, "Libellous caricatures adorn'd the walls; / And greasy pamphlets lay on dirty stalls.") They were the rank outsiders of British society, willing to raise the flag not only for political equality but also, just as scandalously, for religious nonconformism. Many Republicans saw the Anglican Church as its own distinct segment of the British landed gentry—a wealthy beneficiary of an unfair tax policy, an apologist for an antiquated social system, and, too often, a purveyor of religious bigotry.

To be a Republican was to challenge the notion of a divinely sanctioned class structure, the right to rule of Britain's nobility, the ancestral peers and country squires, whose sons attended Oxford and Cambridge before coming into their rightful patrimony—precisely the life that Richard Locke of Burnham had worked so hard to achieve, and that Richard Locke of East Brent was now enjoying. For Richard Adams Locke, to be a Republican was not merely to stand against a political system; it was also to stand against his family.

DURING his time in London Locke wrote for at least two literary journals: a Liverpool publication called the *Bee,* for which he reviewed literature, and the *Imperial Magazine,* founded by the Methodist theologian Samuel Drew, where his chief subjects were biography and Italian history. Still, while Locke would likely have disdained writing for more eminent literary journals such as the *Quarterly Review* and *Blackwood's Edinburgh Magazine*— both of them stoutly Tory in their politics—the *Bee* and the *Imperial* were a long way from the top, not the sort of platform a young writer would most have desired for his work. Though he was intelligent and energetic, and able to write about a wide variety of topics, Locke was having trouble finding his footing in the world of London publishing. London, of course, was a far larger and more bewildering place than the one from which he had come; moreover, he hadn't made the kinds of friendships, so useful in advancing a career, that were often formed among the students in Britain's elite public schools and universities. He must have been living with a real sense of frustration and exhaustion when, at the beginning of 1823, he received an unexpected opportunity: Charles McDowall, a printer and bookseller back in Bristol, offered him the job of editor for a new monthly magazine, to be called the *Bristol Cornucopia.* Becoming editor of the *Cornucopia* meant that he would no longer have to depend for his living on the vagaries of the freelance life. It also meant that he would be leaving London and returning to England's southwest, the land that he knew so well.

In April 1823 McDowall's presses began turning out the first issue of the *Bristol Cornucopia,* a sepia-colored volume of about octavo size, not much larger than one's hand, sold for the price of sixpence. The first issue ran to thirty-two pages, and the second one double that, consisting mainly of essays, poems, and reviews, with subject matter ranging from the history of chemistry to geological theory and the etiology of human depravity. While there is something undeniably invigorating about a magazine in which discussions of Milton and Byron sit side by side with "On the State of Water and Aeriform Matter in Cavities Found in Certain Crystals," much of the writing in the *Cornucopia* seems, by today's standards, almost comically overwrought. "It is generally conceded," begins a review of Milton's poetry, "that even the muse of Homer scarcely wound mightier wings of flame than that which, with solemn and persevering aspiration, bore the genius of Milton above this low diurnal sphere, and made him familiar with regions of glory, of which the Grecian muse never viewed the lightness, nor drank the inspiration."

William Griggs claimed that Locke himself wrote most of the material for the *Cornucopia,* and much of the nonscientific prose does share an overly earnest, self-consciously aesthetic style that can be ascribed to the exuberance of a young writer testing the limits of his own powers. As was common at the time, most of the material is unsigned; the two pieces bearing the initials *R. L.* are the metaphysical essays that lead each of the issues, entitled "Space" and "On the Origin, Nature, and Moral Appliance of Human Knowledge." The essays are recondite, not easily entered; they propose an immanent God, one who inhabits the world everywhere, "as perfect in the centre of a mass of steel or block of marble, as in the 'heaven of heavens.'" The more substantial of the essays, "Space," culminates with the almost Blakean exclamation, "He is in our blood, and in our bones, and in our spirits!" They are two heartfelt reflections on the nature of God and his works that glorify the Divine Being without ever referring to Christ, the Bible, or indeed any Christian teachings.

Perhaps that was what proved to be the problem: perhaps Charles McDowall came to believe that Richard Adams Locke was not hewing closely enough to the "reverence" and "moderation," the celebration of "the grand Doctrines of the Gospel" that McDowall had promised in the prospectus for the *Cornucopia.* If so, McDowell's reaction was the first instance of a lifelong pattern for Locke, of losing editorial jobs after conflicts with publishers. Or maybe the issue was simply financial, as there turned out to be not as many intellectuals in Bristol as McDowall had supposed. In either case, the *Bristol Cornucopia* lasted only two issues. Charles McDowall turned his attentions again to his books and his printing presses, and Richard Adams Locke found himself out of work. It was his first editorial failure, though it was by no means his last; another was to come shortly, just across the county line, back home in Somerset.

A LOCAL newspaper was just then being started in Somerset, to be called the *Bridgwater and Somersetshire Herald,* and an editor was needed. The publishers, Thomas Besley of Exeter and Jeffrey Brinning of South Brent, likely offered Richard Adams Locke the position after hearing of his abilities from his neighbors. Though no copies of the *Herald* survive from the 1820s, for an account of Locke's brief but tumultuous tenure with the paper there are the recollections of a man named James Dare, who had apprenticed for the *Herald* when he was young, and actually set into type many of the editorials written by Richard Adams Locke. After Locke's death in 1871, Dare wrote an article in the *Weston Mercury and Somersetshire Herald* (as the paper was now called) entitled "A Lost Somersetshire Worthy," which extolled the work of this "remarkable individual" and lamented the fact that he was so little remembered even in Somerset. As Dare recalled it, Locke threw himself energetically into the activities of the new paper, and with good reason: after years of disappointing freelance writing and an unsuccessful stint as the editor of a literary journal, he had at last found the job that most suited his talents and interests. He could write about a wide variety of contemporary issues for an interested readership, and his writing, with its earlier tendencies toward grandiloquence, would necessarily be pared and honed by the newspaper's narrow columns.

As was to be expected for someone who had emerged out of the Republican movement, Locke adopted radical editorial positions for the *Herald,* tactfully characterized by Dare as "much in advance of the general political views of the period." Locke's editorials so antagonized the local gentry and clergy that they pressured the publishers of the *Herald* to fire the young editor. Somerset landowners were outraged by his stance against the Corn Laws, which forbade the importation of foreign grain into England unless domestic grain was selling above a fixed price. The local clergy took umbrage at Locke's editorializing against the Test and Corporation Acts, which barred from civil and military office any Briton unwilling to swear allegiance to the Church of England. Roman Catholics were thus prohibited from holding public office, a ban that included university positions. Although they were not denied the vote on religious grounds, Catholics could not serve in Parliament—a particularly contentious situation in Ireland, where Catholics made up nearly three-quarters of the population. Catholic emancipation had long been the most intense political conflict in all of Great Britain, and Locke championed the cause in the pages of the *Herald,* writing a series of editorials that condemned the English clergy as idle and dissolute and contrasted their lavish lifestyle with that of poorly paid Catholic priests in Ireland. These editorials so infuriated the curate of Burnham, a Reverend Trevor, that he initiated a libel action against the newspaper. After a good deal of negotiation Besley and Brinning got the suit dropped on a single condition: that Richard Adams Locke give up his post as editor of the *Herald.*

For the twenty-five-year-old Locke, it must have been a bitter defeat—to have finally found a job he loved, only to be forced from it under threat from political opponents. It was a scenario that would be replayed a decade and a half later, halfway around the world, when he lost his job as editor of the *New Era,* the penny paper he had helped found, after his editorial denunciations of two Democratic power brokers. He was never able to keep a job for long. In his political views he steadfastly resisted the power of authority figures—whether politicians, aristocrats, or clergymen—and so too did he in his own life, at far greater cost, with the publishers who held sway over his future.

Locke continued to write articles for the *Herald* and privately published pamphlets advocating, in William Griggs's characterization, "the most ultra doctrines of Unitarianism and Universalism, in connection with the most Republican principles." Though much of his writing championed Catholic emancipation, he was also a fierce opponent of religious control over civic life, and he took a strong stand against the temporal power of the pope—that is, the right of the pope to rule as sovereign over territory, an issue then very much in dispute. For nearly two years, in the pages of the *Herald,* he conducted a weekly debate on the issue with several Catholic clerics. (Even then, Locke seems never to have declined an opportunity to joust with a clergyman.)

Another controversy arose from a sermon preached by a local minister, Reverend John Matthews of Kilve, advocating the use of philosophy as an aid in interpreting biblical texts. The sermon was so well liked by Matthews's congregants that it was issued in pamphlet form under the title *The Necessity of Philosophy to the Divine.* Locke, unsurprisingly, found little in Matthews's pamphlet to admire; he quickly produced his own pamphlet, called simply *A Review,* in which he derided the sermon as "unconscionably impudent and dogmatical" and argued—in line with Universalist principles of the time—that the Bible itself is sufficient source of religious information. This in turn led to a heated denunciation of Locke by an anonymous pamphleteer (he called himself only "A Defender of the Faith") who suggested that Locke's pamphlet "may have been better entitled A WRY VIEW OF PHILOSOPHY," in so doing making cruel sport of Locke's crossed eyes.

IN 1826, when he was twenty-six, Richard Adams Locke married a local girl named Esther Bowring, eleven years his junior, and the two settled at Mill Batch Farm. He was once again living under the same roof as his siblings and his father; his mother had died nine years earlier, at the age of only thirty-seven. Surely a tension existed between a son returned home after failing to establish himself in the world and a father who did not approve of his son's politics or profession (he could not have had much to say about his fifteen-year-old daughter-in-law, given that his own wife had been fifteen when he married her) and who had chosen not to provide for him in his will.

His father died the next year, at the age of sixty. Richard Adams Locke was now the oldest man living at Mill Batch—though this state of affairs proved temporary, as in 1829 his sister Ann got married and her new husband, John Kent, came to live at the farm. Almost fifty years old, Kent was an itinerant preacher very popular among the faithful of the surrounding area, where he was known as "the apostle of the hill country." Thrown together in that crowded farmhouse were two antipodal brothers-in-law: Kent, a country clergyman of the more exuberant variety, and Locke, who professed a Dissenter theology and had lost his job by antagonizing a local curate.

By that time Richard Adams Locke was cobbling together a living by placing occasional reviews in magazines and writing the sort of anonymous scholarly work, for textbooks and the like, that so often make up the freelancer's livelihood. In August 1830, Esther gave birth to a daughter, Adelaide. Locke was now on the cusp of thirty, and with distressingly few prospects. The family estate, built up over two generations, had not been passed on to him; and in any event, he had no interest in managing land. He considered himself a newspaperman, but he had been ousted from the local paper and in the process had become notorious as a radical and freethinker, which was one thing in London and quite another in a place like Somerset, where everyone, it seemed, knew everyone else, where the church was the hub of town life and the walls were not smeared with broadsheets and graffiti. Memories ran long in Somerset, and even five years after the fact publishers were not interested in hiring someone who had so alienated the most powerful of his newspaper's readers. Nor would Locke likely find employment again in Bristol. Anti-Catholic sentiment ran high there (in 1829 petitions against Catholic emancipation had collected more than 25,000 signatures, and mobs shouting "No popery!" had attacked a Catholic church and the homes of several prominent Catholics), and there would not be much sympathy for a man who had championed emancipation.

Even republicanism offered little of cheer. The movement was losing steam now, having evolved through the 1820s into an electorally based campaign for parliamentary reform, which was encountering seemingly insurmountable obstacles. The new Whig prime minister, Earl Grey, had introduced a reform bill into Parliament to grant representation to rapidly growing industrial cities such as Birmingham, Leeds, and Manchester; though the bill passed the House of Commons, it went down to defeat in the House of Lords. The bill's defeat sparked riots throughout Great Britain, none worse than in Bristol, where on October 31, 1831, mobs ran wild through the city, looting and setting fire to more than a hundred buildings. In the Mansion House along Queen Square, where the mayor had barricaded himself in an upper room, rioters broke down the doors with beams of timber used as battering rams, then swept through the house smashing furniture, windows, mirrors, and chandeliers. Later the Mansion House would be burned down, as would the Bishop's Palace, though not before the books in the bishop's library had been tossed into a bonfire and the wine in his cellars looted and then sold on the green for a penny a bottle. Gangs roamed through prosperous sections of the city, breaking into houses and demanding money under threat of murder; terrified homeowners, locked in their bedrooms, flung out handfuls of silver coins to the crowds below. Looters methodically piled goods stolen from warehouses into wagons and trucks, forming streams of vehicles coming and going and returning again for more, as the owners looked on helplessly. Boys holding torches rushed from house to house, leaping through windows and setting fire to furniture. Before long all the buildings along two sides of Queen Square were aflame, the separate blazes running together into a single immense conflagration, bathing everything in its proximity in a ghastly red light. "One seemed to look down upon Dante's Inferno," a horrified observer would recall decades later, "and to hear the multitudinous moan and wail of the lost spirits surging to and fro amid that sea of fire."

Dawn brought a charge from the assembled dragoons of the 14th Hussars, who swarmed throughout the city and bluntly set about restoring order. By the break of day hundreds of Bristolians lay dead and wounded by sword and fire. It was, wrote a nineteenth-century British historian, "the most disastrous outbreak of popular violence which has occurred in this country during the present century."

The glow from the fires burning in Queen Square could be seen for forty miles around, and East Brent, where Richard Adams Locke and his family were living, was just thirty miles from Bristol. The riot's epicenter was only four blocks from the shop where he had edited the *Cornucopia,* and he had surely strolled often through that beautiful square, now reduced to ashes, surely taken a drink in those tidy pubs now pillaged and burned. Two years earlier Bristol had endured some anti-Catholic riots, but this time the rioters were overwhelmingly Irish. In a single night, Catholics had demolished the goodwill that the long emancipation campaign had managed to foster; now, surely, would come the backlash. What future would there be for a writer who had opposed the claims of Anglican and Catholic alike? He had left Somerset once before, as soon as he had the chance, but over time the ties of familiarity had pulled him back; now, though, those ties were badly frayed. His parents were both dead; the estate would not be coming to him; no reasonable job prospects were on the horizon. He was not a young man anymore, and leaving would get harder with each passing year. They could always go back to London, but he found that his thoughts kept drifting toward America, that beacon of the Republicans: the land of economic opportunity, freed from the weight of aristocracy and prelacy, where he might shed some of the burdens of his own history.

In November 1831, Richard and Esther gathered their belongings into five bags, as much as they could expect to carry, plus the family's bedding; after bundling up Adelaide against the cold, they climbed aboard their hired coach. Bristol was nearly a day's journey, even on the newly tarmacked roads. When they arrived, the coach dropped them at the shipping office. The office was crowded with families like theirs; it was warm from the heat of the bodies. Bags were piled everywhere. Outside, a pall seemed to have settled over the city.

He booked passage on the *James Cropper,* embarking at Bristol, bound for New York.

At sea, the nights were always worst. He lay sleepless in the narrow berth, no more than boards and sacking; his sides ached from the incessant rolling, the sudden, stomach-clenching plunges. Of all the transatlantic trips a ship could make, this one—winter westbound—was the roughest. The trade winds had long since grown frigid, gathering strength as they swept across the ocean, and they seemed to run straight at the face of the ship no matter which way it tacked: the sailors said that a westward passage was like running uphill the whole way. His wife and baby daughter were in the women's cabin at the other end of the 'tweendeck. At least some of his fellow cabin passengers were managing some sleep; the snores, like the waves, rose and fell, maintaining a steady rhythm and then, unexpectedly, turning loud and agitated. At such moments, at least, they drowned out the cries of the pigs and geese and chickens housed in makeshift pens on deck, the animals obviously terrified, as if cognizant of the fate that awaited them downstairs in the galley, sometime before the ship made landfall in New York. Worse still were the nighttime sounds of the ship itself, the rale of the wind as it streamed through the riggings, the creak of the masts twisting, the groans of the hull, its joints wracked by dozens of such hard ocean crossings: a dowager's complaints and, for one listening, a grim reminder of mortality.

Richard Adams Locke was now thirty-one; he had been to London, and to Bristol, and none of it had amounted to anything. His life now was on the water: his wife and daughter asleep in the women's cabin, and, packed in the upper hold, the few books and journals he had managed to carry aboard along with the family's clothes and bedding. Years before he had edited journals of his own, at a time of youthful optimism, when he felt flush with his own powers. Sometimes on the ship he could regain that feeling: evenings when the wine and the talk flowed, the passengers gathering in the saloon for group singing or charades, whatever might distract attention from the dark, churning sea outside. He was the sort of man who could talk about anything, from the latest political scandal or Sir Walter Scott novel to recent discoveries in electromagnetism and scriptural evidence of Christ's divinity. It was easy to lose himself in stories. Inside the cabin, though, it was different, especially when he was lying awake at night, his ears full of the ship's unsteady thrumming, the alcohol still singing in his veins. Then memories would have swirled around him, as foul as the gases that drifted up from the bilge; in such moments, he might have risen from his berth, donned his coat and scarf, and climbed the narrow ladder heading topsides.

The first moment above was like plunging his head into an icy bath. His cheeks instantly began to burn from the cold, and his eyes watered, but the fresh air was a tonic after the suffocating closeness of the cabin. Out here the world had narrowed itself down to renditions of black and white. Beyond the rail of the ship, the North Atlantic roared invisibly. In the distance, in every direction, water blended into sky, the edge of the ocean perceptible only by the absence of stars. He had been watching night skies ever since he was a boy, in the fields around his family's farm in East Brent, but he had never before seen a sky quite like this, so alive, flooded with stars, most splayed out in undifferentiated washes of light, but some of them linked together in his mind as constellations. There was Orion stalking the east, the Dippers to the north, and straight overhead, descending in a line, Aries, Pisces, Aquarius. He scanned the teeming eastern sky—Murzim, Lepus, Eridanus, Cetus: the dog running with the hare, the river opening itself up to the sea monster. And reigning over them all, huge and brilliant, the moon. What was it Shelley had called her? *Orbéd maiden, with white fire laden.* He had read deeply in astronomy, he knew full well that the moon shone purely with reflected light, but at such moments, with his lungs aching, his cheeks wet with spray, he felt he could almost see that fire on the lunar surface: burning white and clear, and seeming almost near enough for warmth.

CHAPTER 4

The Atrocious
Impositions of Matthias

THE WORD *skyscraper* originally referred to the mast of a ship, and though the multitude of ships' masts in the port of New York in the early nineteenth century is invariably described by writers then and now as a "forest," it was at least as much a skyline, a magnificent cluster of spires rising up unexpectedly from the water's edge, defining the essence of the city, its splendor and clamor and measureless ambition, built in pursuit of commerce. Like the later architectural skyline, it was a sight that inspired awe and, invariably, optimism in those who saw it for the first time, from the water, on a ship arriving from far away.

Richard Adams Locke's ship, the *James Cropper,* arrived in New York on January 13, 1832, after a two-month voyage from Bristol. The ship likely moored overnight at Sandy Hook, the spit of land in New Jersey that set the outer limit of New York's waters; at first light of morning the passengers, weary but happy, would have dressed in their best clothes and come on deck to watch the entrance into the harbor. From the Lower Bay the ship sailed into the Narrows, where, after the great expanse of the bay, the land seemed to close down on the water; to the starboard lay the scattered villages of Brooklyn, and to the port side the low hills of Staten Island, the farmhouses and cottages there giving off the early-morning smoke of chimney fires. Beyond the Narrows came the Upper Bay, at the end of which the water forked into two rivers, the East River and the Hudson, then commonly known as the North River. Now, in the distance, came the first sight of New York, at the southernmost tip the greenery of the Battery making a brief pause amid the thicket of masts sprouting from hundreds of ships moored on the narrow wharves that jutted out, fingerlike, from both sides of the island. Manhattan was "belted round by wharves as Indian isles by coral reefs," as it would later be described by Herman Melville, who, like Richard Adams Locke, worked for the Customs Service for two decades when he could not support himself as a writer.

It was no small feat for a captain to successfully navigate New York Harbor, as it abounded with ships, the surface as full of motion and color and bewildering diversity of form as the water below: stately packet ships, flat-bottomed steamboats and ferries belching black smoke, schooners and sloops, tugboats and fishing skiffs and the barks of the oystermen, speedy news boats on their way to meet the oceangoing packets, attaching themselves like remoras on a whale, pausing only long enough to receive the latest batch of European newspapers that within hours would be filleted for items of interest to the readers of New York's merchant papers. As once, it was said, all roads led to Rome, now all waterways seemed to lead to New York. The East River ran into the Long Island Sound, and from there to New England and its fishing fleets and factories; the North River began its journey far upstate, where it linked to the newly opened Erie Canal, extending westward to the farms of the American Midwest; and the harbor itself provided unparalleled access to the Atlantic, because it was large, deep, and almost never blocked by ice, even, as now, in the middle of winter. By the 1830s most of the nation's import business flowed through New York Harbor, with more than 1,400 ships arriving annually from 150 ports around the world, and thousands more from America's own coastal cities. New York's docks presented an ever-changing daily exhibition of hemp, iron, lumber, coal, cotton, tobacco, granite, molasses, coffee, and innumerable other goods dug or cultivated or otherwise taken from the earth.

Even in the early hours the streets and docksides were thronged, a babel of sailors, of carpenters, caulkers, riggers, rope makers, ship owners off to read the merchant papers at one of the local coffee houses, well-dressed families waiting to board a ship or having just disembarked from one. For families like the Lockes, looking to make a home in the city but having no family to call upon or much money of their own, the ill-lit, dingy streets around the waterfront offered numerous boardinghouses where, for anywhere from fifty cents to three dollars a week, payable in advance, guests would be provided a small, damp, poorly ventilated room, with little in the way of sanitary facilities. (Backyard outhouses were the rule; boardinghouses did not supply chamberpots to their guests, the vast majority of whom were too new or simply too poor to have purchased their own; as the saying of the day had it, they were "without a pot to piss in.") Often as not, the paying guests had to share their room with permanent residents such as flies, bedbugs, and wharf rats. Still, despite the lowness of the accommodations boardinghouses were a necessary expedient for many new arrivals, and probably it was in one of them that the Locke family found lodging, at least for a short while, and probably for a time after that in one of the "rookeries" just then becoming widespread in New York—large buildings, such as warehouses, breweries, and churches, converted by enterprising property owners into numerous tiny apartments. The Lockes do not appear to have obtained a fixed residence until sometime between May 1833 and May 1834, when they settled at 18 Duane Street, on the corner of Chatham.

It was one of the noisiest intersections in all of New York. Street vendors assembled there daily, under sun and lamplight, each makeshift stall displaying items for sale: apples and melons carted in from Long Island and New Jersey, coconuts shipped in from tropical islands, homemade buckwheat cakes, ears of corn boiled in the husk and sprinkled with a little salt, shoelaces, pocket combs, boxes of matches split from pine and dipped in brimstone, oysters and chestnuts in the colder months and ice cream and lemonade in the warmer. All of the wares were available for only one cent, as the vendors, men and women alike, beckoned to the hurrying passersby: *A penny apiece! A penny apiece!* The cries resounded through the street, echoing from the stained wooden facings of the buildings pushed up tightly against it. *A penny apiece!* The cries of the vendors were the Locke family's constant companion, their rooster crows in the morning and the lullabies by which three-year-old Adelaide fell asleep at night.

That little apartment above a shabby storefront, so assailed by the noises of the city, was a world removed from Mill Batch Farm, the tidy whitewashed farmhouse with the porch that ran the length of the house, and on some of those clamorous New York days Richard Adams Locke must have thought back to that farm and wondered if they had made the right choice in leaving. Still, he knew, there was no future for them in Somerset; New

York, for all of its difficulties, offered a fresh start. Someday he would move the family out of the city, perhaps buy a house of their own, ideally some-place near the water, where Adelaide could watch the ships coming in from all over the world. It wasn't far off, he knew. He just had to establish him-self first, put together a bit of money.

In New York Richard Adams Locke set himself the task of learning shorthand (several instructional books would have been available to him, perhaps the most famous being Samuel Taylor's *Stenography, Or the Art of Shorthand Perfected*), which he recognized would prove an invaluable skill for a journalist looking for a job. Stenography was surely something of a comedown for him after years of work for newspapers and literary journals, but he had few choices and needed to support his family in whatever way he could. According to P. T. Barnum (who would soon come to know him personally), Locke was at the time "the only short-hand reporter in the city," and before he found regular employment on a newspaper he supplemented his income by working as a legal reporter, furnishing for New York publishers the trial transcripts of celebrated court cases, among them the murder trial of the notorious minister Ephraim K. Avery.

Locke produced that transcript—the full title of which is *Report of the Trial of the Rev. Ephraim K. Avery, Methodist Minister, for the Murder of Sarah Maria Cornell, at Tiverton, in the County of Newport, Rhode Is-land, Before the Supreme Judicial Court of that State, May 6th, 1833*—as a pamphlet for a Cortland Street bookseller named William Stodart. The pamphlet demonstrates why Locke was an especially useful reporter; as a stenographer he could record the full trial transcript (the Avery trial tran-script comprised fifty densely printed pages), while as a journalist he could also provide the colorful detail that brought the trial alive for readers, as, for instance, in his description of Reverend Avery's entrance into court on the opening day of the trial:

> Shortly after the Judges and counsel had taken their seats, the prisoner was brought in; he bowed to each, and sat at the counsel table with per-fect self possession, which was not however characterized by any unbe-coming confidence of demeanor, but appeared rather the result of great mental firmness. In point of health, he seems to have suffered severely since his arraignment in March last; his face is greatly attenuated, and its complexion might almost be described as cadaverous.

On the cover of the Avery pamphlet Locke's name is followed by the title A. B., an abbreviation of the Latin *Artium Baccalaureus,* or "bachelor of arts." This suggests that he was already circulating the story that he had graduated from the University of Cambridge. Bereft of connections and desperately needing work, and with little except his wits to fall back on, Locke must have hoped that the deception would grant him cachet in a profession where Englishmen were not uncommon, but an advanced degree—especially one from an institution as eminent as Cambridge—certainly was. Among the city's more prominent newspaper editors, William Cullen Bryant was the only one who had attended college; most editors had started their careers in business or the military. In the world of New York newspapermen Locke would have met few individuals who knew the first thing about English university life and might have been able to spot an impostor, especially one who so impeccably fitted the role, what with his distinguished ancestry (made even more so by his claims of descent from the great John Locke), his remarkable vocabulary (even by the more literate standards of the age), and his unusual erudition. By this time he was knowledgeable in a broad range of scholarly fields, having written on science, theology, literature, politics, and, most recently, history. In 1834 he produced a thirty-two-page pamphlet, *History of the Polish Revolution, with the Latest Atrocities of the Russian Conquerors, Compiled Upon the Authority of Personal Sufferers,* a moving account of the failed Polish uprising against the occupying armies of Russia. The Poles had fought through the winter of 1830 and into 1831 before finally being put down, and three years later their struggle was still very much on the minds of those, like Locke himself, with Republican sympathies.

History of the Polish Revolution was published anonymously. Locke's political beliefs had made him essentially unemployable back in Somerset, and it only made sense that here in New York, freed of that troublesome history and with a wife and child depending on him, he would be more discreet about revealing them. Later, when he had become editor of the *Sun,* taking the desk of the abolitionist George Wisner, he could state his opinions more openly; for now, though, he was another English immigrant who had arrived in the city with a handful of bags, and who, in his early thirties, was older than most of the men with whom he was competing for work. He would not have wanted to alienate those whose sympathies lay elsewhere, for instance, James Watson Webb of the *Courier and Enquirer,* who sometime around 1834 provided Locke his first regular job in New York.

Colonel Webb, as he liked to be called (he had served in the army on the western frontier, though he never attained any rank higher than lieutenant), presented the very picture of the New York newspaper editor. He stood over six feet tall, and carried himself with an imperiousness that made him look even taller; he had deep-blue eyes, dark wavy hair, and long silvered sideburns, and was known around town, unironically, as "the Apollo of the press." He drank champagne with breakfast and brandy and port at other meals, and had a taste for mutton and for the French pastries made by Delmonico's of William Street. He enjoyed whist and billiards and the novels of Bulwer-Lytton; he dressed expensively and always traveled first-class. He saw himself as a defender of society's natural aristocracy, and as such was a nativist and a racist, even by the standards of his own time. According to Webb, the black man was marked by "debasing ignorance and mental inferiority," his race "the most stupid, ferocious and cowardly of the divisions into which the creator has divided mankind." God-given, like the mark of Cain, this inferiority was a permanent condition, immune to any attempts at social amelioration. Once, on hearing of a proposal to establish a Negro college in New Haven, Webb wondered, "What benefit can it be to a waiter or coachman to read Horace?"

James Watson Webb was also a great believer in the duel, which he regarded as an efficient enforcer of public morality. In 1838 his feud with Congressman Jonathan Cilley of Maine resulted in Cilley's death in a rifle duel with another congressman, W. J. Graves of Kentucky, a friend of Webb's. Four years later Webb fought his own duel with a Kentucky congressman, Thomas F. Marshall. The two men had a long-standing antagonism (among other charges Webb accused Marshall, a temperance activist, of being a former drunk), and finally Marshall challenged Webb to a duel. It was held at dawn, with pistols, in a field in Delaware. Not wanting to kill the congressman, Webb fired into the air and was struck in the hip by Marshall's shot, at which point the duel was stopped by the two men's seconds. Back in New York, Webb was arrested and charged with leaving the state for the purposes of engaging in a duel, the first time the statute had been invoked in the four decades since it had been enacted. He pleaded guilty and was sentenced to the maximum term of two years in the notorious upstate prison Sing Sing; he served two weeks before receiving a pardon from Governor William H. Seward, on the condition that he never again participate in any duels.

James Watson Webb hired Richard Adams Locke to be a metropolitan reporter with a special emphasis on crime stories, including reports from the police court. It was highly unusual for one of the dignified merchant paper to assign a reporter to the crime beat, but by 1834 the *Sun* was already making its influence felt on newspaper journalism in New York. Now, mixed in with the Senate speeches, European correspondence, and the latest commodity prices, the expansive pages of the *Courier and Enquirer* included reports of tenement fires, rabid dogs, thefts of pocket watches and fire snuffers and cases of musk, a cartman who killed another with a blow from his shovel, a husband who killed his wife with a blow from a lead clock weight, a lunatic woman arrested for attempting to cook and eat her baby. Richard Adams Locke now joined George Wisner and his fellow Englishman, William Attree, in the early morning hours in the long yellow courthouse by City Hall, though rather than report all the day's cases, as they did, he generally focused on one or two in greater detail, tending to choose crimes that would be of greater interest to the prosperous readers of the *Courier and Enquirer*: a burglary in one of the better parts of town, for instance, or a pocket picked at the Italian Opera House. But he liked a good story no matter where it happened, such as his item about Eliza Sullivan of the Five Points, a grandmotherly woman who had befriended a young visitor to town named John Cowan. Cowan was in need of lodging for the night, and the kindly old lady insisted that he share her room. Upon awakening the next morning, he found to his horror that she had absconded with not merely the pocketbook in his trousers but the trousers themselves. Fortunately, another resident of the house was able to furnish young Cowan with a substitute pair of pants, "which from their size," Locke reported, "must have occasioned him no little trouble to get into."

His appearance in them at the Police Office satisfied every beholder that they were a tight fit. Indeed he looked as if he had been melted and poured into them; to bring his feet together was utterly impossible, and when he walked he exactly resembled the figure of the Colossus of Rhodes, as represented in pictures.

"He was a little too gorgeous and florid in his descriptions of police scenes," recalled James Gordon Bennett, a Scots immigrant who served for several years as the *Courier*'s Washington correspondent and would later become one of Locke's bitterest rivals, "but otherwise showed learning and science, although out of place." Mostly, however, during his time at the *Courier and Enquirer*, Richard Adams Locke kept his learning under wraps. Once he had written essays on Milton and the nature of God; now he trolled the city's low places, exposing his readers to miseries that were, in a favorite phrase of his, "better imagined than described." While James Watson Webb railed in the accompanying columns against the Democrats, and the foreigners, and the Papists, and the amalgamators, Locke stayed silent, and wrote as well as he could, and went where he was told. In April 1835, long established at the *Courier,* he boarded a carriage for White Plains, where he would report on the trial of Robert Matthews, accused of a murder committed under another name: Matthias the Prophet.

It was in the White Plains courthouse that Richard Adams Locke first met Benjamin Day, who was looking for a reporter to cover the Matthias trial for the *Sun*. Locke accepted the assignment, provided that his name was not attached to the articles, since he was attending the trial under the auspices of the *Courier and Enquirer*. Day agreed to this proviso, and all of Locke's pieces on the Matthias trial carried only the byline "Reported for the Sun" or "Written for the Sun." His trial coverage for the *Sun*, as for the *Courier and Enquirer,* consisted almost entirely of recorded witness testimony, for which his earlier stenographic training proved invaluable. The far more explosive material he was saving for the series of articles, exclusive to the *Sun*, that would shortly follow.

The five installments of the series—the first feature articles ever to appear in the *Sun*—ran on the paper's front page, each one bearing the same eye-catching headline, printed in capital letters: "MEMOIRS OF MATTHIAS THE PROPHET, WITH A FULL EXPOSURE OF HIS ATROCIOUS IMPOSITIONS, AND OF THE DEGRADING DELUSIONS OF HIS FOLLOWERS." Richard Adams Locke (again anonymously) offered the *Sun*'s readers a lengthy history of the Matthias case, exploring the powerful hold he exerted over his wealthy followers, the details of the alleged poisoning of a wayward disciple, and his eventual acquittal on the murder charge and conviction for the lesser charge of assault. Much as he would do later in his moon series for the *Sun,* Locke approached the Matthias series as a dramatic narrative that built slowly and suspensefully to its climax. He began it not with the trial or an account of the alleged murder but in a more literary fashion—with prefatory remarks, draped in the portentous gothic tones of one of the horror stories that Edgar Allan Poe was just then beginning to write:

> Voluminous as is the history of religious delusion, and heavily as its shadows fall upon the human character, it may be questioned whether its pages afford an example arrayed in more appalling gloom, and standing forth in a more startling attitude than the one we are about to unveil in these memoirs. . . . The world has indeed heard that Matthias the pretended prophet is a daring and impudent impostor; that he has deceived and defrauded several intelligent persons, and that he was even suspected of having murdered an infatuated disciple whose extensive property he had previously transferred to himself. But it has not dreamed of those "greater and yet greater abominations" which like the polluted "chambers of imagery" in the visions of Ezekiel, successively reveal their horrors in an increasing magnitude of intensity which the firmest minds will be unable to contemplate without a sensible enervation of their power.

Those horrors included Matthias's sexual claims on his female disciples, several of whom were married, as well as the terrible beating he inflicted on his eighteen-year-old married daughter when she steadfastly refused her father's demand that she give herself to one of his male disciples so that the two might produce "an offspring of incarnate angels." In the upstate farmhouse he had dubbed Mount Zion, Matthias had apparently established for himself a community of seven wives—a "harem," Locke called it—six of them wealthy white women and the seventh a black servant by the name of Isabella Van Wagenen, and "had one appointed to each working day in the week, and the black one consecrated for Sundays." (Isabella Van Wagenen was a former slave who would later join the abolitionist movement, changing her name to the one by which she would be forever remembered: Sojourner Truth.)

For most of the *Sun*'s readers—and likely Benjamin Day as well—the story of Matthias was just a sensational case of murder, one made especially appealing by the air of depravity swirling around it. For many observers, though, the trial became something greater, and Matthias himself a dark symbol of a host of modern ills. Among conservative Christians, he was seen as a warning sign of rising Jacksonian democracy, of abolitionism, individualism, and godless doctrines imperiling social stability. Jacksonians countered that he represented the kind of fanaticism that led to a dangerous moral righteousness. For at least one radical editor, George Henry Evans of the *Workingman's Advocate,* Matthias was a religious con man of the type that was flourishing in "this age of imposture." Others, more sanguine in their outlook, took Matthias's limited popularity, and his subsequent downfall and imprisonment, as an indication of the essential health of American society.

Richard Adams Locke saw something else in the story of Matthias the Prophet. It was not just a cautionary tale about the dangers of religious delusion (although it was that as well), but also a stark illustration of the struggle between the competing claims of religion and science. Long a religious freethinker—one who had managed to alienate himself from both sides of the Protestant-Catholic struggle back in England—and an advocate of the liberating and ennobling power of scientific knowledge, Locke warned in his *Sun* series about the dangers that arose from sacrificing rationality to faith. He pointed out that Matthias had found his followers not among the poor but rather among New Yorkers of wealth, intelligence, and high station; while it might be assumed that such advantages would prevent people from falling victim to this brand of religious imposture, recent history was rife with counterexamples—among them Joanna Southcott, the mystic prophetess of Devon (Locke had been living nearby in Somerset at the time of her death in 1814), who had declared herself to be the woman that the Book of Revelation had foretold would give birth to the future Messiah. Southcott's theories, Locke reminded his readers, had found far more adherents among the English literati than had those of any of the leading scientists working to increase the stores of human knowledge. "Nearly every religious delusion," he wrote, "occupies a position in the imagination which reason and science cannot reach, and stands with a self-consecrated circle which they cannot pass." The fear and mistrust of science, though, could be found not only in religious delusion of the sort exemplified by Southcott and Matthias, but in religious belief generally.

There is, indeed, no religion, however rational and pure, but repudiates the application of reason and science to many of its mysteries as presumptuous and profane. It assumes to have domes and spires too loftily and too brilliantly commingled with celestial radiance, for the inspection of the human intellect. There are lines of demarcation between the kingdoms of reason and of faith, which cannot be crossed by subjects of either, without instant hostilities and deadly warfare; and as faith is generally content with her own fertile dominions, so will she never yield them to the pretensions of her restless neighbor.

The long conflict between "the kingdoms of reason and faith" was a topic about which Richard Adams Locke cared deeply. He would return to it later that year, with far greater effect, in his moon series.

RICHARD Adams Locke's Matthias articles were enormously popular with the readers of the *Sun.* Indeed, the articles were so much in demand that only two days after the series completed its run, Benjamin Day issued it as an octavo-size pamphlet, sixteen pages long, with the same dramatic title as the individual articles. The cover page featured a large illustration of Matthias in his astronomical robe, one hand resting on his double-edged sword, the other holding aloft his prophet's rod, his long hair and beard luxuriant, his eyes menacing under heavy brows. (The *Sun*'s readers had never before seen any images of Matthias, who, as Locke pointedly indicated, "startlingly resembles the most celebrated pictures of Christ, at a mature age, by the old masters.")

The *Sun* printed ten thousand copies of the pamphlet, which Benjamin Day gave to his newsboys to hawk on the streets of the city. That the articles had already appeared in the *Sun* seems to have diminished the popularity of the pamphlet not at all, for the boys sold more than six thousand on the first day alone. Day had priced the pamphlets at three cents per copy, which meant total sales upward of $180; assuming that he maintained the same split in the sale of the pamphlets as he did with the daily papers (with the newsboys keeping one-quarter to one-third of the money they brought in), he had made more than $120 in a single day. (Less than two years before, of course, Day could afford to pay George Wisner a salary of only four dollars per week, and by 1835 twelve dollars was considered a reasonable weekly salary for an editor.) Over the next several weeks the pamphlet continued to sell, in the phrase of the time, like hot cakes; ultimately, according to William Griggs in his account of the moon series, more than forty thousand copies of the pamphlet would be sold. Even allowing for a certain amount of exaggeration on Griggs's part, sales of *Memoirs of Matthias the Prophet* undoubtedly earned the *Sun* several hundred dollars at least, and perhaps even as much as a thousand.

It was a windfall for the *Sun,* and Benjamin Day was, in his own gruff way, overjoyed by the results. He was also instructed by them. Suddenly he understood that enormous profits could be made from material that had appeared in the newspaper, if the right subject matter was given skillful handling; and Richard Adams Locke, the writer whose talents had allowed him this insight, assumed a new importance in his eyes. Locke had by now returned full-time to the *Courier and Enquirer.* Day paid him $150 for his work on the Matthias case—for Locke, it was equivalent to several months' salary—and promised him a similar amount for any other series of popular articles that he might care to write for the *Sun.* Locke set about finding one.

So the summer of 1835 commenced. In June a new play premiered at the Bowery Theatre, a comedy with an unlikely subject—it was called *Matthias the Prophet.* Nearby, the City Saloon was showing Henry Hanington's peristrephic dioramas, or moving scenes of animated nature; the vast canvases, slowly turned and combined with the most convincing light and sound effects, allowed audiences to inhabit a pastoral Italian scene, a shipwreck at sea, and, most entertaining of all, the conflagration of Moscow. Crowds gathered in front of Coleman's bookshop on Broadway, where the front window displayed magnificent color plates from Audubon's *Birds of America.* Everywhere in the city, the talk was of real estate; speculation in land ran rampant, with large swaths of the countryside in upper Manhattan going under the auctioneer's gavel. Immense fortunes were made with the stroke of a pen. "There must come a change," the former mayor Philip Hone worried in his diary, "and when it does, woe to those who are caught!"

In an overcrowded city built mostly of wood, fire was a constant threat. The large fire bell in the cupola of City Hall tolled almost every night, the sentinel stationed beside it shining his lantern, like Paul Revere's compatriots in Boston's Old North Church, in the direction of the blaze. Disasters struck and were averted. A boy playing near a third-story window of the National Hotel on Broadway lost his balance and fell out, and would surely have plunged to his death but for the intervention of the hotel awning below; the boy bounced on the awning for a few moments, as if being tossed by a blanket, and then was rescued entirely unharmed. For nights on end hundreds of young men fought in the streets around the Chatham Market, to the battle cries of "Ireland!" and "America!" Games of roulette could be found on the Bowery, faro on Canal Street, and cutthroat on Park Row. Thousands turned out to watch the foot races on the Hunting Park Course and the Harlem Trotting Course. Regularly collecting the winner's purse, which often totaled several hundred dollars, was the celebrated Stannard, who could run the three-mile course in just over sixteen minutes; his main rival was an Iroquois known only as Barefoot. Up in Harlem, a man named George Crosby rode a horse bareback for a mile in two minutes and forty seconds, a feat that local horse enthusiasts claimed demonstrated the North's superiority over the South in riding. On weekends, when the weather was good, New Yorkers escaped the dirt and smell of the city with a ferry ride across the Hudson River to Hoboken. Not far from the ferry terminal, a winding footpath shaded by large oak trees gradually opened up to reveal the pleasure garden called the Elysian Fields. Its manicured lawn undulating down to the water's edge, surrounded by bucolic meadows and forests, with gravel terraces and a refreshments pavilion, it made a perfect spot for a picnic supper on a warm day. Nearby was the Sybil's Cave, a spacious cavern with a bubbling spring, carved by the proprietor of the Fields out of solid rock.

Among those looking to enjoy the pleasures of the Sybil's Cave on the first weekend of June was William Attree, formerly the police reporter for the *Transcript,* now working for the *Courier and Enquirer.* That Saturday afternoon Attree and a woman named Eveline Reynolds crossed to Hoboken by ferry and then strolled along the river, arm in arm, to the Sybil's Cave. The pair had just entered the cave, with Attree bending down to get Reynolds a cup of water from the spring, when someone leaped out from behind one of the artificial columns supporting the roof and bludgeoned Attree on the back of the head. Attree instantly crumpled to the ground, but his assailant continued to beat him, kicking and stomping him on his head and chest, finally pulling out a knife and stabbing him in the face, the blade passing through the left side of Attree's nose near the bridge and—according to the first physician who attended him—piercing his brain.

Frantic, shrieking in terror, Eveline Reynolds ran from the cave in search of help. She managed to find some men nearby; one of them, as it turned out, was George Wisner, the editor of the *Sun* and Attree's long-time rival at the police court, who by sheer coincidence had been out on the Elysian Fields that same afternoon. Wisner and the others ran back to the cave, but by that time the attacker had escaped.

Two days later Attree's assailant was tracked down and captured in Hoboken, where he was identified as a barber named John Boyd. It turned out that in the *Transcript*'s police column William Attree had reported an assault charge made against Boyd by a prostitute who worked in a brothel on Duane Street (where Attree himself happened to be a regular client); Boyd had been especially infuriated by the story's allegation that his wife supported them both by working as a hairdresser for prostitutes. That Saturday afternoon, he had noticed Attree passing by his Barclay Street barbershop on the way to the Hoboken ferry. Boyd was a member of the Chichesters, a notoriously ruthless Five Points gang; quickly he gathered a few of his Chichester fellows and together they boarded the ferry with their intended victim. Disembarking at Hoboken, they trailed Attree and Reynolds, waiting for the opportunity to strike. Boyd must have walked right by the strolling couple on the path to the Sybil's Cave, a perfect hiding place from which to make his ambush.

Attree's surgeons pronounced his condition so precarious that he might not survive, but he made a remarkable recovery and within a month was back to reporting for the *Courier*. George Wisner, on the other hand, seems to have been deeply unnerved by the events in the Sybil's Cave. (In a *Sun* editorial following the attack, he declared that he was armed and "ready to blow out the brains of any man that lays his hands upon us.") He had passed countless hours sitting beside Attree in the morning court, had developed a certain intimacy with him in the way that old rivals do, and it would not have been surprising if he had begun to contemplate how the victim might just as well have been him, or might the next time *be* him. John Boyd was behind bars, at least temporarily, but his friends still walked free. Nor were the Chichesters the only gang in town. In any of the low places of the Five Points—in the pitch-dark allies, the seamen's bars with walls brightened by pictures of Black-Eyed Susan and Paul Jones the Pirate, the hideous underground dens thick with the smoke of charcoal fires—could be found Roach Guards, Shirt Tails, and Plug Uglies (so called for the oversize plug hats they wore, lined with leather and wool, very useful for protecting the skull during a fight), many of whose members Wisner had publicly named in the police court reports of the *Sun*.

Wisner was living on Chambers Street, about a five-minute walk from the Five Points; more ominously, he was still covering the police court, where every defendant, or defendant's friend, loomed as a potential assassin. It would have been frightening enough were he still single, but he now had a wife and a young son depending on him, and his health, he could tell, was beginning to slip. For the better part of two years he had taken poor care of himself, writing deep into the night and then waking before sunup for court. His constitution had always been delicate, but he was troubled by how weak his lungs had become, how tired he became during his rounds of the city. His large dark eyes seemed now larger against the hollows of his face, darker against the pallor of his skin. Nor was he helping himself by his habit of chewing tobacco; he was little seen anymore without the telltale bulge of a chaw in his cheek. (Wisner was hardly alone in this. After his visit to America, Charles Dickens complained of "the odious practice of chewing and expectorating" he had witnessed in public places.) At the office he and Benjamin Day had taken to quarreling, particularly over slavery, an issue that increasingly dominated Wisner's mind. "He was a pretty smart fellow, but he and I never agreed," Day recalled in an interview years later. "We split on politics. You see, I was rather democratic in my notions; Wisner, whenever he got a chance, was always sticking in his damned little Abolitionist articles."

By the last week of June, less than three weeks after the assault on Attree at the Elysian Fields, George Wisner decided he had had enough. He sat down with Benjamin Day and together they worked out a deal in which Day would pay him five thousand dollars for his half-ownership of the *Sun*—five thousand dollars, when just two years earlier he had been content to work for four dollars a week. It was a fitting payment, he believed, for all his hard work; most important, it was enough to make a fresh start.

Of late, Wisner had been especially interested in the stories he was hearing about Michigan. Brought close by the recently built Erie Canal, the territory had become a magnet for emigrants from upstate New York, including one of his sisters. Perhaps there, in the clean, sharp air of the country, away from the constant pressure of turning out a daily paper, he might regain his health. He had been thinking about becoming a lawyer, maybe even one day going into politics. He was still only twenty-three years old.

With Wisner's departure for Michigan, Benjamin Day had to find himself a new editor. There was, he decided, only one man for the job.

THE story of how Richard Adams Locke came to replace George Wisner as the editor of the *Sun* is, like so much of Locke's life, shadowed by contradiction. As Benjamin Day recalled it, around the time of Wisner's departure Locke came to him looking for work, claiming that James Watson Webb had fired him after discovering that he was the author of the *Sun*'s Matthias series. Locke's assertion that his work for the *Sun* had caused his dismissal might have been accurate, or it might have been an effort to play on Day's sympathies. Benjamin Day, who could not be accused of having an excess of sympathy, always resisted this explanation (in an interview near the end of his life, he used the verb "pretended" in describing Locke's version of events), suspecting instead that Locke had been fired because of a drinking problem—although this notion casts doubts on his own judgment, as it raises the question of why he would choose to hire such a man as his editor. Yet another account has Locke leaving the *Courier and Enquirer* as a result of a conflict with the paper's managing editor, Edward Hoskin, and Hoskin did occasionally appear in an unflattering light in the *Sun*'s pages while Locke was editor there, including, during the moon series controversy, a reference to him as the *Courier*'s "supervising (or supervicious) editor." So Locke was fired because he moonlighted for the *Sun,* Locke was fired because he drank too much, Locke was fired because he couldn't get along with his boss. Each explanation points to a different cause, and each has been advanced in opposition to the others. And each may well be, at least in part, correct.

In May 1835, flush with the money from his Matthias series, Richard Adams Locke moved with his family from Duane Street several blocks north to 30 Franklin Street, between Centre and Elm. The Lockes had finally escaped the incessant noise rising from the Chatham Street marketplace, but their new residence was peaceful only by comparison; it lay across from the State Arsenal and beside the state-owned public yard, later to be taken by the New York and Harlem Railroad for its freight depot. Locke had now been with the *Courier and Enquirer* for the better part of two years, and he must have been feeling frustrated with his situation there. He could not have gotten on well with James Watson Webb, he of the silvery sideburns and piercing blue eyes, who modeled himself on the aristocrats from whom Locke had fled in England; nor could Locke have been proud of his association with a newspaper so closely aligned with the interests of Southern slaveholders and Northern nativists. The *Courier* had provided his family a steady income and given him an entry into the world of New York journalism, but after two years he must have been tired of dissipating his talents on thieves and pimps and wife beaters, when his mind was engaged with larger questions.

How, he may well have wondered, had he come to this? He had a writing style all his own, an erudition that in the newspaper district was surpassed only by that of William Cullen Bryant himself, and he had the ability to capture and hold an audience's attention. The astonishing success of the Matthias series had proven that beyond dispute. For the *Sun* he had lavished thousands of words on a single subject, yet now he was back to turning out his police paragraphs for Colonel Webb. When he was twenty-one he was reviewing works of literature and Italian history; when he was twenty-three he explored the nature of God. It was not merely the hubris of youth to imagine that he would be doing that sort of writing forever. The Matthias series had given him the unexpected opportunity to bring his learning to bear once more on his writing, to address critical issues of science and faith. He had felt liberated, but the feeling had lasted only briefly—until he clapped back on the irons of the police court.

So it would not be surprising if, in his boredom and frustration, he had taken to drinking, most likely at Windust's restaurant on Park Row, a popular gathering place for newspapermen and—this would have been especially appealing to Locke—English actors in town to perform Shakespeare at one of the nearby theatrical houses. (Quotations from Shakespeare adorned the restaurant's walls; above the beefsteak broiler hung these lines from *Macbeth:* "If it were done, when 'tis done / Then 'twere well 'twere done quickly.") Maybe, done in by drink and resentment, Locke missed a few sunrise sessions of the police court; maybe he resisted Hoskin's demands to cover yet another tragedy, to plunge himself again into miseries better imagined than described. (According to James Gordon Bennett of the *Herald,* who had been working for the *Courier* at the time, Locke had wanted to write editorials but was rebuffed by Hoskin.) Locke's position at the *Courier and Enquirer* would already have been growing precarious when Colonel James Watson Webb—not a man who suffered insubordination lightly—learned the name of the anonymous author of *Memoirs of Matthias the Prophet.*

It was May 1835; in a few weeks George Wisner would announce that he was leaving the *Sun* and Benjamin Day would begin to look for another editor. Day had greatly admired Locke's work for the *Courier,* and his coverage of the Matthias trial for the *Sun* had turned a handsome profit for everyone. Now, with the editor's seat unfilled and Locke in need of a job, it only made sense to see if together they might find success anew. He offered Locke the *Sun* editorship at a salary of twelve dollars a week. It wasn't much money, to be sure (five thousand dollars to the poorer, Day was done handing out shares of the paper to his editors), but Locke accepted the offer nonetheless. A decade after he was forced to step down at the *Bridgwater and Somersetshire Herald,* Richard Adams Locke was a newspaper editor once again.

CHAPTER 5

"The Evil Spirit of
the Times"

RICHARD ADAMS LOCKE was not the only new editor in town. Nor,
among the new editors, was he the only immigrant from Great
Britain, nor, remarkably enough, the only new British editor with crossed
eyes. At the beginning of May, just as the *Sun* was winning thousands of
new readers with its Matthias series, a cross-eyed, Scottish-born newspaperman named James Gordon Bennett took a room in a cellar office on
Ann Street, jury-rigged a desk from a pine plank stretched across two
flour barrels, and began to publish a penny paper he called the *Morning
Herald*. Within a matter of weeks it had established itself as the *Sun's*
most dangerous rival, and Bennett himself as Richard Adams Locke's
most capable enemy.

Many New Yorkers considered James Gordon Bennett their enemy, for
Bennett was one of those men who make enemies as naturally—and,
seemingly, as happily—as others make friends. In the course of his long
career at the *Herald*, he suffered numerous public beatings, many of them
administered by rival editors; once conducted a duel with another editor
in Hoboken (though shots were fired, both men escaped unharmed); and
was even the target of an assassination attempt, foiled only when the mysterious package that had arrived at his office began leaking black powder
and was discovered to be a bomb. Once for a full year the city's other papers set aside their differences to join in a campaign intended to put the
Herald out of business forever; over time this struggle became known as
the Moral War, sounding less like a boycott of a hated rival than a crusade

against wickedness itself. In 1842 Bennett was described this way by the editor of the *New York Aurora:*

> A reptile marking his path with slime wherever he goes, and breathing mildew at everything fresh or fragrant; a midnight ghoul, preying on rottenness and repulsive filth; a creature, hated by his nearest intimates, and bearing the consciousness thereof upon his distorted features, and upon his despicable soul; one whom good men avoid as a blot to his nature—whom all despise, and whom no one blesses—*all this* is James Gordon Bennett.

So wrote the twenty-three-year-old Walt Whitman.

Bennett himself would not have been entirely displeased by Whitman's characterization, for he seemed to believe in the Latin maxim that it is an unhappy fortune to have no enemies. He reveled in the invective hurled at him by other editors ("lowest species of scurrility," James Watson Webb called him; "polluter of the press," said Mordecai Manuel Noah) and often tried to provoke it, understanding that people would buy his newspaper just to find out who his next target would be, and that every editorial response from a rival newspaper constituted, for him, free advertising. He ridiculed every sector of society except the readers of the *Herald,* for whom he expressed only the highest respect and affection. He trafficked freely in racial and ethnic slurs. Jews, he once declared, were "without a single redeeming feature, except the beauty, excellence, black eyes, small feet, and fine forms of their women." He called rival editor Park Benjamin, who was physically handicapped, "half Jew, half infidel, with a touch of the monster." In an early editorial he derided the *Sun* as a "dirty, sneaking, drivelling contemporary nigger paper." Elsewhere he observed, "The existing position of the Southern colored races"—that is to say, enslaved—"is their natural position." Raised as a Catholic in Scotland and trained for the priesthood, as an adult he turned against the Church with the special bitterness of the disillusioned former lover. The Catholic Church, said Bennett, "has seen her best day, and aught henceforth to be preserved in Museums, or venerated as an old Gothic edifice, or Grecian temple, but no more."

Bennett delighted in shocking those he considered prudes, using the word *leg* when other newspapers allowed themselves only *limb* (sometimes, as a joke, he used *branch* instead) and, most shockingly, referring to underwear as *pantaloons* rather than by the common euphemism *inexpressibles.* "Petticoats—petticoats—petticoats," he exclaimed in one editorial, "there—you fastidious fools—vent your mawkishness on that!" For years he sold advertising space to the city's most notorious abortionist, Madame Restell of Greenwich Street, whose advertisements promised "a simple, easy, healthy, and CERTAIN remedy," at the price of only five dollars a package. (If that treatment failed—for the remedy was by no means certain—Madame Restell resorted to a painful and risky procedure using a wire.) He specialized in blind items about lecherous clergymen and amorous widows, about adulterous politicians and beautiful young women who sipped champagne in high-priced brothels. He preferred the more gruesome crimes, the more sordid scandals, because they sold more papers and confirmed his belief in the essential nature of human depravity.

In an industry dominated by arrogant, egotistical men, Bennett was the *ne plus ultra.* Early in his career he declared that he intended to be the genius of newspapers, as Shakespeare was genius of the drama and Byron genius of the poem. He bestowed on himself the military title of General, just so that he might outrank his two former employers, Colonel Webb of the *Courier* and Major Noah of the *Star.* Until his marriage at forty-five, he used the newspaper's editorial page as his own lonely hearts column, advertising his charms to the paper's female readers; when he married, he ran news of his honeymoon on the *Herald*'s front page. Bennett was rail thin, even gaunt, for he ate sparingly (he much preferred to work than to eat), and had the slump-shouldered posture common among tall men. His voice was loud, and his Scottish burr was as thick as oatmeal. He had long, wavy hair, a hooked nose, and steel-gray eyes, one of which veered alarmingly toward the other, as if he were unable ever to pull his gaze from the subject that fascinated him the most: James Gordon Bennett himself.

Henry J. Raymond, the legendary founding editor of the *New York Times,* was once heard to cry, "It would be worth my while, sir, to give a million dollars, if the Devil would come and tell me every evening, as he does Bennett, what the people of New York would like to read about the next morning." For Raymond, as for New York's other newspaper editors, Bennett was an especially maddening foe because he was so very good at his job. He believed that newspapers could be, in his words, "the greatest organ of social life" (replacing literature, theater, and, especially, religion), and he never stopped thinking of ways to improve his own paper; many of the innovations he brought to the *Herald* are still in use today. Bennett wrote the first daily Wall Street column, analyzing the latest doings of the stock market; he established the first European bureaus, staffed with regular correspondents; he conducted and published the first interviews with newsmakers; he introduced the use of maps to illustrate war coverage; he was the first to put the news on the front page rather than on page two.

In the early days of the *Herald* he had no money to hire anyone, and so he produced the entire paper by himself. By eight in the morning, when he arrived at his desk, he had already put in several hours of work at home, sustained only by tea and a biscuit. He wrote all morning in the office (where he also sold papers and received advertisements), and after a quick lunch spent the afternoon making his rounds of the city in search of news. After dinner he was back at the office putting the finishing touches on the paper, and then he walked to the printer's to check the page proofs before returning to his tiny apartment at the rear of a tenement building on Nassau Street. He was the *Herald*'s publisher, editor, reporter, proofreader, and business manager. His life was synonymous with his work, and he devoted himself to it with a single-mindedness that observers could not help but find both admirable and slightly appalling. Never before had New York seen an editor so naked in his ambitions, journalistic and personal alike (Bennett made no secret of his intention to become wealthy from the *Herald,* a goal he swiftly accomplished), nor one so willing to indulge the quirks of his own personality, and so eager to avenge his many grievances.

Like Richard Adams Locke, James Gordon Bennett was a British immigrant who had come late to American journalism. He did not arrive from Scotland until he was twenty-five years old, and he was already more than thirty when, in 1827, he was hired as a reporter for the old *New-York Enquirer,* then under the editorship of Mordecai Manuel Noah. Bennett became Noah's assistant after his previous assistant was killed in a duel, but theirs turned out to be a combustible relationship and Noah sent him to Washington to cover the nation's capital. Bennett's letters from Washington were so popular among the paper's readers that Mordecai Noah and later James Watson Webb (who replaced Noah after the *New-York Enquirer* merged with the *Morning Courier*), threatened by Bennett's obvious talent and equally obvious ambitiousness, denied him a byline and made it known that they were giving Bennett the ideas for his pieces when not dictating them outright. Bennett chafed at the constraints and secretly worked to engineer the merger of the *Courier* and the *Enquirer,* two newspapers aligned with the Democratic Party; he believed that the local Democratic leadership would not support the newly created *Morning Courier and New-York Enquirer,* since they had always distrusted James Watson Webb, and would turn to Bennett to start a new Democratic newspaper. Bennett, however, had badly miscalculated. After the merger he left to start his own paper, the *Globe.* But New York's Democrats trusted Bennett no more than they did Webb (they could tell that Bennett, whatever his gifts as a newspaperman, was at heart an opportunist), and the *Globe* did not long survive.

For the first time in years Bennett was without a regular job. He wrote to Vice President Martin Van Buren (whom he had strongly supported in his bid to replace John C. Calhoun) seeking a consulship in the state of Bremen, but never received a reply. He applied for a reporter's job at the *Washington Globe,* a position for which he was brilliantly qualified, but the *Globe*'s powerful editor, Francis P. Blair, merely directed him to a small Philadelphia daily paper, the *Pennsylvanian,* which needed an editor. In the spring of 1834 Bennett became a partner in the paper, but once again he managed to alienate himself from the local Democratic establishment and by the end of the summer the *Pennsylvanian* had disappeared, and Bennett's investment with it.

Penniless now, and a publishing failure twice over, at the end of 1834 Bennett returned to New York, where he applied for a job with the *Sun.* It must have been a distasteful errand for the proud Bennett, having to humble himself before a publisher so much younger than he and, in his estimation, so much less deserving of success. Benjamin Day, always a shrewd judge of talent, was inclined to hire him but was unwilling to overrule the vehement objections of George Wisner, who disapproved of Bennett's sympathy for the Southern cause (Bennett had spent time in the South as a young reporter for the *Charleston Courier,* and had adopted the racial attitudes of a plantation owner), but likely also feared being overshadowed by him. Ultimately Day turned down Bennett's request, pleading a lack of funds. It was a kind enough excuse, but James Gordon Bennett was not one to forget a slight, and the rejection helped fuel the antipathy he held for the *Sun* for the rest of his life.

After the publishers of the city's other penny paper, the *Transcript,* likewise turned him away, Bennett approached the young printer Horace

Greeley and proposed that they start a daily newspaper together. Greeley had been a partner in Horatio Sheppard's ill-fated *Morning Post,* and a few years later he would found his own very successful paper, the *Tribune* (which, ironically, would merge with the *Herald* in 1924, creating the *New York Herald Tribune*). He seemed a promising candidate for such a partnership, but, like Wisner, Greeley was leery about throwing in his lot with a supporter of slavery—and one of such challenging disposition to boot—and he too said no.

James Gordon Bennett was now forty years old, and quickly running out of options. For the better part of two years he had offered his talents to anyone who would take them, and in return had received little more than rebuffs and false promises. He had no doubt that he would start another paper, for that was what he was meant to do. But his experience had been bitter and his lessons hard won; he saw now that to succeed he could depend on no one but himself. For the first time in his life he might run a newspaper as he, not some highbrow editor or hypocritical politician, wanted it to be run: the way a newspaper should be run. It would cost a penny—for the penny paper was the wave of the future—but unlike the other penny papers his would not be directed solely at a working-class audience. Rather than win his readers through crass appeals to party or class, he would give the people the latest news from around the city, taking them, for the first time, inside the downtown countinghouses and the society balls and even the annual church meetings, in addition to more of what they really wanted—crime stories, of course, but written stylishly, with a sense of drama, not those shabby little police court columns; sharp-witted provocations; and scandals like they had never even imagined. Nor would he focus on the city's merchants; once enough readers had been won, the merchants would come flocking to him with their advertisements. He would not limit himself at all; limitations, he believed, were for lesser men. Alone in his dingy room, he nursed his grudges as other men did their drinks—slowly, to let the happy feeling last.

In the spring of 1835 Bennett scraped together five hundred dollars and hired the firm of Anderson & Smith to print his newspaper, which he had decided to call the *Morning Herald*. He took the cheapest office he could find near the newspaper district, just a small, dark room, not even on street level; he improvised a desk and brought in a single wooden chair. It was, for the moment, all he would need. By the end of the first week of May 1835, he was ready to deliver his *Morning Herald* to the world.

The *Herald,* Bennett grandly declared in the first issue, was "equally intended for the great masses of the community—the merchant, mechanic, working people—the private family as well as the public hotel—the journeyman and his employer—the clerk and his principal."

> We shall support no party, be the organ of no faction or coterie, and care nothing for any election or any candidate, from President down to constable. We shall endeavour to record facts on every public and proper subject, stripped of verbiage and coloring, with comments, when suitable, just, independent, fearless, and good-tempered. If the "Herald" wants the mere expansion which many journals possess, we shall try to make it up in industry, good taste, brevity, variety, point, piquancy, and cheapness.

At once Bennett began launching volleys against the city's other newspapers, starting with the *Herald's* chief rival, the *Sun,* "with its brace of blockheads for editors and lead of dirty and indecent police reporters." The *Sun,* he declared, was produced by "the garbage of society—a set of poor creatures whose light is going down faster than it ever went up; whose paper is too indecent, too immoral for any respectable person to touch, or any family to take in." Referring, presumably, to Wisner's abolitionist sentiments, Bennett called the *Sun* a "decrepit, dying penny paper, owned and controlled by a set of woolly-headed and thick-lipped Negroes." (In response the *Sun* asserted that Bennett's "only chance of dying an upright man will be that of hanging perpendicularly upon a rope.")

The *Sun's* Matthias pamphlet, Bennett claimed, "is full of exaggeration, folly, and falsehood, and is written in the vilest taste of the Police Office literature." The *Herald,* unlike the other penny papers, would not feature a police office column at all; it would not be "inundating the town with indecent and filthy police reports of drunkards, blacks, and negresses." Bennett had loftier aims for his crime stories; he disdained the usual run of wife beaters and shoplifters, preferring, whenever possible, stories that involved prostitutes (the more elegant the bordello the better) and profligacy of any kind among the rich and famous. For several days running the *Herald's* news columns led off with lengthy articles about a trial under way in New York's circuit court, in which a man named

George Barnard was suing a woman by the name of Mary Power for a breach of promise of marriage. The two, who lived in the upstate town of Hudson, had begun a romantic relationship (or, as Bennett preferred, "the gentleman commenced making love to the lady") when Mary was just twelve years old. Sometime later George moved to New Orleans on business, and over several months they maintained a regular correspondence, with numerous letters sent on each side. In one George proposed marriage, and in another Mary (who had earlier declined his proposals) agreed. Many weeks passed without George coming to visit Mary, even though he had since moved back to New York City, just a few hours' sail from Hudson. Finally Mary wrote that another man had proposed to her, and she asked George to release her from their engagement. George replied that he could not do this without receiving a sizable payment as compensation for his "loss of time, and expense of feelings" during the years of their courtship. Mary refused to pay and married her new suitor; George took her to court for breach of promise. Day after day Bennett provided all the details of the court proceedings, culminating in the jury's decision in favor of George Barnard, with an award of one thousand dollars. The verdict, Bennett thundered, was "one of the most strange hallucinations on the subject that has ever yet taken place in this or any other country." He declared it a mockery of justice—and he published all of the letters that had passed between the two lovers, in full, so that his readers might see it for themselves.

By July 1835, just two months after the *Morning Herald* began publishing, Bennett could claim a daily circulation of seven thousand, almost as great as that of the *Sun,* which by then had been publishing for nearly two years. Well into his middle age, James Gordon Bennett had found his true path as a newspaperman. With the *Herald* he could at last display his remarkable gift for reading the public's desires, a gift that the *Times's* Henry Raymond would later complain had been bestowed on him by the devil.

FOR much of the summer of 1835 New York sweltered under a thick gray slate of a sky, the air a stifling haze that by evening thickened into a fog so dense, as one visiting Yankee was heard to remark, that you could drive a peg into it and hang up your hat. Old-timers said the weather recalled that of 1811, a summer memorable mostly for the appearance of the Great Comet, a comet so large and spectacular that for weeks it could be seen with the naked eye. Now New Yorkers awaited another celestial visitor, Halley's Comet, which the famed English astronomer Sir John Herschel, watching the skies from his observatory in South Africa (an observatory that Richard Adams Locke would shortly make the focus of endless speculation), had predicted would be arriving sometime soon.

The city's papers were filled with stories of horses dropping dead in the street from exhaustion, of laborers suddenly taking sick and dying, according to the common belief of the time, from a too rapid consumption of ice water. On Elm Street a policeman was set upon from behind and drenched with a shoeful of the brown, stinking water that ran in the gutters after a thunderstorm. The temper of the city grew short, the general mood as foul as the smells that rose up from the streets and pervaded every home, mansion, and shanty alike. Many New Yorkers expected a reprise of the events of the previous summer, when, night after terrifying night, white mobs, some of them several thousand strong, had roamed the streets looting and burning the homes, stores, and churches of blacks and abolitionists. Before the week was over the attacks were being carried out with an almost military precision, with preestablished targets, runners passing information among the roving bands, and horse carts chained together to form primitive but effective barricades shielding the work of destruction. The rioters had been inflamed by newspaper reports that the Reverend Samuel H. Cox, a local minister, had advocated the "amalgamation" of blacks and whites and, most gallingly, claimed that Christ was a colored man. As the riots nightly raged, the *Commercial Advertiser* published false reports that black gangs, "breathing violence and revenge," were threatening to burn down the city, while the *Courier and Enquirer*'s editorials seemed calculated to egg on the rioters in their destruction. "How much longer are we to submit?" asked James Watson Webb, inveighing against the president of the American Anti-Slavery Society, whose dry-goods store was a prime target of the mobs. "In the name of the country, in the name of Heaven, how much more are we to bear from Arthur Tappan's mad impudence?"

Now, in the summer of 1835, a new and even more menacing threat had arisen. Back in May the American Anti-Slavery Society had initiated a full-scale campaign to flood the South with antislavery literature. By the end of July some 175,000 copies of the society's magazines had passed through the New York post office on their way to Southern destinations.

There they were met with organized resistance such as might greet the advance guard of an invading army. In Charleston, the mailbags containing the abolitionist literature were stolen from the post office; the next night a crowd of thousands raised effigies of Arthur Tappan and William Lloyd Garrison, the abolitionist leader from Boston, and ceremoniously burned the magazines, to great shouts and cheers, in an enormous bonfire. The flames soon spread everywhere: all through August the Southern night was illuminated by the flickering glow of torchlight parades. Nearly every city, large and small, held its own anti-abolitionist rally. Newspaper editors urged the passage of state laws making it a crime punishable by death to circulate abolitionist literature south of the Potomac; the governors of the offended states would have the authority to demand that the North extradite these "fugitives from justice," and if they were not handed up, to offer a reward for their capture and transport to a Southern jail. In Norfolk, Virginia, a rally was held to raise money "for the heads of Garrison, Tappan & Co." Residents of a parish in Louisiana put up a reward of fifty thousand dollars for the capture of Tappan dead or alive. (When informed of the bounty that had been placed on his head, Tappan managed to joke, "If that sum is placed in the New York Bank, I may possibly think of giving myself up.")

New York was a center of the cotton trade, and seven thousand Southerners were said to be living there, among them any number of potential conspirators; whispers began to circulate that a team of assassins from New Orleans had secretly arrived in the city to murder Tappan. Philip Hone worried in his diary that "the least spark would create a flame in which the lives and property of Arthur Tappan and his associates would be endangered." James Watson Webb printed a letter from a North Carolinian who claimed to have encountered a group of men heading for New York to capture Tappan, to which Webb had appended a taunting message: "Keep a look out, Arthur—a large reward is offered for you— before you are aware, you may be *boxed*." According to Webb, Southern slaves were "as well off as it is probably practicable for that race to be under any circumstances. They are fed, clothed and treated in all respects, with a care and kindness that made them happy and contented with their lot." The abolitionists, on the other hand, "ought to be honest and acknowledge their real character—the worst enemies the slaves have in the country."

In the *Evening Star,* editor Mordecai Manuel Noah proudly affirmed his quarter century of opposition to "every attempt to create excitement, or produce unhappy difficulties on the Slave question" and opened the columns of the newspaper to the citizens of the South; he was, he said, "happy to make the paper the medium of communication through which their sentiments can be heard, and their wishes made known to the people of the United States." Noah also issued a veiled threat of attacks like the ones of the previous summer: "The immediate abolitionists hold a large caucus this day—we know where they meet. . . . If they are determined to go on and keep up this excitement, their deeds be on their own heads." The *Transcript* similarly threatened the visiting British abolitionist George Thompson: "If he ventures too far even here in promulgating his wild and objectionable doctrines, he may involve not only himself, but also many respectable citizens who have unfortunately been made converts to his peculiar faith, in consequences the most dreadful and alarming." Even the more progressive-minded William Leggett of the *Evening Post* (filling in for the traveling William Cullen Bryant), while criticizing Southern censorship of abolitionist literature, felt obliged to add that "we deprecate, as earnestly and sincerely as any person can, in the north or south, the conduct of the abolitionists."

"If our feeble voice might prove of any avail," wrote Leggett, "we should exert it with all our power to dissuade the misguided men engaged in the abolition cause from prosecuting their designs, when certain ruin must be the consequence, even to the poor wretches in whose behalf they fancy themselves labouring."

Of all the daily newspapers in New York, only one maintained a firm and unapologetic stance against slavery: the *Sun.* If Benjamin Day had believed that Richard Adams Locke would take a less forceful position on the issue than had George Wisner, he was relieved of that idea soon enough. Locke filled the *Sun*'s columns with news of outrages committed against Southern abolitionists, "the Excitement against the Anti-Slavery advocates," he called it, "which has made murder and outrages almost as common in some of the slave holding states as slavery itself." The "Excitement," though, was not confined to the South, as was shown in the story of a New Jersey mob who surrounded the house of a black man accused of an unspecified offense; the mob was composed entirely of Quakers. "The evil spirit of the times," Locke observed, "appears to be pervading all classes, sects, and communities of the country." He was right. The next few months would witness more than one hundred riots, most of them directly related to issues of race and slavery; it was the most violent period in America since the days of the Revolution.

Locke decried the atmosphere of threat and menace that was rising against all those, South or North, who dared to stand against popular opinion on slavery: "With all our boasting about the glorious government under which we live, the sanctity of our laws, and the safety of the persons and property of our citizens under their protection, there is not another government in Christendom in which there is in reality less security against rapine or murder, or in which they are more winked at and even commended, if they are the offering of any popular prejudice, than in this our *free* and *happy* land." In the face of New York's overwhelming sympathy for the Southern cause (an anti-abolition rally held in the Park later that summer would draw a crowd of nearly ten thousand), Locke railed against the threats made upon Arthur Tappan and other abolitionists. "Let them invite the abduction and murder of a citizen of the North by offering money for him," he warned, "and they would see in what latitude 'true chivalry' is found. 'The very stones would cry out' against such an outrage. From the Potomac to the St. Lawrence, from Lake Michigan to the Atlantic, every man would be roused, and a deep and thundering burst of indignation would go forth that would shake the Blue Ridge from its base." From the offices of the *Sun,* in the cheerless summer of 1835, a New Yorker could hear the distant rumblings of civil war.

Perhaps Locke's strongest and most comprehensive statement on slavery came in response to a reader's letter canceling his subscription to the *Sun,* "as you have come out in favor of the abolitionists."

"We have complied with the gentleman's request," Locke began his reply, "and ordered our carrier to leave him the Sun no longer." He acknowledged that the Northern states had no legal right to enforce abolition in the South, because slavery was "an evil which the south has inherited, and which can only be eradicated by the slave-holders themselves." Still, he felt it perfectly within his rights to call for the abolition of slavery in the District of Columbia ("to wipe away the foul stain from the capitol of our country"), his argument growing into a stirring, full-throated condemnation of slavery of the sort that never appeared in the editorial columns of a New York daily newspaper. Other editors paused for a perfunctory disapproval of Southern slavery on their way to a denunciation of abolitionists or a defense of states' rights; this was something entirely different. Slavery, Locke declared,

is at war with the genius of our government—it scoffs at our national declaration, and brands us with hypocrisy before the nations of the earth. It paralyzes the power of our free institutions at home, and makes them a "hissing and a bye-word abroad." It is sheltered under the wings of our national eagle, republican law is its protector, republican equality its advocate, republican morality its patron, and republican freemen its body guard. It is a sin in itself apart from the rigors incidental to its administration. It wrests from our fellow men the legacies which God Almighty has bequeathed them—inalienable birth-right endowments, exchanged for no equivalent, unsurrendered by volition, and unforfeited by crime. It derides the sanctity with which reason, religion and law have invested domestic relations—annihilates marriage— makes void parental authority—invites the violation of chastity by denying it legal protection, and bids God speed to lust as it riots at noon day, glorying in the immunities of law. Its baneful influence is beginning to be felt in every part of the Union. At the north the press lowers under a censorship, and the freedom of speech, that glorious privilege of American citizens—is trampled under the feet of a ruthless mob. At the south the mechanic arts and all vigorous enterprise is crushed under an incubus—a thriftless agriculture is smiting the land with barrenness and decay—prodigality, in lavishing upon the rich the plundered earnings of the poor, is accounted high souled generosity— revenge is regarded as the refinement of honor—aristocracy entitled republicanism, and despotism chivalry.

"Such is slavery," Locke concluded, "and such *we* shall ever call it, the loss of a few subscribers to the contrary notwithstanding. We have stopped the gentleman's paper, as we said in the beginning of this article, and if there are any more of our subscribers who think that to tell the *truth* is to be an abolitionist, we shall be happy to stop theirs also."

Though the question of slavery dominated the city's attention in the summer of 1835, it was one slave in particular, Joice Heth, who became the focus of its curiosity and wonder, her sitting room the destination of immense crowds that came to see her day after day, for as long as she remained on view. She had been brought to New York by P. T. Barnum, a twenty-four-year-old would-be promoter who had arrived in the city only recently with his wife and daughter from the village of Bethel in western Connecticut. Within a matter of days Barnum had produced an attraction that captivated the city as had no other in recent memory—at least until later that same month, when Richard Adams Locke unveiled his moon series in the *Sun*.

These two great impositions on the public (as the saying of the day had it) would, in their denouements, entangle Barnum, Locke, and Bennett in an elaborate series of deceptions and exposures. By that time, however, Barnum was already moving on to the next attraction. With Joice Heth he had successfully re-created himself as a showman, setting in motion a career that would eventually make him a multimillionaire, a friend of presidents and royalty, and arguably, for a time, the most famous American in the world.

It had all begun years before, as in so many American success stories, with a single plot of land on which he could build.

CHAPTER 6

The Prince of
Ivy Island

P. T. BARNUM WAS not born into wealth, although he grew up believing that he was. He was born—or, as he liked to put it, made his first appearance on the stage—in the village of Bethel, Connecticut, on July 5, 1810, not long after the town's Independence Day celebrations had been completed. "The smoke had all cleared away," he wrote in his autobiography, "the drums had finished their rattle, and when peace and quiet were restored, I made my *début*."

Though Bethel had been settled since the seventeenth century, modern ways had arrived there only fitfully, and its daily life was not much different from that of more recently settled frontier towns. For the women of the town, days were filled with an exhausting array of household chores, few of them lightened by any mechanical conveniences, from washing and ironing clothes to making soap and candles, milking cows, churning butter, and preparing meals in a large iron pot suspended in the fireplace; the men, by and large, worked in the fields or in the town's main industry, the manufacture of combs and hats. Children ate their meals with lead spoons, on pewter plates sold from the backs of wagons by itinerant peddlers. Everyone, clergymen included, drank the hard cider they called "gumption." Physicians made house calls on horseback, carrying their calomel, jalap, and Epsom salts, the mainstays of their practice, in their saddlebags. In the spring it was customary for the townspeople to be bled: the ill for cure, the healthy for prevention. Anyone found guilty of offending public morals was apt to find himself locked up in the public stocks. Sunday mornings were spent in the town's Presbyterian meeting-house, a church building without a steeple or a bell or, for that matter, a stove. During the New England winters, the congregation would shiver through the pastor's two-hour sermons, providing a literal manifestation of the name by which such fervent believers were known among the less devout: bluenoses. When one of the brethren, imbued with the spirit of reform, proposed installing a stove in the church, the congregation voted down the notion overwhelmingly. "A pretty pass, indeed," Barnum recalled the congregants grumbling, "when professing Christians needed a fire to warm their zeal."

The presiding spirit of the town was Calvinist, the world seen as a dark, brooding place of sin and judgment, of souls foreordained by God to heaven or hell, where dead babies were condemned to damnation (because they had not yet had the opportunity to accept Jesus Christ as their savior) and the pope was understood to be the antichrist. All through Barnum's childhood, Connecticut was in the grip of the nationwide religious revival that became known as the Second Great Awakening, meant to hasten the second coming of Christ; at night the low hills around Bethel often reverberated with the sounds of raucous camp meetings led by traveling preachers who promised eternal woe for those unfortunate souls not among God's elect. Barnum himself attended many of these meetings as a boy, returning home

> almost smelling, feeling and tasting those everlasting waves of boiling sulphur, and hearing the agonizing shrieks and useless prayers of myriads of never ending sufferers, including mothers and their children, or perhaps children whose saved mothers were complacently watching their eternal agonies from the battlements of heaven, and with my eyes streaming with tears, and every fibre of my body trembling with fear, I have dropped upon my bended knees and fervently prayed this cold, stern God to let me die immediately, if thereby it was possible to save my soul and body from His endless wrath.

It was a vision of the world that Barnum found first terrifying and then infuriating, and against which he would struggle for the rest of his life. Like Richard Adams Locke, P. T. Barnum was a religious freethinker (both men advocated the doctrines of Universalism, though only Barnum actually belonged to that denomination) who opposed the undue influence of religious officials on civic life and enjoyed nothing more than holding them up to ridicule. Like Locke he propounded his beliefs first in newspaper editorials and later in pamphlets, including a widely distributed essay entitled *Why I Am a Universalist*. Even more forcefully, Barnum fought against the dark spirit of Puritanism by the example of his own life, which was richly devoted to joyfulness and laughter. God had granted people the gift of amusement, he contended; to deprive them of that pleasure—to reduce life, as had the stern churchmen of his childhood, to an endless round of drabness and drudgery—was little short of evil. It was a belief succinctly captured in the motto he had emblazoned on his private carriage when he came into wealth: *Love God and Be Merry.*

P. T. Barnum had been named for his maternal grandfather, Phineas Taylor (his family members always called him Taylor), and from his namesake he inherited both his Universalism and his love of a good joke. Bespectacled, with unruly hair and devilishly arched eyebrows, Phineas Taylor made his living buying and selling land, but his greater talent seems to have been for practical jokes. According to Barnum, his grandfather "would go farther, wait longer, work harder and contrive deeper, to carry out a practical joke, than for anything else under heaven." He enjoyed nothing better than sitting around the wood stove at the country store with the other local wags, telling tales of their adventures—the stories growing funnier, and more improbable, with each round of Santa Cruz rum or Holland gin—while endlessly devising practical jokes to play on each other and the store's customers, sparing few their comic attentions, and all the better if the victim happened to be a clergyman. Phineas Taylor was said to be the first person the infant Barnum ever recognized (not surprising, given the hours he spent happily in his grandfather's arms being fed lumps of sugar), and Taylor was unquestionably the guiding spirit of his life. The very first sentences of Barnum's autobiography, *The Life of P. T. Barnum, Written by Himself,* were devoted not to his parents or the circumstances of his birth, but to Phineas Taylor.

It was Phineas Taylor who first told the four-year-old Barnum about Ivy Island—five acres of land that his proud grandfather had bequeathed him as a gift for carrying his name, which he would inherit when he turned twenty-one. Though few details were forthcoming, according to everyone Ivy Island was the most valuable farm in Connecticut. Scarcely a week went by that the young Barnum was not reminded by someone of the value of his holdings. Phineas Taylor delighted in telling acquaintances, whenever his grandson was around, that this was the richest boy in Bethel, for he was the owner of Ivy Island. Barnum's father hoped he would see fit to support the family when he came into his inheritance; Barnum solemnly pledged that he would. His neighbors worried aloud that he would not want to play with their children because he was propertied and they were not; Barnum promised his playmates that he would give them a piece of Ivy Island so that they might become rich too.

One summer day when Barnum was twelve years old, he asked his father for permission to visit Ivy Island. To his surprise, his father replied that he would soon be mowing a meadow near there; he could come along and help out, and during lunchtime take a break to inspect his property. For three nights Barnum was so excited he could barely sleep. His head was filled with visions of Ivy Island, which his youthful imagination had turned into a kind of storybook version of the biblical land of milk and honey, the landscape dotted with caverns overflowing with diamonds and emeralds, mines encrusted with gold and silver.

Finally the long-awaited day arrived. "Now, Taylor," his mother advised him before he set off, "don't become so excited when you see your property as to let your joy make you sick, for remember, rich as you are, that it will be nine years before you can come into possession of your fortune."

All that morning Barnum worked the meadow with the men; noontime could not come fast enough. After a quick lunch under a shady tree, his father gave him permission to leave, enlisting one of the hired hands, an Irishman named Edmund, to lead the young man to his property. Edmund leaped into service, grabbing an ax to take along with them. When Barnum asked what the ax was for, Edmund replied that he thought the young man might like him to cut a few pieces of timber from Ivy Island, so that he might see how superior it was to any other. This answer seemed to Barnum perfectly reasonable, and the two started out.

As they reached the north edge of the meadow, he noticed that the ground was becoming damp; as they pressed on a bit farther, the ground turned muddy and before long it had dissolved into swampland. With each passing step earth increasingly gave way to water, and eventually Barnum was able to keep moving forward only by leaping from bog to bog, often missing his step and splashing down into water as high as his waist. The hot sun glinted off the water, shining on the tall ferns and cattails that grew everywhere; from all around came the hum and whir of unseen insects. Edmund, his stride longer and more assured, was already far ahead. Once Barnum was set upon by a nest of hornets, one of which stung him on the nose, causing him to plunge into the water up to his neck. After a quarter hour of painfully slow trekking, his nose throbbing, his ankles aching, the boy finally saw Edmund waiting for him on dry land. With a last heave he crawled out of the swamp, covered with mud, gasping for breath, and, as he recalled years later, "looking considerably more like a drowned rat than a human being."

There, Edmund pointed out to him; there it was, on the other side of the creek. Now the real purpose of the ax was revealed, as Edmund used it to fell a small tree that he then laid over the creek, providing them a bridge to Ivy Island.

Edmund helped him across and Barnum was, at very long last, standing on his own property. He turned to look at what lay all around him, his heart sinking at the realization. The fabled Ivy Island, wellspring of so many childhood fantasies, was nothing more than a forlorn patch of land overgrown with ivy vines, from which protruded a few stunted trees.

It was so clear now: Ivy Island was the greatest of all his grandfather's practical jokes, carefully prepared for the better part of a decade. In a sickening moment, too, Barnum understood the truth of the name Phineas Taylor had bestowed upon the land. Any place called *Ivy* Island, after all, would naturally be covered in ivy; and it could not be called Ivy *Island,* of course, unless it was completely surrounded by water. His own excitement and pride had prevented him from seeing that. How important he had felt then, and how foolish now. Imagine: diamonds and emeralds—in Connecticut! He could provide no help for his father, no gifts for his friends, and everyone but him had known it all along. In shame he cast his eyes downward, where to his horror he saw an enormous black snake slithering toward him, its head raised up, menace in its eyes. With a shout Barnum scurried back across the fallen tree to the other side of the creek. For the rest of his long life, he would never again set foot on Ivy Island.

As time went on, P. T. Barnum seems to have been able to laugh with the others at the fun that had come at his expense; in Bethel the laughter about Ivy Island would not fade away for another five years. Still, as the literary critic Van Wyck Brooks noted in his essay on Barnum, "One seldom hears of a grandfather outwitting an infant in arms, of a mother conspiring to jeer at her own offspring, of a whole family, in fact, inviting the village to make game of its youngest and most helpless member." It is surely too simple to surmise that Barnum's later vocation as a showman, and his undying love of the hoaxes that he termed humbugs, arose from a need to fool others as he had once, as a boy, been so grievously fooled—but an event as remarkable as this one could not have failed to leave traces on its young victim. The motives of his family members in maintaining the long deception must not have been malicious; they loved their Taylor deeply, and none of them more than the man who had purchased the land and set the joke into motion. With Ivy Island these Connecticut Yankees were, in a sense, welcoming the young man into the tribe; and like all tribal initiations this one contained important lessons, no less powerful for being unspoken. This, the people of Bethel were telling him, is how life is: things are rarely as they seem, and fortunes are not handed over to the undeserving. Shrewdness, like temperance and prudence, is a virtue. Keep your wits about you, lest you fall prey to others.

That knowledge, as deep and solid as land, was Barnum's inheritance.

NOT long after the Ivy Island incident, Barnum's father, Philo, opened a country store in Bethel and brought in his son to work as a clerk. Though it may be too strong to call Philo a ne'er-do-well, he had already tried and failed at a variety of trades, and when he died a few years later he left behind him a drawer full of unpaid debts—among them one to his own son, who had to work extra hours to earn the money to buy the shoes he wore to his father's funeral. Perhaps Philo was concerned that his son would follow in his own wayward path; even as a teenager Barnum showed an aversion to manual labor and clearly was never going to earn a living, as most of the village men did, in field or factory. In any case, Philo's decision proved to be an inspired one. Behind the counter of a store, Barnum proved to be efficient and capable, and no longer easily fooled; he was, in the widely used phrase of the day, up to snuff. Before long he was running the store by himself—his father had gone on to open a tavern, where he spent most of his time—and he reveled in the new adult responsibility, displaying a merchant's proud strut, his pen thrust jauntily behind his ear, as he weighed out ten-penny nails or drew from large kegs of molasses and rum. ("I suppose I have drawn and bottled more rum than would be necessary to float a ship," Barnum would later say.)

As was typical of the period, the store carried just about everything needed for running a household, from groceries and dry goods to hardware and a thousand small items known collectively as notions. For these the customers paid variously in cash, credit, and, most challeng-ingly, barter, which meant that rates of exchange had to be quickly fig-ured, involving not just butter and eggs but also beeswax, feathers, and ax handles. Nor was the offer of trade always on the up-and-up; some-times the sharp young proprietor would measure a farmer's truckload of oats or rye only to find it several bushels shy of the number claimed, or cut open a bundle of rags, solemnly declared by the woman who brought it in to contain entirely linen and cotton, only to discover worthless woolens, or that the bundle's weight had been augmented by a pile of gravel or ashes.

In *The Humbugs of the World,* his high-spirited dissection of cons and tricksters past and present—séance rappers, faith healers, lottery sharks, diviners, false prophets, and numerous others—Barnum included a sec-tion on food adulteration, expensive products ingeniously stretched or even replaced with cheaper ones: black tea made green by being cooked with plaster of Paris and Prussian-blue paint powder; cayenne mixed with corn meal and salt; pepper blended with dust; coffee ground up with chicory root, dandelion root, peas, beans, parsnips, even horse livers, all of them baked to the proper color and consistency. Much of this informa-tion he seems to have garnered from direct experience during his years as the proprietor of a country store in the Nutmeg State—the very name of which was derived from the legendarily crafty Yankee peddlers who were said to sell fake nutmegs carved out of wood. "Otter" hats might be made from beaver or rabbit; clocks ran slow or fast, if at all; and fabric colors billed as "fast" more accurately foretold the speed with which they ran in the wash. Incidents of deception were surprisingly common, and a store-keeper had always to be on the qui vive, even when dealing with towns-people who were seemingly above reproach. Barnum loved to tell the story of a grocer who doubled as the deacon of the town's church. One morning, before breakfast, he called down to his clerk:

"John, have you watered the rum?"
"Yes, sir."
"And sanded the sugar?"
"Yes, sir."
"And dusted the pepper?"
"Yes, sir."
"And chicoried the coffee?"

"Yes, sir."

"Then come up to prayers."

PHILO died in September 1826, just a few months after his son turned sixteen. Before long Barnum left the store in Bethel and went to work at another country store in the nearby town of Grassy Plain. There he met a seamstress from Bethel named Charity Hallett (known to all as "Chairy") who had come to Grassy Plain to buy a bonnet. Barnum was immediately struck by the girl's rosy cheeks, pale complexion, and beautiful white teeth (enough of a rarity in a country village of the time that he recalled the detail decades later), which provoked in him, as he charmingly described it, "a state of feeling quite new to me." Their relationship proceeded slowly, due in part to resistance from Barnum's mother and other relatives, who felt that the promising young man should set his sights higher than a local seamstress. The two did not marry until three years later, in a ceremony in New York to which none of Barnum's side of the family had been invited.

By that point Barnum had left the store in Grassy Plain to become a clerk in a grocery store run by a former Bethel neighbor, Oliver Taylor, in Brooklyn. In 1826 Brooklyn consisted of a few neighborhoods near the docks, surrounded by a collection of independent villages with names such as Flatbush and Gravesend. Thanks to the newly established Fulton Ferry service to New York, Barnum could easily cross the East River to Manhattan, where he happily partook of the night life available there, often squiring visiting Connecticut friends to the theater, of which he had come to fancy himself a discerning critic. As a boy Barnum had once accompanied his grandfather on a business trip to New York, but the excitement of that brief stay could hardly have compared to that felt by a young man living in the city for the first time, with his own money in his pocket. It is not hard to imagine Barnum strolling up Broadway of an evening, peering into the windows of the exquisite little shops offering the latest fashions from Paris and London (differing in every way from the country stores he knew), admiring the great stone spires of Trinity Church and St. Paul's Chapel (the Bethel church had not even had a steeple), letting himself drift along with the crowds that surged all the way up the avenue to Niblo's at Prince Street, the most celebrated eating house in the city, where those with enough money could feast on shad and grouse and venison, and in the warmer months stroll in the landscaped gardens under showers of fireworks. Surely he stopped at Scudder's American Museum in the park behind City Hall to see the tens of thousands of items on display there, including remarkably preserved animal specimens—petrels and hummingbirds and toucans and grebes, snakes and alligators, an ostrich, a five-legged sheep, a dog-faced monkey, even an Indian elephant—as well as genuine antiquities and curiosities, from a piece of the damask bed curtains under which Mary, Queen of Scots, had slept to a chunk of Plymouth Rock: gazing at it all in what must have been a kind of rapture, beholding, for an admission price of just twenty-five cents, the miraculous nature of the world. Just fourteen years later he would become the new owner of the museum, renaming it Barnum's American Museum, where, at the top of that grand marble structure on the corner of Ann Street, he would bring the first limelight to Broadway, its dazzling blue-white light soaring into the night sky and visible for miles in every direction, his prospects by then having become just as bright, and seemingly as limitless.

After working for a year at Oliver Taylor's grocery, Barnum left to open his own porterhouse (he was then seventeen years old), which a few months later he sold at a sizable profit. For a while after that he worked at a local tavern, but he found himself becoming homesick, feeling more acutely than ever his distance from Charity. When he received a letter from his beloved grandfather Phineas, offering him free use of half of a Bethel carriage house, he went back home to open a fruit and confectionery store that also did a brisk trade in oysters and ale. Still, even this was not enough to fully engage his attention, and before long he had taken up a more stimulating sideline: managing lotteries.

"Advertising is like learning," Barnum once counseled a would-be showman, "a little is a dangerous thing." Having become a lottery manager, he immediately blanketed the state with huge placards and brightly colored handbills and took out large newspaper advertisements awash in exclamation points, all of them proclaiming the unrivaled good fortune of his lottery office (he had bestowed on it the name "Temple of Fortune"), which he said was overseen by the trustworthy-sounding—though imaginary—proprietor "Dr. Peter Strickland." *Another mammoth prize—huzzah Dr. Strickland*, trumpeted one advertisement. *A fortune for a dollar—apply to Fortune's favorite, Dr. Strickland.* Before long Barnum had hired agents throughout the state, and they were selling as much as two thousand dollars of lottery tickets per day. His own profits were, he later wrote, "immense."

Despite Connecticut's Puritan heritage, lotteries had long been highly popular there, raising money for a variety of public institutions, including churches. (As a writer of the time noted, "People would gamble in lotteries for the benefit of a church in which to preach *against* gambling.") Still, resistance to lotteries was beginning to build. By the beginning of the 1830s a newly energized revivalism was sweeping across the state, and a ban on lotteries seemed the least of the measures looming on the horizon. There was even talk of forming a Christian political party, with the goal of reestablishing the old alliance between church and state. (In Connecticut the Congregational Church was not disestablished until 1818; before that time church membership was a requirement to hold public office, churches ran the public schools, and the church itself was supported by public taxation.) Barnum bitterly opposed all such ideas. He had long ago freed himself from the hellfire of those childhood camp meetings, and by political inclination he was a Jacksonian Democrat; like many of his fellow dissenters and Democrats, he was alarmed at the prospect of a religious coalition controlling the state's political life. Never one to shy away from expressing his opinion, Barnum sent several strongly worded letters to the Danbury newspaper, the *Recorder,* setting forth his concerns about the threats to freedom posed by undue religious excitement, and reciting the evils committed throughout history whenever religion had been joined with political power. To his great indignation, the letters were not published. Barnum was convinced that the editor of the *Recorder*—perhaps even the press generally—was being muzzled by the forces of religious orthodoxy. Liberty itself seemed now at stake, and he felt a duty to alert the public to the growing danger. So he purchased a printing press and a set of types, and took on a new occupation: P. T. Barnum became a newspaper editor.

The name of the paper that Barnum founded in October 1831 was the *Herald of Freedom.* Published weekly, the *Herald* was, in contemporary fashion, four pages long, most of it taken up by advertisements from local merchants and tradesmen offering butchering and blacksmithing, soapstone furnaces, peddlers' wagons, coffins ("made at the shortest notice"), and farms for sale. The news pages contained political speeches as well as reports on the doings of the Connecticut legislature, many of them written by Barnum himself—no mean feat for a twenty-one-year-old storekeeper with limited education—and like New York's mercantile press, they carried clippings from foreign newspapers. The real energy of the

The Prince of Ivy Island

Herald of Freedom, however (and the primary reason it found subscribers throughout Connecticut and in fifteen other states), came in Barnum's vigorous and untiring excoriation (much like that of another crusading young editor, Richard Adams Locke of the *Bridgwater and Somersetshire Herald*) of conservative politicians and orthodox clergymen.

On the front page beneath the masthead, the *Herald* carried a quote from Thomas Jefferson, "For I have sworn upon the Altar of God, eternal hostility against every form of tyranny over the mind of man," and inside Barnum promised that the *Herald* would oppose "all combinations against the liberties of our country." This meant not only standing against any effort to reestablish the old church-state alliance in Connecticut (in one item, for instance, he denounced a proposal that would have allowed the state legislature to hire chaplains with public funds) but also ridiculing what he saw as the superstition and fanaticism of the revivalist movement. The *Herald of Freedom* regularly included stories of suicides and murders, of people gone mad—all of these tragedies, Barnum claimed, brought on by the sermons of fear-mongering evangelists. In one especially horrific case, a girl in New Haven, convinced that she carried an intractable evil inside her, attempted to cut out her own heart with a razor. That, raged Barnum, was the hateful consequence of these "*hireling Priests,*" these "relentless savages who would reduce every peaceable dwelling to an insane house, and make every father a *murderer* of his own innocent and helpless offspring, rather than fail in establishing their heart-rending, barbarous and unfeeling creed."

Given the ferocity of his invective and the often personal nature of his attacks—various news items accused ministers, by name, of drunkenness, philandering, seducing their female servants, even robbery—it is not surprising that during his three years as editor of the *Herald of Freedom* Barnum was sued for libel three times, twice successfully. The first case resulted from his accusation that a local butcher was acting as a spy within the state Democratic caucus, for which he was ordered to pay a $215 fine. It was an even more serious matter when he pronounced Seth Seelye, one of Bethel's leading citizens and soon to become deacon of the church, "guilty of taking usury of an orphan boy."

The outcome of the case could hardly have been doubted: Seth Seelye was a highly respected merchant from a prominent family (two of his sons would go on to become presidents of Amherst and Smith colleges) and an outspoken member of the Congregational Church; Barnum, on the other hand, came from questionable stock, had enriched himself from lotteries,

and was a believer in the heresies of Universalism. Barnum was found guilty of libel, and after a tongue-lashing by the judge he was fined $100 and sentenced to sixty days in the Danbury jail.

Where others might have been chastened, or at least demoralized, by the guilty verdict, Barnum emerged from the Seelye trial exultant; he reveled in the publicity it had brought him (not to mention the hundreds of new subscribers for the *Herald of Freedom*), and in his newfound status as a martyr for freedom of speech—a view of the case that Barnum himself took every opportunity to encourage. "The same spirit governs my enemies that imprisoned Sellick Osborn and burnt to death Michael Servetus by order of John Calvin," he declared in a letter written to a supporter in Hartford. As a Democratic editor who had been imprisoned for libel in Connecticut two decades earlier, Sellick Osborn provided a fitting comparison, but Michael Servetus's fiery death at the hands of inquisitors in Geneva bore scant resemblance indeed to the conditions that met Barnum in the Danbury jail, where the walls of his cell had been freshly papered, and a new carpet laid down. For the two months of his stay he received a steady stream of well-wishers, and continued to edit the *Herald of Freedom* all the while.

At sunrise on the day of his release, a group of Barnum's friends gathered on the Danbury green to raise the flag and fire a salute in his honor. For hours they braved the cold of the December morning, until shortly before noon, when a "Committee of Arrangements" marched across the green to the jail. There they met a delighted Barnum, requesting that he accompany them to the nearby courthouse. Passing through the cheering crowd that had gathered outside to meet him, they entered the same courtroom in which Barnum had received his sentence two months earlier. The program began with the singing of a musical ode composed for the occasion, followed by the democratic anthem "Jefferson and Liberty" and a long oration on freedom of the press by the Universalist minister Theophilus Fisk, after which a choir sang "Strike the Cymbal" as the crowd, now numbering several hundred, filed out of the courthouse and proceeded to a banquet in a nearby hotel. For hours they feasted, sang, gave speeches, and raised toasts (Barnum, "the fearless advocate of truth and liberal principles"; Barnum, "a terror to bigots and tyrants"). Then, when the celebrations were ended, from outside the hotel came the roar of cannon fire and the lively strains of a brass band, and Barnum was escorted, like the giant-slaying hero of a fairy tale, to a coach drawn by six horses. Forty riders on horseback preceded the coach, at the very front a marshal bearing the American flag, while behind followed sixty carriages filled with supporters. The hundreds who remained sent up three cheers as the procession started off, seeming less a political march than a circus parade, the horses high-stepping, the band playing patriotic tunes all along the three-mile route to Bethel, where at the village limits the band broke into a spirited rendition of "Home, Sweet Home." All of this Barnum happily chronicled in the following week's edition of the *Herald of Freedom,* in an item he headlined "The Triumph of the People."

BETHEL, however, turned out to be not as sweet a home as he had hoped. Though he had some supporters, the Seelye case had agitated the community, unearthing a not very deeply buried vein of Puritanism there. His store was struggling, largely because of his customers' debts, which Barnum was often kind-hearted enough to forgive or simply too amiable to pursue. ("By friendship," he wrote in the margin of his accounts book, canceling one debt; "by being a damn clever fellow," he wrote, canceling another.) In January 1833, one month after his triumphant release from jail, he sold the Bethel store, having concluded that the mercantile life was not, as he put it, "my natural sphere." Five months later Charity gave birth to their first child, a daughter named Caroline, a joyous event for the couple but one that also deepened Barnum's financial woes. Making matters worse, the following year the Connecticut legislature prohibited lotteries, his primary source of income; the Temple of Fortune was forced to shut down, leaving him with numerous unpaid debts. His own fortune, accumulated almost overnight, had vanished just as quickly—and the *Herald of Freedom,* a source of personal satisfaction but never a going concern, was draining away whatever funds he had left. On November 5, 1834, he put out his last issue.

Without his store or newspaper, Barnum's ties to Bethel were growing thin. The village had been a wonderfully intimate sideshow in which to make a debut, to discover his voice and develop his talents, but now he required the brighter lights, and larger audiences, that could only be provided by the main stage. That winter he and Charity packed up their belongings and said their good-byes. Having already gained and lost one fortune, Barnum headed to New York City to seek another.

AT the age of twenty-four P. T. Barnum was tall and sturdy, his broad frame having not yet taken on the impressive stoutness of his later years. He still did not know exactly what line of work he would pursue, but he had come to recognize something important about himself: that he was no longer interested in any job offering a fixed salary, but only one that would allow him to earn money according to his own abilities. For by this time Barnum surely sensed the greatness that lay within him. He had, he knew, been blessed with an unusual amount of energy, as well as a bottomless curiosity, an intelligence not always distinguishable from cunning, and an outsized ambition that had inevitably pushed him beyond the few scattered homesteads of Bethel. And it may have been dawning on him, too, that he had an unexpected gift: the uncanny ability to read the public's desires, to know what people wanted even before they knew it themselves, a talent so rare and profound that it would not be inappropriate to call it genius.

The Barnums took up lodging in a house on Hudson Street, and he set out to look for work. For a time he found employment as a "drummer" for a cap store on Chatham Street, earning a small commission for every paying customer he persuaded to come in; the job came naturally for someone as gregarious as he, but all the while he kept searching for something better. Every morning at sunrise, just as the newsboys were piping their first sleepy cries, he handed over a penny for the *Sun* and opened the paper to the "Wants" section. "Fortunes equalling that of Croesus, and as plenty as blackberries, were dangling from many an advertisement," Barnum would later recall, but all the opportunities, when he pursued them, turned out to be not as golden as had been promised. Time and again he trudged up dark, rickety stairways inside dingy waterfront boardinghouses, only to find that he was required to invest his own money in the production of some new invention, or patent medicine, or other get-rich-quick scheme of dubious merit. One time he applied for a job as a bartender at Niblo's Garden. The owner, William Niblo, was willing to hire him, and though he needed the job very badly Barnum turned it down, balking at Niblo's condition that he remain for at least three years: even then, at his lowest ebb, he was leaving himself available for greater things.

In the spring of 1835, after receiving several hundred dollars for old debts from the Bethel store, Barnum opened a boardinghouse on Frankfort Street. It quickly became a popular destination for travelers from Connecticut, and soon he used the profits from the boardinghouse to buy an interest in a grocery store on South Street. At last he was earning a steady income, able now to support his family, but he could not help feeling dissatisfied again. He was back in the same mercantile trade he had disavowed in Bethel, one that he knew was not well suited to his talents or disposition.

He felt himself, for perhaps the first time in his life, adrift. Still, he continued attending to the boarders with Charity, continued to mind the store, all the while keeping his eyes open, waiting for something to happen.

In July an acquaintance from Connecticut named Coley Bartram came to shop at Barnum's grocery store. The men got to chatting, and soon discovered that they shared a taste for speculative opportunities. Bartram told Barnum that he had recently sold his interest in, as he put it, an extraordinary Negro woman. Her name was Joice Heth, and he believed her to be 161 years of age; even more extraordinary, he believed that she had been the nursemaid of none other than George Washington. Together with a business partner, R. W. Lindsay, Bartram had purchased the rights to exhibit Joice Heth; Mr. Lindsay was now going it alone in Philadelphia, but he had little enthusiasm for the life of a showman and was eager to sell the contract and return home to Kentucky. Perhaps Barnum might be interested?

Bartram pulled out the July 15, 1835, edition of the *Pennsylvania Inquirer* and directed his attention to an advertisement displayed there. Barnum read it with growing excitement:

CURIOSITY.—The citizens of Philadelphia and its vicinity have an opportunity of witnessing at the Masonic Hall, one of the greatest natural curiosities ever witnessed, viz., JOICE HETH, a negress aged 161 years, who formerly belonged to the father of George Washington. She has been a member of the Baptist Church one hundred and sixteen years, and can rehearse many hymns, and sing them according to former custom. She was born near the old Potomac River in Virginia, and has for ninety or one hundred years lived in Paris, Kentucky, with the Bowling family.

All who have seen this extraordinary woman are satisfied of the truth of the account of her age. The evidence of the Bowling family, which is respectable, is strong, but the original bill of sale of Augustine Washington, in his own handwriting, and other evidence which the proprietor has in his possession, will satisfy even the most incredulous.

At once Barnum felt himself cease to drift. All the disappointments of the previous few months, all those wretched interviews with charlatans and cheats, seemed now somehow worthwhile, because they had brought him to this: this was what he had been waiting for all along. Immediately he began to consider potential venues in which Joice Heth might be shown in New York, discarding some possibilities, keeping others.

William Niblo had just added a beautiful saloon to his restaurant, and perhaps he would be interested in exhibiting her there—this female Methuselah. She could sing some old-time hymns during her performances, which would endear her to audiences, but she should also relate stories of how she had helped raise General Washington, for people would love to hear about the father of his country when he was just a boy. Barnum could feel his imagination filling like a sail, propelling him forward.

YEARS later, looking back on the Joice Heth affair, recalling the many layers of deception it had entailed, P. T. Barnum would say that the exhibition had been "the least deserving of all my efforts in the show line." It was the only one that caused him even the slightest bit of shame. Even so, he still felt a certain affection for the Heth tour because it had been his first, the one that established him as a showman. There had been other attractions, of course, in those early years: Signor Vivalla and his spinning plates; Henry Hawley, with his Western tall tales; John ("Master") Diamond, the best of all the Ethiopian breakdown dancers; clowns, singers, magicians galore. Without the start Joice Heth had given him, however, he never could have gotten the museum six years later—Barnum's American Museum, the largest and most glorious jewel in his crown.

But of course, looking back on it, there had been another deception as well, one with roots even more ancient. It was the fall of 1841, when he first chanced to discover that Scudder's American Museum was up for sale. He knew at once—just as he had known when he first heard from Coley Bartram about Joice Heth's contract—that he must have it. Still, as always, there was the problem of money. His most recent variety acts had failed, and he had been reduced to writing advertising copy for the Bowery Amphitheatre. But he was determined not to let this opportunity pass him by.

A wealthy merchant named Francis W. Olmsted owned the building on Broadway in which the museum's collections were displayed; Barnum decided that the clearest route to the purchase went through him. So he sat down and wrote a letter to Olmsted, informing him that he wished to buy the collections. He admitted that he had no cash to put down, but he pointed out that he had things perhaps even more valuable: tact and experience, and a devotion to business. He suggested that Olmsted buy the museum's collections himself and sell them to Barnum on a payment schedule; Barnum would additionally pay rent for the use of the entire building, providing the convenience of a single permanent tenant. If he missed even a single payment,

P. T. Barnum, the self-styled "Prince of Humbugs."
(Courtesy of the New York Public Library.)

he promised, he would vacate the premises and make no claim on whatever had already been paid. "In fact, Mr. Olmsted," Barnum continued with all the earnestness at his disposal, "you may bind me in any way, and as tightly as you please—only give me a chance to dig out, or scratch out, and I will either do so or forfeit all the labor and trouble which I may have incurred."

Barnum carried the letter to Olmsted's suite of rooms on Park Place and handed it to a servant. Then he returned home and waited anxiously for a reply. After two days it came: Mr. Olmsted would see him the following day.

Barnum arrived punctually for the meeting, which pleased his host. Francis Olmsted was an older man with an austere, aristocratic demeanor; beneath that exterior, however, Barnum thought he could detect a certain openheartedness, even traces of good humor, that made him feel surprisingly comfortable. The two men sat down, and Olmsted asked Barnum to tell him about himself. Barnum related the details of his upbringing in Bethel, his background in business, the exhibitions he had managed.

Olmsted eyed him closely. "Who are your references?"

"Any man in my line," Barnum replied at once. He rattled off several names, prominent among them William Niblo, who had become a good friend after the Joice Heth exhibition, and Moses Yale Beach, the publisher of the *Sun,* who had recently bought the paper from Benjamin Day—the *Sun* had always been a reliable source of free publicity.

Olmsted asked Barnum to have the men visit him the next day. The day after that, he should return again to receive his answer.

Barnum somehow managed to get through the next two days, his attention entirely focused on the morning when he would arrive again at Park Place to learn his fate.

"I don't like your references, Mr. Barnum," Olmsted announced as soon as he had entered the room.

Barnum was momentarily confused. Could any of his friends have betrayed him? Did one of them want the collections for himself? He murmured only, "I regret to hear it."

Olmsted's grave expression gave way to a smile. "They all speak too well of you," he said, adding with a laugh, "In fact, they talk as if they were all partners of yours, and intended to share the profits." Then, turning to business, he laid out the terms of the deal: the rooms to be leased, the rent to be paid, the accountant who would oversee the payments. It was all acceptable to Barnum. He could barely believe it: the American Museum was at last within his grasp.

But there was one thing more, continued Olmsted. Promises were all well and good, but he needed some form of collateral, something of value to ensure his side of the deal. It had to be something that, if necessary, Olmsted could claim outright—nothing with a mortgage on it. "If you only had a piece of unencumbered real estate that you could offer as additional security," Olmsted told him, "I think I might venture to negotiate with you."

On this last point Olmsted was adamant; the deal itself hinged on the security. There, in those expensive downtown rooms, Barnum suddenly felt himself poised at the turning point of his fortune. In his mind he raced back over his past, going over all that he had gained and lost, searching for anything that he might grasp on to, to pull himself out of the mire in which he currently struggled, up to the high ground he had always envisioned for his future. Surely there was something he could find. At one time, as a boy, he had considered himself wealthy; now, as a man, he might actually become it. He knew at once what he must do. Everything in his life had led him to this moment.

"I have," said Barnum, "five acres of land in Connecticut which is free from all lien or encumbrance."

CHAPTER 7

Strange Attractions

WHEN P. T. BARNUM first laid eyes on Joice Heth, she looked to be a thousand years old. She was reclining on a high lounge in an exhibition room in Philadelphia's Masonic Hall, where Barnum had arrived after a long and tiring journey from New York. Coley Bartram, he now saw, had not been exaggerating: everything about Joice Heth evoked antiquity. With her wizened face, toothless mouth, and impossibly slight frame (advertisements put her weight at only forty-nine pounds), she seemed to have been shrunken by a great expanse of time, like an Egyptian mummy just exhumed from its sarcophagus. Her eyes, totally sightless, had sunk so deeply into their sockets that, from Barnum's vantage point, they seemed to have disappeared. She lay on her right side with her knees drawn up toward her chest, her left arm—the arm, like her legs, was paralyzed—draped over her chest, her knobby fingers drawn tightly together. A thatch of gray hair sprouted unkempt from her head. Standing with the rest of the crowd, Barnum took all this in with great interest, noting to himself that the nails of her left hand had grown to a length of four inches, that the nails on her big toes were nearly a quarter-inch thick.

Although the thought seems not to have occurred to him (if it did, he never let on), P. T. Barnum was examining this woman much as other white men were then doing in slave marketplaces elsewhere in the United States: scrutinizing the body with an eye toward the profit that might be wrought from it—although this would-be buyer was looking for precisely the opposite attributes. Barnum, after all, wanted not youth but age, not vigor but feebleness, not strength but fragility. In Joice Heth he had found just what he was hoping for, a perfect combination of mental acuity and physical decrepitude. Though blind and paralyzed in nearly all of her limbs, the old woman had not lost her power of speech, and Barnum was struck—as were all who came to view her—by how sociable she was, how she kept up an almost constant conversation on a wide variety of topics. She sang old Baptist hymns for her visitors, she discoursed on religious subjects, she related charming anecdotes about her young charge George Washington, whom she referred to always as "little George." She laughed often at her own remarks, with a heartiness that belied the frailty of her body, and (as observers often remarked) gave every indication of good cheer. It is, of course, possible that Joice Heth was naturally garrulous and truly enjoyed the attention being paid her at long last. But it is also indisputable that she had lived out her life as a slave in Virginia and Kentucky, and over those many years she had surely learned how to act for the white people who controlled her fate. The songs and the stories had gotten her off the plantation, a place where she now lacked all practical value, and had landed her on this comfortable couch in a big northern city, and were keeping her well fed and warmly clothed; and she would continue telling those stories and singing those songs for as long as she possibly could.

Barnum was exceedingly impressed by Joice Heth, but before he set out to purchase her contract from R. W. Lindsay he needed to be sure of what he was getting. He asked Lindsay for proof of Joice Heth's extraordinary age, and in return was shown a faded, crumbling piece of paper mounted under glass. Dated February 5, 1727, the document appeared to be a bill of sale for a slave named Joice Heth, "aged fifty-four years," who had been purchased for thirty-three pounds by Elizabeth Atwood of Virginia from her brother-in-law, Mr. Augustine Washington—the father of the future president. Lindsay explained that Atwood was a near neighbor of the Washington family, and that when "little George" was born, Joice Heth, as the family's former nurse, was called on to help care for the new baby.

The story seemed plausible enough to Barnum, but there was still something else he didn't understand. How, he wanted to know, had the existence of this remarkable woman not been made public until now? Lindsay told him that Joice Heth had long ago been purchased by a Kentucky slaveholder named John S. Bowling, and she had been living quietly in one of the outbuildings on Bowling's estate. Her true age had been uncovered only recently by Mr. Bowling's son, who had been doing some research in the Virginia state records office when he found an old bill of sale for a woman named Joice Heth. Realizing that this was very likely the Joice Heth owned by his family, he excitedly returned home and confirmed the information with Joice Heth herself, who by his calculation had been alive for no less than 161 years.

"This whole account appeared to me satisfactory," Barnum would later write. Of course the account was absurd: a woman with a life span approximately four times that of the average—and who just happened to have been the nursemaid of George Washington, the most revered of all Americans past or present. Nor could an authentic-looking bill of sale have provided conclusive evidence, as the practice of prematurely aging documents—by immersing them in tea or tobacco water, burning them, rubbing them with dirt, and various other stratagems—was hardly unknown at the time, especially to someone as well versed in the arts of deception as P. T. Barnum; and even if the document itself was authentic, there was no proof that this elderly black woman was truly the "Joice Heth" recorded there. For such a shrewd Yankee trader, Barnum seems to have been unusually credulous in the matter of Joice Heth. More likely, he recognized the fraudulence of the account offered by Lindsay—as one showman speaking to another, with a little nod and an implied wink of the eye—but he always denied this, firmly attesting to his belief in what he had been told. Barnum would thus have been, in a sense, enchanted by Joice Heth and by the prospect of the career that now awaited him: he had a vested interest in the truth of her story and was not keen on being convinced otherwise.

Having decided that Joice Heth would make a worthwhile investment, Barnum now turned to the matter of price. By Lindsay's estimation, Joice Heth was worth three thousand dollars, but Barnum, with his long experience in horse trading with farmers and peddlers (combined with Lindsay's desire to forgo the life of a showman and return home to Kentucky), was able to negotiate the price down to one thousand. He had only five hundred dollars in cash, but he left Philadelphia with a signed contract from Lindsay giving him the rights to Joice Heth if he obtained the remaining five hundred within ten days.

Hurrying back to New York, Barnum first consulted with Charity on the new venture, which would require all the money they had saved from their boardinghouse and grocery; it was a risk, he admitted, because at any moment the old woman might die and cause them to forfeit their investment. (Barnum had not yet figured out how to make money from Joice Heth even after her death.) Charity, younger and less worldly, deferred as usual to her husband's business instincts, which were mostly (though not always) sound. Having gained his wife's endorsement, Barnum next set about raising the rest of the money; with his gift for salesmanship, this proved not very difficult. Eloquently evoking the "golden harvest" that the Joice Heth exhibition would produce, Barnum convinced a friend to lend him the five hundred dollars, at which point he hastened again to Philadelphia to sign the contract.

There has long been some dispute as to whether, in handing over his thousand dollars to R. W. Lindsay, P. T. Barnum had in effect become a slave owner. (One biography of Barnum, for instance, states that he "became Joice Heth's sole owner," while another has it that he "overnight became showman and slaveholder.") Barnum himself muddied the question in his autobiography, *The Life of P. T. Barnum, Written by Himself,* when he wrote, rather imprecisely, that the contract with Lindsay meant that he had "become her owner." Elsewhere, however, he referred to himself not as the owner but as the "proprietor of the negress," and in the first edition of the book Barnum presented in full the contract he had signed with Lindsay, which made clear that he was simply purchasing the right to exhibit Joice Heth for the ten months that still remained of the twelve originally contracted by R. W. Lindsay; after that time, all claims to Joice Heth would revert to her owner, John S. Bowling of Kentucky.

Still, even if he was not legally her owner, Barnum was nonetheless proposing to earn his living on the labors—even if those labors consisted only of singing and storytelling—of a slave. This was not a situation that seems particularly to have troubled him, at least at the time. For all his passionate advocacy of the freedoms of religion and expression, Barnum's views on racial issues were not especially distinguished, even by the standards of the age. His early livelihood had come, in part, from the comical derogation of blacks—he often employed blackface performers in his traveling shows—and as late as the 1870s he was exhibiting a mentally retarded black man named William Henry Johnson as a putative "missing link" between man and monkey, dressing him in mock African costume (Johnson had been born in New Jersey) and calling the "marvellous creature" only by the name What Is It? Unlike many of his fellow Universalists, Barnum did not support the cause of abolition until near the start of the Civil War, when he became an abolitionist as well as a champion of extending the vote in Connecticut to blacks. Once, in Great Britain in 1844, he became involved in a heated debate with a group of Scotsmen who were espousing abolition. Barnum took great exception to their criticism of Southern slavery, arguing that slave owners had an economic interest in caring for their slaves and were compelled by law to provide for their comfort into old age (his own history with Joice Heth must have crossed his mind in saying this), and further asserting that "if the blacks were unceremoniously set free and there was no army to protect the whites, the blacks would murder them and take possession of their property." "I am no apologist for slavery," he explained afterward to the New York newspaper the *Atlas,* "and I abhor its existence as much as any man. But the rabid fanaticism of some abolitionists is more reprehensible than slavery itself and only serves to strengthen instead of weaken the fetters of the enslaved."

A far greater blot on Barnum's character can be found in an unsigned article published in the *Atlas* the following year, when he was a regular contributor to the paper. The article (or "sketch," as Barnum would refer to it in his autobiography) related incidents in his early career as a showman, including the time he spent touring the South with a circus company. During the winter of 1837, while in Mississippi, Barnum made two notable purchases: the first one a steamboat, named the *Ceres,* so that the troupe might avoid having to travel on the region's muddy roads; and the second one a black man to serve as his valet. At some point during the tour Barnum suspected the valet of thievery when several hundred dollars went missing from one of his pockets; Barnum, the article reported, searched "the nigger" and found the money, whereupon he "gave him fifty lashes, and took him to New Orleans, where he was sold at auction." Later, when the company had finished its tour and Barnum sold the *Ceres,* he took his payment in "cash, sugar, molasses, and a negro woman and child. He shipped his sweets to New York, sold his negroes in St. Louis, and arrived in the city in June, after a very successful tour." (While Barnum mentioned the *Ceres* in his autobiography, the story of the valet and the mother and child, unsurprisingly, did not appear in any of the various editions; however, he cited the *Atlas* article in the book, and neither there nor anywhere else did he dispute the truth of any of its "numerous anecdotes.")

So the Joice Heth tour was not, as Barnum claimed in a post–Civil War edition of *The Life of P. T. Barnum, Written by Himself,* "the least deserving of all my efforts in the show line"—not when compared with his subsequent tour of Mississippi. Still, there was plenty in the Joice Heth tour of which he might later feel ashamed. At Philadelphia's Masonic Hall

Barnum had Joice Heth carefully bundled up and carried to a railroad car where, as James Gordon Bennett reported in the *Herald,* the other passengers "gazed, wondered, looked" at her, and "some laughed." Barnum was bringing Joice Heth to New York, that most Southern-leaning of all Northern cities, a city where the evil of slavery was still very much an open question.

FORTUNATELY, William Niblo did not remember Barnum from their meeting earlier that year, when he had rejected Niblo's offer of a bartending job. Barnum seems never to have second-guessed that decision—second-guessing was not really part of his nature—and he would certainly have been glad of it now, when he was coming to Niblo as a full-fledged showman with an exhibition that he was convinced would prove a sensational money maker. Niblo must have felt likewise, for he agreed to put up Joice Heth in one of the rooms that adjoined his saloon and begin exhibiting her there as soon as possible. He would provide the exhibition room, pay for all advertising and other expenses, and handle ticket sales, in return for half the proceeds. This turned out to be a highly lucrative deal for Niblo, but it was no less a coup for Barnum, still unknown in New York, to be associated with such an illustrious showman.

William Niblo—Billy, as his friends called him, and everyone wanted to be his friend—was an Irish immigrant who had worked his way up to become the owner of the most fashionable entertainment spot in the city. In 1823 he had purchased the site of a former stud farm, occupying a full city block, and set about creating the greatest pleasure garden that New York had ever seen. Over the next few years he turned what was already a beautiful setting into a kind of enchanted landscape, planting exotic flowers and trees (in which he hung small cages full of singing birds) and designing serpentine walks lined with statuary, above which glowed particolored glass lanterns. In 1827 Niblo added a theater, the Sans Souci; in 1829 he converted the theater into a handsome saloon (a term that then referred not to a barroom but to a large entertainment hall), built a hotel, and named the property after himself: Niblo's Suburban Pleasure Garden, he called it, though it was known by all simply as "Niblo's Garden." For fifty cents patrons could stroll through Niblo's immaculate grounds, where in the evenings there were fireworks displays; or, if they preferred, take a table in one of the ivy-covered, latticed boxes that surrounded the gardens, where they might order a lemonade and a frosted cake, a port-wine negus, or any of the other refreshments served by Niblo's legion of black waiters, each of whom wore a white apron and a blue sash with a numbered badge, so that any patron, if displeased with the service, could report the offending waiter to Mrs. Niblo. An extra twenty-five cents gained admission to the saloon, which nightly featured gymnasts, polka dancers, contortionists, pantomimists, opera singers, and other purveyors of light entertainment. Off the saloon were separate viewing areas, usually occupied by painstakingly crafted dioramas that gave viewers the impression of being present at the Great Fire of London, the exodus of the Israelites from Egypt, and other memorable historical events. They were halls of grand deception, and in one of them Joice Heth performed her engagement at Niblo's Garden.

On August 10, Joice Heth—plainly exhausted by the trip up from Philadelphia—was carried in a sedan chair to her new accommodations next to the saloon; there she could rest until Barnum had completed the arrangements for the exhibition. Immediately he commissioned a woodcut portrait of her, to be featured on advertising posters. The portrait shows Joice Heth in a three-quarter profile that highlights her great spray of wrinkles, rendered in stark white against the severe darkness of her face and arms; her arms are crossed in front of her, her good right hand resting on the paralyzed left one, positioned so as to emphasize the extraordinary length of her nails; she is wearing a lacy bonnet and a checked dress, looking just as prim and respectable as any other regular churchgoer. Next Barnum hired an assistant, a former courthouse clerk from upstate named Levi Lyman, and together the two men blanketed the city with the posters, which announced the arrival at Niblo's of "the greatest curiosity in the world, and the most interesting."

With his public advertising campaign under way, Barnum now turned to the city's newspaper editors. Part of P. T. Barnum's brilliance as a promoter lay in his early recognition of the power of what he liked to refer to as "printer's ink." With Joice Heth's engagement at Niblo's Garden, he first put into practice the expert manipulation of the press that would mark his career for decades, lavishing newspapers with paid advertisements in exchange for a constant stream of free publicity, cultivating friendships with editors to such a degree that one of his address books contained a separate category with the heading "Newspapers friendly." (Just a few days before his death in 1891, Barnum sent a letter to his business partner, James A. Bailey. "I am indebted to the press of the United

States," he wrote, "for almost every dollar which I possess and for every success as an amusement manager which I have ever achieved.")

Before Joice Heth's engagement at Niblo's began, Barnum decided to invite the city's leading newspaper editors to private meetings with the star attraction. He was counting on the intense rivalry among the editors to help create his publicity, for he knew that each one would want to be the first to bring his readers an account of "Lady Washington"—as Joice Heth had begun to call herself—and none would want to be seen as having been excluded from the great curiosity just arrived in town. As he had anticipated, the editors of nearly all the daily papers hurried over to Niblo's (it is not known if Richard Adams Locke was among them, though a subsequent item in the *Sun* describing Joice Heth's appearance suggests that he was); there each man was met by Billy Niblo, exuding his usual charm and hospitality, who led him to the viewing room where Barnum had arrayed Joice Heth, in the phrase of the day, in her best bib and tucker. He had bought a new dress for her and carefully reviewed her best stories, mostly about the young George Washington, one of them a retelling of what was already, by the 1830s, a mythic American tale, although in Joice Heth's version the cherry tree was replaced by a peach tree. She also had tales of her conversion to Christianity and her baptism in the Potomac River, as well as some stories she had not recalled during her tour with R. W. Lindsay, the best of them involving her childhood on the isle of Madagascar—where, as it turned out, she had been a princess.

The newspaper editors listened to Joice Heth's stories, they asked her questions, they inspected her certificate of baptism and the bill of sale from the Washington family. They were, to a man, impressed with what they had seen—but Barnum, just to be absolutely certain (or so claimed his assistant Levi Lyman in a story he gave the *Herald* the following year), took each editor aside and promised him money in exchange for a positive newspaper review. It is not exactly clear if this money constituted outright bribery, or if it was simply a promise of paid advertisements for his paper—Barnum did, in fact, place scores of ads in New York's newspapers throughout Joice Heth's engagement at Niblo's—but in either case, as Lyman recounted to James Gordon Bennett, "the expense of making these sudden conversions" was "considerable." The amount Barnum was said to have given the newspapers reads almost like a bar graph of their relative importance at the time. According to Lyman's account, Webb's *Courier and Enquirer* would end up receiving the most money of all,

$49.50. Noah's *Evening Star* received, precisely enough, $31.46. William Leete Stone's *Commercial Advertiser* got an even $30, and three other mercantile papers a good deal less. The *Sun,* as further evidence of its growing prominence in the city, received $42, while its penny-paper rival the *Transcript* received $21.75. (The *Herald,* which published the information, is conspicuously missing from the list.)

Immediately the publicity items (or "puffs," as they were known) began to appear. The *Daily Advertiser* told its readers, "We venture to state, that since the flood, a like circumstance has not been witnessed equal to the one which is about to happen this week. Ancient or modern times furnish no parallel to the great age of this woman." "This old creature is said to be 161 years of age," observed the *Courier and Enquirer,* "and we see no reason to doubt it. Nobody indeed would doubt it if she claimed to be five centuries." "We can have no doubt that she is 160 years of age," agreed the *Evening Star,* citing the bill of sale from George Washington's father as proof. The *Commercial Advertiser,* while allowing for some possibility of exaggeration, was scarcely less enthusiastic in its pronouncement: "She is evidently very old, and although we are not prepared to say that all doubt is removed touching the amazing protraction of existence assigned to her, we have no difficulty in believing that she has actually lived considerably more than a century."

Barnum and Lyman had done their work well. Just a few days before, no one had heard of Joice Heth; now, it seemed, all of New York was talking about her. "The arrival, at Niblo's Garden, of this renowned relic of the olden time has created quite a sensation among the lovers of the curious and the marvellous," Richard Adams Locke wrote in the *Sun* (going on to add that "a greater object of marvel and curiosity has never presented itself for their gratification"). Barnum was pleased enough with his work to allow himself a bit of hyperbole: "Victoria herself would hardly have made a greater sensation."

By the second week of August, New Yorkers were arriving at Niblo's Garden less to see the Grand Military Band play patriotic music to the accompaniment of fireworks and the release of colored pigeons, or Dr. Valentine present his "amusing eccentricities," or Signor Il Diavolo Antonio and His Three Sons (direct from Drury Lane in London) perform on the "flying rope," than to see for themselves the ancient woman the posters and newspapers had so loudly heralded. Originally Barnum had intended for Joice Heth to be on view fourteen hours a day, from eight in the morning until ten at night, but it quickly became apparent that any woman as old as she (even one, as Barnum's advertisements claimed, whose "health is perfectly good") could not bear up under such a demanding schedule, and before long he had reduced her visiting hours to six per day, six days a week, allowing her a day of rest on the Sabbath. His agreement with William Niblo had been for a two-week engagement; however, business proved so brisk that Niblo extended Joice Heth's stay to near the end of August, beyond which she could not continue, as Barnum had already booked other engagements for her. Exactly how many people came to see Joice Heth at Niblo's is not known, but the demand was clearly overwhelming: with an admission price of twenty-five cents per person (twelve and a half cents for children), Barnum estimated that each week he and Niblo divided gross receipts of fifteen hundred dollars.

If there were New Yorkers who disbelieved Joice Heth's purported age, they kept silent; not until later in the year, after Barnum took Joice Heth to New England, would doubts be raised about the authenticity of her story. In New York in 1835, it was accepted wisdom—at least among the city's white residents—that black people were constitutionally different from whites. Such a belief was necessary to tolerate what would otherwise have been intolerable: the manifest horrors of slavery. The differences between the races were thought to encompass a broad range of attributes, physical and emotional, including the diminished capacity among black people for basic human emotions; many whites allowed themselves to believe, for instance, that a slave would not feel anguish at being separated from a spouse or child when sold to another owner—the possibility that George Wisner had once entreated his readers to consider. Given the notion of such overwhelming difference, it was not difficult for whites to imagine that some blacks, like Joice Heth, might attain an astonishing longevity. The racial stereotypes of the age, which had fostered so much delusion throughout the society, did so inside Niblo's as well, creating a powerful (and, for her exhibitors, extremely lucrative) gullibility that would not have been possible if Joice Heth had been white.

Day after day, the people kept coming to see Joice Heth. The room in which she lay was dimly lit, and nearly bare except for her couch and the documents of her enslavement displayed on the walls. Visitors arrived frequently, singly or in pairs, sometimes in small groups, and though they might have entered laughing or talking, on seeing the still, sightless woman on the couch most grew momentarily silent, hushed by the presence of one who had somehow escaped mortality's grasp. But either Barnum or Lyman was always there to relate the story of how her remarkable age had been discovered, and Joice Heth's own open, friendly manner soon prompted visitors to begin asking questions about her life, all of which she answered gladly and without hesitation. Some visitors just gazed in wonder as she went about her daily activities: praying, eating, smoking her pipe. (She claimed to have been a pipe smoker for 120 years; "if tobacco smoke is a poison," noted a correspondent to the *Evening Star,* "then it is a *very slow poison.*") Some of a more religious inclination sang or prayed with her, the low, thrilling chant of the hymns echoing through rooms more accustomed to polkas and patriotic airs. A good many knelt beside her to stroke her rough, leathery hands; ordinarily they would not have cared to touch the hands of a slave, but these hands were different; they were the hands that had once held George Washington, and in touching Joice Heth the visitors felt the past draw suddenly near, almost as if they were touching the great man himself (he whose portrait hung in almost every house), and kneeling beside her they felt something approaching veneration, as though this slave were a kind of reliquary, preserving the remains of a departed saint.

On August 8, two days before Joice Heth arrived in New York, the *Sun,* having outgrown its tiny office on William Street, moved to a three-story building at the corner of Nassau and Spruce streets. Just four days later, in the early-morning hours of Wednesday, August 12, one of the most destructive fires ever seen in the city swept through the printing district of Lower Manhattan. AWFUL CONFLAGRATION, screamed the *Sun's* headline of the following day. IMMENSE DESTRUCTION OF PROPERTY, AND LOSS OF LIFE.

The fire had begun on the second floor of a six-story building at 115 Fulton Street and quickly spread to the surrounding buildings on Ann, Nassau, and William streets. Nearly all of the buildings contained businesses associated with the printing trades—booksellers, binderies, newspapers, print shops—and, feeding on the seemingly limitless supply of paper, the fire grew with terrifying speed, consuming whole blocks of new five- and six-story brick buildings. Five people perished in the flames, including two printers living on the fifth floor of 115 Fulton, one of whom, Daniel Wyatt, was attempting to carry the other, an elderly man named

David Carlisle, on his back to safety when he lost his balance and fell into the burning mass below. More than thirty buildings were destroyed, including the printing offices of thirteen newspapers. Among these was the building at 34 Ann Street, the third floor of which was occupied by the firm of Anderson & Smith, which printed both of the *Sun*'s penny-paper rivals, the *Transcript* and the *Morning Herald*.

The publishers of the *Transcript* were still at work when the fire broke out, and, seeing the glow rising from Fulton Street, they managed to rescue most of the newspaper's supplies before the flames reached their building. They soon found new offices on Pearl Street near City Hall; it was only by chance that their new double-cylinder printing press (with a price tag of nearly three thousand dollars) had not yet been installed in their Ann Street offices.

James Gordon Bennett was not so fortunate. He lost everything in the fire: his books, types, papers, and printing press. Just as he was finally beginning to prove himself as an editor, showing the world the kind of newspaper he could produce, he was once again ruined. He had sunk all of his money (what little he had) into the *Morning Herald,* and after only three months of publication he had not recouped enough to replace what had been lost.

Those three months, however, had changed him forever. He could no longer imagine himself without the *Herald,* could no more abandon it than he could abandon his own life. The morning after the fire, Bennett stopped briefly at Ann Street to inspect the charred remains of his printing plant, and then, having ascertained the extent of the damage, he strode over to the *Sun*'s new office to place a classified ad—a typically bold pronouncement, but overly confident in its prediction of a quick return:

A CARD—James Gordon Bennett begs leave to inform the public that the press, type and materials of the Herald establishment having been destroyed in the great fire on Wednesday morning in Ann Street, the publication of the Herald will be resumed in a few days, as soon as materials can be procured.

In that day's edition the *Sun* published a full accounting of the fire, including the names of the dead and the circumstances in which they died, and a street-by-street inventory of the businesses that had been destroyed. By the end of the week Richard Adams Locke was publicizing a charity campaign for the neediest of those thrown out of work by the fire, calling on the *Sun*'s readers to be "possessed of that milk of human kindness, which soothes, whilst it nourishes, the lips of the afflicted." All over the city New Yorkers looking for the latest developments turned to the *Sun* (its circulation spiked in the aftermath of the fire) rather than the merchant papers, which had shown themselves inadequate to the journalistic demands of the new city. This New York was noisy and crowded and chaotic, haunted by disease, riven by ethnic conflict, and grievously divided over the central issue then facing the nation. No longer would currency conversion tables and outdated foreign news suffice. Like the man in the story by old New York's favorite writer, Washington Irving, the merchant papers had been in a sleep of years, and while they slept everything around them had changed.

Now, in New York, the verities of the past were giving way as quickly as the wooden houses torn down to make room for modern structures of brick and stone. The surrounding countryside, little altered since the retreat of the glaciers, was everywhere being sold and built upon. The earth was in upheaval, the water polluted, the air a carrier of plague, fire a constant threat. Expanding ever northward, the city had grown too large to be traversed by foot. Now it was populated by strangers; a New Yorker could walk the streets all day and never see a familiar face.

Ships sailed into New York Harbor every day from all over the world, arriving in a city that was said to rival Babel in the number of tongues its inhabitants spoke—and, one might add, in the height of its buildings. To live there was to embrace the new and the exotic, and New Yorkers, priding themselves on their sophistication, flocked to see all the latest attractions the city's promoters supplied. Some, like Joice Heth, were human curiosities, but at least as often the natural world proved just as astonishing in its productions. Traveling menageries brought African creatures whose forms beggared the imagination, among the most remarkable being the giraffe ("cameleopard," as it was often called), gnu ("horned horse"), and the orangutan ("wild man of the woods"). On display at Scudder's American Museum was a sculpture of the Virgin Mary carved from a single elephant's tusk; the tusk itself, taken from the greatest of all animals, was at least as spectacular as the sculpture. Scudder's Grand Cosmorama included in one of its gaslit cases a view of an exploding volcano. There were technical marvels as well, such as the electrifying apparatus featured at Peale's Museum; at night Peale's presented Afong Moy, "the Chinese

Lady," whose performance reached its climax when she removed her shoes to expose her bound feet. Balloonists thrilled crowds with their daring, constantly modifying their crafts to attain ever greater heights and distances. The twin conquerors of the period—science and exploration—had revealed to New Yorkers the very strangeness of the world, where the exotic merged with the commonplace, and nearly anything, it seemed, was possible.

On August 26, the *Sun* introduced its readers to the first of the remarkable discoveries that had recently been made on the moon.

Part Two

———◆———

THE MOON

CHAPTER 8

Celestial Discoveries

IN THE SUMMER of 1835 Richard Adams Locke was thirty-four years old, and at the height of his powers—editor of the most widely read newspaper in the city. As New York newspaper editors went, Locke cut a decidedly unimposing figure, being of slim build and middling stature (Edgar Allan Poe, who stood five foot eight, guessed Locke to be an inch shorter than himself), nowhere near as tall as James Gordon Bennett or James Watson Webb, and without Webb's military bearing, or the literary glamour of the *Evening Post*'s William Cullen Bryant, or the aristocratic burnish of Mordecai Manuel Noah of the *Evening Star*. Still, he had a certain presence. In *The Literati of New York City* Poe observed that Locke's eyes contained a "calm, clear *luminousness*"; there was "an air of distinction about his whole person," as though he had carried with him to New York, along with the family's five bags and bedding, some of the genteel manner of the world he had left behind.

Despite the often heated attacks Richard Adams Locke launched from his desk at the *Sun,* many of them directed against the city's other newspapers, there are no recorded instances of his being involved in physical confrontations, a rarity among the high-strung New York editors of the time. (Even James Gordon Bennett, who was not known for his graciousness toward rivals, acknowledged that Locke was "very gentlemanly in his manners.") In a world of furious self-promotion, he always avoided the spotlight, preferring to declaim from offstage, a consequence, perhaps, of the crossed eyes and scarred face that had marked him since childhood. ("His face," Poe did not fail to observe, "is strongly pitted by the smallpox.") Though a newspaper editorship was among the most visible positions in the city, providing a useful stepping-stone for many editors in their postjournalistic careers, Richard Adams Locke never ran for public office, never parlayed his contacts into lucrative business opportunities, never wrote his memoirs or collected his writings for publication; indeed, nearly all of his best work was written anonymously—including, of course, the moon series that made him, for a time, famous.

The other leading editors in town were not just editors but publishers, owning a stake in the newspapers for which they worked, but at the *Sun* Benjamin Day had retained all equity, which left Locke to make ends meet on a newspaperman's salary of twelve dollars a week. As a consequence he was always short of money, a condition that would plague him to the end of his life. It was one thing to be living on a shoestring as a young writer on London's Grub Street, but by now he was into his middle age, and at the end of an evening, returning home from work, he would walk up Broadway, passing the gaslit mansions along the park—through the open windows he could look in on elegant drawing rooms, their chairs and sofas covered in European silk, on the walls bronzes and busts and cameos, and mirrors whose frames shone with ormolu—back to that apartment by the Public Yard where Esther and Adelaide awaited him. The apartment was barely large enough for the three of them, and he and Esther were hoping for more children, perhaps even many more. (Two years later a son would arrive—another Richard Locke, the fifth consecutive generation to carry the name—followed by four more children in quick succession, the last one, Walter, born when Locke was forty-six years old.)

Always, always there was the problem of money. Locke would agree with Shelley that luxury is the forerunner of barbarism; he had no use for the vast acreage his grandfather had owned or the outsize manor house, its ceilings buttressed by massive timbers and thick slabs of stone on the floors—but surely he might find a way to set his family's finances aright. It was inevitable that Locke's thoughts would turn to his grandfather, the great man of the family, who had written numerous works of history and geography, from which he proudly claimed never to have earned even a sixpence—and did not have to, because he had made a fortune in land. There it was, the eternal paradox: the rich man spends his days thinking about books, while the poor writer spends his days thinking about money.

Recently, of course, Richard Adams Locke had managed to earn a bit extra—the $150 Benjamin Day had paid him for his Matthias series. That money had gotten the family out from under the maddening din of

Chatham Street; another such windfall might get them out of Manhattan entirely, maybe across the Narrows to Staten Island. Day had promised him still more if he could come up with another series that sold as briskly as the Matthias one had, and in idle moments, as he pursued his daily rounds, he considered possibilities.

For the past several years Locke's reading had focused almost entirely on the natural sciences. Science was his true intellectual love, even more than literature or politics, and astronomy in particular had long held a special interest for him. When he was seventeen, shortly before he left East Brent for London, he had composed an epic poem entitled "The Universe Restored," in six cantos of nearly a thousand lines each, that put forward his own theory of the ceaseless destruction and reproduction of the universe. Under his editorship the pages of the *Sun* often carried news of the latest astronomical developments. It might have seemed curious material to give the readers of the *Sun,* who were accustomed to news made much closer to home, but those were the journals he was reading and could draw upon for his items—and, in any case, almost everyone these days had at least a passing interest in astronomy, thanks in part to the imminent arrival of Halley's Comet, an event awaited with excitement as well as a certain trepidation, for there was still a tendency to see comets as omens of disaster, portents of God's wrath: an age-old imposition of religion onto science of the very sort that Richard Adams Locke had long found so objectionable.

The idea for his moon series came to him as he was leafing through an old volume of the *Edinburgh New Philosophical Journal,* the distinguished British quarterly of arts and sciences; he had been a regular reader of the *Journal* back in England, and had brought several copies with him aboard the *James Cropper.* He was perusing the premiere issue, published in 1826, when he came upon a brief article entitled "The Moon and its Inhabitants." The article reported that the German astronomer Wilhelm Olbers considered it "very probable" that the moon was inhabited by rational creatures, its surface covered by a vegetation very much like that of the earth's; the astronomer Franz von Paula Gruithuisen likewise maintained that he had recently discovered "great artificial works in the moon, erected by the Lunarians," and was at present considering the possibility of communicating with the inhabitants of the moon—perhaps by means of an immense geometrical figure to be built on the plains of Siberia. That idea had met with the approval of "the great astronomer Gauss" (the mathematician and scientist Carl Friedrich Gauss), who believed that "a correspondence with the inhabitants of the moon could only be begun by means of such mathematical contemplations and ideas, which we and they must have in common."

Locke had found this item near the back of the journal, as part of a survey of various disciplines under the heading "Scientific Intelligence." Toward the front was a longer article by the Scottish astronomer Thomas Dick about a new telescope he had invented, which he had dubbed the "aërial reflector." In the past decade Thomas Dick had risen from obscurity (he had until recently been a schoolteacher in Perth) to become one of the most widely read authors in the field of science. The book that had made him famous was called *The Christian Philosopher, or, The Connection of Science and Philosophy with Religion.* First published in 1823, it had gone through several editions since then, at least one of which (the one Richard Adams Locke had read) contained a statement of Dick's beliefs about life on the moon. In an appendix called "On the means by which it may probably be ascertained whether the Moon be a habitable world," he proposed that a vast number of astronomers be enlisted worldwide to maintain continuous observations of the moon's surface; over time, he believed, these observations would reveal changes on the surface brought about by "the operations of intelligent agents," a forest being cut down, for example, or a city being built on what had earlier been only an open plain. Even if the lunarians themselves were not seen, their presence could be inferred, just as a sailor passing an uncharted island concludes that it is inhabited after noting the presence of huts and cultivated fields. If such a plan were to be put into effect, he wrote, "there can be little doubt that direct proofs would be obtained that the Moon is a habitable world."

Immense Siberian figures, astronomers the world over watching for signs of lunarian cities: it was all, Locke thought, utterly absurd. Yet these were respected scientists, their views aired in prestigious journals. They were so very confident in their predictions of lunar life; they believed it was only a matter of time until, in Thomas Dick's mathematical phrase, "direct proofs" were obtained and humanity knew itself to be alone no more. Life discovered elsewhere in the universe: what a sensation that would make. Locke began to imagine how such an event might be reported in the newspapers—the triumphant announcement, the awestruck descriptions of the fantastic become real. He could picture the exclamatory headlines, the long columns of black type, each day's account concluding with that most captivating of phrases: *To be continued*. It would be the most remarkable news story in the history of the world.

And all the better, for his purposes, for being entirely untrue.

KNOWING the great success that his Matthias pamphlet had enjoyed, Locke asked three hundred dollars for this new series—exactly double what he had received for the earlier one—a high price, to be sure, but one to which Benjamin Day readily agreed. (Ultimately, Day later recalled, he would pay Locke "between $500 and $600" for the moon series. It was an enormous sum, equivalent to about a year's wages for Locke, but for Day it would still prove very cheap.)

Did Benjamin Day know from the outset that the series being proposed by Richard Adams Locke was fictitious? This has never been established— neither of the two men ever publicly discussed the matter—but it seems scarcely possible that Day had not known. Day himself never claimed as much, and none of his actions in the aftermath of the series are indicative of a publisher who has been grievously fooled by his editor. He never expressed misgivings about paying Locke double his original asking price; nor did he fire Locke, who continued as the *Sun*'s editor (writing several important features for the paper) until 1836, when he left to start his own penny paper, the *New Era*. And if one of the stories that subsequently arose about the Moon Hoax is true—that of the Yale astronomers who came to the *Sun* offices seeking proof—then Benjamin Day had to have been in on the game. Day was a shrewd, hard-nosed entrepreneur who had envisioned the *Sun* primarily in business terms from the very beginning, when he had conceived of the newspaper as a means of advertising his struggling print shop. In the summer of 1835 the *Sun* had been publishing for less than two years, and though it had become unexpectedly successful, the paper's future remained uncertain. It was engaged in a fierce battle for the city's readers, not only with the old guard of merchant newspapers but with two aggressive new penny dailies as well. Just that summer a pair of entrepreneurs, hoping to capitalize on his work, had started a penny paper they called the *True Sun;* that piratical venture hadn't lasted a week, but there were rumblings of other papers to come, and some of them would undoubtedly prove more enduring. Not all of the papers could survive, even in a city as large as New York. The Matthias series had greatly improved his paper's chances;

Day had every confidence that this one would as well, and he accepted Locke's proposition.

Perhaps, as seems most likely, Richard Adams Locke told Benjamin Day straight out about the details of his scheme. Or else he simply outlined the fantastic nature of the series, leaving unspoken the question of its authenticity—and, like P. T. Barnum accepting R. W. Lindsay's assurances about Joice Heth's age, Day saw the glittering opportunity that lay before him and did not inquire further.

THE first item, published the morning of Friday, August 21, attracted little attention among the *Sun's* newsboys (who much preferred news of a more sordid nature), and among the paper's readers as well. Headlined "Celestial Discoveries," it was the lead story, although unlike nearly all of the other twenty-seven items on the page it comprised only a single sentence, one said to have been taken from the venerable Scottish newspaper the *Edinburgh Courant*. According to the *Courant*—or so claimed the *Sun*—an "eminent publisher" in Edinburgh was reporting "astronomical discoveries of the most wonderful description" made by Sir John Herschel at his observatory at the Cape of Good Hope, using an enormous telescope that worked on "an entirely new principle." The excerpt from the *Courant* ran only forty-two words, and in its brevity left much unsaid: the source of the original report (the "eminent publisher"), the "new principle" on which the telescope worked, and, most centrally, the "wonderful" discoveries that Sir John had made. Those details would have to await further updates, the next one of which—truly the first installment of the moon series—arrived four days later.

ON August 25, the *Sun* announced on its news page that it was beginning the publication of a series of articles, entitled "Great Astronomical Discoveries, Lately Made By Sir John Herschel, L.L.D., F.R.S., &c. at the Cape of Good Hope," which had recently appeared in the *Supplement to the Edinburgh Journal of Science* and had been furnished to the *Sun* by an unnamed "medical gentleman" just returned from Scotland. The forthcoming articles, trumpeted the *Sun,* would reveal "celestial discoveries of higher and more universal interest than any, in any science yet known to the human race," discoveries that "cannot fail to excite more ardent curiosity and afford more sublime gratification than could be created and supplied by any thing short of a direct revelation from heaven."

According to the *Sun,* the remarkable information contained in the series had been provided to the *Edinburgh Journal of Science* by Dr. Andrew Grant—a character of Richard Adams Locke's own creation—who was serving as amanuensis to Sir John Herschel at his observatory at the Cape of Good Hope. Dr. Grant had thus been an eyewitness to the otherwise scarcely believable events described in the *Supplement.* He had stood by Herschel's side as the eminent astronomer made the final adjustments to his telescope before directing it at the moon; he was there to record how Sir John, at last satisfied with the preparations, had solemnly adjourned for several hours, so that he could prepare his own mind for the great revelations he felt certain would follow. "Well might he pause!" exclaimed the anonymous author of the *Supplement.* "He was about to become the sole depository of wondrous secrets which had been hid from the eyes of all men that had lived since the birth of time. He was about to crown himself with a diadem of knowledge which would give him a conscious pre-eminence above every individual of his species who then lived, or who had lived in the generations that are passed away."

Having set the scene, the *Supplement* next provided its readers a brief taste of the "wondrous secrets" that would soon be revealed:

To render our enthusiasm intelligible, we will state at once that by means of a telescope, of vast dimensions and an entirely new principle, the younger Herschel, at his observatory in the Southern Hemisphere, has already made the most extraordinary discoveries in every planet of the solar system; has obtained a distinct view of objects in the moon, fully equal to that which the unaided eye commands of terrestrial objects at the distance of a hundred yards; has affirmatively settled the question whether this satellite be inhabited, and by what orders of beings; has firmly established a new theory of cometary phenomena; and has solved or corrected nearly every leading problem of mathematical astronomy.

Before all that could be explained, however, it was first necessary to describe the invention of John Herschel's revolutionary telescope. For years the great astronomer had worked on telescope design, following the course set by his astronomer father William in his own efforts to observe the moon; his latest instruments had allowed an unprecedented view of the lunar landscape, but beyond a certain point his progress had been stymied. Herschel was confronting the optical problem that had bedeviled astronomers since the dawn of telescopes: the more highly an image is magnified, the dimmer it becomes. The *Supplement* cited a kind of honor roll of astronomers—Huygens, Newton, Gregory, William Herschel—all of whom had fruitlessly searched, like medieval alchemists seeking the philosopher's stone, for the right compound of materials to overcome this essential problem. John Herschel had used the most sophisticated materials that modern chemistry could provide; in the *Supplement*'s romantic description, he "had watched their growing brightness under the hands of the artificer with more anxious hope than ever lover watched the eye of his mistress." But while he might have taken satisfaction in the knowledge that his telescopes provided him a more intimate view of the moon than had been gained by anyone before him, he was still denied an answer to the most interesting question of all:

> Whether this light of the solemn forest, of the treeless desert, and of the deep blue ocean as it rolls; whether this object of the lonely turret, of the uplifted eye on the deserted battle-field, and of all the pilgrims of love and hope, of misery and despair, that have journeyed over the hills and valleys of this earth, through all the eras of its unwritten history to those of its present voluminous record; the exciting question, whether this "observed" of all the sons of men, from the days of Eden to those of Edinburgh, be inhabited by beings like ourselves.

The age-old problem of creating magnification and light, like that of creating gold from lead, had long seemed insoluble. And yet somehow John Herschel *had* solved it, had succeeded where so many men before him had failed—had discovered life on the moon. But how had he done it? The key moment, reported the *Supplement,* had occurred three years earlier during a conversation between Herschel and Sir David Brewster, the eminent Scottish scientist and one of the world's great experts in the field of optics. (Significantly for Richard Adams Locke's purposes, the real-life Brewster was also among the leading scientific advocates of the idea of lunar life.) The two learned men had been chatting—Sir John had just complimented Sir David on his article on optics for the *Edinburgh Encyclopedia*—when Herschel off-handedly remarked on the great convenience offered by the old style of tubeless telescope. Such a telescope, he observed, was actually highly practical, because the astronomer did not have to contend with the enormous weight of the tube. Sir David had agreed, and the conversation then turned to the perennial problem of the paucity of light under great magnification. Herschel was silent for several moments, deep in thought. Might it not be possible, he finally asked, to effect a transfusion of *artificial light* through the focal object of vision?

Taken aback by the originality of the idea, Brewster was himself momentarily silent, before raising a few tentative objections involving the refrangibility of rays and the angle of incidence. Herschel, however, had already considered those problems, and he confidently brushed them aside with a reference to the Newtonian reflector, which had used additional lenses to correct for them. Now he continued, the excitement in his voice growing, "Why cannot the illuminated microscope, say, the hydro-oxygen, be applied to render distinct, and, if necessary, even to magnify the focal object?"

The hydro-oxygen microscope was not a creation of Locke's; it was one of the most heralded scientific instruments of the age. To operate the microscope, the scientist first placed the object to be viewed on a glass slide; streams of hydrogen and oxygen were then directed against a piece of lime, the resulting reaction producing an intense light that projected an image of the object through the microscope's lens and onto a distant screen. In this manner, objects so small as to be invisible to the naked eye could be magnified, breathtakingly, to a dimension of several feet. As the *Times* of London wrote about the hydro-oxygen microscope in 1833, "It can, in truth represent objects five hundred thousand times larger in size than they really are. Thus the pores of the slenderest twig and the fibres of the most delicate leaf expand into coarse net work. The external integuments of a fly's eye, filled with thousands of lenses, appear the dimensions of a lady's veil—that gentleman yclept the flea, swells into six feet—worms seem like boa constrictors: while the population of a drop of goodly ditch water presents such shapes as Teniers should have seen before he pencilled the grotesque monsters who troubled the sleep of St. Anthony." In an age when microscopes were still rare and wondrous instruments, the hydro-oxygen microscope had so captured the interest of the public that in New York—as Richard Adams Locke well knew—a demonstration of the microscope was one of the featured attractions at Scudder's American Museum on Broadway.

Essentially, Herschel's idea (as supplied to him, of course, by Locke) was to take the lunar image produced by the telescope and then transmit that image through a hydro-oxygen microscope. This way, he would not only illuminate the image, thus resolving the problem of available light, but would additionally magnify it, so that—as the *Supplement* quoted him as remarking—he could study even the entomology of the moon, in case there happened to be insects living on its surface. It did not take David Brewster long to grasp the import of the idea, and when he did the effect was extraordinary: "Sir David sprung from his chair in an ecstacy of conviction," reported the *Supplement,* "and leaping half-way to the ceiling, exclaimed, 'Thou art the man!'"

At once the pair set to work on the new "hydro-oxygen telescope." For several weeks they experimented on every aspect of the instrument, until at last they deemed it ready. But even this singularly powerful telescope still brought Sir John's view of the moon's surface no closer than forty miles: not close enough to detect life. A much stronger lens would have to be cast, but this would require a great deal of money. So, according to the *Supplement,* John Herschel brought his plan for a new telescope to the Royal Society, where it was enthusiastically approved, with the chairman promising to convey Herschel's request to the King himself. Informed that the new telescope would require an estimated $70,000 [*sic*] to build, King William IV (popularly known as "the sailor king," in recognition of his long naval career) wanted to know if it might improve the nation's navigational abilities. Assured that it would, His Majesty promised whatever funds would be required for the completion of the work.

Several more months of experimentation followed, until finally the perfect combination of materials for the lens—two parts crown glass to one part flint glass—was achieved. The renowned glass house of Hardy and Grant (the latter partner being the brother of the *Supplement*'s correspondent, Dr. Andrew Grant) was hired to oversee the casting of the lens; after the glass produced by the first cast was found to be seriously flawed, the second proved virtually perfect. John Herschel had succeeded in fashioning a truly mammoth lens: twenty-four feet in diameter, six times the size of the one used in his father's largest telescope. After polishing, the lens weighed more than seven tons and produced a magnifying power of 42,000 times, capable, in Herschel's estimation, of observing objects on the moon as small as eighteen inches in length. Next came the construction of a suitable microscope and the mechanical framework for the telescope as a whole, undertakings that were quickly completed. The great telescope was at last ready.

With that Richard Adams Locke ended the first installment of the *Sun*'s moon series, an ingenious amalgam of technical detail and lyrical fancy that Locke, like Herschel working on his prodigious telescope, had crafted down to the smallest detail. The result was a narrative that seemed—to anyone not learned in astronomy and even to some who were—utterly believable.

THERE really was a Sir John Herschel, of course, and he really was in South Africa, having sailed there from England in 1833 to set up an observatory at the Cape of Good Hope. While in South Africa, Herschel intended to perform a years-long survey of the southern skies, the project to serve as an extension of the surveys his father had earlier made from the Northern Hemisphere. It was, like so much else of his astronomical researches, an act of filial piety—for unlike Richard Adams Locke, as a young man John Herschel had passed up the work that held the most interest for him and had instead returned home to take over the family business: he was an astronomer because his father was.

William Herschel had been an unheralded amateur astronomer (he earned his living as a church organist in the city of Bath) when in 1781, using a telescope he had built himself, he discovered a new planet that came to be known as Uranus, after the Greek god of the skies. The shock of that discovery can hardly be overstated. Since the earliest days of stargazing, humans had seen only five planets in the skies above the earth; so prevalent was the idea that the solar system ended with Saturn that astronomers had not even tried to search for others. With Herschel's discovery, a seventh planet had been added, and the solar system was suddenly twice as large as had been thought before. On the basis of that single discovery, King George III appointed Herschel to be the first King's Astronomer, with an annual stipend of £200 and a generous allowance with which to build more of his own telescopes.

Five years after his celebrated discovery, William Herschel moved with his sister Caroline (also a noted astronomer) from Bath to the town of Slough, near the royal house at Windsor, where over the course of his life he made several other major discoveries, including moons of Saturn and Uranus, infrared radiation, and the motion of the solar system. In 1816 Britain's Prince Regent, George IV, made him a knight of the Royal Guelphic Order; he would also help found the Astronomical Society of London, which subsequently became the Royal Astronomical Society, the seal of which still features an illustration of his famous forty-foot telescope. (That telescope was also the subject of the first woodcut illustration ever printed in the *Sun*, two weeks after the paper's founding.)

Unlike William, who had grown up poor, his son John was born in 1792 into a world of privilege. John was a shy, lonely boy, with no siblings, few friends, and a distant relationship with his parents. He attended a school in Slough run by a friend of his father's, while receiving private tutoring from a Scottish mathematician; he quickly showed himself to be a brilliant student, and indeed something of a prodigy. At seventeen he entered St. John's College of the University of Cambridge (unlike Richard Adams Locke, he actually did attend Cambridge), where he and a classmate translated into English Sylvestre Lacroix's book on differential calculus, which quickly became the standard textbook of its kind in Great Britain. He also wrote a mathematical paper that won him the Royal Society's Copley Medal. He would seem to have been a natural mathematician, but in fact his greatest interest was chemistry, and over the course of his life he made several notable contributions to the chemistry of photography, among them the invention of a process for making photographs on glass plates—his first pictures having been made of his father's forty-foot telescope.

John Herschel did not, however, become either chemist or mathematician. His father, for reasons that remain murky, wanted John to enter the Church (it may have been because he believed that a churchman would have spare time to devote to astronomy), but this was a path that the young man seems never to have seriously contemplated. As a compromise John began to study law, though he could manage this pursuit for only eighteen months, at which point he went back to St. John's to become a math tutor. The following year, 1816, he was elected to a position on the St. John's faculty; he looked to be headed for a bright academic career, but in the summer of that year he made a decision that would change his life forever.

That summer, John joined his father on a trip to the coast of Devon, where it became clear to him that William, now seventy-eight years old, was in poor health. William Herschel had devoted himself to his work with extraordinary diligence (once, in his younger days, he had sat at his telescope for seventy-two hours straight—and then slept for twenty-six), but he had not begun observing full-time until he was forty-three years old, and much of his research was still uncompleted. As his powers began to fail him, William had grown desperate to find a successor, someone whom he might entrust with his astronomical researches. John was pained at seeing his father in such distress, for despite the lack of warmth in their relationship he had always admired his father, and felt keenly the responsibility of being the great man's son. After a good deal of agonizing, he concluded that there was no recourse but to take the position himself: to move back to Slough and, under his father's direction, become an astronomer.

So began years of intensive astronomical training, learning the correct techniques for everything from grinding and polishing mirrors to making celestial observations—which culminated, finally, in his assuming his father's ambitious project of "sweeping" the northern skies: proceeding from zone to zone, cataloguing all of the objects to be seen there, recording new ones and reexamining those observed earlier. William Herschel died in 1822, and for the better part of the next two decades John Herschel's own work was a tribute to his father's. From 1825 to 1833 he undertook two monumental tasks—a list of 2,300 nebulae and star clusters, and an immense catalogue of double stars—each of them a review and extension of his father's earlier observations. It was grueling work, but he pursued it with conviction, rarely giving up even a single night of available viewing; as he wrote in his diary, he regarded the completion of the work "not as a matter of choice or taste, but a sacred duty which I cannot postpone to any consideration." Where William had loved nothing better than to sit at his telescope hour after hour (his head draped with the black hood that he always wore to block out light and preserve, as he put it, "tranquility of the retina"), John was often bored by the glacial pace of astronomical research, and his diaries are marked by entries such as this one: "Sick of star-gazing—mean to break the telescope and melt the mirrors." (After he returned from his four years in South Africa he would never again sit behind a telescope. His life as a working astronomer was over at forty-six, an age when his father's had scarcely begun.)

By 1833 Sir John Herschel—like his father, he had been made a knight of the Royal Guelphic Order—was the most famous astronomer in the world, and perhaps the most famous scientist of any kind. (His renown during the nineteenth century has been compared to Einstein's in the twentieth.) He spoke six languages and enjoyed writing and translating poetry. He had long since shaken off his childhood shyness, and was

The great astronomer Sir John Herschel, around the time of his South African expedition.
(Courtesy of the Library of Congress.)

known as something of a raconteur, with a love of stories, riddles, and parlor games such as charades; he was cheerful, disarmingly modest, and interested, apparently, in everything. He cut a dashing figure in British society, with his dark, tousled hair, prominent sideburns, and large, soulful blue eyes. (In later life those pale eyes would seem to grow lighter still, their brilliance intensified by the lines and shadows deepening his face, and he would let his white hair grow long, the combination imparting to him a kind of leonine majesty—an aspect memorably captured in a series of photographic portraits taken by Julia Margaret Cameron.) At the age of forty-one, he could easily have turned away from astronomy and devoted himself to work that held a greater interest; still, there was one more astronomical task he felt obliged to complete. His father's celestial observations, for all of their thoroughness, had been limited to the objects that could be seen from England. Those in the Southern Hemisphere, beyond the range of even his mighty telescope, had eluded him. For years William Herschel had painstakingly swept the northern skies; now, in what he saw as the culmination of his father's work, John Herschel would do the same with the southern.

In November 1833 the Herschel family—John, his wife Margaret, and their three young children—accompanied by a nursemaid and two assistants (neither of them named Grant), boarded the ship *Mountstuart Elphinstone*. They would arrive in South Africa two months later, after a difficult journey that Herschel passed in typically eclectic fashion, by making observations of everything around him: the temperature of the air and sea, the bird life passing overhead, the optic nerve of a dolphin caught by the sailors, even, when nothing else presented itself, his own pulse rate. He had brought with him two telescopes, the larger one a twenty-footer, with which he planned to conduct his surveys. Over the next four years he would use those telescopes to catalog 1,707 nebulae and 2,102 double stars, map the Large Cloud of Magellan and the Orion Nebula, reexamine the inner moons of Saturn (not seen since his father had observed them in 1789), estimate the luminosity of nearly two hundred stars, draw and measure Halley's Comet, and much more. About the only celestial object to which he paid little attention, in fact, was the moon.

JOHN Herschel had been very busy in the year before his expedition to the Cape. There was so much to attend to, from preparing his telescopes (he ground the mirror for the twenty-footer himself) to packing up the family house at Slough. He was also burning the midnight oil to complete his remaining scientific work, including a new book he called *A Treatise on Astronomy*. Intended for interested laypeople as well as his fellow astronomers, the book provided a lucid exposition of the latest astronomical thinking on a vast array of subjects, from the magnitude of the earth to the motion of the sun and moon, from the physical characteristics of comets to the distribution of the stars in the heavens.

A Treatise on Astronomy was issued in the United States in 1834. It quickly became one of the most popular astronomical books of the day, encouraging a public fascination with astronomy that would culminate with the appearance of Halley's Comet, which Sir John had predicted for September or October 1835. The growing interest in astronomy had not gone unnoticed by the new editor of the *Sun*, Richard Adams Locke, who was, like so many scientifically minded people, an admirer of Sir John Herschel. As one who kept up with all the latest astronomical reports, Locke was well aware that Sir John was presently working at the Cape of Good Hope—a spot so distant that a letter sent there would require months for a reply—and that the world still awaited, with great anticipation, the news of his latest discoveries.

CHAPTER 9

A Passage to
the Moon

Among the other Americans who read John Herschel's *A Treatise on Astronomy* in 1834 was a young short-story writer in Baltimore named Edgar Allan Poe. Like Richard Adams Locke, Poe was a longtime astronomy buff and he read Herschel's book with great interest, paying special attention to its discussion of the possibility of future explorations of the moon; as he later wrote in his essay on Locke in *The Literati of New York City,* it was a theme that "excited my fancy." Having finished *A Treatise on Astronomy,* Poe decided to create a moon story of his own, which he called "Hans Phaall—A Tale." While John Herschel was not the protagonist of "Hans Phaall," his book was its inspiration, and indeed provided the text for many of the story's scientific passages (a fact that Poe would never reveal). "Hans Phaall" was published at the beginning of the summer of 1835, and Locke's *Great Astronomical Discoveries* at the end. Two moon stories appearing only two months apart, each one involving John Herschel—the coincidence seemed to Poe so unlikely that for years he insisted that his story had been plagiarized by Richard Adams Locke. Poe found it even more galling that Locke's story had achieved international renown, while his—which he considered far more deserving—languished in obscurity. It was, for Poe, one more reason to despise the literary world, yet another defeat in a life full of reversals.

In 1834 Edgar Allan Poe was living in a little brick house on Amity Street with his aunt Maria Clemm and his twelve-year-old cousin Virginia, whom he would marry shortly after she turned thirteen. He was a most

"The Bard": Edgar Allan Poe, in a rare photograph taken near the end of his life.
(Courtesy of the Library of Congress.)

incongruous figure—a moody, half-starved writer haunting the cheerful streets of Baltimore, a city that one guidebook of the time called "conspicuous, as well as for the rapidity of its growth, as for its present splendour and prosperity." Broad avenues sloped down to the harbor, where steamers and schooners and clippers unloaded their wares into tidy brick warehouses stacked together as tightly as crates; the city's markets were abundantly supplied with fresh local food, including the much-celebrated blue crabs and oysters pulled from the waters of the Chesapeake. To the north stood the tall steeple of St. Paul's and the grand marble column of the Washington Monument, surmounted by a statue of the Father of the Country himself, who seemed to gaze in approval over the picturesque city below.

Those proud edifices of church and state, however, held little interest for Edgar Allan Poe. He preferred the clutter of E. J. Coale's bookstore on Calvert Street, which carried the latest foreign books and magazines, or the hush of the library on Fayette Street, where he could read volumes of poetry or science without having to buy anything; or, when a few coins jingled in his pocket, Widow Meagle's Oyster Parlor on Pratt Street, where in the evenings, by the warmth of the fire, he liked to recite his own poems—his voice, everyone remarked, had a pleasing, almost musical quality—the performances earning him a sobriquet from the other patrons that he must have cherished: "the Bard." He wore linen shirts with Byron collars and a nattily tied black stock, a black double-vested waistcoat buttoned tight across his chest, over it a black frock coat (all of his clothes were old but still dapper, carefully mended and regularly brushed for him by his aunt), his long, silky black hair combed back over his ears, looking every inch the magnificent poet he believed himself to be. He was as proud a man as could be found in the city, an aristocrat in manner if no longer in means. Once he had lived in a large house surrounded by fig trees and raspberry bushes, his needs attended to by his stepfather's black servants, but those days were long gone. The prosperous Richmond merchant John Allan, bowing to his wife's pleas, had taken in the two-year-old orphan Edgar Poe, and for a time he had provided well for the boy, but as the years passed their relationship had grown increasingly bitter, fouled by resentment and misunderstanding. In 1834 John Allan died, leaving behind eight houses and an estate worth three-quarters of a million dollars, but to Edgar, living on the brink of starvation, he gave not a penny. For the rest of his life Poe would sign his work simply E. A. Poe or Edgar A. Poe, expunging from print the name he had inherited, with so little else, from his stepfather.

He had endured, by then, so many losses. His mother Eliza, a highly praised actress, had died of tuberculosis at the age of twenty-four, orphaning three children under five years old. By that time his father David Poe, also an actor (though by all accounts a far less winning one than his wife), had deserted the family, not to be heard from again. Later there would be two other women, one his stepmother and the other the mother of a friend, each of whom provided him much-needed maternal devotion, and each of whom died young. More recently his older brother Henry, arrived from Richmond to live with the Clemms in Baltimore, had died of tuberculosis while Edgar cared for him in the room they shared. (His beloved Virginia would eventually succumb to the same disease; she died, as had his mother, at the age of twenty-four.) "I think I have already had my share of trouble for one so young," he wrote once in a letter to John Allan.

In 1834 Edgar Allan Poe was already twenty-five, but despite all his furious exertions his life had amounted to little. He had been a fine student at the newly founded University of Virginia, but John Allan had withdrawn him after only a year there; Allan had refused to provide sufficient funds to cover his school expenses, and during the year Poe had accumulated more than two thousand dollars in gambling debts, in the misguided hope that he might win enough to pay off what he owed. After leaving the university he had returned to Richmond to stay at John Allan's house, but after two months of conflict—the endless rehashing of grievances: the stinginess of the older man, the ingratitude of the younger—he fled in rage, his only plan for the future to be free of his stepfather's supervision. "My determination is at length taken," he wrote in a letter he left for Allan—"to leave your house and endeavor to find some place in the wide world, where I will be treated—not as *you* have treated me." He gave the address of a nearby tavern to which he requested that Allan send his clothes and books and enough money to pay for travel to a northern city, where he might start over. He hoped, he said, that Allan would comply with his requests "if you still have the least affection for me," but Allan wrote back only to dismiss them: "After such a list of black charges," he remarked sarcastically, "you Tremble for the consequence unless I send you a supply of money." Two days later Poe wrote his stepfather again, the combative tone of the earlier letter replaced now by frank desperation: "I am in the greatest necessity, not having tasted food since Yesterday morning. I have no where to sleep at night, but roam about the Streets— I am nearly exhausted—I beseech you. . . . I have not one cent in the world to provide any food." To this plea for help Poe received no response; having finished reading it John Allan turned over the page and scrawled on the back a single mocking retort: "Pretty Letter."

Poe's disappearance in the ensuing weeks has given rise to various legends, among them accounts of extended drinking bouts, of having his portrait painted by Henry Inman in London, even of his boarding a schooner to Greece—in the fashion of his hero Lord Byron—to help in the fight for national independence. In fact Poe did talk his way onto a ship, not a schooner but a coal barge, and bound not for Greece but for Boston.

Boston was a city that had always held great meaning for him, for it was where he had been born and where his mother had given some of her greatest performances, including acclaimed turns as Ophelia and Juliet; he still had the little watercolor she had painted of Boston Harbor, which she had left to him with the inscription, "For my little son Edgar, who should ever love Boston, the place of his birth, and where his mother found her *best,* and *most sympathetic* friends." In Boston he managed to obtain occasional work as a clerk, but nothing that might sustain him. (What little money he had he used to publish his first volume of poetry, *Tamerlane and Other Poems,* a forty-page booklet bound simply in paper, its author named only as "A Bostonian"; not surprisingly, the unassuming-looking little book received no critical attention.) After several fruitless months in Boston, hungry and exhausted and not knowing where else to turn, Edgar Allan Poe did what so many other poor young men with few prospects have done: he enlisted in the army.

Stationed first in Boston and then at various forts in the South, Poe distinguished himself in the military as he had in school. He rose quickly through the ranks, eventually earning a promotion to sergeant major, the highest rank available to a noncommissioned officer. Still, the life of a soldier was not well suited to one with such a consuming literary ambition, and after two years of service (he had signed up for five) Poe sought his discharge, which, he learned, could be obtained only with a letter from his stepfather. His appeals to John Allan were met with silence, until finally Allan consented to provide the letter, but only on the condition that Poe enroll as an officer candidate in the United States Military Academy at West Point.

Poe thrived at first within the strict discipline of the academy, but the ill health that would plague him for the rest of his life was beginning to emerge; as he complained in a letter to Allan: "I have no energy left, nor health, if it was possible, to put up with the fatigues of this place." His discovery that John Allan had remarried, to a much younger woman with whom he hoped to produce a rightful heir (Allan had sired two illegitimate sons before his first marriage) led to an exchange of mutually accusing letters and, ultimately, Poe's decision to withdraw from West Point—which once again required a letter from his stepfather. This time, however, Allan adamantly refused to provide one; in the long struggle between the two men, the final break was now at hand. Poe, who was growing increasingly unhappy and unwell at West Point (and beginning to seek comfort in brandy, which only worsened matters), decided that he had no recourse but to procure his own dismissal by refusing to attend class or perform his duties. He set himself to his task with characteristic willfulness, earning, in a single month, an impressive sixty-six misconduct citations (the next most troublesome cadet received a mere twenty-one). Brought before a general court-martial on charges of gross neglect of duty and failure to obey an officer, Poe pleaded guilty and was dismissed. After eight months at West Point he left with little more than the uniform on his back. He sailed down the Hudson for a brief, illness-wracked stay in New York before boarding a steamboat for Baltimore, where he found lodging with his late father's widowed sister Maria Clemm and her young daughter: the two who would provide him a family for nearly all of the eighteen years that remained to him.

Poe had published a second book of poems just before entering West Point, and yet another while enrolled there. (He dedicated the book to his fellow cadets, who had collected the money to pay for its publication.) In the four years since his departure from the University of Virginia he had managed to produce three volumes of poetry, but none had earned for him the reputation he felt certain he deserved. He gloried in his writing even when no one else did, when his books, so lovingly composed, were derided or, even worse, ignored. He had been so often abandoned by those who once cared for him; by early adulthood he was already an intimate of wasting illness and death. Perhaps this was why he held so desperately on to his pride, for it was all he had left. Constantly he measured the distance between his present location and the golden city he imagined in his future, his own El Dorado; constantly he appraised his own position relative to those whom he considered inferior. He both needed and disdained the goodwill of others; he was supremely sensitive to slights, whether real or merely perceived, and, as Richard Adams Locke would discover, he nursed a lifelong obsession with writers he believed to be plagiarists.

It was worse, of course, when he drank. Though Poe was not a regular drinker, during especially difficult periods of his life he was prone to binges. Those were the times when he unleashed the full fury of his despair, when his charcoal eyes took on a strange shine and he mocked and abused everything around him. "He did not drink as an epicure, but like a barbarian," wrote one of his later admirers, Charles Baudelaire. "As soon as alcohol had touched his lips he went to the bar and drank glass after glass until his good Angel was drowned, and all his faculties were destroyed." Often the alcohol set him to roaming the streets, where he brooded over old battles and lost himself in reveries; surely too in his solitary wanderings he comforted himself with the happy memories he retained from his boyhood. Most of them centered on the Allan house in Richmond, that brick mansion with the mahogany staircase and mirrored ballroom. Outside the air was sweet with raspberry and jasmine from gardens overlooking the green valley that rolled down to meet the James, the little houses of Manchester perched as delicately as river birds along the south bank, and off in the distance, gleaming white, the state capitol with its triangular portico and Ionic columns, like a temple atop one of the hills of Rome. He had been given his own bedroom, with a well-stocked wardrobe (even as a boy he was something of a dandy) and a comfortable lounge, where by the glow of an agate lamp he stayed up reading books he borrowed from his stepfather's library, discovering then the work of Byron and Milton and Keats, the poets who would, *in absentia,* become his lifetime companions. Perhaps his favorite place of all, though, was the wide porch that ran along the second floor of the house. There John Allan had installed a powerful telescope, and young Edgar spent many hours gazing at the night sky, when he first acquainted himself with the stars and the planets, and, as he wrote in his tale "Hans Phaall," begun in Baltimore in 1834, "the wild and dreamy regions of the moon."

In the summer of 1833, a short-lived Baltimore weekly called the *Saturday Visiter* sponsored a literary contest, offering a prize of one hundred dollars for the best story. The *Visiter*'s judges were three of the city's most respected literary figures, among them a writer named John Pendleton Kennedy, who would become one of Poe's most important benefactors. On the day of the judging, the panel met in the home of one of its members, John H. B. Latrobe. The men retired to the back parlor, where a table had been "garnished," Latrobe recalled, "with some old wine and good cigars." Thus fortified, they settled into easy chairs to begin their deliberations. Latrobe, as the panel's junior member, opened the packets that had been delivered to the *Visiter* and read aloud each of the submitted stories. The rejections basket quickly began to fill up. Many of the stories were discarded after only a few lines had been read; a few were set aside for later consideration, but upon further review these too were deemed unworthy of the hundred-dollar prize. The judges had just about decided not to award a story prize at all when Latrobe noticed another submission that had been left unread, perhaps, as he would later explain, because it looked so different from the rest. The other stories had been written on letter paper in the florid cursive script of the time, but Poe submitted a small bound notebook into which he had painstakingly copied out six stories in distinctive block letters, as if to imitate typographical printing. On the front page he had inscribed a title: *Tales of the Folio Club*. The other writers had produced manuscripts; Poe had created a book.

Latrobe began to read Poe's stories aloud, and before long the room had fallen respectfully silent except for the sound of his voice and an occasional interjection from one of the other judges: "Capital!" one of them might be moved to exclaim. "Excellent!" "How odd!" When Latrobe had finished reading and laid down the book, the judges understood, without a word having been spoken among them, that the contest had come to an end. In Poe's stories there was none of the sentimentality or cliché that had marred the other submissions. Instead, the language was richly styled (the judges were all impressed by what Latrobe termed the author's "classic diction"), the writing passionate yet always controlled, and the plotlines deeply imaginative. In the span of a half dozen stories, Poe had managed to create his own world—utterly strange yet believable, and altogether fascinating. For the judges, the question was no longer which writer should win the prize, but only to which of Poe's stories the prize should be awarded.

After some discussion, the judges awarded the hundred dollars to the story "MS. Found in a Bottle," a harrowing first-person account of a shipwreck off the coast of Java and the survivor's subsequent encounter with a phantom ship inhabited by an ancient crew. At the close of the story the narrator's ship gets caught in a whirlpool and goes down, its only remaining traces the manuscript itself, which he has placed in a bottle and thrown into the sea. The story anticipated "Hans Phaall" because it was Poe's first attempt to infuse a fanciful narrative with scientific and technical erudition in order to create the effect he called "very close verisimilitude," leading the reader to believe that the story, however unlikely its events may seem, could well have happened in just this way. It was a technique to which he would return again and again in his stories, especially in his hoax stories, perhaps most memorably in the "Balloon Hoax" that he modeled on Richard Adams Locke's Moon Hoax, and in his own moon story (he was then calling it simply "Hans Phaall—A Tale"), on which he was about to begin work.

MANY years later, in an address to a Poe memorial service held in Baltimore in 1875, John Latrobe would recall that Edgar Allan Poe came to visit him at his law offices shortly after the *Saturday Visiter* contest in 1833. During that visit Poe began to describe a story he was writing about a balloon voyage to the moon. According to Latrobe, Poe became very excited as he recounted it, speaking rapidly and even clapping his hands or stamping his foot for emphasis. This behavior sounds like Poe, and the conversation between the two men surely did occur. However, recent scholarship has decisively shown that Latrobe's chronology was faulty (understandable after an interregnum of more than four decades) and that the meeting took place no earlier than 1834. During the conversation Poe is said to have mentioned the Richmond journal the *Southern Literary Messenger,* which was not founded until May 1834. Furthermore, Poe could not have begun "Hans Phaall" in 1833 because he drew heavily on John Herschel's *A Treatise on Astronomy,* which did not appear in the United States until 1834.

It is possible that Poe began work on "Hans Phaall" as late as 1835, in which case he might have been influenced by a balloon story called "Leaves from an Aeronaut" (its author's name was given only as "D.") that appeared in the January 1835 issue of the New York monthly the *Knickerbocker.* (There is little doubt that Poe saw the story, for he avidly read the literary journals and the *Knickerbocker* was the leading one of its time.) Like "Leaves from an Aeronaut," Poe's "Hans Phaall" begins with a four-line poetic epigraph, and like the earlier story, it presents a first-person account of a secretly prepared balloon flight, with detailed descriptions of the physical phenomena encountered during the flight, including—in both stories— the use of a test pigeon, the unexpected appearance of a "double horizon," and the fearsome sight of a thunderstorm raging below the balloon. But while D.'s aeronaut is content to ascend five miles into the atmosphere, Hans Phaall sets his sights on the moon.

Poe's story opens in the Dutch city of Rotterdam, where a large crowd in the town square suddenly beholds an unexpected sight. "Ten thousand faces were upturned toward the heavens" (in "Leaves from an Aeronaut," the balloonist preparing for his flight is "the focus of ten thousand eyes") as a large balloon descends from the sky. Inside the basket is a very strange-looking old gentleman, no more than two feet tall, dressed in brightly colored satin clothing. Pulling a leather pocketbook from his jacket, he takes from it a thick letter tied with red tape, and from his lofty perch drops it at the feet of the astonished burgomaster below; then, his mission accomplished, he soars away again, disappearing behind the cover of a cloud. The letter has been written by a bellows mender named Hans Phaall (the Latin word for bellows, as Poe undoubtedly knew, is *follis*), formerly of Rotterdam, who had mysteriously disappeared from the town some five years earlier. It relates Hans Phaall's strange tale—his "unparalleled adventure," as Poe would call it in a late version of the story's title.

As the story begins, the bellows-mending business has been very slow, and Hans Phaall is besieged by bill collectors. One afternoon, having momentarily eluded his creditors, Hans ducks into a bookshop where he happens upon an obscure pamphlet of "speculative astronomy." He soon finds himself absorbed in the work, and by the time he returns home he has concocted a daring plan to escape his debt. He will build a balloon, but not just any balloon, because (as he reveals later in the story) he is "determined to depart, yet live—to leave the world, yet continue to exist. . . . I resolved, let what would ensue, to force a passage, if I could, *to the moon.*"

Secretly, so as not to excite the attention of his creditors, Hans and his wife (she is a capable woman, he assures the reader, and will get along perfectly well without him) sell whatever property they can and use the money to purchase fine cambric muslin, strong twine, a large wicker basket, and everything else he will need to construct "a balloon of extraordinary dimensions." Under cover of darkness, he transports these supplies to a secret location east of Rotterdam, along with an unspecified quantity of materials he will identify only as "*a particular metallic substance*" and "*a very common acid,*" which, when combined, form a gas much lighter than air. More darkly (for his scientific program has a sinister aspect as well), Hans has also purchased five large iron casks, which he fills with cannon powder and buries near the balloon, leaving visible only a short section of fuse.

At last his preparations are complete. It is the first of April, a rainy, starless night. (Surely it is not a coincidence that Poe begins the main action of his story on April Fool's Day.) Hans Phaall sets to work inflating his balloon with the aid of his three creditors, whom he has inveigled to help him with an invention that he promises will be a sure money maker. By daybreak the balloon is fully inflated and the basket loaded with provisions, which include 175 pounds of ballast, an apparatus for the condensation of air, various devices for conducting experiments in the upper atmosphere, food and water, and his traveling companions—two pigeons and a cat.

After surreptitiously igniting the fuse leading to the cannon powder, Hans hops into the basket and cuts the cord. The balloon shoots into the sky, its takeoff followed almost immediately by a deafening roar from the earth below: an explosion of burning wood and scattering metal and mangled limbs (for his creditors have now met their violent end), the blast sending up such a mighty concussive force that Hans Phaall, like one of the slapstick comedians of a later century, is thrown out of the basket and quickly finds himself dangling upside down, hanging on only by an entangled left foot. His situation has become unexpectedly desperate, but Phaall—showing, under the circumstances, a remarkable sangfroid—manages to pull himself back to the safety of the basket by jury-rigging a grappling hook out of his cravat and the belt buckle of his pantaloons. Before long he has regained his composure and given himself over fully to his voyage, his narration of which will include an account of his sighting of the North Pole (a view never before beheld by human eyes), the changes in the appearance of the earth's surface at different altitudes, his experiments with gravity, and his terrifying encounter with a meteor shower. All the while the balloon is rising ever closer to its destination, the moon.

In the climactic moment of the story, Hans Phaall awakens to find that the balloon has undergone a *bouleversement,* a reversal of position caused by the shrinking gravitational pull of the earth relative to that of the moon, so that the earth has suddenly disappeared, hidden behind his balloon overhead, while the moon itself now lies directly below. The next day—just nineteen days since his departure from Rotterdam—Phaall successfully lands on the moon, avoiding the immense volcanoes that cover the lunar surface and tumbling into the center of "a fantastical-looking city," where he finds himself surrounded by a large crowd of silent, grinning, earless little creatures. His voyage, "undoubtedly the most extraordinary, and the most momentous, ever accomplished, undertaken, or conceived by any denizen of earth," has reached its end.

THOUGH Edgar Allan Poe would make vigorous claims for its originality, "Hans Phaall—A Tale" was by no means the first literary account of a lunar voyage. Ludovico Ariosto's sixteenth-century epic poem *Orlando Furioso,* for instance, includes a trip to the moon in a chariot driven by four swift red horses. Two centuries later, a chariot also figured in the novel *The Consolidator,* by Daniel Defoe; this one was mounted atop two large wings, each of them powered by a mysterious fuel discovered by the lunar inhabitants themselves. In Francis Godwin's *Man in the Moone: or A Discourse of a Voyage Thither by Domingo Gonsales, the Speedy Messenger,* published in 1638, the eponymous hero uses a harness rigged up to a flock of trained geese; having gotten into some trouble with the British navy, Diego Gonsales believes that the geese—he refers to them by the Spanish word *gansas*—are carrying him to safety on a nearby mountain, and is bewildered when they soar past the mountaintop and keep on rising. Little does he suspect that the *gansas* are going into hibernation, and that they do so each year on the moon. For the lunar voyage of *L'Autre Monde: Les etats et empires de la lune,* the seventeenth-century French writer Cyrano de Bergerac (on whom, of course, Edmond Rostand based his famous play) imagined a flight suit made of vials filled with dew, the idea being that the heat of the sun will draw the dew into the air. When that scheme delivers the narrator no farther than Canada, he next sets to work on a flying machine. A group of carousing soldiers, trying to turn the contraption into a fiery dragon, load it up with firecrackers; the resulting explosion thrusts the machine aloft, each new explosion setting off additional ones, the force propelling the flying machine higher and higher, until it has left the earth's atmosphere and, freed of gravity's pull, sails all the way to the moon—becoming, in effect, literature's first rocket ship.

Horses, wings, geese, dew, firecrackers: Edgar Allan Poe, for his part, seems to have been the first writer to imagine a voyage to the moon in a hot-air balloon. In writing "Hans Phaall" he was unquestionably aware of his literary forebears, for in a lengthy appendix that he wrote for a subsequent publication of the story Poe, ever competitive, took time to disparage several of those earlier works. Though he grudgingly acknowledged that Godwin's tale about Diego Gonsales and his *gansas* was "somewhat ingenious" and "not without some claim to attention," in general he found it a "naive specimen" marred by numerous scientific errors. Cyrano's tale he dismissed as "utterly meaningless," while another, more obscure work, "The Flight of Thomas O'Rourke," he tossed aside with the single phrase "not altogether contemptible." Poe did point out, correctly, that in each of the earlier stories the writer's motive was primarily satirical rather than scientific— the author was describing the customs of the moon as a way of commenting on those of the earth. In "Hans Phaall," on the other hand, Poe devoted most of his attention to the flight itself, including several pages of technical discussion about how such a voyage might be accomplished. As Poe saw it, "Hans Phaall" was unique in the annals of literature for its emphasis on what he proudly called "*verisimilitude,* in the application of scientific principles (so far as the whimsical nature of the subject would permit,) to the actual passage between the earth and the moon."

In his appendix to "Hans Phaall" Poe also referred to a review in the *American Quarterly Review* of a recent novel about a lunar voyage in which flight was made possible by a newly unearthed metal (dubbed "lunarium"), on which the moon exerted a powerful magnetic attraction. The very notion of it was "stupidity," Poe fumed, "more deplorably ill conceived than even the *ganzas* of our friend the Signor Gonzales." Poe did not deign to name the book, referring to it only as "a certain 'Journey' of the kind in question," but it was *A Voyage to the Moon,* a short novel published in 1827 by "Joseph Atterly," the pseudonym of George Tucker, a professor at the University of Virginia. Although Poe dispatched Tucker's novel with a few rapier sentences, and further condemned the re viewer's own "absurd ignorance of astronomy," the detailed summary of the book in the *American Quarterly Review* was actually one of the important sources he drew on for his writing of "Hans Phaall." He seems to have picked up from it a number of ideas he would later incorporate into his story, including the use of an exotic metal to power the lunar flight (the "*particular metallic substance*" from which Phaall generates the gas for his balloon), an air condenser to allow for respiration in space, a meteor shower produced by lunar volcanoes, a *bouleversement* that takes place while the protagonist is asleep (both protagonists initially mistake the moon below them for the earth), and many more.

Poe's appendix to "Hans Phaall" appeared in his first story collection, *Tales of the Grotesque and Arabesque,* published in 1839. It would be another seven years before he mentioned his most important source for "Hans Phaall": John Herschel's *A Treatise on Astronomy.* In his 1846 essay "Richard Adams Locke," Poe wrote that he had read the American edition of Herschel's book and had been "much interested in what is there said respecting the possibility of future lunar investigations." He extended this remark to note, "The theme excited my fancy, and I longed to give free rein to it in depicting my day-dreams about the scenery of the moon." But these two sentences do not begin to acknowledge the debt he owed John Herschel. In writing "Hans Phaall" Poe had not merely been inspired by *A Treatise on Astronomy;* he had in fact lifted whole passages from it.

For example, in discussing the largest segment of the earth ever seen from the air John Herschel wrote:

> The convex surface of a spherical segment is to the whole surface of the sphere to which it belongs as the versed sine or thickness of the segment is to the diameter of the sphere.

As Hans Phaall looks down at the earth from his balloon and attempts to calculate what segment of its surface he can see, he explains to the reader:

> The convex surface of any segment of a sphere is, to the entire surface of the sphere itself, as the versed sine of the segment to the diameter of the sphere.

In the section of *A Treatise on Astronomy* that discusses the use of a barometer, Herschel wrote:

> From its indications we learn, that when we have ascended to the height of 1000 feet, we have left below us about one thirtieth of the whole mass of the atmosphere:—that at 10,600 feet of perpendicular elevation . . . we have ascended through about one third; and at 18,000 feet (which is nearly that of Cotopaxi) through one half the material, or, at least, the ponderable body of air incumbent on the earth's surface.

Continuing his calculations, Hans Phaall notes:

> From indications afforded by the barometer, we find that, in ascensions from the surface of the earth we have, at the height of 1000 feet, left below us about one-thirtieth of the entire mass of atmospheric air; that at 10,600 we have ascended through nearly one-third; and that at 18,000 which is not far from the elevation of Cotopaxi, we have surmounted one-half the ponderable body of air incumbent upon our globe.

These are just two excerpts from as many as a dozen passages in which Poe closely paraphrased, or copied outright, the work of John Herschel. Sometimes, however, he could not find what he needed in Herschel, and when this happened he turned to other sources, chiefly the 1819 edition of Abraham Rees's *Cyclopedia or Universal Dictionary of Arts and Sciences, and Literature*. The *Cyclopedia* entry on the moon, for instance, contains the following sentence, describing some of the German astronomer Johann Schröter's observations of the moon:

The two cusps appeared tapering in a very sharp, faint prolongation, each exhibiting its farthest extremity faintly illuminated by the solar rays, before any part of the dark hemisphere was visible.

That sentence appears, in its entirety, in Poe's story, as Hans Phaall muses on the meaning of Schröter's work; it is part of three long paragraphs, totaling more than four hundred words, that Poe took from Rees's *Cyclopedia,* changing or adding a word or phrase here or there ("I thought," "I supposed," "my ideas on this topic") as necessary to suggest that they originated not with an encyclopedia but with Hans Phaall.

Of course, "Hans Phaall" is a long story, the great bulk of which was written by Edgar Allan Poe himself, and its "design is original," as Poe asserted in his appendix, in the conception of a balloon ride to the moon and in its emphasis on the technical aspects of the flight. But the genre of the lunar voyage was hardly a new one, while a story that gave a detailed description of a balloon ride ("Leaves from an Aeronaut") appeared in a major literary magazine about the time Poe was setting to work on his own story. Those two stories share certain incidents, as does Poe's story and a recent novel about a trip to the moon, a long review of which he acknowledged having read. Moreover, virtually all of the scientific passages in "Hans Phaall," in which Poe took such pride, were lifted directly from other sources. So too, as it turned out, were important elements of his critique of the moon series of Richard Adams Locke, the writer whom he believed had stolen his idea for a moon story: that being one early battle in Poe's lifelong campaign against plagiarism.

"Hans Phaall—A Tale" appeared in the June 1835 issue of the *Southern Literary Messenger,* the Richmond journal for which Poe would shortly be hired as editor. The story received little notice beyond the immediate region, but in Virginia and Maryland the critical response was generally favorable. The Richmond *Whig* called it an "extraordinary production ridiculed by some" with "a great deal of nonsense, trifling and bad taste before Hans Phaal [*sic*] quits the earth," but having scenes in outer space that "exhibit genius and invention"; those parts of the story the *Whig* found "wonderfully approximating to truth, and penetrative of the mysteries of creation." (Poe was very pleased by this review, writing of it to the *Messenger*'s publisher, "I will take care & have the Letter inserted in all the Baltimore papers.") The Baltimore *Patriot* praised the story's "hairbreadth 'scapes and stirring incidents," and hoped that the author would someday provide readers an account of Hans Phaall's journey back to the earth, echoing a sentiment expressed in the editorial introduction to the issue of the *Southern Literary Messenger* in which the story appeared. "Mr. Poe's story is a long one," wrote the *Messenger*'s editor,

> but it will appear short to the reader, whom it bears along with irresistible interest, through a region of which, of all others, we know least, but which his fancy has invested with peculiar charms. We trust that a future missive from the lunar voyager will give us a narrative of his adventures in the orb that he has been the first to explore.

Poe seems to have had every intention of writing a sequel to "Hans Phaall—A Tale." Indeed, at one point in the story, Hans remarks about his balloon, "I wished to retain with me as much weight as I could carry, for reasons which will be explained in the sequel." The second part of that sentence, the reference to a "sequel," was cut by Poe from the 1839 version of the story, replaced by the phrase, "for the obvious reason that I could not be *positive* either about the gravitation or the atmospheric density of the moon."

Sometime between 1835 and 1839, then, Poe gave up on the idea of writing a sequel to "Hans Phaall," a second story that would finally allow him to entertain his "day-dreams about the scenery of the moon." (In fact, as he would later admit, "The chief design in carrying my hero to the moon was to afford him an opportunity of describing the lunar scenery.") Ironically, the demise of the second story was connected to his original idea for the first one, which did not involve a balloon flight at all. Instead Poe, having been inspired by Herschel's *A Treatise on Astronomy,* imagined a story about a man who discovers a fantastical world on the moon by means of an extraordinarily powerful new telescope.

Poe recognized at once that the story would be successful only if readers so trusted the science of the story that they would give themselves over to its flights of fancy. But would they willingly suspend disbelief about a telescope powerful enough to detect life on the moon? He discussed his idea with a few friends in Baltimore (among them John Pendleton Kennedy, one of the judges of the *Saturday Visiter* contest), who advised him that the optical problems presented by such a telescope were so obvious and so widely recognized that readers would never believe one could really exist. Reluctantly concluding that his friends were right, Poe shelved his plans for the telescope story and decided instead "to give what interest I could to an actual passage from the earth to the moon."

Scarcely two months after "Hans Phaall" appeared in the *Southern Literary Messenger,* a series of articles began to run in the *Sun,* reporting the lunar discoveries that had been made with a powerful new telescope—one said to have been invented by none other than John Herschel. Even from Baltimore Poe could tell that, unlike "Hans Phaall," the series was receiving an astonishing amount of attention. The *Sun*'s moon story—so rife with blunders, like all the others—was on everyone's lips, and his own, which he knew to be superior in so many ways, had already been forgotten. Someone in New York was growing wealthy while he remained obscure, still wandering the nighttime streets, gripped by his dark memories—which now included those long-ago evenings on John Allan's porch, when he had gazed at the moon in wonder, little knowing that one day it too would be lost to him.

CHAPTER 10

"If This Account Is True, It Is Most Enormously Wonderful"

O N WEDNESDAY, August 26, the *Sun* brought to New York the first accounts of the remarkable lunar discoveries that had, it said, recently
appeared in the *Edinburgh Journal of Science*. The *Journal*'s correspondent, Dr. Andrew Grant, amanuensis to Sir John Herschel himself, had
earlier described how the new telescope came to be invented. Now Dr.
Grant reported the events of the previous January 10, when John Herschel
directed his telescope at the moon. At exactly half past nine, Sir John removed the screen from the hydro-oxygen microscope (which was serving
both to illuminate and further amplify the image produced by the telescope), and immediately the wall opposite displayed the distinct image of
a steep shelf of basaltic rock, greenish brown but thickly covered with
bright red flowers that precisely resembled the *Papaver rhoeas* that grows
so abundantly in Europe and Asia. It was, noted Dr. Grant, "the first or-
ganic production of nature, in a foreign world, ever revealed to the eyes of
men": a field of poppies.

The reference to poppies was surely Richard Adams Locke's little joke,
akin to (though more subtle than) Edgar Allan Poe's launching of his
hero's journey on April Fool's Day; for as soon as Sir John had finished
adjusting his telescope fantastic images of the lunar landscape began to
pour forth, streaming through the telescope and then projected onto the
walls of the room, as vivid and strange and beautiful as one of those

dreams lately described by Thomas de Quincey in his *Confessions of an English Opium-Eater*. The poppies confirmed what Herschel and his three assistants had hoped for, though not dared to believe: that the moon did possess an atmosphere capable of sustaining life. Still, Herschel's group was not prepared for what came next, as the telescope, in its slow transit of the moon's surface, came upon a forest—a *lunar forest*—the trees standing as tall and dignified as the yews in an English churchyard. For long minutes the astronomers examined the forest, the telescope charting seemingly endless miles, until finally they decided to reduce the magnifying power of the microscope to enlarge the viewing area, at which point it became evident that the telescope's course had been gradually descending a mountainous area just along the Mare Nubium, and had now come to the edge of a lake, or, as Grant pointedly called it, an "inland sea."

By 1835 the world's astronomers, while still divided over whether the moon was devoid of water, generally agreed that the so-called lunar "seas" (Mare Nubium, Mare Angius, Mare Tranquillitatus, and so forth) were really nothing more than basaltic plains formed by ancient volcanic eruptions. A basaltic plain, however, can hardly inspire the romantic imagination, and so Richard Adams Locke had taken it upon himself to fill those plains with water, turning them back into actual seas. The water shone as blue as that of any of the earth's oceans, and broke in gentle waves on the brilliant white sand of the shore that enclosed it, which was itself girded by high outcroppings of green marble ("wild castellated rocks," as Locke described them, calling to mind images of turrets and battlements), in the distance mile after mile of white gypsum cliffs. Hundreds of thousands of miles away, in the telescope room of their Cape Town observatory, the astronomers gazed in silent wonder at the colorful images that revolved around them, each one slowly dissolving into the next, as though the room had been transformed into a magnificent kaleidoscope.

Before long the room began to glow red as the telescope swept across giant formations of quartz, which Herschel pronounced to be the wine-colored amethyst variety, as they were colored the ruby of claret. From there the observations passed through the Mare Fecunditatis, the "Sea of Fertility," though, as Grant remarked, never had a name been so inappropriately bestowed: the region appeared to be a great desert of chalk and flint. But even the most unappealing lunar expanses had to be observed and recorded, and patiently the astronomers continued their trek, with three hundred miles passing under their lenses before the desert finally gave way to a great oval valley surrounded by hills "red as the purest vermilion." At the foot of the hills lay a wooded area thirty miles long and nearly twenty across, the picturesque copses including trees of every description. The region seemed to be bursting with life—and indeed it shortly proved to be the one that, as Grant reported, "blest our panting hopes with specimens of conscious existence."

For there, in the shaded woods of that red-hilled valley, Sir John Herschel and his cohort first beheld lunar animals. They could clearly make out a herd of large brown quadrupeds; with their curved horns, humped shoulders, and shaggy fur, the animals closely resembled earthly bison, although they possessed a "fleshy appendage" over their eyes, like a hairy veil, which Sir John quickly identified as a "providential contrivance" to protect the eyes from the moon's extremes of light and darkness.

The next animal they observed, reported Grant, "would be classified on earth as a monster." It was a bluish gray and was about the size of a goat, with a goat's head and beard—but it had, protruding from the center of its head, a single horn. The horned goats seemed to prefer the glades to the woods, racing fast over the gently sloped ground, pausing a while to nibble on the grass, then bounding and springing about as playfully as kittens. They provided the astronomers no end of amusement, and in their honor Sir John named the region the "Valley of the Unicorn."

By now the astronomers had been at the telescope for many hours, they were as exhausted as they were exhilarated by what they had seen, and with the moon moving swiftly into its descent, they concluded their evening's viewing, toasting their success with congratulatory bumpers of East India ale.

The following two nights were unfavorably cloudy, but Sir John Herschel's lunar observations began again on the night of January 13, when, reported Grant, "further animal discoveries were made of the most exciting interest to every human being." With that promise, the second installment of the *Sun*'s moon series came to an end.

IT was a rainy day, that Wednesday, and a bit cooler, providing a welcome respite from the heat of the summer. The sky over New York was a gray slate, the streets a dingy brown, so far removed from the bright colors of Richard Adams Locke's imagined lunar realm. He was living, in those hectic weeks, in two worlds at once, one outside and one inside him, as he worked furiously to keep the moon series coming (it would not do to miss a day just because he hadn't finished the next installment, not when the *Sun* claimed to have the entire *Edinburgh Journal of Science* account in its possession), writing whenever he could spare a few moments from the news of the city.

From his office in the *Sun* building on the corner of Spruce and Nassau, Locke could hear the murmur rising from the Park as final preparations were made for the mass meeting—"monster meetings," they had been called back in his native England—that would be held the next day to place New York on record as supporting the South's right of self-determination. He had witnessed some monster meetings in his youth, and heard about many others; in England, stories were still told of the Peterloo Massacre of 1819, how the great orator Henry Hunt had bravely exhorted the crowd, "Be firm!" as the cavalry charged, their sabers turning that Manchester field red with blood. Those meetings had declared universal suffrage a right fundamental to the expansion of human liberty; tomorrow's mass meeting would give consent to precisely the opposite. The resolutions that doubtlessly would be approved by acclamation had already been distributed and printed in the papers; he could scarcely imagine a drearier set of propositions than these, which condemned the cause of abolitionism and "recognized as lawful the condition of Slavery in the Southern States." The mayor himself, Cornelius Lawrence, would chair the meeting, while the chief justice and all two dozen judges of the state's Court of Errors had agreed to attend, standing together on the platform being assembled in the Park, less than two blocks from where Locke worked.

When he could, he dreamed a world of poppy fields and unicorns. He pored over his copy of Charles Blunt's lunar map, charting where each new discovery would be made, read and reread his astronomy books, studying the moon's librations, the refraction of rays, the correct working of lenses and reflectors. The words flowed so smoothly from his pen onto the page. His was the self-assured hand of a natural writer; that could be seen in the delicately curled serifs he placed at the feet of his capital letters, the slender loops of the *f*'s, the crosswise slashes of the *t*'s extending from one word into the next: the handwriting that Edgar Allan Poe would later call "clear, bold, and forcible" and "indicative of his fine intellect" (the science of autography, like phrenology, being very much in vogue). He only wished he had more time to write; as editor of the *Sun* there was always something to attend to. The office was a constant hubbub, what with people constantly coming in to purchase copies of the paper, deliver advertisements, or pass along the latest rumors. It was difficult enough to turn out his daily paragraphs, much less produce a series, thousands of words long, from his own imagination. The best time to work was late at night in the stillness of the apartment, away from the chatter of voices and the clank and whir of the printing press. There was something soothing about the scratching of the pen, its metal nib, sharp as a needle, depositing threads of ink on the page like stitches on a sampler. Already the moon series gave every indication of surpassing the Matthias series in popularity, and New Yorkers had yet to discover the many astronomical wonders he still had in store. There, in the quiet of his room, he could almost hear the buzzing as it arose from all parts of the city, combining into one great reverberation, the sound large enough to drown out—if only temporarily—those awful noises coming from the Park.

"The night of the 13th was one of pearly purity and loveliness," reported Dr. Andrew Grant from John Herschel's Cape observatory. "The moon ascended the firmament in gorgeous splendor, and the stars, retiring around her, left her the unrivalled queen of the hemisphere."

Sir John had decided to devote that evening to an investigation of the moon's western regions. The telescope room was soon illuminated by the blue-white gas flame of the hydro-oxygen microscope, and within moments the viewing wall was presenting a mountain scene: three mountain chains that met at a common point, two of them rounded into loops, so that it all resembled an immense ribbon tied into a bow. Beyond the mountains, near the crater called Endymion, luxuriant green fields grew, their tall grasses undulating in an invisible breeze, an expanse that Herschel and his assistants thought must closely resemble the prairies of the American West. It seemed a likely spot in which to encounter more of the hairy bison that had been discovered in the Valley of the Unicorn, and many such herds did make their appearance, as well as reindeer, elk, moose, horned bears, and, most astonishingly, biped beavers—beavers that walked upright on their hind feet. (They walked, marveled Grant, "with an easy gliding motion.") The beavers carried their young in their arms and made their habitats not in the crude mud-and-branch dams of their earthly counterparts, but in actual huts, the roofs of which emitted trails of smoke; their occupants, like primitive man in his caves, had discovered the secret of fire.

From the Endymion, the astronomers next proceeded southward toward the Cleomedes crater, following the course of a broad river that wended its way for about twenty miles before flowing into the largest lake they had yet seen on the moon. The lake contained numerous small islands, most of them actively volcanic, hiding themselves from the astronomers' attentions behind a veil of smoke and ash. Near its western edge lay a large oval-shaped island, ringed by velvety brown hills that were crowned with tall quartz crystals so richly yellow and orange that the astronomers at first thought them to be on fire. The crystals formed natural spires that rose above the low woods "like church steeples," noted Grant, adverting once more to his (and of course Locke's) English origins, "in the vales of Westmoreland." On this island the group observed for the first time lunar palm trees, bedecked with large crimson flowers. They also saw an elegantly striped quadruped, about three feet high, like a species of miniature zebra; blue and gold pheasants; and on the lakeshore, multitudes of shellfish of all shapes and sizes. The island's bounty certainly merited further observation, but by now the hour was growing late and Sir John ordered the telescope to be redirected toward the Langrenus crater, a region for which he had especially high hopes.

(Here ended Thursday's installment of *Great Astronomical Discoveries*; on its news page the *Sun* apologized for the brevity of that day's portion— the article ran just two columns, in comparison to Wednesday's four—and promised its readers that the next issue would bring the account of the discoveries which had earlier been promised. The moon story picked up again on Friday, with a fourth extract, brief but highly spectacular, from the *Supplement to the Edinburgh Journal of Science*.)

After a short delay in redirecting the telescope and focusing its lenses again, the astronomers found themselves gazing upon a dark, narrow lake. At the lake's edge a border of woodland opened onto a grassy plain bounded on three sides by red hills like those that surrounded the Valley of the Unicorn, the semicircle forming a kind of natural amphitheater, as steeply pitched as the Roman Colosseum but far larger, two thousand feet high and six miles wide. (In recognition of those hills, John Herschel denominated the region "the Ruby Colosseum.") The high red wall of the hills plunging down to a fringe of trees and the lush greensward of the plain, a sliver of lake glimmering beyond it: the telescope's reflectors had transformed the viewing wall into a kind of artist's canvas, the scene it displayed as vivid and dramatic as any of the great Turner landscapes, one that set the group's hearts racing with the prospect of someday showing it to their countrymen back in England.

The astronomers could have long stood in silent appreciation, but the lateness of the hour compelled them to move on with their observations. Soon they had discovered a new variety of animal life, this one a quadruped to which even the mythical gryphon might defer, its body brindled with white and brown patches like a deer but having a head much like a sheep's, except for its two spiral horns, as smooth and white as ivory. Still the telescope continued its steady passage, and before long another animal had come into view. Seeing it, the astronomers could not help but laugh: in that lunar meadow, contentedly grazing, stood a flock of sheep. Even under the closest scrutiny the sheep exactly resembled those of their home country, and appeared to be such large and healthy specimens that, as Grant remarked, they "would not have disgraced the farms of Leicestershire, or the shambles of Leadenhall market."

From the grassy plain Herschel and his party next explored the opening to the lake, where the valley dramatically narrowed, seeming to give itself over to the authority of the cliffs, the dark crags jutting out like medieval ramparts, crested on top by trees that formed a kind of forest in the sky, making a tableau almost gothic in its stark, brooding beauty. For several moments all was still; then, suddenly, four flocks of large winged creatures could be seen descending in a slow, even motion from the cliffs to the plain, where they landed and, their wings disappearing behind them, began walking, erect and dignified, toward a nearby forest. ("Now, gentlemen," exclaimed Herschel, "we have here something worth looking at.") To enable closer inspection, the telescope was fitted with the strongest available lens, the H. z., which provided a viewing distance of eighty yards. Some of the winged creatures had disappeared from the telescope's sight, but a cluster of six remained, allowing the wonderstuck astronomers to examine them. They stood about four feet tall and were covered with short copper-colored hair. Their faces were simian in feature, something like that of an orangutan, though with a larger forehead and a more gracefully formed jawline. In their general symmetry, the relationship between body and limb, they were far superior to the orangutan—so much so, joked one of Herschel's assistants, a Lieutenant Drummond, that if it were not for their wings, "they would look just as well on a parade ground as some of the old cockney militia!"

The next view obtained by the astronomers was even more revealing. A group of the creatures had crossed the lake and were lying along the opposite shore. The astronomers could now see that their wings resembled those of a bat, composed of a semitransparent membrane formed into curvilineal segments and attached to the back of the animal. The structure allowed for impressive expansion and contraction; some of the creatures entered the lake to bathe, and in returning to the shore spread their wings to shake off the water, much as ducks do, and then just as quickly closed them again, whereupon the wings rested snugly on their backs. Several of the creatures were observed making emphatic gestures with their hands and arms, clearly engaged in conversation.

These were, then, rational beings; on the moon, that perennial object of earthly wonder, intelligent life had at last been discovered. For some moments the astronomers scarcely breathed, observing the startling scene, but eventually the import of what they had found began to sink in, and what Grant called "our paralyzing astonishment" began to subside, and together they denominated this unexpected new creature Vespertilio-homo, or man-bat.

The recumbent man-bats apparently engaged in other activities beyond bathing, but these were not specifically described for the readers of the *Edinburgh Journal of Science*. Dr. Grant was a scientist but he was also an Englishman, and he carried out his duties with a propriety that would have met the approval of the young princess who, two years hence, would assume the British Crown:

> Our further observation of the habits of these creatures, who were of both sexes, led to results so very remarkable, that I prefer they should first be laid before the public in Dr. Herschel's own work, where I have reason to know they are fully and faithfully stated, however incredulously they may be received.

Here a series of asterisks was inserted into the text, indicating expunged material, followed by an additional observation by Andrew Grant, sounding a bit shaken by the scenes he had witnessed: "They are doubtless innocent and happy creatures, notwithstanding that some of their amusements would but ill comport with our terrestrial notions of decorum."

The editors of the *Edinburgh Journal of Science* now interrupted the narrative to affirm that they had faithfully obeyed the injunction of their Cape correspondent, and had omitted the indicated passages, which they acknowledged were "highly curious." They assured their readers, however, that this and other prohibited material would one day be published by Dr. Herschel, accompanied by certificates of authenticity furnished by the civil and military authorities of the Cape colony, as well as several ministers, who, under the strictest secrecy, had been permitted to visit the Herschel observatory and would attest to the wonders they had seen. With that the editors returned their columns to Andrew Grant, though only long enough for him to report that the following night proved to be hazy and not conducive to close observation. Shortly after midnight, however, the last mists dissipated and the astronomers resumed their work, orienting themselves to the crater called Tycho, where, noted Grant, "they added treasures to human knowledge which angels might well desire to win."

By Friday the rain had stopped and the heat returned; New York's damp houses stood baking in the sun like bricks in a kiln, its streets once again filling with the sounds of commerce. "Ice! Rockland ice!" was a much-anticipated cry in the summer, heralding the arrival of the heavy blocks hauled in covered wagons from Rockland and other counties up the North River, so that the city's residents—those who could afford it—might relieve the heat with a glass of iced water; and "Here's cherries!" from the women with their children alongside, peddling the fruit for twelve cents a pound, making their rounds with their baskets and scales; and from the ice-cream men and the hot-corn girls, and those selling sand or matches, buying rags or grease, looking to sweep chimneys or mend locks or sharpen knives, everything that might be required for the proper running of the city's households. In the morning hours, especially, the streets were alive with a medley of cries, but this week the ones most avidly awaited were those of the highest pitch, made by the newsboys with their papers, proclaiming the latest discoveries from the moon.

The boys sold as many papers as they could carry, the pockets of their trousers growing heavy with pennies; and then they returned to the *Sun* office for more and more copies until by the middle of the day there were no more papers to be had. The *Sun* building, William Griggs recalled, "was besieged by thousands of applicants from dawn to midnight," who stood waiting in noisy clusters for more newspapers to arrive. In their size and raucous good cheer, the crowds resembled those P. T. Barnum had produced just a few weeks earlier in front of Niblo's Garden, drawn together by the prospect, however improbable it might seem, of something strange and new. In their excitement, the crowds were also prone to what Griggs referred to as "spontaneous mendacity"—tale-telling that, in retrospect, seems befitting of its subject. Griggs, a close friend of Richard Adams Locke, heard of many such incidents, and personally witnessed two. In the first, a man announced to the skeptics in the crowd that he owned a copy of the *Supplement to the Edinburgh Journal of Science* from which the *Sun* had been publishing excerpts, and so far he had found no errors or lapses in the newspaper's reprint. A rather more elaborate story was supplied by an elderly gentleman dressed in "a fine broadcloth Quaker suit," who asserted that he himself had seen the great telescope described in the *Sun*. He had been in London the year before, he explained, and his business had taken him to the East India docks, where he watched as the seven-ton lens and the rest of the enormous telescope apparatus was loaded onto a ship bound for the Cape of Good Hope. Of course, he hastened to add, he had high hopes even then for this powerful instrument in the hands of such a capable astronomer as John Herschel; still, he could never have dreamed that Sir John would produce anything like the astonishing discoveries recently revealed in the pages of the *Sun*.

Among those listening to the man in the Quaker suit was Richard Adams Locke, who was out in front of the *Sun* building with a group of friends, smoking a cigar and surveying the scene. Locke did not reply to the elderly gentleman but simply regarded him, Griggs noted, with "a look of mingled astonishment and contempt."

Richard Adams Locke had little time those days to witness the effects of his work; he was too busy writing the articles for which the crowds outside hungered, even as he continued to perform his regular editorial duties—duties that had now grown enormously as a consequence of those very articles. The *Sun* office was being deluged with letters from outside the city, some of which contained money, from correspondents who had heard about the *Great Astronomical Discoveries* series and wanted to purchase back copies. The daily editions of the papers were all gone, having long since sold out; Locke, however, was now able to inform them that the entire series would soon be available in pamphlet form.

The pamphlet, *A Complete Account of the Late Discoveries in the Moon,* was issued on Saturday morning, August 29. The haste with which it had been produced was evident—simply printed, it had no illustrations, just the title followed by eleven dense pages of text. The pamphlets sold for twelve and a half cents apiece in the *Sun* office, but the demand quickly became so great that before long they could also be purchased in bookstores and from enterprising newsboys. Twenty thousand copies sold almost instantly in New York (even though the series had already been published there), and soon the *Sun* was producing another edition for national circulation. In all, *A Complete Account of the Late Discoveries in the Moon* would sell, by one estimate, more than forty thousand copies. Benjamin Day himself put the number at sixty thousand: equivalent, in today's population, to over one million copies.

In Locke's first installment of the moon series, published the previous Wednesday, the editors of the *Supplement to the Edinburgh Journal of Science* had referred to "engravings of lunar animals and other objects" produced by a Herbert Home, Esq., who had accompanied Dr. Herschel from London to the Cape. Immediately the *Sun* began receiving requests for those engravings from readers, ideally engravings produced in lithograph form, so they might display them at home, alongside their looking glasses and mourning pictures.

Lithographs to accompany a news story: this was a venture that Benjamin Day had not considered before, and one that instantly appealed to him. Day himself was occupied in supervising the *Sun*'s overworked printing press, as well as with various other business matters, so he entrusted the job to Locke, who hurried down to the offices of Norris & Baker, the Wall Street lithographers. The drawings, it was agreed, would be executed by Mr. Baker, one of the principals of the firm, whom the *Sun* extolled as "the most talented lithographic artist in the city." Baker applied himself to the job with relish, working on it around the clock, so that on Saturday morning—just twenty-four hours after the first appearance of the man-bats—the *Sun* was able to offer, for twenty-five cents, a lithograph entitled *Lunar Animals and Other Objects, Discovered by Sir John Herschel in His Observatory at the Cape of Good Hope and*

The Lunar Animals *lithograph issued by the* Sun *at the end of August 1835,*
featuring a variety of man-bats, water birds, and unicorns.
(Courtesy of the Library of Congress.)

Copied from Sketches in the Edinburgh Journal of Science. It was, the
Sun assured its readers, "a most splendid and beautiful print." Baker
proved himself worthy of the *Sun*'s praise, in the lushly detailed lunar
panorama he produced on such short notice. As was to be expected, the
featured players were the man-bats, more than two dozen of whom could
be observed flying, bathing, and conversing—though, needless to say, not
engaged in any of the activities that had so distressed Dr. Grant. The high
stone walls of the Ruby Colosseum formed a natural backdrop for the
tableau, with added visual drama provided by a rushing cataract, white
foam spraying up from its base. Scattered about the river and hills was a
kind of menagerie of lunar animals, including numerous water birds, the
blended quadruped with the spiral horns, and, serenely observing the ac-
tivity from the riverbank, several unicorns. (In this last detail the artist
was taking some liberties: the man-bats and the unicorns had been
sighted in two different locations.)

Baker would shortly produce another lithograph, *Lunar Temples*, depicting the even more extraordinary variety of man-bats later observed
by Herschel and his team (which Locke would describe in Saturday's fifth
installment). It is not known exactly how many copies of the lithographs

were sold, though Horace Greeley, who purchased a copy himself, was stunned by the demand for them, writing in the *New-Yorker* that they were selling "faster than all the Bible Societies in the universe could give away the Sacred Book." As each lithograph cost twice the price of a pamphlet, the number sold was presumably a good deal lower than sixty thousand, but given the enormous public interest it was certainly substantial. P. T. Barnum, who knew a great deal about the merchandising of hoaxes, estimated in his book *The Humbugs of the World* that the *Sun* ultimately sold no less than fifty thousand dollars worth of Moon Hoax materials—this coming just a few months after Benjamin Day had fretted about spending five thousand dollars to buy out George Wisner's half share of the paper.

ON Friday, the day before the pamphlet and the lithograph went on sale, Benjamin Day led the *Sun*'s news page with an item he called simply "Our Circulation." He began with the announcement that he would soon be enlarging the pages of the *Sun*. Recently, he lamented, he had been forced by a lack of space to *refuse* (the italics were his) yearly and sometimes even monthly advertisers; there simply was not enough room in the paper to include them. The enlarged *Sun*, made possible by the recent surge in the paper's circulation, "will at once accommodate our advertising friends." The great circulation, however, had brought its own complications, and therefore the *Sun* would no longer be able to accept advertisements that came in after six o'clock in the evening, because a day's edition required at least ten hours to print. That was a problem he hoped would soon be remedied, as he was presently negotiating the purchase of a new and even faster printing press, powered by a steam engine.

Now Day came to the heart of the matter, the topic promised in the item's headline. The *Sun*'s total circulation, he proudly announced, had risen to 19,360, with 17,440 of those papers sold in New York and the remainder in Brooklyn and surrounding cities. It was, as he surely knew, a cataclysmic number, one that must have sent shock waves through the city's newspaper district, where none of the *Sun*'s six-penny competitors had a circulation of more than a few thousand. The readership numbers being generated by the *Sun* had never before been seen in New York, or anywhere else. Even the mighty *Times* of London, Great Britain's paper of record since 1788, in a city six times larger than New York, could claim a daily circulation no greater than 17,000.

Founded less than two years earlier by a printer hoping to advertise his struggling print shop, the *Sun* was now the most widely read newspaper in the world.

How many of the *Sun*'s readers truly believed what they were reading in *Great Astronomical Discoveries*? No one can state this with any degree of accuracy, but contemporaneous accounts suggest that the number—at least for a while—was very high indeed. "As these discoveries were gradually spread before the public," Edgar Allan Poe wrote in his essay on Richard Adams Locke, "the astonishment of that public grew out of all bounds." Those who doubted the veracity of the *Sun*'s account numbered, according to Poe, "not one person in ten," and most strangely, "the doubters were chiefly those who doubted without being able to say why— the ignorant, those uninformed in astronomy, people who *would not* believe because the thing was so novel, so entirely 'out of the usual way.'" (Poe himself reported that "a grave professor of mathematics in a Virginian college told me seriously that he had *no doubt* of the truth of the whole affair!")

Poe's assertions were echoed by Benson J. Lossing in his 1884 *History of New York City*. Lossing was twenty-two years old when the moon series appeared in the *Sun,* and in his history he recalled how "the construction of the telescope was so ingeniously described, and everything said to have been seen with it was given with such graphic power and minuteness, and with such a show of probability, that it deceived scientific men. It played upon their credulity and stimulated their speculations." Horace Greeley, who was then editing the weekly paper the *New-Yorker,* remarked on the "unquestionable plausibility and verisimilitude" of the series; those who were fooled by it comprised, in his estimation (like that of Poe), "nine-tenths of us, at the least." P. T. Barnum declared that "the majestic, yet subdued, dignity" of Locke's work "at once claimed respectful attention; whilst its perfect candor, and its wealth of accurate scientific detail, exacted the homage of belief from all but cross-grained and inexorable skeptics."

Whether or not readers entirely believed it, *Great Astronomical Discoveries* was the first news story to be avidly read and discussed by all New Yorkers—not just the merchants perusing the six-penny papers for the latest currency tables or the mechanics opening the penny papers to the police office reports—but everyone, wherever people talked about the news: in the Chatham Market and the Merchants' Exchange alike, around the cloth-covered tables of Delmonico's and the pine tables of countless waterfront boardinghouses, on any of the hundred omnibuses rumbling up and down Broadway, in the Bowery taverns where the cartmen and firemen ate freshly killed oxen, and in the more genteel establishments where talk of the moon was punctuated by the delicate clinking of hammers chipping off pieces of ice for chilled drinks. In Bowery Village, at the corner of what today would be Eleventh and Broadway, a nurseryman named Michael Floy noted in his diary on Sunday, August 30: "A great talk concerning some discoveries in the moon by Sir John Herschell [*sic*]; not only trees and animals but even men have been discovered there." (Floy, who was an amateur astronomer and mathematician, did not believe the moon stories. "It is all a hoax," he wrote, "although the story is well put together.") On lower Broadway, a much wealthier and more prominent New York diarist of the time had recently set down his thoughts on the *Sun* series. Philip Hone— former auctioneer, former mayor, and perhaps New York's leading citizen— had returned on Friday to his mansion near Park Place from a vacation at the Marine Pavilion in Rockaway (where the amusements had included trotting races, sea bathing, and "champaign" dinners). That evening Hone made a lengthy entry in his diary with the heading "Lunar Discoveries":

> An exceedingly well written article is going the rounds of our papers, extracted from the Supplement to the Edinburgh Journal of Science, purporting to be an account of the "Great Astronomical Discoveries lately made by Sir John Herschel LLD—FRL at the Cape of Good Hope." The astronomer, the son of the great Herschel who gave his name to the last discovered Planet, who if this wonderful story be true is as much greater a man than his father, as the moon is greater than said Planet, was sent to the Cape by the British Government to observe a transit of Mercury and took with him a telescope of his own construction to which the largest instrument of that kind heretofore made bore no more comparison than a pippin to a watermelon. With this gigantic telescope, he and his companions began their operations by peeping in a manner rather indelicate into the moon, that renowned Repository of Lovers' Vows, and discovered something more than the hoary Sabbath breaker and his wearisome bundle of sticks. For wonderful to relate,

Mountains of Amethyst, Rivers whose "Sands were Diamonds," Trees of a grandeur and beauty unknown as yet to mortal Eyes, were rendered as visible as Greenwich Hill, the Thames and Hyde Park to the Cockneys of London, and to fill up the measure of mortal wonderment, Shrubs, animals and even Birds were clearly discerned, and the Reader would hardly be more surprised to learn that the organs of smelling and hearing had been gratified by the magical process of reducing the 240,000 miles which intervene between the moon and our Planet to a reasonable speaking distance.

In sober truth, if this account is true, it is most enormously wonderful. And if it is a fable, the manner of its relation, with all its scientific details, names of persons employed, and the beauty of its glowing descriptions, will give this ingenious history a place with Gullivers Travels and Robinson Crusoe, and the reading world will divide with its author their admiration of the fine writing of Swift and DeFoe and the mendacity of Baron Munchausen and Ferdinand Mendez Pinto.

Up the Long Island Sound in New Haven, Connecticut, interest in the moon story was absolute. On Saturday the city's *Daily Herald* began running the series—a practice soon to be followed by newspapers around the country—on its front page, under the headline "New Discoveries in the Moon," crediting the "extraordinary celestial discoveries" not to the *Sun* but to the *Edinburgh Journal of Science*. In publishing the series the newspaper was responding to public demand, for by then the local campus was already gripped by moon fever. "Yale College was alive with staunch supporters," a student of the time later recalled.

> The literati—students and professors, doctors in divinity and law—and all the rest of the reading community, looked daily for the arrival of the New York mail with unexampled avidity and implicit faith. Have you seen the accounts of Sir John Herschel's wonderful discoveries? Have you read the Sun? Have you heard the news of the man in the Moon? These were the questions that met you every where. It was the absorbing topic of the day. Nobody expressed or entertained a doubt as to the truth of the story.

Yale was then the leading center of American astronomy, the possessor of the Clark telescope, the most powerful in the country. (So great was the college's enthusiasm for astronomy that the tower of its Atheneum had recently been remodeled to serve as an observatory.) Among the distinguished figures in Yale astronomy were two professors, Denison Olmsted and Elias Loomis, who would soon become implicated—rightly or not—in the clamor surrounding Herschel's purported discoveries. Not long after the series appeared in the *Sun,* a story began making the rounds that the two learned astronomers had traveled by steamboat to New York, where they showed up unannounced at the *Sun* office to demand that they be given a copy of the *Supplement to the Edinburgh Journal of Science* for inspection. There they were met by Benjamin Day, who, in his typically gruff manner, declared himself to be highly indignant that they should doubt his word on the matter. "I suppose the magazine is somewhere upstairs," he told them, "but I consider it almost an insult that you should ask to see it." Instead, he directed them to his editor, who was interested, he said, in "the matter of the moon" and had overseen the publication of the *Supplement;* he could be found downstairs, smoking a cigar and gazing at the crowds.

Richard Adams Locke was by nature more mild-mannered than Benjamin Day, but, in this case at least, no less cagey. Having been apprised by the professors of their mission, he informed them that, unfortunately, the *Supplement* was in the hands of a printer on William Street; he would, however, be happy to provide them the address. The pair immediately set off—but not as fast as Locke himself, who raced to William Street to alert the printer about the arriving delegation.

The printer greeted the Yale professors with the news that he was very sorry, but the *Supplement* had been sent on to another shop for proofreading; perhaps the gentlemen might inquire there. And so it went, with Olmsted and Loomis endlessly frustrated in their quest to lay their hands on the elusive *Supplement,* until finally they had to leave to catch the afternoon steamboat back to New Haven. It was an embarkation they absolutely could not miss, for that very evening they hoped to become the first astronomers to observe the return of Halley's Comet. (In fact Olmsted and Loomis did claim that honor, sighting the comet on Monday, August 31, the day the final installment of the moon series was published.)

The story of the Yale astronomers first appeared in an item that ran the following week in Mordecai Noah's *Evening Star;* it was then repeated by James Gordon Bennett in the *Herald,* and has since become one of the staples of Moon Hoax lore. Day himself spoke of the incident at some length (he was clearly still amused by it) in an interview he gave on the *Sun*'s fiftieth anniversary in 1883. For their part, Olmsted and Loomis firmly denied having been fooled by the proprietors of the *Sun,* and insisted that at no time had they believed the lunar discoveries attributed to Sir John Herschel. In September 1835, as the story became widely circulated, their cause was taken up in a letter sent to the New Haven *Daily Herald,* signed only "Yalensis." (The authorship has been attributed to Olmsted and Loomis themselves, but this is not clear from the text.) Yalensis pronounced the *Evening Star* item "entirely erroneous" and assured the readers of the *Daily Herald* that "the Professors of Yale were not deceived by the article in question for a single moment, as many of the inhabitants of New Haven, who inquired their opinion, will be ready to testify." Anyone with a knowledge of optics and astronomy, claimed Yalensis, would perceive that the author of the moon series was ignorant of the finer points of those two sciences—and yet the very success of his endeavor was, ironically, a testament to the achievements of science itself: "We cannot, however, but regard the general credit given to his statements, as favorable to the reputation of science in the age in which we live, since its real discoveries have of late been so extraordinary that no creation of the imagination seemed too wonderful to be believed."

Not since ancient Greece had the power of science so captured the popular imagination; never had the possibilities it offered seemed so limitless. Thanks to the recent invention of hot-air balloons, human beings were now able to fly. Ships and trains—and even newspaper presses—were powered by the force of an immaterial substance: steam. The dread disease smallpox (which had left a permanent imprint on Richard Adams Locke, one of its last victims in England) was now preventable with a vaccination obtained from, of all things, a virus found on cows' udders. Not content with transforming human life, science was now extending itself to discover new, undreamed-of varieties of life. No more than six months earlier, the *Sun* had carried on its front page a large drawing of the creatures—"animalcules," they were called—that could be seen in a single drop of water by means of the hydro-oxygen microscope then on exhibit at the American Museum. The accompanying article reported that the size of the animals "surpasses the conception of the human mind"; ten thousand members of a single species were, together, no larger than a single grain of sand. Yet the animals had distinct, even complex bodies, complete with what looked like tiny claws and wings and antennae. They came in a bewildering diversity of forms: one seemed to resemble a miniature sea serpent, another a triangle, still others a funnel or a bell, while some, noted the article, "cannot be compared to any object familiar to our senses." If these tiny wonders could be detected in a single drop of water, then why should it not also be possible that the hydro-oxygen microscope, in combination with a powerful new telescope, might discover equally astonishing creatures on the earth's closest neighbor?

Life, it seemed, was everywhere, in even the most unexpected places. In worlds distant and near at hand, modern science was only now beginning to perceive the variety of forms that God had bestowed on the universe, or so held the article of faith shared by theologians and scientists alike. Science, they believed, was bringing man ever closer to God's greatness, and perhaps, with the aid of science, humanity might more powerfully do God's work. Shortly after the publication of the *Sun* articles, Sir Francis Beaufort, the hydrographer to the Royal Navy, wrote to his friend John Herschel in South Africa to ask if he had heard about the discoveries claimed in his name. Sir John replied that he had, and that he had further heard something even more remarkable—how an American clergyman had informed his congregation that, given the late wonderful discoveries, he expected that one day he would be calling on their generosity to help purchase Bibles for the unenlightened inhabitants of the moon.

CHAPTER 11

The Picturesque
Beauty of the Moon

LIKE MOST OF the astronomers of his time, John Herschel was a devout Christian, and nothing in any of his scientific discoveries (those of the genuine variety) ever caused him to question that faith. He also believed in life on other worlds, a supposition based less on his astronomical research than on his deeply held religious convictions. In one passage from *A Treatise on Astronomy*, after marveling at the glory of the stars and planets, he asked the reader:

> Now, for what purpose are we to suppose such magnificent bodies scattered through the abyss of space? Surely not to illuminate our nights ... nor to sparkle as a pageant void of meaning and reality, and bewilder us among vain conjectures. Useful, it is true, they are to man as points of exact and permanent reference; but he must have studied astronomy to little purpose, who can suppose man to be the only object of his Creator's care, or who does not see in the vast and wonderful apparatus around us provision for other races of animated beings.

He was not certain about the existence of lunarians, but he kept an open mind on the question. The final paragraph of his chapter on the moon in *A Treatise on Astronomy* begins, "If there be inhabitants on the moon . . . ," and in his magisterial *Outlines of Astronomy*, published in 1849, he noted that while there were no indications of water on the visible side of the moon, "It by no means follows . . . that the other is equally devoid of them, and equally unfitted for maintaining animal or vegetable life."

John Herschel's uncertainty was not shared by his astronomer father William, who from the outset of his career in the 1770s had been using his homemade telescopes to look for signs of life on the moon. In this endeavor he had met with a surprising amount of success, as almost immediately he found what looked to him to be a lunar forest, while later on he noted in his journal the apparent discovery of canals, roads, pyramids, and even towns. William Herschel never published these findings, however— he seems to have doubted their accuracy and worried about how the rest of the astronomical community might view him as a result—and not long after his discovery of Uranus in 1781, he began to direct his attention away from the moon to his many other celestial projects. Still, efforts to find lunar life went on.

In 1791 the German astronomer Johann Hieronymus Schröter (known as "the Herschel of Germany," in part because both men enjoyed the patronage of King George III) published his *Selenotopographische Fragmente,* the most detailed mapping of the moon's surface yet produced. Schröter was convinced that he had detected evidence of a lunar atmosphere, one apparently free from rain and snow, as it gave no sign of having any clouds. Fortunately enough for the moon's inhabitants, water-carrying vapors rose from the lunar valleys, then fell again like dew to nourish the fields that he imagined to be just as fruitful as Italy's famously abundant Campanian plain. On the moon, Schröter declared, "nature has ceased to rage." The weather there was "mild and beneficial," ideal for "the calm culture of rational creatures."

Johann Schröter died in 1816; like William Herschel, he had long since moved on from moon gazing to other astronomical projects, notably a search for evidence of atmosphere on other planets. It is his lunar observations, however, for which he is best remembered, and which served to inspire a cadre of younger German astronomers, probably the most enthusiastic of whom was Franz von Paula Gruithuisen. A physician as well as an astronomer, Gruithuisen published no fewer than 177 papers in his lifetime, the most memorable one entitled "Discovery of Many Distinct Traces of Lunar Inhabitants, Especially of One of Their Colossal Buildings" (1824). Gruithuisen seems to have had none of William Herschel's circumspection about publishing his lunar discoveries, and proudly announced sighting "great artificial works on the moon erected by the lunarians," including roads, cities, and "a system of fortifications thrown up by the selenitic engineers." There was even a star-shaped structure that he interpreted to be a lunar temple, an idea that Richard Adams Locke would resurrect in his moon series.

Gruithuisen's observations clearly owed more to fancy than to empirical evidence, and even the most confirmed of his fellow believers viewed his findings with skepticism. Still, his paper was widely discussed throughout Europe, and the extravagance of his conclusions did little to diminish interest in the idea of discovering life on the moon—nor in the even more ambitious project of communicating with its inhabitants, for which purpose the German mathematician Carl Friedrich Gauss is said to have proposed the construction of a vast geometrical figure on the plains of Siberia. Though this idea has been widely attributed to Gauss, its origin is actually rather murky, as is the origin of an idea long associated with the Viennese astronomer Johann Joseph von Littrow, to contact the lunarians by setting ablaze a massive kerosene-filled trench in the Sahara. But whether the geometrical-figure scheme originated with him, Gauss seems to have had few qualms about the basic concept of extraterrestrial communication. In 1818 he invented the heliotrope, a land-surveying instrument that uses a mirror to reflect sunlight over very long distances; four years later, in a letter to his astronomer friend Wilhelm Olbers, he noted, "With 100 separate mirrors, each of 16 square feet, used conjointly, one would be able to send good heliotrope-light to the moon." It would be, Gauss added, "a discovery even greater than that of America, if we could get in touch with our neighbors on the moon."

Like so many of his countrymen, Wilhelm Olbers was a believer in lunar life. In a letter to Gruithuisen he wrote, "I hold it to be very probable that the moon is inhabited by living, even rational creatures, and that something not wholly dissimilar to our vegetation occurs on the moon." Privately, though, he was critical of the highly speculative claims Gruithuisen made for his work, and in a February 1827 letter to Gauss complained that the two had been associated with Gruithuisen in "an English journal article."

Olbers was referring to the fact that in October 1826, several of the latest developments in lunar research—Gruithuisen's observations, Gauss's proposal for the geometrical figure in Siberia, and his own ideas about vegetation on the moon—had been collected in a brief article entitled "The Moon and its Inhabitants," published in the premiere issue of the

Edinburgh New Philosophical Journal. It was the very article that Richard Adams Locke would happen upon nearly a decade later, which would provide the inspiration for his series about the remarkable creatures discovered on the moon.

THE idea that life exists not just on the earth but throughout the universe—what has come to be called the plurality of worlds doctrine, or simply pluralism—originated long before the nineteenth century. In ancient times the Epicureans had propounded a theory of extraterrestrial life ("We must believe that in all worlds there are living creatures and plants and other things we see in this world," wrote Epicurus), a view that was just as strongly derided by Aristotle and Plato. For many centuries afterward, the plurality of worlds remained a purely philosophical question; it was given new life in 1543 by Nicolaus Copernicus's controversial theory that the earth is just one of the planets circling the sun and not the center of the universe. (If the earth resembled the other planets in this one crucial respect, then perhaps the other planets resembled the earth in another.) The pace of the debate quickened with the invention of the telescope, as astronomers came to understand the vastness of the universe and made the first tentative efforts at determining the physical conditions on the other planets in the solar system. The Catholic Church, however, saw little reason for discussion. The Church was deeply troubled by what it saw as the theological implications of pluralism, particularly in relation to the crucifixion of Christ: the significance of his sacrifice would seem to be diminished if the earth was only one of many worlds under God's care. In 1600, the astronomer Giordano Bruno was burned at the stake in Rome's Campo de Fiori for the crime of heresy, which included his passionate advocacy of pluralism. (Bruno's countryman Galileo, who had his own problems with the Church, remained an agnostic on the question.)

Less than a half century after Bruno's death, the book *The Discovery of a World in the Moone, or, A Discourse Tending to Prove That 'Tis Probable There May Be Another Habitable World in That Planet* became one of the most influential works of popular science of its time, and the first to set the case for pluralism before the public. Issued anonymously in England in 1638, *The Discovery of a World in the Moone* was written by John Wilkins, a young Anglican clergyman who later became bishop of Chester. Wilkins directly addressed the theological objections to the idea of life on other worlds, providing counterarguments that would still be used by pluralists two centuries later. No one, he pointed out, could state with certainty that the creatures living on these other worlds were men. "There is a great chasm betwixt the nature of men and angels," he wrote. "It may be the inhabitants of the planets are of a middle nature between both these. It is not impossible that God might create some of all kinds, that so he might more completely glorify his nature." If these creatures were not human, Wilkins continued, then they would not need to be saved by Christ. If they were human, then perhaps they had not sinned and were not in need of saving. And even if the creatures of other worlds were indeed human and were in need of salvation, then Christ might have died for them as well. What churchman would be willing to state with certainty that the influence of the Son of God was limited to the earth alone, and could not extend even into space?

The pluralist position was further enhanced in the middle of the following century, when the Scottish astronomer James Ferguson published his *Astronomy Explained upon Sir Isaac Newton's Principles*. The book's title notwithstanding, Ferguson took pluralism far beyond Newton's own speculations, proclaiming the certainty of life throughout the reaches of space. The universe, he contended, contains "thousands of thousands of Suns . . . attended by ten thousand times ten thousand Worlds . . . peopled with myriads of intelligent beings, formed for endless progression in perfection and felicity." Among those peopled worlds was unquestionably the moon, Ferguson declared, the surface of which, with its mountains and valleys, more closely resembled the earth than did any other celestial body.

Ferguson had a gift for communicating complex concepts to laypeople, and *Astronomy Explained* eventually appeared in seventeen editions. Among its devoted readers was the Bath church organist William Herschel, who purchased the book in 1773 and is said to have taken it to bed with him along with "a bason of milk or a glass of water" (as noted by his sister Caroline) for several months as he worked his way through it. By the time he discovered Uranus in 1781, Herschel was already a confirmed pluralist, and in his letters and published papers he made numerous references to the inhabitants of Mars, Jupiter, Saturn, and the planet of his own discovery. By the 1790s he was developing his remarkable thesis that the sun was not an immense fireball but a "large and lucid planet," composed of a cool, dark nucleus surrounded by a luminous layer of clouds that shielded the interior from the tremendous light and heat generated by the exterior. (He thought sunspots were regions of the dark nucleus glimpsed through holes in the clouds.) From this idea Herschel proceeded to the even more striking supposition that the sun might be inhabited. "Its similarity to the other globes of the system," he wrote in a 1795 issue of the Royal Society's *Philosophical Transactions,* "leads us to suppose that it is most probably . . . inhabited . . . by beings whose organs are adapted to the peculiar circumstances of that vast globe."

By the early decades of the nineteenth century, pluralism had made the leap from heresy to conventional wisdom—preached in sermons, printed in textbooks, evoked in poems. (Pluralist sentiments can be found in the work of, among other poets, Wordsworth, Byron, Shelley, and Coleridge.) Not only did the idea seem to better comport with modern scientific discoveries, such as the discovery of microscopic creatures, but it seemed to posit a grander, more expansive notion of God as truly infinite and omnipotent, caring for unimaginably tiny animals even as he oversaw the vastness of the heavens. The Glasgow minister Thomas Chalmers made this point explicitly in his highly influential collection of sermons published in 1817 as *A Series of Discourses on the Christian Revelation Viewed in Connection with the Modern Astronomy.* The telescope "led me to see a system in every star," Chalmers wrote, while the microscope "leads me to see a world in every atom." God was certainly capable of caring for the earth amid the plenitude of the heavens, for "magnitude does not overpower him, minuteness cannot escape him, and variety cannot bewilder him." Thomas Chalmers was so mesmerizing a speaker that crowds would wait for hours to hear him preach, and his written work was just as popular. *Astronomical Discourses* (as the book came to be known) sold twenty thousand copies in its first year of publication, six thousand in its first ten weeks alone. The impact of Chalmers's book, reported the British critic William Hazlitt, "ran like wild-fire through the country." It met an equally enthusiastic reception in the United States; first published there in 1817, it stayed in print for more than four decades. "All the world," proclaimed Edward Hitchcock, the president of Amherst College, "is acquainted with Dr. Chalmers' splendid Astronomical Discourses."

In the early nineteenth century, any tension between the dictates of science and religion—one grounded on experiment, the other on revelation— was felt less in astronomy than in the much younger science of geology. Fossils were being found deep in the earth and on the tops of mountains, and their location and apparent age both seemed to call into question the biblical account of the Great Flood, a centerpiece of Christian natural history. Moreover, many of the fossils were clearly of animals that no longer existed (for a while some theologians tried to argue that living examples of these animals had simply not yet been discovered on earth, but the fossilized remains of mammoths were not so easily explained away), which inevitably raised the issue of why God had mandated the extinction of species in a world that he had created according to his own design and, having finished, pronounced "good." Perhaps most troubling was the growing understanding among geologists of how the layers of the earth had been formed, as the result of infinitesimal changes taking place over very long periods of time, which indicated that the earth itself was far older than had ever been imagined, indeed many millions of years old, and had not in fact been created (as was famously calculated by James Ussher, the archbishop of Armagh, Ireland) on October 23, 4004 B.C.— sometime in the midafternoon.

Some theologians would try to reconcile old dogma and new science with the theory of "progressive" creation, in which God provides new species to replace ones that have been lost. But this idea was neither scientifically adequate nor theologically satisfying, and eventually the friction between the opposing ideas became insupportable and the ground gave way, as in one of those earthquakes that science had come to understand as a prime cause of geological change, cleaving the terrain and leaving the two camps to gaze warily at each other across the divide. On one side were those who no longer believed in the literal truth of the Bible's creation story, having determined that the earth was colossally old (an understanding that would prepare the way for the theory of evolution), and on the other, those who insisted on a six-thousand-year-old earth in the face of all the scientific evidence to the contrary.

In astronomy, though, the ground was still reasonably stable, and the sky above looked as full of life as ever. Much of the most popular and highly regarded astronomical writing of the time was being produced by theologians, while the astronomers were, by and large, a pious lot who would have readily concurred with the assertion made in 1802 by William Paley in his landmark *Natural Theology* that astronomy "raises to sublimer views of the Deity than any other subject affords" and "shows, beyond all other sciences, the magnificence of his operations."

Even among astronomers, it was widely held that science was not an equal partner with religion, but rather—in the commonly used trope of the time—its handmaiden. The belief was perhaps most forcefully expressed in the work of the Scottish schoolteacher Thomas Dick, especially in his first book, *The Christian Philosopher; or, the Connection of Science and Philosophy with Religion.* (Among that book's many readers was Richard Adams Locke, who paid special attention to its appendix on the probability of life on the moon.) Theology, wrote Dick, "ought to be viewed as the most varied and comprehensive of the sciences; as embracing, within its extensive grasp, all the other departments of useful knowledge, both human and divine," while science was properly "subservient to the elucidation of the facts and doctrines of religion, and to the accomplishment of its benevolent designs." For Dick, there could be no genuine conflict between faith and reason because God had designed the laws by which the universe functioned; careful inquiry would allow the scientist to lift the veil of ignorance and perceive ever more clearly the greatness of God's work.

Published in 1823, *The Christian Philosopher* became an instant hit in Great Britain and the United States and established Thomas Dick as the most eloquent advocate of the idea of extraterrestrial life. The Almighty Being, Dick insisted, would not have created an entire universe devoid, except for one tiny planet, of creatures capable of receiving his moral government. Nor would he have created an infinitude of stars and planets, most of which exist beyond our sight, simply to provide a twinkling canopy for the earth's night sky. (This was the assertion John Herschel would later echo in *A Treatise on Astronomy.*) The stars were made not for useless splendor, but for the enjoyment of their own intelligent beings, on whom God can bestow his benevolence and who can, in return, adore him and sing his praises. In Dick's cosmology, the universe is not the cold, silent, desolate expanse imagined by those who believe the earth to be the only world in all of creation; it is instead a joyfully buzzing place inhabited by an inconceivably large number of creatures (in a later work he would estimate the number to be sixty quadrillion in the visible universe alone) that together encompass a thrilling variety of orders, from the tiniest animalculum all the way up to the seraph and the archangel. Intelligent life exists literally everywhere: on each planet, on every star, on comets, possibly on asteroids, likely on the sun, and—most assuredly—on the moon.

Unlike some of his German colleagues, Thomas Dick was skeptical about the idea of communicating with the lunarians by means of a large geometrical figure, not so much for the absurdity of the project as for the unlikelihood of its ever getting built. "Our terrestrial sovereigns are much too engaged in plunder and warfare to think of spending their revenues in so costly an experiment," he declared; "and, therefore, it is likely that, for ages to come, we shall remain in ignorance of the genius of the lunar inhabitants." The "genius" of the inhabitants of the moon, their "intelligence," their "sensitivity," were assertions often repeated in Dick's work; in a later book called *Celestial Scenery; or, the Wonders of the Planetary System Displayed,* he went so far as to suggest that the moon "may contain a population of intelligent beings far more numerous, and perhaps far more elevated in the scale of intellect, than the inhabitants of our globe." Exactly how numerous? The mathematical calculation of extraterrestrials was one of Thomas Dick's specialties, and in *Celestial Scenery* he determined that if the moon were as densely populated as England (exactly why it should be as crowded as England is left unstated) it would be home to no fewer than 4.2 billion inhabitants, more than five times the current population of the earth.

For Dick, the intelligence of those inhabitants was directly related to the physical conditions in which they lived. That was perhaps the central tenet of his philosophy: God would not create beautiful worlds without also placing there beings intelligent enough to appreciate them. In *The Christian Philosopher* Dick referred only in passing to the "sublime scenery" of the moon, but in a later book, *The Sidereal Heavens,* he lavished praise on its "beautiful diversity . . . of plains and valleys surrounded with circular ramparts of hills; of mountains towering far above; and vales and caverns sinking far below the general level of the lunar surface, with many other varieties." All this, he noted, could be espied through a telescope; one had only to imagine those grand contours being covered with vegetation (grass, flowers, and trees) to create on the moon "a scene of picturesque beauty and magnificence." Like Johann Schröter, Dick believed that the moon contained an atmosphere—different in composition from the earth's but capable of sustaining life nonetheless—and that the atmosphere was cloudless, for, as he noted, "all the parts uniformly present a clear, calm, and serene aspect, as if its inhabitants enjoyed a perpetual spring."

Dick took bitter exception to the theory (by this time widely agreed on by scientists) that the moon's surface was pocked with the remains of extinct volcanoes. Volcanoes, he reminded his readers, were not a feature of the original earth, when man existed in paradise; rather, they were brought forth only after the Great Flood, along with other natural disasters such as earthquakes and hurricanes, as a representation of man's sinful nature. "To suppose, therefore," Dick declaimed, "that such destructive agents exist in the moon, would be virtually to admit that the inhabitants of that planet are in the same depraved condition as the inhabitants of this world." This was a notion he found unthinkable (he was deeply offended by Gruithuisen's claim to have seen fortifications on the moon, which he called a "pretended discovery"). As opposed to the intelligence of the lunar creatures, though, for the innocence of lunar creatures Dick marshaled no evidence, presented no lines of reasoning; he maintained the idea simply as an article of faith, an expression of his confidence in the benevolence of God's design. If the inhabitants of the moon were morally corrupt, then so might be those on all the other stars that beautify the night sky—and the idea of a fallen universe, populated by untold billions of sinners, was more than he could bear.

Thomas Dick was not at all frightened by the prospect of actually meeting the inhabitants of distant worlds; indeed, he seemed to relish the thought of it. Like the other pluralists of his time, he acknowledged that there might be marked physical differences between extraterrestrials and the people of earth, but he did not recoil from them. "It is not improbable," he wrote, "were we transported to those abodes, that we should feel more at home in their society and arrangements than we are now apt to imagine." Nor did he believe that we would encounter any difficulties in communicating with the extraterrestrials, once we came to understand their language (or, in the absence of language, other means of communication), because, as he put it, "certain relations, sentiments, dispositions, and virtues" must be held in common by intellectual and moral creatures everywhere in the universe. All had been made by the same God, and all were rational enough to behold his work and bestow on him their love.

To nineteenth-century readers, it was a profoundly comforting sentiment. Man was *not* alone in the universe, as had been preached for centuries, not a solitary pilgrim traveling through a vast, cold, windswept realm; those lights off in the distance were the warm glow of untold hearths. Better still, our new neighbors were friendly. (It is not hard to fathom how Dick's readers might have harbored a fear of being colonized or enslaved by a distant, more powerful race.) And even if the extraterrestrials were not yet practicing Christians, one can imagine a bevy of church societies, like that of John Herschel's putative American clergyman, buying subscriptions to send Bibles to the inhabitants of Mars or Jupiter, who already upheld the traditional Christian virtues and prayed to the God of the Christians. However initially strange or unsettling the inhabitants of other planets might seem, there was no reason to fear them; they were, Thomas Dick assured us, "beings not much unlike ourselves."

Although Thomas Dick's books were highly popular in his native Great Britain, his message found an even more receptive audience in the United States. In his book *The Humbugs of the World* P. T. Barnum described how Dick's writings

> were read with the utmost avidity by rich and poor, old and young, in season and out of season. They were quoted in the parlor, at the table, on the promenade, at church, and even in the bedroom, until it absolutely seemed as though the whole community had "Dick" upon the brain. To the highly educated and imaginative portion of our good Gothamite population, the Doctor's glowing periods, full of the grandest speculations as to the starry worlds around us, their wondrous magnificence and ever-varying aspects of beauty and happiness, were inexpressibly fascinating. The author's well-reasoned conjectures as to the majesty and beauty of their landscapes, the fertility and diversity of their soil, and the exalted intelligence and comeliness of their inhabitants, found hosts of believers; and nothing else formed the staple of conversation, until the beaux and belles, and dealers in small talk generally, began to grumble, and openly express their wish that the Dickens had Doctor Dick and all his works.

Thomas Dick's extraordinary appeal for the Americans of the time is not surprising, given that the United States was among the most thoroughly Christianized nations in the Western world, the place, observed the young French writer Alexis de Tocqueville, "where the Christian religion has kept the greatest real power over men's souls."

In the years since the American Revolution, religious denominations had founded virtually all of the country's private colleges, organizing them to meet the "spiritual necessities" of the new nation and supporting them as a "child of the church." Well into the nineteenth century, their character and curriculum were still determined by their denominational parents; in science courses, William Paley's *Natural Theology* was the standard text. As a modern historian of the subject has observed, in the American colleges of the time "the forces of irreligion, of rationalism, and of deistic thought were effectually checked on a hundred fronts," thus ensuring that "the menace of free thought no longer threatened the citadels of faith." This was true throughout the country, from the newly founded frontier colleges of the West to the most well-respected institutions of the East. In the early years of the nineteenth century, the president of Yale, the Reverend Timothy Dwight, had successfully suppressed ideological challenges launched by freethinking students inspired by the French Revolution, turning the college into what one observer approvingly called "a perennial fountain of orthodoxy." (Not surprisingly, Dwight was a confirmed pluralist who once noted of the moon, "It is most rationally concluded that Intelligent beings in great multitudes inhabit her lucid regions, being probably far better and happier than ourselves.")

For much of the rest of the century, American science would labor under the fundamental precept of natural theology: that the proper function of science is to illuminate God's design. As late as 1854 Benjamin Pierce, the distinguished Harvard mathematics professor and founder of the college observatory, could confidently assert that he and his fellow scientists were capable of providing eternal proofs of God's existence. Science is "the history of the works of the Deity," declared Edward Hitchcock, longtime professor of natural history at Amherst College and later its president. The scientist, he added, "receives with gratitude and joy those richer disclosures of truth which revelation brings. To its authority he bows reverently and rejoicingly, and counts it the best use he can make of science to render it tributary to revelation and to the cultivation of his own piety."

Of all the sciences, only astronomy was widely understood to be spiritually ennobling. Edward Everett, the Harvard professor turned congressman, declared that astronomy in particular is "well adapted to arrest the attention of minds barely tinctured with scientific culture, and even to touch the sensibilities of the wholly uninstructed observer." No other science, another lecturer told a class of "young ladies" in 1833, was "more calculated to exalt the soul and fill it with sublime conceptions of the great Author of nature, than Astronomy." It was, agreed other lecturers, "the queen of the sciences," "the only *perfect* science." Geology carried the whiff of heresy; biology was not for the squeamish; chemistry required too much knowledge to be comprehended. Astronomy, however, demanded little more than a telescope and an artistic soul. The young Brooklyn poet Walt Whitman captured the popular temper when he wrote in *Leaves of Grass* of listening to "the learn'd astronomer" present his proofs and figures. Although Whitman "became tired and sick" from the presentation (ever the experientialist, he preferred just to look up in silence at the stars), he reported that the rest of the audience greeted the astronomer "with much applause in the lecture-room."

The public's fascination with all things astronomical only intensified with the publication of John Herschel's *A Treatise on Astronomy* in 1834 and reached even greater heights the following year, thanks to the imminent arrival of Halley's Comet. In the summer of 1835 a group of entrepreneurs, seeking to cash in on the excitement, set up a telescope in the Park and charged six cents for a view of the night sky unmatched anywhere in the city. Years later P. T. Barnum would recall the "peculiar mania of the time," in which "the whole community at last were literally occupied with but little else than 'star-gazing.'" The excitement came to a crescendo at the end of August, when Richard Adams Locke introduced his man-bats to New York.

CHAPTER 12

"The Astronomical Hoax Explained"

Locke's man-bats made their New York debut on Friday, August 28, and by Saturday they were the talk of the town. Temporarily forgotten were the tales of abolitionist outrages, reported in the merchant newspapers and taken up on countless street corners: abolitionists seating blacks next to whites in church, encouraging blacks to dress as dandies and parade up Broadway, asking their own daughters to marry blacks. Even the ancient slave Joice Heth, whose unlikely appearance had amazed the city just two weeks earlier, seemed nearly as remote as George Washington himself. Now crowds of excited New Yorkers thronged the *Sun* offices, laying down their shillings for the *Complete Account of the Late Discoveries in the Moon* pamphlet, their quarters for the *Lunar Animals* lithograph, or their pennies for the current issue of the *Sun,* to read about the latest discoveries from the moon.

Saturday's installment was relatively brief, most of it taken up by Andrew Grant's close descriptions of the moon's surface. The writing was vivid enough, and contained much that was unexpected, but it was not what the *Sun*'s readers were hoping for, not after the much more sensational material, some of it so racy as to require expurgation, that had been presented in the previous installment. The man-bats, having taken their star turn the day before, now delayed their second entrance while the astronomers continued their survey of the lunar world.

Even without the immediate presence of living creatures, the moon presented a magnificent spectacle, and from their distant observatory the astronomers took it all in with what Grant called a "reverential confidence in the illimitable power of the Creator." (Here Richard Adams Locke was again making sly reference to the theological assumptions underlying the work of many of the day's leading scientists.) The telescope's gaze traversed a magnificent lunar ocean, the Mare Serenitatis, and then passed along Bullialdus, an active volcano standing at the edge of another large lunar sea. To the west the astronomers came upon a ring of bright hills, composed of either white marble or semitransparent crystal, which bounded a patchwork of green valleys that were "of paradisiacal beauty and fertility, and like primitive Eden in the bliss of their inhabitants" (as Locke pointedly characterized them, using another bit of religious imagery), for it was in one of those idyllic valleys, at the culmination of a long night of observing, that Sir John and his cohort once again discovered intelligent lunar life, or at least the vestiges of it. There they beheld an immense stone structure, a perfect equilateral triangle; and though the building's function could not have been immediately evident, Grant at once pronounced it to be a "temple."

Locke's decision to introduce a lunar temple was surely prompted by the German astronomer Franz von Paula Gruithuisen's earlier claim to have observed one on the moon. (Gruithuisen had figured prominently in the *Edinburgh New Philosophical Journal* article, "The Moon and its Inhabitants," that had inspired the moon series in the first place.) In his description of Grant's subsequent attempt to make sense of the temple, Locke again invoked the prevailing creed of the time, natural theology, in which the scientist's proper role was to reveal the presence of God through a greater understanding of his works. Unsure about the exact purpose of the building, whether religious or scientific in nature, Grant dodges the question by pronouncing it "a fane of devotion, or of science, which, when consecrated to the Creator, *is* devotion of the loftiest order; for it exhibits his attributes purely free from the masquerade, attire, and blasphemous caricature of controversial creeds, and has the seal and signature of his own hand to sanction its aspirations."

The lunar "temple" was made of polished sapphire, its lustrous blue flecked with gold that shone in the sunlight. Huge square columns, seventy feet high, stood along the temple's three sides, but even more remarkable was the roof, made of some kind of yellow metal and encircled by a series of triangular planes, set at various angles to resemble flames; from the center of the roof rose a large copper-colored sphere, around which the fire raged "as if hieroglyphically consuming it." It was a disturbing tableau, made especially so by the absence of any living creatures in the vicinity of this carefully wrought structure. Shortly afterward the astronomers found two other buildings nearby, each of them exactly like the first. What, they wondered, had become of the makers of these huge, elaborate temples? And what was the meaning of the central image displayed there, a globe engulfed by flames? Was it a memorial for a catastrophe that had befallen their world, or—more troubling to contemplate—an augury of one yet to arrive on ours?

With these questions, Locke brought Saturday's installment to a close, leaving readers to ponder the answers they hoped would be revealed on Monday, when the *Sun* would publish the last of the excerpts from the *Supplement to the Edinburgh Journal of Science.*

On Saturday the echoes of Benjamin Day's thunderclap item of the day before, "Our Circulation," were still reverberating through New York's newspaper district. After less than two years of publication (its second anniversary would arrive the following Thursday), the *Sun* had achieved a paid daily circulation of almost twenty thousand—nearly five times greater than that of its largest six-penny rival, and nearly ten times that of the majority of the city's daily papers. Just who, Day's competitors must have been asking, *were* all these readers? Some, undoubtedly, were readers of the six-penny papers, who now took the *Sun* in addition to their morning copy of, say, the *Journal of Commerce* or the *Courier and Enquirer.* But far more numerous were those who had never before thought of themselves as newspaper readers, the very people Benjamin Day had hoped to reach when he first conceived of his new penny paper back in that tiny William Street print shop. Though New York had grown dramatically over the previous decade and a half, its population more than doubling (from 123,000 to 270,000), the circulation of the merchant papers had remained essentially constant. The thousands of new arrivals to New York had been drawn by the city's rapidly expanding economy, but they had little interest in the economic news offered by the six-penny papers; on the other hand, they were extremely interested in reports of life on the moon. New York's proud merchant editors must have bitterly resented the fact that this sensational and clearly lucrative story (one that had been extracted from a foreign journal, no less, which was their own specialty) had been discovered by the penny *Sun.* It was a galling development—but not so galling that they would, as a consequence, deny themselves the most talked-about news story of the age.

Before the week was out, many of the city's six-penny newspapers had begun to reprint the moon series on their own front pages.

Among the first to do so was the largest evening newspaper in New York, the *Evening Post*. On Friday, the day Locke introduced the man-bats to New York, the *Post* ran the first installment of *Great Astronomical Discoveries*. Inside, an editorial explained that the paper was copying the series just as it had been presented in the *Sun,* without feeling the need to "accompany it with any comments to shake the faith which credulous readers may be disposed to place in its authenticity." For the moment, at least, the *Post* was maintaining a position of neutrality about the veracity of the articles, stating that "The story is certainly, as the old newspaper phrase goes, 'very important, if true.' And if not true, the reader will still be obliged to confess that it is very ingenious."

On Saturday the *Commercial Advertiser* began running the series as well, in deference, noted its editor William Leete Stone, to "the request of many friends." Stone apparently felt obligated to print the moon story despite the fact that he personally disbelieved it; in the item accompanying the first installment he pointed out that the construction of such a massive and expensive telescope could not have escaped the notice of the British press. Still, Stone praised the story as "wonderful" and "ingenious," and suggested, in a sort of backhanded tribute to Locke's work, that it was not original to the *Sun* but had come instead from Great Britain. "We think we can trace in it marks of transatlantic origin," he wrote. (The merchant editors' many misjudgments about the moon series can be traced at least partially to their long-standing underestimation of the writers for the penny papers, whom they regarded as hacks possessing little culture or erudition; as Horace Greeley of the *New-Yorker* admitted, "We did not dream that any of the ordinary penny literati were capable of so magnificent a hoax.")

The city's oldest daily newspaper, the *Daily Advertiser,* likewise began running the series on Friday. "No article, we believe, has appeared for years, that will command so general a perusal and publication," stated the editorial that accompanied the first installment. "Sir John has added a stock of knowledge to the present age that will immortalize his name, and place it high on the page of science." A rival morning paper, the *Mercantile Advertiser,* quickly followed suit, declaring of the *Supplement,* "It appears to carry intrinsic evidence of being an authentic document." The *American,* an evening paper, ran the series as well, and another morning paper, the *Journal of Commerce,* began making its own plans to reprint it.

One of the city's smaller dailies, the *Spirit of '76,* generously complimented the *Sun* on its success: "Our enterprising neighbors of the *Sun,* we are pleased to learn, are likely to enjoy a rich reward from the late *lunar* discoveries. They deserve all they receive from the public—'they are worthy.'" The *Sunday News,* for its part, believed that John Herschel was the source of the story, but admitted to some skepticism about all he claimed to have seen; still, Sir John's reputation preceded him, and the paper was willing to withhold judgment until more information was available. "Our doubts and incredulity may be a wrong to the learned astronomer," wrote the *News* editorialist, "and the circumstances of this wonderful discovery may be correct. Let us do him justice, and allow him to tell the story in his own way." At the *New-Yorker,* Horace Greeley informed his readers (many of them, presumably, from out of town and not regular readers of the *Sun*) that John Herschel had been "successful in constructing a telescope of extraordinary power," with which "he has been enabled to discover not merely land and water, but clouds, tides, trees, verdure, rocks, and at last animals, in the moon, and to examine them carefully and almost minutely." Greeley concluded the item by declaring, "The promulgation of these discoveries creates a new era in astronomy and science generally."

Among the city's major six-penny papers, only the largest—the *Courier and Enquirer*—remained silent about the *Sun* series. This was not surprising, since the *Courier*'s editor, James Watson Webb, was unmatched in his disdain for hoi polloi who read, and wrote, the penny papers. For many months after the *Sun*'s founding Colonel Webb had refused to mention the new paper in his columns, as though it simply did not exist. Finally, in April 1834, when the pretense could no longer be sustained, Webb had composed an editorial lamenting the success of the newspaper he referred to as "penny trash." As late as February 1835 Webb had maintained in print that the *Courier and Enquirer* had the largest circulation of any newspaper in the city. (An indignant Benjamin Day offered Webb a wager of one thousand dollars that the *Sun*'s circulation was not just larger than the *Courier and Enquirer*'s but twice as large; Webb never took Day up on the bet.) At the time of the moon series Webb was occupied with important matters of his own, chiefly the Native American Democratic Association, which he had helped found a month earlier to aid in the fight against immigration and, he contended, the subversion of American political institutions by agents of the Roman Catholic Church.

Besides the *Sun* there were two other penny papers in New York, although only one of them was able to publish. As August drew to a close,
James Gordon Bennett was still tending to his beloved *Herald* in the wake
of the fire that had devastated the printing district earlier that month. (No
longer, he had decided, would the paper be called the *Morning Herald;*
just the *Herald* would do splendidly. His was a newspaper to be savored
all day long.) Bennett had found new offices in the basement of a building
on Broadway, and it is not difficult to imagine his frustration as he
awaited the installation of his double-cylinder printing press. Just when he
was catching up to the *Sun*, the Ann Street fire had wiped him out; and
then, when he could not respond, the *Sun* had come up with this new bit
of crowd-pleasing humbug. Bennett was certain that he knew who was
behind the moon series, and it was not John Herschel.

The city's other penny paper, the *Transcript*, was more fortunate than
the *Herald*, as it had managed to survive the fire and keep publishing. The
Transcript had been founded the year before by two former *Sun* printers;
they had learned well from Benjamin Day's example, and for a while their
paper had been able to keep pace with the *Sun* through lively local news
and sports reporting, as well as police court coverage by the blustering
Englishman William Attree. Now, thanks to the moon series, the *Sun* had
shot ahead once again and the *Transcript* needed to respond. It chose to
do so not with condemnation (of the sort that James Gordon Bennett
would so richly dole out) nor with duplication, but with satire. By Saturday the *Transcript* was lavishing tribute on John Herschel's wonderful discoveries, about which only a few persons in the city—"we believe a very
few"—harbored any doubts. And why should they? "The account, we
confess, is marvellous," declared the *Transcript*, "but not therefore necessarily false." In fact the *Transcript* knew the story to be true, for it had its
own Cape correspondent, a man who, like Dr. Andrew Grant, had been
with Sir John Herschel at his observatory; his name was Captain Thomas
Tarbox. Captain Tarbox confirmed the story told by Andrew Grant,
though he had some discoveries of his own to reveal, which for some reason had been overlooked by the *Edinburgh Journal of Science.*

According to Captain Tarbox, the intelligent creatures who had so enchanted the astronomers were not in fact man-bats but rather human beings, and their "wings" were really nothing more than large sleeves, which
were worn, according to contemporary lunar fashion, by males as well as
females. The men and women addressed each other by leaping up and

striking the soles of their feet with their hands; one especially eager young gentleman, on meeting a young lady, leaped so energetically into the air that he managed to disarrange her dress, a faux pas for which she boxed his ears, making them ring so loudly that the captain swore he could hear them all the way down at the Cape of Good Hope.

By the second installment of Captain Tarbox's account, editor Asa Greene was in full voice, creating a pitch-perfect lampoon of Andrew Grant's highly precise, occasionally orotund style. Tarbox had been present when the astronomers encountered that first poppy field, but unlike Dr. Grant he opted to close his eyes, fearing the sleep-producing effect of the *Papaver somniferum*. When he was sure the poppies were safely out of sight, he opened his eyes again, whereupon

I beheld the most magnificent flower that mortal eye ever rested upon. At least, I have seen nothing like it, though I have circumnavigated the globe seven times, and have visited every land from Dan to Beersheba, and from Kamtschatka to Terra del Fuego. It was a most gorgeous flower, waving on the top of a stalk seventy-seven feet high, and as large as the main-mast of the ship Sally, in which I made my last voyage to the East Indies. Its petals were of a beautiful and most dazzling white, interspersed here and there with stripes of yellow and purple; each petal being two feet six inches in width and eight feet ten inches in length. It belonged to the thirteenth *class* and first *order,* of Linnæus. The *stamens* were two feet in length, and about the size of my wife's pudding-stick, the shape whereof they very much resembled. The *pistil,* in size, would have served as a club for Hercules.

Captain Tarbox's account (entitled *More Lunar Discoveries, NOT contained in the Supplement to the Edinburgh Journal of Science*) was published in three installments, and for the first week it constituted the *Transcript*'s entire response to the *Sun* series. Unlike so many of the six-penny papers, the *Transcript* resisted reprinting the series until the following Wednesday, September 2, when it ran the opening excerpt of *Great Astronomical Discoveries* on its front page, alongside the first installment of a story that had not previously been seen in a New York newspaper. That story, which now bore the simple title *Lunar Discoveries,* presented a lengthy account of a balloon trip to the moon; its author was given as "Baron Hans Phaall, *the celebrated Dutch Astronomer and Aeronaut.*"

On Monday morning, the last day of August, Locke's man-bats made their final appearance in the pages of the *Sun*. At the edge of the forest surrounding the valley where the three triangular temples had been found (now dubbed by Sir John "the Vale of the Triads"), the astronomers came upon several groups of winged creatures that closely resembled the ones earlier seen in the Ruby Colosseum. These man-bats, however, were taller than the others, somewhat lighter in color, and according to Andrew Grant, "in *every respect* an improved variety of the race." They were highly sociable creatures and pleasingly well mannered; the astronomers observed many instances of a man-bat selecting the choicest specimen from a pile of the gourdlike fruit that constituted their diet and then tossing it to another who had none. As far as the astronomers could tell, these man-bats did not engage in any activities of art or industry, but rather spent their time happily collecting fruit, eating, bathing, and, as Grant remarked, "loitering about upon the summits of precipices."

Although the man-bats were unquestionably the highest order of creature in the valley (at one point Grant refers to them as "semi-human beings"), they were not its only denizens. Many of the animals that had been discovered elsewhere on the moon Sir John and his assistants found here too, as well as several new species of quadrupeds, the most impressive among them being a large white stag with antlers as black as ebony. Several times that elegant creature trotted over to nibble some vegetation alongside a group of seated man-bats; on those occasions the astronomers could see not a trace of fear in the stag or animosity in the man-bats. Indeed, all the creatures of the moon seemed to be living in what Grant termed a "universal state of amity," the contemplation of which gave great pleasure to the astronomers watching from earth, that larger but evidently less favored world. Thomas Dick and his fellow religious astronomers had apparently been correct in their suppositions about the moon being a kind of paradise, its inhabitants as blissful as those of "primitive Eden," in Andrew Grant's telling phrase. Now, in reflecting on all he had seen there, Grant found himself turning to the aid of the poets. When in the future, he wrote, he would "eye the blue vault, and bless the useful light" (as Alexander Pope had rendered Homer's line from the *Iliad*), he knew that he would recall the scenes of beauty and grandeur he had witnessed on the face of the moon; and never again would he think of Lord Byron's couplet, "Meek Diana's crest/ Sails through the azure air, an island of the blest," without exulting in the knowledge of its truth.

Exhausted by their evening's labors, Herschel and his three assistants made some final notations and then retired to their nearby bungalow. The next morning the astronomers were awakened by the excited shouts of some passing Boer farmers that the "big house" (as they quaintly termed it) was on fire. Sir John leaped from his bed and ran to the window, where to his horror he saw the observatory enveloped in thick black smoke. The telescope's great lens, which as a rule was lowered during the day, had unaccountably been left in a vertical position, which concentrated the rays of the sun. Everyone rushed to the burning observatory, whereupon the lens was immediately turned and the fire extinguished with water from a nearby brook. Fortunately, the building had been covered in a thick coat of Roman plaster or it would have burned to the ground. As it was, by the time the last of the flames had been put out much of the plaster had vitrified into blue glass, the hydro-oxygen microscope's reflectors had fused into useless clumps of metal, and the observatory's viewing wall, "on which had been exhibited so many wonders that will ever live in the history of mankind," had been totally destroyed. Masons and carpenters were summoned from Cape Town, and within a week the telescope was again ready for use, but by then the moon was invisible and John Herschel had redirected his attention to the planets.

Not until March was the weather again favorable enough for lunar observations, by which time Herschel was too absorbed in his cataloguing of the southern skies to explore the moon further. However, his assistants were eager to reacquaint themselves with their newly discovered lunar world, and on one of those clear nights, when Sir John was otherwise occupied, they turned the gaze of the retooled telescope back to the moon. In one of its northern regions they found several new species of horned animals and the ruins of three more triangular temples, but they made their most exciting discovery near the Atlas crater, where they found a third, highly superior variety of Vespertilio-homo. Though these man-bats were no larger than those seen earlier, they were far more beautiful: "scarcely less lovely," noted Grant, "than the general representations of angels by the more imaginative schools of painters." Their social life seemed to be regulated by rituals like those of the man-bats living in the Vale of the Triads, but their works of art were far more numerous, and executed with such skill that only the most expert of observers would be capable of describing them. As a result, Andrew Grant had decided to bring his correspondence to a close, and "let the first detailed account of them appear in Dr. Herschel's authenticated natural history of this planet."

So concluded the *Supplement to the Edinburgh Journal of Science,* but for an additional forty pages of mathematical notes that the editor of the *Sun*—that is to say, Richard Adams Locke—chose to omit because they did not add to the story's general interest. However, he included as an addendum a page from those notes, presenting a new geometrical approach to calculating the height of lunar mountains, so that the newspaper's readers might have a look at the great astronomer's work. "For ourselves," admitted the *Sun*'s editor, "we know nothing of mathematics beyond counting dollars and cents."

On the last morning of August, James Gordon Bennett awoke early, as he always did. He washed with cold water, a practice he had learned as a boy on a farm north of Aberdeen. *Cold water ablutions over the whole person every morning, cold or hot, summer or winter, wet or dry:* it was one of the rules for living that he would share with his readers a few years later, after the *Herald* had achieved its well-deserved success, that they might become as healthy and happy as he was. At five o'clock the sky was just growing pink; within the hour the sun would appear beyond the river, gilding the masts of the ships berthed at Peck Slip. To all outward appearances it was a morning like any other, but inside, surely, he felt that his birthday had come a day early, because today, at long last, the *Herald* was returning to New York.

Bennett took his usual breakfast of tea and a biscuit (*Strict temperance in eating and drinking, but not tetotalism toward good cooking and choice wines*) and set to work. Early morning was when he wrote his lighter paragraphs, the ones that so amused New Yorkers with their insouciance and daring. Among today's items was the case of a local barber pleading for leniency from a judge on the grounds that he had been shaving him for nearly two years. "He was dealt with," remarked Bennett, "with the keenness of razor, and compelled to pay a fine for his *barbar*ous actions." A geranium, he had heard, was growing on Broadway that had been taken from the tomb of Napoleon on St. Helena. Elsewhere on Broadway, at the City Saloon, the artist Hanington was still pleasing the crowds with his peristrephic dioramas, the latest of which was a representation of the Great Deluge, complete with waters and rainbow. Now, Bennett informed his readers, "Hanington has some idea of getting up a diorama of Herschell's lunar discoveries." (He proved to be correct about this: the new diorama would premiere before September was out.)

When his work was completed, Bennett left his room on Nassau Street and strode around the corner to his office at 202 Broadway, a former coal cellar that managed to retain its impressive dankness even in the heat of the summer. There he joyfully received his first copies of the newly reborn *Herald*.

"We are again in the field," he had proclaimed in the lead editorial, "larger, livelier, better, prettier, saucier, and more independent than ever." He reminded his readers that before the fire the *Herald* had reached a daily circulation of nearly seven thousand; soon, he vowed, its circulation would soar to twenty-five thousand, and that was "no astronomical dream—no Herschell discovery in the moon." He bade his readers a cheerful good morning and urged them to bring him the latest news on any subject, "barring always discoveries in astronomy, which our friends of the Sun monopolize."

Several times in that maiden issue he referred to the series that had propelled the *Sun* to such an unprecedented circulation—it was clearly working on his mind—as in one of the financial articles, when he reported that "a few large capitalists" were causing fluctuations in the stock market by making unscrupulous offers to young or otherwise naive merchants, attempting to "dazzle them with such visions as Doctor Herschell says he saw in the moon." This, however, was but little in comparison with the long item that ran below the headline "The Astronomical Hoax Explained," in which Bennett offered his readers what he claimed was the real story behind the *Sun* series. Like so much of James Gordon Bennett's *oeuvre,* the story was an intoxicating mixture of truth, half-truth, and outright libel.

The revelation came right at the beginning: "The town has been agape two or three days at the very ingenious astronomical hoax, prepared and written for the Sun newspaper, by Mr. Locke, formerly the police reporter of the Courier and Enquirer." As Bennett well knew, this was a bombshell sentence, for it was the first time Richard Adams Locke had been publicly named as the author of the moon series. "Mr. Locke is an Englishman by birth," continued Bennett, warming now to his subject, "a graduate of Oxford or Cambridge—was intended for the Church, but in consequence of some youthful love affair, getting a chambermaid in some aukward [*sic*] plight, abandoned religion for astronomy."

Having thus made free with the facts of Locke's history, Bennett next related how he and Locke had become acquainted when they both worked for the *Courier and Enquirer*. He had been impressed with Locke's talents and sympathized with him in his conflict with the *Courier*'s managing editor, Edward Hoskin, "a man," Bennett noted, "utterly incompetent to measure the extent of Mr. Locke's genius and acquirements." After Locke was dismissed from the *Courier and Enquirer* he had come to see Bennett, who was just starting up the *Herald*. Now Bennett claimed, astonishingly, that he was the one who suggested to Locke the idea of writing about Matthias the Prophet ("I told him a famous thing might be made out of the affair of Matthias"). During that conversation, Locke said that he had recently been "engaged on some scientific studies. He mentioned optics, and I think astronomy, as the particular branches." The two men saw each other again shortly afterward, Bennett said, at which point Locke was already busy "concocting his recent ingenious discoveries in the moon."

Still, Bennett continued, despite its "superlative drollery" Locke's work contained several telling mistakes, including a description of shadows on the moon ("incorrect on mathematical principles," he asserted) and the identification of John Herschel as an LL.D., a degree that the great astronomer did not possess. Perhaps most egregiously, the alleged "supplement" was said to have been issued by the *Edinburgh Journal of Science*—a publication, Bennett pointed out, that no longer existed.

In fact the *Edinburgh Journal of Science* had ceased publishing three years earlier, in 1832. It is possible that Richard Adams Locke was unaware that the journal was defunct, as he had left for New York in 1831, before it stopped publishing. However, in his 1852 account *The Celebrated "Moon Story," Its Origins and Incidents*, William Griggs suggested that Locke had simply erred in setting down the journal's name, and that he had really meant the *Edinburgh New Philosophical Journal*, the periodical that had published the views of Gruithuisen and his colleagues about the habitability of the moon. In either case, the misattribution was a major blunder on Locke's part, one serious enough to have derailed the moon series before it even began; but as Griggs pointed out, the series was so sensational, and Locke's writing of it so convincing, that no one seems to have noticed the mistake until James Gordon Bennett did—after *Great Astronomical Discoveries* had already concluded its run.

Despite his criticisms Bennett was unstinting in his praise of Locke's literary ability; "ingenious," he called him, "original," "brilliant." He always maintained a respect for his rival editor—this was, for Bennett, highly uncharacteristic—as well as a certain empathy, for though the two men could not have been further apart on the contentious issue of slavery, nor more different in their personalities, they had an unusual measure of shared experience, even beyond the odd coincidence that both were cross-eyed. (Locke's strabismus had resulted from a case of childhood smallpox; Bennett claimed that his had come from reading too much as a boy.) Both men were expatriate Britons; both had grown up on family farms; both resisted the careers urged on them by their fathers; both emigrated to America to find work as journalists; and both condemned the undue influence of religious authorities. The respect Locke had earned was indicated by the fact that Bennett (who had earlier called Benjamin Day and George Wisner "the garbage of society") referred to him always as "Mr. Locke" or, more familiarly, "Richard." So concluded Bennett's exposé of the "Astronomical Hoax":

> Mr. Locke, however, deserves great credit for his ingenuity—his learning—and his irresistible drollery. He is an original genius, and very gentlemanly in his manners. If he would come out and tell the public frankly the whole secret history of the hoax, he would lose nothing in character or in talents. We tender to him cheerfully the columns of the Herald for that purpose.

By the end of the day James Gordon Bennett had received his response from Richard Adams Locke, by way of an open letter delivered to the editor of the *Evening Star*. "SIR," it began:

> Some paragraphs, written by Mr. James Gordon Bennett, were put into my hand this morning, which, strangely enough, attribute to *me* the astonishing astronomical discoveries lately made at the Cape of Good Hope by Sir John Herschel. Mr. Bennett, in seeking for notoriety has found a mare's nest. I beg to state, as unequivocally as the words can express it, that I did *not* make those discoveries, and it is my sincere conviction, founded on a careful examination of the internal evidence of the work in which they first appeared, that, if made at all, they were made by the great astronomer to whom all Europe, if not incredulous America, will undoubtedly ascribe them. I have sought in vain for those discrepancies in the account which some half informed persons pretend to have detected. Nothing is said about those "shadows in the Moon," which Mr. Bennett, with an affectation of science says "are mathematically

incorrect"; and in the full work published this morning in the Sun office, the most scientific reader will find ample internal evidence to demonstrate its consistency and plausibility. . . .

Mr. Bennett takes the most indecorous liberties with the biography of so obscure an individual as myself. He says that after taking my degree at one of the English Universities, I took an unwarrantable degree of liberty with some chamber-maids. This is as untrue as it is impertinent. To give plausibility to his theory of the authorship of the astronomical discoveries, he says that I sometime since informed him I was directing my attention to astronomy and optics. I am sorry to be compelled to give this statement a flat contradiction. I said not a syllable to him upon the subject. If I mentioned my immediate pursuits at all, it was that I was engaged in writing a Latin Grammar. Optics indeed!—only think of two men squinting so curiously and contradictorily as we undeniably do, putting our noses together and discussing optics! Mr. Bennett's hypothesis is too ridiculous to receive any further notice from

Your obedient servant,
RICHARD ADAMS LOCKE

James Gordon Bennett reprinted Locke's letter in the next day's *Herald*—followed by his own response, of course, for he was not one to cede the last word. He had been delighted to receive such a clever, not to mention prompt, reply to his charges ("Good! excellent! admirable!" his response began), but clearly he was also taken aback by the vehemence with which Locke denied being the author of the moon series. Bennett had a dilemma: if any newspaperman in New York had the erudition and command of language to pull off such a magnificent hoax, it was Richard Adams Locke; but Locke, with his English background and knowledge of science, might equally well have been the one to receive a new scientific pamphlet from some "medical gentleman" just arrived from Scotland, as the *Sun* had claimed. Perhaps, Bennett mused, the truth lay somewhere in the middle. "Our friend Richard," he now hastened to clarify,

says we "attribute" to him "the astonishing discoveries made at the Cape, &c." We did no such thing. We only said he did the writing part—he dressed up the materials, he clothed the skeletons taken from scientific works with flesh—the bat-wings and golden hair and angel's apparel. The mathematical part was furnished by a gentleman recently from England, who has seen some private letters detailing the actual discoveries (modest they are in comparison to the Sun's account) which Sir John J. H. Herschell has made.

Bennett had earlier commended Locke for his "gentlemanly" manners, and these were on full display in the *Evening Star* letter. To the accusation of past impropriety with a chambermaid Locke had responded first with humility ("so obscure an individual as myself"), then with wit (the twinned use of the word *degree*), and then stout denial; most impressively, he had done so without resorting to invective of his own. James Gordon Bennett was used to being ignored by his rivals, or replied to with the insults that were the New York newspaper editor's stock in trade. ("Turkey buzzard," Mordecai Noah called him; "moral pestilence," said James Watson Webb; "lizard looking animal," said Benjamin Day.) Locke had chosen a finer course; if he were not careful, Bennett must have sensed, he would find the city turning against him. The *Herald*'s editor made a tactical retreat. "As to the 'indecorous liberties' we took with his 'biography,' 'the chambermaid, &c.' we take that back," he wrote. But he still insisted that Locke had claimed to be "very much engaged in optics and similar pursuits."

That last riposte by Locke, regarding their conversation about optics, must have been especially consternating for Bennett. To deftly parry his assertion with an amusingly self-deprecating reference to their mutual strabismus ("two men squinting so curiously and contradictorily as we undeniably do"), and then to dismiss the whole of the charges as unworthy of his further attention: Richard Adams Locke was exhibiting a rhetorical sophistication rare among New York editors. Nonetheless, Bennett remained convinced that the facts of the case were against him. "The whole note of Mr. Locke," he concluded, "furnishes 'ample internal evidence' for the belief we had that he has had a finger at least in this astronomical pie. He does not deny the thing plumply. He need not be ashamed of it, neither need he squint so awfully at us about the chamber-maid. We can return the look with seven per cent. interest. We still persist in our belief."

As he had promised in his letter, Richard Adams Locke did not again publicly respond to James Gordon Bennett's accusations. Thus he left the field to his adversary, who took full advantage. Day after day, Bennett hammered away at the *Sun*, denouncing it as a lying, swindling paper unfit to receive the public's trust; in the process he won the *Herald* legions of new readers, who considered it well worth a penny to find out what Bennett would say that morning. Once he tried his hand at satire, producing an item he called "A Better Story—Most Wonderful and Astounding Discoveries by Herschell the Grandson, LL.D., F.R.S., R.F.L., P.Q.R., &c. &c. &c." Like the *Transcript*'s earlier account by "Captain Tarbox," this item purported to bring news of additional discoveries from the observatory at the Cape of Good Hope. The first of the sightings was "the Editor of the New York Sun, seated on a three legged stool, with a great sledge hammer in his hand, forging 'truths,' in the same manner that Jove forged thunderbolts." Bennett's touch was not as light as Asa Greene's; he was much better at direct attack, as with the item in which he railed against the newspaper he called "the impudent Sun—the unprincipled Sun—the mercenary Sun—the low bred Sun—the Sun that hoaxes the public—that tells untruths for money—that cheats the whole city and country."

"Why still persist in cheating the public?" he asked in another item. "How many prints and pamphlets have they yet unsold?"

Bennett knew Richard Adams Locke to be an honorable man, and in emphasizing the profits the *Sun* had reaped from the moon series he seems to have been trying to prick Locke's conscience, like a constable badgering a wavering conspirator into a confession. James Gordon Bennett had made his name from insult, but he was equally adept at the calculated flattery that, by the 1830s, was already becoming known as the "soft soap."

> Mr. Locke has exhibited great ingenuity in the general keeping of the account. He wrote it, as we learn, to amuse a vacant hour, and out of the vigor and fulness of a vivid imagination. He has certainly exhibited talent of a very remarkable kind. Knowing as we do the amiableness of Mr. Locke's character, we do not charge him with the intention to deceive the public. He had no money making motive in the affair. It was as far as he is concerned, a mere *jeu d'esprit*, but the motives of the Sun editors are far different.

By the "Sun editors" Bennett was referring not to Locke but to Benjamin Day and, most likely, Day's brother-in-law Moses Yale Beach, a paper mill owner brought on to help manage the *Sun*'s financial affairs: men, Bennett believed, who cared little for truth and much for money. There was no harm in publishing Locke's *jeu d'esprit* and enjoying for a day or two the folly of those who believed it. "But now," he thundered, "when that paper in order to get money out of a credulous public, seriously persists in averting its truth, it becomes highly improper, wicked, and in fact a species of impudent swindling."

"Mr. Locke himself," Bennett assured his readers, "would never sanction such a course."

For his part, Mr. Locke was saying little. In those turbulent early September days, he was navigating a treacherous passage between truth and duty. Benjamin Day was his employer; the man had hired him at a time of great exigency, when he had been thrown out of work with a wife and daughter dependent on him, and that counted for a great deal. Moreover, Day had paid him well for the moon series, had purchased it as rightfully as any storekeeper buying a barrel of whiskey or molasses to resell at a profit. Locke felt himself bound to silence by contract, and at least as much by honor. The secret, he believed, was no longer his to tell.

There had been enough calumny in Bennett's first charges that Locke felt he must respond, both to clear his name and protect his wife's dignity— that outrageous claim about the chambermaid—and also to set the record straight about those allegedly incorrect "mathematical principles." Still, there was less to his *Evening Star* letter than it initially appeared. He had tried to uphold the *Sun*'s position without being overtly untruthful, by denying that he had made any "discoveries" (which of course he hadn't) rather than denying having written the series itself. At the same time, he had acknowledged some doubt about the genuineness of the discoveries by inserting the careful phrase "if made at all." (Bennett had picked right up on that: "*If* do you say?" he had crowed, before quoting Shakespeare: "'An if is your only peacemaker, much virtue in *if*.' *If* is also an astronomer and a great one. Is it not, Richard?")

When Locke was asked about the series, as he so often was those days, he tried as best he could to express no opinion on the subject, telling all who asked that the mails would soon arrive from Europe and the facts of the matter would then be known. What else could he say? He had not thought the series would be believed in the first place. Of course he had put a great deal of care into the writing, but he had never intended that it be taken as a genuine scientific work. If he had, he would not have filled the lunar "seas" with actual water, contrary to what all respectable modern astronomers believed about them. Nor would he have carefully graduated Herschel's discoveries, beginning with nonorganic matter (the basaltic rock), proceeding through plants (the poppy flowers) to trees, and finally to animal life of ever-greater intelligence, culminating with the man-bats, who themselves appeared in three varieties of increasing sophistication. While this steady progression made for excellent suspense, keeping the *Sun*'s readers in anticipation of what marvel would be discovered next, it was highly improbable that actual astronomers would make their discoveries in such a convenient order. This was the most obvious flaw of all in the series, but no one had even noticed it.

By the beginning of September a distressing word was starting to be heard around town in connection with his name: *hoaxer.* Meanwhile, Benjamin Day was growing rich from newspapers and pamphlets and prints. The *Sun*'s circulation had risen as quickly as a hot-air balloon shed of its ballast; now the *Herald* was rising in pursuit, with James Gordon Bennett in the basket below happily throwing darts in all directions. Unlike Bennett, Richard Adams Locke had never cultivated a public identity. Bennett had left the *Courier and Enquirer* when James Watson Webb refused to grant him a byline; Locke, on the other hand, had always preferred anonymity. He was not at all comfortable with the attention he was suddenly receiving; his good friend William Griggs remarked later that Locke had "suffered severely from the determined inquisitiveness of which he was necessarily the object."

The talk around town was that he had begun drinking more heavily. One evening he was having a drink in the taproom of the Washington Hotel on Broadway, when he was joined by a reporter friend of his named Finn. The two had worked together briefly at the *Sun* before Finn left to take a job at the six-penny *Journal of Commerce*. Finn mentioned that one of the *Journal*'s editors had instructed him to procure back copies of the *Sun,* so that they might reprint the moon series in the *Journal of Commerce*. The story, Finn said, was already being set into type and would likely appear the next morning.

Perhaps it was just a bit of advice to a journalist friend not to publish a false story; or perhaps, with his tongue loosened and his will weakened by drink, he could no longer hold the secret inside him.

"Don't print it right away," said Richard Adams Locke. "I wrote it myself."

CHAPTER 13

Moonshine

T HE SUMMER, at long last, was coming to an end. The heat departed as suddenly as it had arrived; now the mercury struggled to reach sixty during the days, and the nights hinted of frost. Cloaks and gloves appeared once more on the city's streets, along with black beaver hats and the new short-napped castors that were, this season, à la mode. In the countryside that rolled out beyond Fourteenth Street, the trees were tinged with red and gold, though the pastures remained as green as ever, nourished by the summer rains that seemed so long ago. "We hope that old winter will have more consideration for poor humanity, than to think seriously of commencing his career for two months to come, or to insist upon staying where he cannot but perceive he is altogether unwelcome," Asa Greene remarked in the *Transcript*. He could not resist adding, "We hope the late 'discoveries in the moon' have had nothing to do in this early recurrence of cold weather."

The *Transcript* could now, in September, feel a bit more comfortable in its joke. Rather than respond gratefully to a fellow journalist's warning, Finn of the *Journal of Commerce* had taken Richard Adams Locke's admission as a scoop, and the *Journal* ran an article that denounced the series as a hoax (though the paper continued to reprint it nonetheless), and named Locke as its author. With two of the city's newspapers having thus identified him, Richard Adams Locke became the most famous—or notorious—newspaperman in New York. "The name of the author of the 'Moon Hoax' was on everybody's lip," the magazine *Every Saturday* would recall years later.

In hindsight, Richard Adams Locke must have seemed the obvious culprit. Not only was he the editor of the newspaper to which the Edinburgh supplement had allegedly been provided, but he was well-known for his learnedness, at least within the few blocks of New York's newspaper district. (No one seems to have been aware that he had not attended "one of the English Universities," as he vaguely expressed it in his letter to the *Evening Star.*) Moreover, Locke's Matthias pamphlet had demonstrated that he could comfortably handle the demands of a long narrative. By September, then, with Locke under heavy suspicion and the man-bats having produced their artwork in the shadow of their temples (a scene that even the most credulous reader might find difficult to credit), the moon series retained few supporters among the city press. Even the *Daily Advertiser,* once its strongest advocate, now acknowledged that the series was an "article of fiction." New York's other newspapers branded it a hoax, if a particularly ingenious one.

That charge was soon taken up by newspapers around the country. "The Great Hoax," the series was called in the *Indiana Democrat* of Indianapolis; "Stupendous Hoax," said St. Louis's *Missouri Republic;* "A Consummate Hoax," declared the Mobile *Daily Commercial Register and Patriot.* But even as they denied the truth of the story, America's newspapers could not resist printing it. Throughout the month, as the mail from New York traveled farther west, newspapers brought the series to readers in Boston, Providence, Philadelphia, Baltimore, Cincinnati, Chicago, and many smaller cities and towns. *Great Astronomical Discoveries* became the most widely circulated newspaper story of its time. "With our American papers, it seems to be a subject that never tires," Locke observed in the *Sun,* adding an apt citation from *Hamlet:* "They resume it again and again, as if their appetite had increased by what it fed on." New York's editors, having envied the *Sun* its moon series in August, now had to see it again in September, in the newspapers they received in free exchange from around the country. "Our exchange papers are filled with the clever hoax of discoveries in the Moon," noted the *Evening Star.* "We wish for the sake of news, that the moon would stand still."

For its part, the *Sun* did not admit to having perpetrated a hoax (a decision so important would presumably have been made by Benjamin Day himself), but as the month went along its denials became less insistent. On Tuesday, September 1, the day after the series concluded, the *Sun* had issued its strongest defense of the series—though without ever quite claiming it to be genuine. Instead, the paper focused attention on its rivals, praising the newspapers that had accepted the discoveries as "the sensible, candid and scientific portions of the public press" and condemning its more skeptical contemporaries as those "to whom none of those attributes can be ascribed." To profess disbelief of the Herschel series, the *Sun* seemed to be saying, was to cast oneself with the enemies of science, even of reason itself.

As might be expected, given Richard Adams Locke's political beliefs, much of the *Sun*'s argument for the series—specious as Locke surely knew it to be—was framed by the conflict between science and religion. Ignorance, he pointed out, had always found cause to doubt the most important scientific discoveries, but in matters of religion it "could swallow any dogmas, however great, that are given upon the authority of names." He recalled how "those who in a former age imprisoned Galileo for asserting his great discoveries with the telescope, and determined upon sentencing him to be burnt alive, nevertheless believed that Simon Magus actually flew in the air by the aid of the devil." New York's newspapers were hardly immune from what he termed "the most improbable credenda of extravagant systems of faith." The *Journal of Commerce,* he noted, had denounced the moon series, and yet that paper—the two editors of which were both devout Christians—"believes and defends the innocence of the murderer Avery." (Reverend Ephraim K. Avery was the Methodist minister acquitted by a Rhode Island jury of the murder of a young woman; Richard Adams Locke had served as court reporter for the trial.)

Locke concluded the item with a reference to the mathematical calculations, said to have been extracted from a page of John Herschel's notes, that had appeared the day before in the *Sun*. He claimed to have received assurances from "several eminent mathematicians" that the work was correct, and indeed "the greatest mathematical discovery of the present age." These testimonials he asserted as evidence of the *Supplement*'s authenticity. "We did not make it," Locke insisted about the work, "for we know nothing of mathematics whatever." While the first part of that statement may have been true enough, the same cannot be said for his conclusion: "therefore, it was made by the only person to whom it can rationally be ascribed, namely Herschel the astronomer, its only avowed and undeniable author." As Locke surely understood, there was no logical reason why, if the calculations had not been made by the editor of the *Sun*, they had therefore been made by John Herschel. In fact, he had taken the calculations from a recently published paper by Wilhelm Olbers (the German astronomer mentioned alongside Gruithuisen and Gauss in the *Edinburgh New Philosophical Journal* article "The Moon and its Inhabitants")—a paper, presumably, that had not yet been read by those "several eminent mathematicians."

Locke was working too hard, reaching too far, to make his claims for the genuineness of *Great Astronomical Discoveries;* surely he was growing tired of having to defend a proposition that could not be truthfully defended. Indeed, in his subsequent comments on the topic he sought to shift the discussion away from the authenticity of the moon series to the other subject that so occupied the city's attention: the abolition of slavery. By the end of the week the *Sun* was asserting:

> We go from the genuineness of the discoveries because we like a sprinkle of the marvellous and because we hope that, by directing all eyes to the ladies and gentlemen of the moon, there will be less devilment practiced on earth. We are curious to know whether *Lynch Law* exists amongst our Lunar neighbors, or whether they have not yet arrived at that degree of *refinement!*

"Lynch law," a term that seems to have entered into common usage in 1835, referred to mob violence, most often directed against blacks and abolitionists. ("Lynching" at that time applied to many kinds of violence and not just to hanging, as the term came to be understood later.) All through that autumn, alongside its regular coverage of local crime and entertainment, the *Sun* carried news of the latest outrages: a former seminarian in Kentucky seized by a mob and whipped until nearly dead, the Boston abolitionist William Lloyd Garrison paraded about the city with a noose around his neck, a Presbyterian minister hanged in Louisiana for distributing abolition pamphlets. As always, the *Sun* directed much of its outrage against the newspapers sympathetic to the Southern cause—those whom Locke denounced as "the purchased, the collared, the hungry pack of New York editors, who, under the plausible pretext of crying down the immediate abolitionists, have been struggling to destroy the moral sense of the community with regard to the iniquity of slavery." For instance, a long article in the *Courier and Enquirer* had asserted the right of slaveholding states to demand the extradition of the abolitionist leader Arthur Tappan to the South (where he would surely face execution, if not by legal decree then by Lynch law). "What if we were to write an article," the *Sun* inquired, "to prove that the British government at Botany-bay has an international right to one of the Courier editors?"

On September 16, the *Sun* brought together the two issues by means of a curious apologia for the moon series: it had provided a welcome respite from the nationwide conflict over slavery.

Most of those who incredulously regard the whole narrative as a hoax, are generously enthusiastic in panegyrizing not only what they are pleased to denominate its ingenuity and talent, but also its useful effect in diverting the public mind, for a while, from that bitter apple of discord, the abolition of slavery; which still unhappily threatens to turn the milk of human kindness into the rancorous gall. That the astronomical discoveries have transiently had this effect, is obvious from our exchange papers; for abolition and astronomy being the only matters of exciting interest on the tapis, all the brilliant editorializing which have been expended on the latter, would have become inflammable matter devoted to increase the combustible horrors of the former. Who knows, therefore, whether these discoveries in the moon, with the visions of the blissful harmony of her inhabitants which they have revealed, may not have had the effect of reproving the discords of a country which might be as happy as a paradise! which has valleys not less lovely than those of the Ruby Colosseum, of the Unicorn, or of the Triads; and which has not inferior facilities for social intercourse, to those possessed by the vespertiliones-hominem, or any other hominem whatever?

Richard Adams Locke, who daily chronicled in the *Sun* the horrors being visited on slaves and abolitionists, surely did not believe that his moon story would have any discernible effect on the enduring institution of slavery; but in September of 1835, as race riots still raged throughout the country, he must have found some brief pleasure in imagining that it might.

By the middle of September the moon story had grown beyond the confines of journalism and entered the realm of popular culture. On September 14, just two weeks after the final installment of *Great Astronomical Discoveries,* a play inspired by the *Sun*'s series premiered at the Bowery Theatre. The Bowery had opened in 1826 as one of New York's largest and most fashionable theaters—it was the first in the country to have a stage lit entirely by gas—and within its first four years had twice burned to the ground. The rebuilt theater, like so many of the city's newer structures, was designed in the Greek Revival style; modeled on the Temple of Theseus in Athens, it had great Doric columns and a portico patriotically ornamented with a large golden eagle. The interior was just as magnificent, especially the boxes, painted gold in the front and a delicate pink in the back (to show off their occupants to best advantage), where tickets cost seventy-five cents; tickets for the gallery cost a quarter, while down in the pit, where the newsboys reigned, a seat could be had for just three and a half cents.

The Bowery's program usually comprised a selection of short plays, which by the middle of September included the new comic extravaganza *Moonshine, or Lunar Discoveries,* written by the manager of the theater, Thomas Hamblin. It starred Henry J. Finn (not the Finn who worked for the *Journal of Commerce*), the immensely popular actor who was reprising his role as Major Jack Downing, a character originally created by the Maine humorist Seba Smith. In *Moonshine,* the sharp-witted Major Downing becomes embroiled in a series of comical misadventures with the lunar inhabitants King Moonshine, Prince Mooncalf, and Lord Pigeon Wing. The actual plot of the play is no longer remembered (it seems to have eluded even some of those in the audience), but in the climactic scene Major Downing, having failed to bag a flock of man-bats with his rifle, blows them up with a highly combustible bundle of abolitionist tracts. *Moonshine,* the *Sun* declared, was "the most amusing thing that has been on these boards for a long time," and it played to overflow audiences for the length of its run at the Bowery—one that was all too brief, because the next week Finn had to leave town to play an engagement elsewhere.

Fortunately, New Yorkers could soon enjoy another spectacle inspired by Locke's moon series. At the City Saloon on Broadway, the resident artist Henry Hanington had long been delighting crowds with his moving dioramas (peristrephic dioramas, he called them), vast rotating canvases with sound and light effects carefully designed to create the illusion of reality. Hanington had made a great hit with "The Deluge," his rendering of the biblical account of the Great Flood, from the darkening of the heavens to the advent of the rainbow and the return of the dove. It was followed by the equally dramatic (if less morally elevated) "The Storm and Shipwreck," with its remarkable effects of rain and lightning and thunder. A more relaxing tone was then established with the pastoral "Scene in Italy," a trip through the Italian countryside that culminated in a funeral procession of monks by torchlight, who laid their companion to rest to the solemn tolling of the abbey bell. The final diorama, "The Conflagration of Moscow," depicted the burning of Moscow by the city's residents as Napoleon's army approached; in the climactic scene, conducted to the sound of distant explosions, a Russian patriot set fire to the castle of his ancestors and then fled to the surrounding forests to join the struggle against the French invaders.

On September 28, these dioramas were joined by another, called "Lunar Discoveries," which illustrated "the reported Lunar observations of Sir John Herschell." It was the most ambitious spectacle that Henry Hanington had yet conceived. Painted on more than one thousand feet of canvas, the diorama managed to portray the entire lunar landscape, from the Ruby Colosseum to the Vale of Triads: all the mountains, volcanoes, lakes, and rivers of the moon, and its various inhabitants as well, which could be seen, promised the advertisements, "with their natural motions to resemble life." (Hanington's renderings of the man-bats were apparently so realistic that during one performance a Newfoundland dog belonging to an audience member began to howl whenever one of them appeared. The dog was "baying at the moon," joked one observer.)

For Richard Adams Locke, who was among the thousands of New Yorkers to attend a showing of Hanington's dioramas that month, it must have been a deeply affecting experience to see the work of his imagination—work that had become such an object of contention and controversy—so exquisitely rendered on the artist's immense canvas. There, spread out before him, were the crystal mountains, the hills of amethyst and topaz. The island volcanoes actually seemed to be erupting with smoke and streams of what appeared to be genuine lava; the lunar cataracts rushed and roared; golden pheasants filled the groves with their sweet music; the winged man-bats soared high overhead.

It was, reported the *Sun*, "the most unique and beautiful spectacle ever beheld."

AMONG the many avid readers of the moon series was Caleb Weeks of Jamaica, Long Island, who shortly afterward embarked on a ship bound for Cape Town. Weeks was locally prominent as the owner of a menagerie—a traveling collection of animals, something of a precursor to the modern-day circus. In the 1830s, menageries were a highly competitive but flourishing business; they enjoyed a near-universal appeal, as they were at once unabashedly showy (a menagerie would often make its entrance into town as a long caravan of brightly painted wagons, its arrival heralded by a marching band) and at the same time unassailably educational, introducing their patrons to the wonders of the natural world. By 1835 sixteen traveling menageries were competing for the public's attention, including James and William Howe's New York Menagerie, which boasted an elephant, two leopards, a camel, a gnu, two ostriches, a pelican, several guinea pigs, and an albino raccoon. The rival Boston and New York Menagerie had much the same brood (not, it seems, the albino raccoon), along with a polar bear, a tapir, an ichneumon, and a display of wax figures. Another menagerie had a rhinoceros said to have been purchased from the Crown Prince of Calcutta. Caleb Weeks's own menagerie had been the first to exhibit a giraffe, perhaps the most astonishing of all the African mammals. (The giraffe proved to have an unforgivingly delicate constitution, for it soon died; its skeleton, however, was carefully preserved and displayed for many years afterward.) The proprietor of a menagerie had always to be scouring the world in search of never-before-seen creatures to capture the public imagination—and so Caleb Weeks had set out to Cape Town, in the hopes that in the jungles of southern Africa he might find an animal that was as remarkable as the giraffe, but also more durable.

At his hotel, Weeks inquired at the front desk about where he might find Sir John Herschel, the eminent British astronomer. He was delighted to learn that Sir John was in that very hotel, and would cordially agree to meet him. The name of that hotel is no longer known, but it would have been one of the few grand hotels that Cape Town could then offer, the type that attempted to re-create at the farthermost tip of Africa the splendor of English club life, with thick draperies and plump chairs and sideboards groaning with decanters of brandy and Madeira: grand enough that John Herschel visited nearly every afternoon (his observatory was some five miles away), sitting in a cozy back parlor where he smoked his daily pipe and read the journals newly arrived from Europe and America.

Much like his fellow showman P. T. Barnum, Caleb Weeks was a man who enjoyed nothing better than a jest. (His obituary described him as "a person possessed of a fund of humor and merriment rarely met with.") Entering the parlor where the world-famous astronomer awaited him, he identified himself and solemnly announced that he had the honor of presenting Sir John with the American report of his "great astronomical discoveries."

Surprise passed across John Herschel's face, his large pale eyes growing briefly larger. He was certainly flattered by the attention, he said after a moment, but he could not conceive how there might be an American report of his activities, as he had not yet written a report on the subject himself.

That might well be, Weeks answered, but the information must have gotten out somehow, because here was the full account in print—and with that he presented Herschel with the issues of the *Sun* containing installments of the moon series, and the pamphlet *A Complete Account of the Late Discoveries in the Moon.* Then, with a bow, he excused himself and left the astronomer to his reading.

Weeks rejoined the other members of his expedition in the hotel's public room; no more than a few minutes later John Herschel strode into the room in a state of great excitement. "This is a most extraordinary affair!" he exclaimed. "Is this really a reprint of an Edinburgh publication, or an elaborate hoax by some person in New York?"

He could not say for certain, Caleb Weeks replied; all he knew was that every word of the articles was believed in New York—and, as the well-known maxim had it, "what everybody says must be true."

Sir John laughed at this, and invited Weeks and his party back to his private room, where he peppered them with questions about the story. Weeks related the events in as much detail as he could provide—he was, by every account, a skilled raconteur—and Herschel listened with mounting surprise and amusement. For the duration of Weeks's stay, Sir John sought him out to ask him new questions about the series, at one point good-naturedly remarking that he feared the actual results of his observations at the Cape would be considered very humble compared to those ascribed to him in the American account.

That was the first time that John Herschel heard about Locke's moon series, but it was by no means the last. Not long after Caleb Weeks's visit, Herschel received the letter from the royal hydrographer, Sir Francis Beaufort, asking if he knew about the discoveries claimed in his name; it was in his reply to Beaufort that Herschel recounted the anecdote about the American clergyman who anticipated raising funds from his congregation to send Bibles to the moon. Months later, on August 21, 1836—as it happened, one year to the day from the *Sun*'s first announcement of the forthcoming series—Herschel wrote another letter on the subject, this one addressed to the editor of the *Atheneum,* the respected London journal of science, literature, and the arts. The letter seems to have been provoked by a recent English publication of the moon series, very likely the pamphlet

Some Account of the Great Astronomical Discoveries Lately Made by Sir John Herschel at the Cape of Good Hope, published in 1836 by the prominent London bookseller and publisher Effingham Wilson.

As I perceive by an Advertisement in one of the London Newspapers now before me that the nonsense alluded to in the heading of this letter after running the round of the American and French journals has at last found a London Editor, it appears to me high time to disclaim all knowledge of or participation in the incoherent ravings under the name of discoveries which have been attributed to me. I feel confident that you will oblige me therefore by inserting this my disclaimer in your widely circulated and well conducted paper, not because I have the smallest fear that any person possessing the first elements of optical Science (to say nothing of Common Sense) could for a moment be misled into believing such extravagancies, but because I consider the precedent a bad one that the absurdity of a story should ensure its freedom from contradiction when universally repeated in so many quarters and in such a variety of forms. Dr. Johnson Indeed used to say that there was nothing, however absurd or impossible which if seriously told a man every morning for breakfast for 365 days he would not end in believing— and it was a maxim of Napoleon that the most effective figure in Rhetoric is Repetition. Now I should be sorry, for my own sake as well as for that of truth, that the world or even the most credulous part of it, should be brought to believe in my personal acquaintance with the man in the moon—well knowing that I should soon be pestered to death for private anecdotes of himself and his family, and having little intention and less inclination to humour the hoax, should come to be looked on as a very morose and uncommunicative sort of person when it was found that I could or would say no more about him than what is already known to all the world—vis that he

"drinks claret"

"Eats powdered beef turnip & carrot"

and that "a cup of old Malaya Sack"

"Will fire the pack at his back."

John Herschel was not an especially vain man, not the sort who worried overmuch about prestige or reputation. Still, he was the preeminent astronomer of his time, recipient of all the scientific honors the Crown had to offer; he had traveled to the other side of the world to honor and extend his father's valuable research, and it would only be natural if at a certain point he became angry that, through no fault of his own, his good name had been inextricably linked with these "incoherent ravings." Despite his jocular allusion to the old English verse about the claret-drinking man in the moon, the tone of his letter was unmistakably harsh and revealed, perhaps, more of the great man's distress than he might have wished: for, having written it, Herschel reconsidered and decided not to send the letter.

He did, however, send a different letter—a private one, not meant for public consumption. It was dated January 10, 1837; by then nearly a year and a half had elapsed since the first publication of the moon series, during which time John Herschel had clearly been asked more about it, not just on a few occasions but again and again, from correspondents around the world. At the end of an otherwise cheerful letter to his Aunt Caroline, Herschel added an exclamatory postscript, describing a situation he surely had not envisioned on that pleasant afternoon with Caleb Weeks: "I have been pestered from all quarters with that ridiculous hoax about the Moon—in English French Italian & German!!"

ENGLISH, French, Italian, German: by the time John Herschel sent his complaint to his aunt, the series about his supposed lunar discoveries had been published in those languages and many more besides. Within months of its publication, leading newspapers in London, Edinburgh, and Paris had received copies of the *Sun*'s pamphlet and reprinted it without reference to its New York origins. While the newspapers' editors had likely read about the moon series in the American papers, the pamphlet provided the story whole and complete—and even if the editors personally believed the lunar discoveries to be a hoax, it made a far more interesting story for their readers if the account were presented just as it had been received, as a "supplement" to the *Edinburgh Journal of Science*. Even the newspapers of Edinburgh, which undoubtedly recognized the story as not emanating from their city, published it, as William Griggs recounted, "with all the gravity and reserve of a synod or council of sages." Before long the series had spread across Europe, appearing in newspapers in Germany, Switzerland, Italy, Spain, and Portugal. In some of the interior parts of Germany, Griggs claimed in his 1852 account, the story had not yet been contradicted, and nearly two decades later was still taken by much of the populace as gospel.

Portrait of a man-bat, from an edition of the moon series published in Naples.
(Courtesy of the New York Public Library.)

In 1836 a complete German edition of the story was published in Hamburg under the title *Neueste Berichte vom Cap der guten Hoffnung über Sir John Herschel's astronomische Entdeckungen*. In Italy two editions were published, one in Naples and one in Milan; the Naples edition, entitled *Delle scoperte fatte nella luna del Dottor Giovanni Herschel*, featured a large illustration of a Vespertilio-homo; this man-bat, though, bore little resemblance to Locke's description, as he had shoulder-length hair and a full beard, and for some reason balanced himself on one foot, arms raised gracefully above him, as though preparing for a grande jeté. A less fanci-

A busy lunar landscape, as depicted in a Welsh edition of the moon series. Note the plume of smoke issuing from the hut of the biped beavers.

(Frontispiece of *Hanes y Lleuad* © The British Library Board. All Rights Reserved.)

ful illustration could be found in the pamphlet *Hanes y Lleuad; yn gosod allan y rhyfeddodau a ddarganfyddwyd gan Syr John Herschel*, published in the Welsh town of Llanrwst. That delightful pen-and-ink drawing, its lines as thick and sturdy as those of a medieval woodcut, depicted four of the Vespertilio-homo in animated conversation in the shade of a tree, the group framing a seated mother man-bat cradling her baby; elsewhere, other man-bats frolic at the water's edge among various shore birds, in the background a hairy bison and several of the biped beavers, their hut issuing a plume of smoke, just as was described in the text.

In France, no fewer than four editions of the complete moon series were issued, three from Paris and the other from Bordeaux. When the French astronomer François Arago first read the story, likely in one of the newspapers, he became immediately incensed at the liberties that had been taken with the reputation of his friend John Herschel. Arago was the country's leading astronomer, serving simultaneously as director of the Paris Observatory and permanent secretary of the Académie des sciences; he was himself a pluralist who believed in the possibility of life on comets as well as the sun ("If one asked me whether the sun can be inhabited by beings organized in a manner analogous to those which populate our globe," he wrote, "I would not hesitate to make an affirmative response"), but he understood at once that these discoveries did not bear the stamp of John Herschel's work. Considering himself duty-bound to defend the honor of his friend, he brought the matter directly to the academy. He entreated his colleagues to condemn what he believed was a malicious defamation of Sir John Herschel, who of all men should be immune from such ridicule, who was at that very moment—and here Arago's voice surely rose to fill the hall—engaged in an invaluable scientific mission in one of the remotest regions of the earth, labors from which all mankind would benefit, and it was the solemn responsibility of their Academy to protect him from such a poisonous attack as this one. That he was correct in his interpretation would be immediately apparent from the translation that he held in his hand. With that, François Arago commenced to read aloud *Great Astronomical Discoveries,* all eleven thousand words of it. The other members of the Academy apparently found the story less invidious than did Arago; his reading was met by "repeated interruptions from uncontrollable and uproarious laughter." In the end, however, Arago got his wish: the French Academy of Sciences passed a resolution that officially declared the lunar discoveries "utterly incredible."

By the end of September 1835, the *Sun* had still not admitted its role in the alleged discoveries; in print, as in private, Richard Adams Locke continued to counsel patience. Perhaps he was waiting for Benjamin Day to release him from his silence; perhaps he hoped the furor would soon abate. "Certain correspondents have been urging us to come out and confess the whole to be a hoax," he acknowledged in one item;

> but this we can by no means do, until we have the testimony of the English or Scotch papers to corroborate such declarations. In the meantime, let every reader of the account examine it, and enjoy his own opinion. Many intelligent and scientific persons still believe it true, and will con-

tinue to do so to their lives' end; whilst the scepticism of others would not be removed though they were in Dr. Herschel's observatory itself.

In that same item, Locke wrote that some readers had suggested that the entire series was but "an elaborate satire upon the monstrous fabrications of the political press of the country"—with the different species of lunar animals meant to represent various newspaper editors. Locke did not give any credence to this rather antic theory, although he did amusedly confess that the "idea of intended satire somewhat shook our own faith in the genuineness of the extracts." Still, it was the first time that he had referred to the possibility of the moon series being a satire; with this reference, at last, he was edging closer to the truth.

Meanwhile, at the *Herald*, James Gordon Bennett kept up his relentless cannonade. "The hoax is now complete," he wrote on September 3. "The Sun can never thrive hereafter upon the moon or any other planet. It will sink—it has already sunk to its original inanity and insipidity. A newspaper can only attain a sterling character by a sustained and sustaining intellect. People are already beginning to be disgusted with its monstrous mendacity." Two days later, Bennett told his readers he had learned that Richard Adams Locke was completing a novel "on a subject similar to that of his recent able invention of astronomy." Of course, Bennett well knew that Locke had not written any such novel (nor would he ever write one); he was simply joking, teasing the *Sun* about the fiction of the moon series, but in his jest he had hit upon a genuine insight. "Mr. Locke," Bennett declared, "has opened a new vein, as original, as curious, as beautiful, as any of the greatest geniuses that ever wrote. He looks forward into the future, and adapts his characters to the light of science." It was, pronounced the item's headline, a "New Species of Literature." Bennett dubbed this genre the "scientific novel," but readers of a later age would know it instead as science fiction.

As his rival and admirer James Gordon Bennett had so presciently observed, with *Great Astronomical Discoveries* Richard Adams Locke might well be considered the originator of American science fiction. This was a distinction, however, that history would more often accord to the author of "Hans Phaall—A Tale," the short story that the *Transcript* finished serializing on the very day Bennett's item appeared. At the end of the final installment, the *Transcript* raised the question of a sequel: "And now, as regards the residue of the adventures and doubtless highly important dis-coveries of Hans Phaall in the moon, will they not be published, as were the preceding, in the Southern Literary Messenger?"

Less than a week later, the author of "Hans Phaall" (who was now an editor of the *Southern Literary Messenger*) wrote a highly agitated letter to a friend, one that contained a question of his own. "Have you seen the 'Discoveries in the Moon'?" he asked.

"I am convinced that the idea was stolen from myself."

CHAPTER 14

Monck Mason's Flying Machine

IN THE LATE SUMMER of 1835, walking to work, Edgar Allan Poe had to pass a strangely familiar sight. The offices of the *Southern Literary Messenger* stood right next door to the storehouse of Ellis & Allan, his late stepfather's tobacco brokerage firm, a place he had often visited as a boy. On those warm mornings, when all the windows in Richmond's business district were thrown open, he would arrive at the corner of Fifteenth and Main and smell again the distinctively sweet, faintly licorice scent of Virginia tobacco; at such times he must have felt himself momentarily plunged back to the happier days of his childhood, though the memories were darkened now with resentment about the patrimony he had been denied.

Poe was twenty-six years old, and still unable to support himself by his writing. In early August, the publisher of the *Southern Literary Messenger,* Thomas Willis White, had hired him as assistant editor at a salary of $520 a year. The offer could not have come at a better time—an entry in the diary of his friend John Pendleton Kennedy noted that Poe had been living "in a state of starvation"—but he had accepted the job with misgivings because it meant moving to Richmond, leaving behind his aunt Maria Clemm and his young cousin Virginia, for whom he had recently developed strong romantic affections. The separation from his Baltimore family grieved him no end, and contributed to the ill habit he had lately acquired, of drinking in the morning before work, which in turn contributed to the black moods of despair that increasingly overtook him.

"My feelings at this moment are pitiable indeed," he wrote to Kennedy on September 11. "I am suffering under a depression of spirits such as I have never felt before."

He had no time now, or energy, for writing poetry or tales. His days were instead filled with the routine tasks of office work, filling subscriptions, maintaining correspondence, correcting proofs, though he did manage to write frequent book reviews, a task that he always undertook with great seriousness. No matter how hard he worked, the pile of mail on his desk seemed never to diminish, the pace of books arriving for review never slackened, the shouts for copy from the printers in the front room never grew less insistent. At the end of August a letter from Aunt Maria, suggesting that she and Virginia might go live with his cousin Neilson Poe, sent him into a greater depression. His skin, always strikingly pale, now seemed even paler; he must have been biting his nails to the quick, as he always did when he was nervous or agitated.

His state of mind grew even worse when he learned that one of his stories had been ill used by newspapermen in New York. In his September 11 letter to John Pendleton Kennedy, in which he described himself as "miserable" and "wretched" and begged Kennedy for some form of consolation, Poe still took time to inquire:

> Have you seen the "Discoveries in the Moon"? Do you not think it altogether suggested by *Hans Phaal?* It is very singular,—but when I first purposed writing a Tale concerning the Moon, the idea of *Telescopic* discoveries suggested itself to me—but I afterwards abandoned it. I had however spoken of it freely, & from many little incidents & apparently trivial remarks in those *Discoveries* I am convinced that the idea was stolen from myself.

Poe's conviction was surely strengthened by the response he received from Kennedy the following week, with its reference to the series that had recently concluded in the *Transcript:* "More than yourself have remarked the coincidence between Hans Phaal & the Lunar Discoveries and I perceive that in New York they are republishing Hans for the sake of comparison." The "coincidence" between the two stories must have made a very strong impression on Poe; he would return to it in print on at least three occasions: in 1839, in the appendix of his first short-story collection, *Tales of the Grotesque and Arabesque;* again in 1844, in the letters from New York that he wrote for the *Columbia Spy* newspaper of Pottsville, Pennsylvania (later collected under the title *Doings of Gotham*); and once more in 1846, in the essay on Locke for his *Literati of New York City* series, published in the Philadelphia fashion magazine *Godey's Lady's Book.*

In one of his *Columbia Spy* letters, Poe claimed that in the fall of 1835 he had included in the *Southern Literary Messenger* a critique of the many "philosophical blunders" of the moon series. (By philosophical Poe meant scientific; science was then widely known as "natural philosophy.") However, the issues of the *Messenger* from that period do not reveal any such critique, and Poe did not repeat this assertion in his other discussions of the moon series. But he never stopped insisting that the series was rife with scientific errors, and always maintained that he had recognized them right away. "No sooner had I seen the paper than I understood the jest," he recalled in his essay on Locke, adding pointedly, "which not for a moment could I doubt had been suggested by my own *jeu d'esprit.*"

Poe must have found it supremely galling to watch helplessly from Richmond as *Great Astronomical Discoveries* created an international sensation—this story that he considered to be so riddled with flaws, so less worthy of acclaim than his own. The divergent responses given the two stories was a subject that he long mused about, and over time he came to understand that he had made two critical mistakes with "Hans Phaall." First, he had published it in a literary journal, whereas the moon series had appeared in a newspaper; readers of a literary journal would immediately assume that a story was fiction, while newspaper readers would assume that it was fact. Second, the author of the moon series had maintained a serious tone throughout, never letting on to his readers that what had been written was anything less than the absolute truth; Poe, on the other hand, had begun "Hans Phaall" with a comic scene—the one in which the strange creature appears over Rotterdam in a balloon—imparting to his story a tone that was (as he would later ruefully characterize it) "half plausible, half bantering." These two issues, in Poe's view, had doomed "Hans Phaall" to be nothing more than a short story, when what he had really wanted to create, he understood now, was a hoax.

For the rest of his life Edgar Allan Poe would be fascinated by hoaxes. He would produce several of his own, of varying degrees of seriousness, including the first book of prose he ever published, the novella entitled *The Narrative of Arthur Gordon Pym,* a seafaring adventure purportedly written by the sailor Pym himself. As he had with "Hans Phaall," Poe labored to give his narrative the highest possible degree of realism—and once again accomplished this at least in part by plagiarizing authoritative sources. Many of the passages that described the South Seas were taken, sometimes virtually word for word, from encyclopedias and earlier travel narratives. All told, as much as one-fifth of the entire book came from elsewhere. Nonetheless, only a few reviewers believed the story to be true; many more identified it as fiction dressed up as fact. One New York newspaper, the *Gazette,* even raised the possibility that its author was "the very ingenious" Richard Adams Locke, a notion that would certainly have infuriated Edgar Allan Poe. Locke, however, quickly disavowed responsibility for what he called "this new hoax," writing in the *New Era* that he "verily believes that the merit of it, be it what it may, is entirely due to Mr. Edgar A. Poe."

In 1840 Poe attempted another novella, *The Journal of Julius Rodman.* Published in several installments in *Burton's Gentleman's Magazine,* it was said to be a firsthand account of an eighteenth-century expedition across the Rockies. In what had become his standard practice for adventure stories, Poe took numerous passages from other books, relying perhaps most heavily on the 1814 *History of the Expedition Under the Command of Captains Lewis and Clark.* (This at a time when he was castigating Henry Wadsworth Longfellow for allegedly having "purloined" a poem by Tennyson, a very faint likeness that Poe nonetheless labeled "bare-faced and barbarous plagiarism.") Though *The Journal of Julius Rodman* was not very successful as a work of literature (Poe never completed it), in one instance it succeeded utterly as a hoax: Rodman's "journal" was cited in a report issued by the U.S. Senate Select Committee on the Oregon Territory, which asserted that "nothing yet appears, either in the journal or related to it, calculated to excite suspicion with regard to its authenticity."

Poe wrote other hoax stories as well, among them a story about a chemist who discovers a method of changing lead into gold, which Poe hoped would provide a check on the gold fever then gripping the country. His most ambitious one, though, was published in New York in 1844, nearly nine years after Locke's moon series had brought home to him the power of a well-conceived hoax. Like "Hans Phaall," it was a story about a balloon voyage, but unmarred by what Poe now saw as the imperfections of his earlier one: a story that he felt certain would dwarf the moon series in its impact, and prove his superiority as a hoaxer once and for all.

On the morning of April 6, 1844, amid a driving rainstorm, Edgar Allan Poe arrived by steamship in New York. He had been to New York before—those terrible few weeks some thirteen years earlier, when he stayed over after his expulsion from West Point, sick and shivering, the only sure thing in his future the wrath of his stepfather—but now he entered the city as a married man, accompanied by his wife Virginia, whom he affectionately called "Sissy." (His aunt Maria Clemm—"Muddy," Poe called her—was still in Philadelphia, and he hoped soon to earn enough money to send for her.) Within a matter of hours Poe had found a room for them in a boardinghouse on Greenwich Street, just a couple of blocks from the North River. It was an especially unlovely part of town, its side streets a haven for wharf rats, the seamen's bars selling watered beer and brandy that was nothing more than whiskey colored red with oak juice. The boardinghouse itself was old and shabby, its color a forlorn brown, but the room was clean and the board very generous. "Last night, for supper," Poe wrote to his aunt the next morning, "we had the nicest tea you ever drank, strong & hot—wheat bread & rye bread—cheese—tea-cakes (elegant), a great dish (2 dishes) of elegant ham, and 2 of cold veal, piled up like mountains and large slices—3 dishes of the cakes, and every thing in the greatest profusion. No fear of starving here."

Starvation was not an idle worry, as after the trip up from Philadelphia Poe had only four and a half dollars remaining from the eleven with which he had started out. (It was slightly less than he had anticipated: he had paid twenty-five cents for an umbrella for Sissy, who, he was pleased to note, had not been coughing as much of late.) Still, he felt in excellent spirits. He thought he could borrow three dollars from a friend, an amount that would hold them over for at least a fortnight. Even more promising, he had an idea for a story that he was sure he would be able to sell. He had been planning the story for a long while, had made certain of every particular, so that no one reading it could tell that it was entirely untrue. It concerned a new type of steering balloon, designed and flown by the illustrious aeronaut Monck Mason, which had just completed the first ever transatlantic crossing. The air, like the earth and water before it, had now been conquered by science. It was a remarkable story, Poe told himself confidently, and there was only one proper venue for it.

He paid a visit to the offices of the *Sun*.

In 1844 Benjamin Day was no longer the publisher of the *Sun*, having sold his share of the newspaper six years earlier to his brother-in-law Moses Yale Beach. Physically, Beach was Day's opposite—he was a broad-shouldered, handsome man with wavy hair and rakishly long sideburns—but like Day he was a Connecticut Yankee who prized the values of thrift, hard work, and a positive balance sheet. The recession of 1837 had dramatically reduced the profitability of the *Sun*—it had scared Benjamin Day into selling the paper—and in the years since then, Beach had sought to recoup his investment with content he believed would have the widest possible appeal, introducing romantic fiction and giving even greater attention to crime stories and coverage of sports and entertainment. He was also, as it turned out, not averse to the idea of another hoax. Although Beach did not assume full ownership of the *Sun* until 1838, he had begun working for the paper in 1835, not long before the publication of the moon series, and he surely remembered how lucrative a proposition that had been. He offered Edgar Allan Poe fifty dollars for his story. That was not an especially generous offer (a decade earlier Locke had received more than ten times that amount for his series), but Poe accepted the money gladly; the payment would allow Sissy and him to rent their own apartment and bring Muddy up from Philadelphia as well.

On Saturday, April 13, exactly one week after Poe's arrival in New York, the *Sun* brought out a single-page extra edition given over almost entirely to the balloon story. Six headline decks thundered the announcement in bold capital letters, each line printed in a different typeface, some italicized and some not, accompanied by a forest of exclamation points, the whole of it looking less like a newspaper headline than a broadside announcing the arrival of a menagerie or minstrel show.

ASTOUNDING NEWS!
BY EXPRESS VIA NORFOLK
THE ATLANTIC CROSSED IN THREE DAYS!
SIGNAL TRIUMPH OF MR. MONCK MASON'S FLYING MACHINE!!! ...
FULL PARTICULARS OF THE VOYAGE!!!

The story itself was nearly five thousand words long, divided into two main sections. The first part was said to have been written by an "agent" of the *Sun* in South Carolina, identified only as a "Mr. Forsyth," who had also arranged to transmit the exciting news by horse express, so that the *Sun*'s readers could have it before the regular mail had arrived from Charleston. Forsyth triumphantly announced Monck Mason's remarkable achievement ("The great problem is at length solved!" he proclaimed. *"The Atlantic has been actually crossed in a Balloon!"*), and then briefly related the details of "this most extraordinary voyage."

According to Forsyth, Mason's journey had begun in Wales on Saturday, April 6, at eleven o'clock in the morning (more or less exactly the moment that Poe himself had arrived in New York), and ended in Charleston, South Carolina, the following Tuesday at two o'clock in the afternoon: a mere seventy-five hours from shore to shore. The balloon's passengers were the celebrated Monck Mason and his fellow balloonists Holland and Henson, the historical novelist William Harrison Ainsworth, two members of the English peerage, and two seamen hired for the trip. Forsyth then described, often in highly technical language, the history and development of Mason's new balloon, the *Victoria,* and the genesis of the history-making balloon flight. The original plan had been simply to cross the English Channel to Paris, though the balloon's passengers had obtained passports good for all parts of the Continent. In doing so they believed they were preparing for all eventualities—but "unexpected events," remarked Forsyth, "rendered these passports superfluous."

The story's second section was composed of journal entries made during the trip, the bulk of them written by Monck Mason. The *Victoria,* Mason related, had lifted off in fine English weather; it rose higher and higher, the countryside below revealing itself with ever greater boldness, showing dramatic crags and pinnacles that "resembled nothing so much as the giant cities of eastern fable." In half an hour the balloon had reached the Bristol Channel, and its happy passengers had just given nine cheers and dropped a ceremonial bottle into the sea, when "an unforeseen accident occurred which discouraged us to no little degree." A sudden swaying of the balloon car dislodged the steel rod that connected the rudder to the propeller. As Mason struggled to reattach it, a strong wind blew the balloon out over the Atlantic. By the time the rod had been secured, the balloon was drifting off the southern coast of Ireland. This was when Harrison Ainsworth made his extraordinary suggestion: rather than beat their way back toward Paris, they should take advantage of the prevailing winds and attempt to reach North America. In Mason's estimation, it was a bold but "by no means unreasonable or chimerical proposition." Together the two men convinced the other passengers of the soundness of their new plan, and with that they set their course due west.

In a nice touch by Poe, Monck Mason's rather matter-of-fact journal entries (the type that would be expected from an experienced aeronaut) were interspersed with far more animated ones from the novelist Harrison Ainsworth. "The last nine hours have been unquestionably the most exciting of my life," he declared in his first entry. "I can conceive nothing more sublimating than the strange peril and novelty of an adventure such as this. May God grant that we succeed!" On the afternoon of the third day, the travelers sighted the coast of South Carolina. "We have crossed the Atlantic," marveled Ainsworth, "fairly and *easily* crossed it in a balloon! God be praised! Who shall say that anything is impossible hereafter?"

"The Journal," reported the *Sun*, "here ceases." The remainder of Poe's story described securing and deflating the balloon and temporarily lodging its passengers at Fort Moultrie, near Charleston. (Poe had been stationed there briefly during his army days.) More information would be forthcoming in the *Sun* on Monday, and with that Forsyth concluded his account, his final words on the subject as enthusiastic as those set down midflight by Harrison Ainsworth: "This is unquestionably the most stupendous, the most interesting, and the most important undertaking, ever accomplished or even attempted by man. What magnificent events may ensue, it would be useless now to think of determining."

Poe had long reflected on the success of Richard Adams Locke's moon series, and in designing his balloon story he clearly appropriated some of Locke's techniques. Just as Locke had established the credibility of his story by ascribing the lunar discoveries to a prominent astronomer, John Herschel, so too Poe wrote about a real-life balloonist, Monck Mason. And as the first installment of Locke's series had described the invention of Herschel's new telescope, the first part of Poe's story focused on the construction of Mason's new flying machine. There was, however, one critical difference: Richard Adams Locke had created his story nearly from scratch. John Herschel had not invented a "hydro-oxygen telescope"— no one had—and he was not even particularly interested in the moon as a subject of astronomical research. On the other hand, Poe chose for his hoax a type of balloon that *did* exist and had actually been flown by Mason.

In November 1836 Mason and two other aeronauts had made a balloon trip across the English Channel from London to the German town of Weilberg, a trip like the one described in Poe's story, which included a change in course due to shifting wind currents and a decision to proceed to a new destination. (Like the passengers in Poe's story, Mason and his partners had originally intended to fly to Paris.) Later that year Mason wrote up a report of the trip as a pamphlet with the title *Account of the late Aeronautical Expedition from London to Weilburg, accomplished by Robert Holland, Esq., Monck Mason, Esq., and Charles Green, Aeronaut.* Poe put innumerable details from Mason's *Account* into his story, from the operation of the balloon's guide rope to the equipment carried onboard (barometers, telescopes, even a device for warming coffee with slack lime). Originally published in London in 1836, Mason's pamphlet was not reprinted in New York until the following year. This was certainly the version Poe read, as the discrepancy in dates seems to have confused him slightly: in his balloon story he made note of the Weilberg expedition but misidentified it as having taken place in 1837.

Poe drew even more heavily on another pamphlet. In 1843, at London's Royal Adelaide Gallery, Monck Mason exhibited a model of a balloon that he had recently built; the pamphlet that accompanied the exhibition, *Remarks on the Ellipsoidal Balloon, propelled by the Archimedean Screw, described as the New Aerial Machine,* described the new balloon and explained the history of its construction. Poe must have found the technical nature of the pamphlet appealing because he took from it all the basic details for his own balloon story. Mason's balloon was "an ellipsoid or solid oval; in length, 13 feet 6 inches, and in height, 6 feet 8 inches." Poe's too was an ellipsoid, and "its length was thirteen feet six inches—high, six feet eight inches." The weight of Mason's flying apparatus was seventeen pounds with "about four pounds to spare"; Poe's was "seventeen pounds—leaving about four pounds to spare." So it continued for the rest of the elements of the balloon's design, from its "frame of light wood" (as described in both accounts) to its rudder made of "a light frame of cane covered with silk."

In all, more than one-quarter of Poe's balloon story was taken from the two earlier Mason pamphlets. Nor was his borrowing limited to the text of the story. The extra edition published by the *Sun* also included a large engraving of the steering balloon *Victoria*—copied almost exactly from the one on the frontispiece of Mason's *Remarks on the Ellipsoidal Balloon*.

POE wrote an account of the Balloon Hoax (as it almost immediately came to be known) in his second letter to the *Columbia Spy*, published in May 1844, one month after his Monck Mason story appeared in the *Sun*. "The 'Balloon-Hoax,'" he asserted, "made a far more intense sensation than anything of that character since the 'Moon-Story' of Locke."

> On the morning (Saturday) of its announcement, the whole square surrounding the "Sun" building was literally besieged, blocked up—ingress and egress being alike impossible, from a period soon after sunrise until about two o'clock P.M. In Saturday's regular issue, it was stated that the news had been just received, and that an "Extra" was then in preparation, which would be ready at ten. It was not delivered, however, until nearly noon. In the meantime I never witnessed more intense excitement to get possession of a newspaper. As soon as the few first copies made their way into the streets, they were bought up, at almost any price, from the news-boys, who made a profitable speculation beyond doubt. I saw a half-dollar given, in one instance, for a single paper, and a shilling was a frequent price. I tried, in vain, during the whole day, to get possession of a copy.

Having recounted the morning's events (Poe's assertions of the hoax's great success were as fictional as the hoax itself), he then turned once again to the "gross errors" of Locke's series in comparison with the perfect verisimilitude of his own story. "As for internal evidence of falsehood, there is, positively, *none*—while the more generally accredited fable of Locke would not bear even momentary examination by the scientific." If there were those who disbelieved the balloon story, the blame can be laid at the doorstep of the *Sun*, which had published the moon story in the first place. "The *success* of the hoax," he wrote, referring to Locke's moon series,

> is usually attributed to its correctness, and the consequent difficulty of detecting a flaw. But we rather think it attributable to the circumstance of this hoax being first in the field, or nearly so. It took the people by surprise, and there was no good reason (apart from internal evidence) for disbelief. It was therefore believed, although abounding in gross er-

rors, which should have caused it to be discredited at once; while, on the other hand, the "Balloon-Story," which had *no* error, and which related nothing that might not really have happened, was discredited on account of the frequent previous deceptions, of similar character, perpetrated by the "Sun."

Few of New York's other newspapers paid any attention to the balloon story, and those that did immediately denounced it as fraudulent. In the *Herald,* James Gordon Bennett called it "a ridiculous hoax," "blunderingly got up" and "preposterously issued." The *New-York American* observed that "the express which has hardly outstripped the regular mail, must also have brought along a woodcut of the balloon, as the Sun has the picture as well as the story—one as good as the other." Nor was the criticism confined to New York. In Philadelphia, the *Saturday Courier* reprinted a portion of the story but advised, "We think every intelligent reader will be disposed to regard this attempt to hoax as not even possessing the character of pleasantry. The celebrated 'Moon Hoax,' issued from the office of the New York Sun, many years ago, was an ingenious essay; but that is more than can be said of this 'Balloon Story.'"

The *Courier's* comment indicates that the Moon Hoax was still fresh in people's minds, as Poe had suggested, but there may have been another reason for the general skepticism. In Poe's account of the scene at the *Sun* building, he presents himself as a mere bystander, watching in amazement as his work creates a frenzy. A rather different version of the morning's events has been supplied by a prominent New Yorker of the time, Thomas Low Nichols, in his memoir *Forty Years of American Life.* Nichols was a novelist and newspaper editor, as well as a practitioner of what was then known as hydropathy, or the "water cure." During Poe's years in New York, the two men often saw each other socially (Nichols's wife and fellow hydrotherapist, Mary Sargeant Gove Nichols, wrote her own "Reminiscences of Edgar Allan Poe" and was herself a subject of Poe's *Literati of New York City* series). Poe praised Thomas Low Nichols in the *Columbia Spy* as "a man of much talent." In his memoir, published in 1864, Nichols returned the compliment, calling Poe "a man of rare genius," although one "with some grave faults of character and one great misfortune—a temperament so sensitive that a single glass of wine made him not merely intoxicated, but insane." The single incident Nichols related about Edgar Allan Poe involved the publication of the balloon story.

The publisher, as is the American custom, had brought it out as an extra; and Poe, crazed by a glass of wine, stood on the walk before the publisher's door, and told the assembled crowd that the extra was a hoax, as he personally knew, for he had written it himself. The crowd scattered, the sales fell off, and the publisher, on going to the door, saw the author making what he conceived to be the necessary explanation.

This would seem highly curious—even scarcely believable—behavior for the author of such a carefully designed hoax, but Poe's career was riddled with acts of self-sabotage, often provoked by drink, which he came to regret when sober. Such may have been the case here. Since his earliest days as a writer, Poe had taken extreme pride in the quality of his work, which he believed would allow him to rise above the mass of ordinary people whose taste he disdained but whose acclaim he thirsted for like wine. ("I love fame," Poe once confided to Mary Gove Nichols. "I dote on it—I idolize it—I would drink to the very dregs the glorious intoxication.") The pride, the vanity, the desire for fame: that powerful combination may have caused Poe to proclaim to the crowd assembled before the *Sun* building that he was the true author of the balloon story, especially if, as Thomas Low Nichols claimed, he was drinking at the time. Indeed, subsequent events seem to suggest that Nichols's version is the more likely one. For if Poe's account were accurate—if his hoax had created an "intense sensation," with New Yorkers paying up to fifty cents for a single copy—then Moses Beach, enterprising business-man that he was, would have attempted to keep alive the possibility of the story's veracity in order to extend the controversy (and the sales) as long as possible. But this path would not be available once word got around town that the author had very publicly admitted to perpetrating a hoax. (Richard Adams Locke had made his admission in private, to a single reporter.)

In its very next issue the *Sun* printed a retraction of the story, some-thing it had never done with the moon series:

The mails from the South last Saturday night not having brought con-firmation of the balloon from England, the particulars of which from our correspondent we detailed in our extra, we are inclined to believe that the intelligence is erroneous. The description of the balloon and the voyage was written with a minuteness and scientific ability calculated to obtain credit everywhere, and was read with great pleasure and satisfaction. We by no means think such a project impossible.

For the Balloon Hoax, there would be no pamphlets or lithographs; no reprints in newspapers around the country and around the world; no theatrical parodies; no peristrephic dioramas portraying Monck Mason's voyage across the Atlantic. Within weeks Poe's hoax was largely forgotten, except for his report of it in the *Columbia Spy*. "Poe's account of the publication of his own *Balloon Hoax* is extremely interesting," Thomas Mabbott, an editor of the collected *Columbia Spy* letters, remarked nearly a century later. "From my own reading in various papers I have the impression that fewer people were fooled than Poe could have wished."

In 1844, the year of his Balloon Hoax, Poe published an odd little essay called "Diddling Considered as One of the Exact Sciences." (The title is a play on Thomas de Quincey's "Murder Considered as One of the Fine Arts.") As a genre, the humorous essay was not ideally suited to Poe's talents, and this example is today little remembered, but "Diddling" is notable for the insight it gives into Poe's longtime fascination with hoaxes—what one of his most sympathetic biographers termed "a childish and almost unbalanced delight in a hoax of any kind."

"Man is an animal that diddles," declares Poe at the outset of the essay, "and there is *no* animal that diddles *but* man." A crow may thieve, a fox may cheat, but only a man may diddle. Poe himself does not provide the etymology, but the word *diddle* can be traced to the British playwright James Kenney's 1803 farce *Raising the Wind,* which featured a good-natured swindler by the name of Jeremy Diddler. A diddle is a kind of swindle, and Poe's essay is full of examples of small-time swindles: a shopkeeper tricked into providing free whiskey, a ship's captain deceived into paying a fake bill of charges, attendees of a camp meeting convinced to pay a toll to cross a free bridge. In each case the diddler has concocted a story that causes the unsuspecting listener to hand over his possessions willingly, even cheerfully. The anecdotes all seem very lighthearted, and Poe's sympathies throughout clearly lie not with the victim of the diddle but its perpetrator. The diddler possesses all of the attributes that Poe so esteemed: he is ingenious; he is audacious; he is persevering; he is nonchalant ("He is cool," Poe observes admiringly, "cool as a cucumber"); he is original. He also takes great pleasure in his own work. Having finished his daily labors, Poe informs us, the diddler goes home at night, locks the door, undresses, puts out the candle, gets into bed, and then, alone in the darkness, he grins. "A diddle," Poe informs us, "would be *no* diddle without a grin."

The diddler is a man who lives by his wits. The tools of his trade are intelligence, cunning, and bravado, which he uses to concoct a story so authentic-seeming that the listener cannot help but believe it. To diddle, then, is not merely to swindle, but to do so by creating a carefully planned, artful deception—by producing a kind of hoax.

According to Poe, the hoaxer is the extraordinary, the superior man, for with his hoax he has managed to rise above the foolish, credulous mass of people. (In his account of the Balloon Hoax, Poe refers to them as "the rabble.") He has achieved his success not by being born into it (an especially sensitive topic for Poe, given how little he received from his wealthy stepfather) or by cultivating friendships with more successful men (Poe was forever railing against the clubbiness of the literary world), but by earning it: his success is a reflection of his own brilliance.

"Diddling," then, helps explain Poe's complicated response to Richard Adams Locke. Poe's finely tuned sense of literary competitiveness caused him to disparage Locke's most celebrated work as shoddily constructed, if elegantly delivered, but he also could not help but admire what he saw as Locke's consummate skill as a hoaxer: his calm, his audaciousness, his ingenuity. Sometimes one of those feelings was ascendant in Poe, and sometimes the other—as in his 1841 *Autography* series, when he extolled Richard Adams Locke, then a journalist about to give up journalism forever, as "one among the few men of *unquestionable genius* whom the country possesses."

POE loved all kinds of puzzles, but he was especially devoted to codes and ciphers. In 1840 he invited the readers of the Philadelphia newspaper *Alexander's Weekly Messenger* to send him their own ciphers—pieces of prose written with replacement alphabets—which he promised he would be able to solve. The more interesting solutions he printed in *Alexander's* along with his comments. The series grew so popular that he repeated it the following year in another Philadelphia publication, *Graham's Lady's and Gentleman's Magazine*. Soon he was so deluged with submissions that he had little time for his own writing, but he felt obligated to solve all he had received. "Nothing intelligible can be written," he pronounced in a letter to a friend, "which, with time, I cannot decipher."

For Poe, no greater intellectual pleasure could be found than in matching wits with a capable adversary. Of course he greatly enjoyed perpetrating his own hoaxes—a diddle would be *no* diddle, after all, without a grin—but he also loved to expose the hoaxes of others, taking them apart to reveal their inner workings. This was what he strove to do in his dissection of the flaws of Locke's moon series, and, in a more literal manner, in his famous exposé of Maelzel's automaton chess player, which would be his one true success in the world of hoaxes.

By the time Edgar Allan Poe focused his attention on it in 1836, the automaton chess player had been fascinating audiences for three-quarters of a century. Invented in 1769 by the Hungarian engineer Baron Wolfgang von Kempelen, it was a life-size wooden figure resplendently attired in traditional Turkish garb: a white turban, ermine-lined jacket, billowing trousers, and white gloves, its left hand holding a long, thin pipe. (The automaton was popularly known as "the Turk.") It sat at a wooden cabinet four feet long, two and a half feet deep, and three feet high—the dimensions would be critical to the efforts to solve the mystery—on top of which had been affixed a chess board. At the beginning of every performance, Kempelen ceremoniously opened the doors of the cabinet, one by one, illuminating the inside with a candle to reveal a complicated-looking mechanism of gears and levers, like that found inside a clock or music box. Then, after closing the cabinet again, he announced that the automaton would play a game of chess against anyone in the audience who dared to challenge it. When a volunteer had been found, Kempelen wound up the figure with a large key, whereupon it briefly surveyed the board and then, its gears whirring, reached out a delicately carved hand and made its first move.

At the end of the game the Turk had nearly always emerged victorious, even against some of the strongest chess players in the world. Audiences were mystified. Could the Turk really be, as the entire performance suggested, a thinking machine? And if not, were the Turk's moves secretly controlled by its creator? Or did the cabinet, seemingly filled with machinery, instead conceal a person inside it—a small child, or a dwarf, or even (according to one of the more outlandish notions) a chess-playing monkey?

The Turk was an immediate sensation, but over time Kempelen grew uncomfortable at being so closely identified with his remarkable creation (he had, he believed, more important work still to accomplish), and the

Turk's performances grew more sporadic. Eventually Kempelen dismantled it, and for many years nothing more was heard of the chess-playing automaton—until 1809, when Kempelen's son sold its disassembled components to a Bavarian engineer named Johann Nepomuk Maelzel. Maelzel was a distinguished engineer and brilliant inventor, but his even greater talent was as a showman. For years he toured the Continent, exhibiting the Turk in London, Paris, Amsterdam, even, it has been said, arranging a game against Napoleon. He was, however, a man of expensive tastes, and his debts began to pile up. When those debts were compounded by lawsuits, he set sail in 1826 for the United States, where he and his celebrated chess player toured for more than a decade. Their appearances were confined mostly to large cities such as New York, Boston, and Philadelphia, but in December 1835 the Turk played a short engagement in Richmond, Virginia, where on numerous occasions the audience included Edgar Allan Poe.

Poe never played against the Turk himself, preferring to remain unseen among the crowd, a slight, serious-looking figure carefully studying the Turk's operations, scrutinizing Maelzel's every move. In the April 1836 issue of the *Southern Literary Messenger* he published an essay entitled "Maelzel's Chess-Player," in which he boldly claimed to have solved the mystery.

By this time the Turk had been the subject of a great deal of learned speculation, going back at least to 1789, when Joseph Friedrich, Freiherr zu Racknitz, wrote a book that concluded—correctly—that the automaton's moves must be controlled by an operator hidden inside the cabinet. The breakthrough moment came in 1821, with the publication of an anonymous pamphlet (its author was a twenty-year-old Cambridge undergraduate named Robert Willis) entitled *An Attempt to Analyse the Automaton Chess Player of Mr. De Kempelen, with an Easy Method of Imitating the Movements of that Celebrated Figure.* Willis carefully explained how the cabinet was actually larger than it appeared to be, large enough for a normal-size man to be concealed inside it; he also provided illustrations that demonstrated the positions the man would have to assume to remain hidden as each of the several cabinet doors was opened. The pamphlet was reviewed later that year in the *Edinburgh Philosophical Journal,* among the editors of which was Sir David Brewster (the same David Brewster whom Richard Adams Locke put to work inventing the hydro-oxygen telescope with John Herschel). In his 1832 book *Letters on*

Natural Magic Brewster himself wrote a lengthy analysis of the chess-playing automaton, though it was little more than a gloss on Willis's previous work. Just as Brewster had relied heavily on Willis, so did Poe rely heavily on Brewster in his explanation of the Turk's operations. And much as he had in his appendix to "Hans Phaall," with its slighting remarks about earlier stories of lunar voyages (some of which he had drawn from for his own story), Poe acknowledged his debt by disparagement: Brewster's analysis, he claimed, was "very cursory and inattentive."

Poe's discussion begins with the assertion that the Turk cannot be a calculating machine because a single chess game provides far too many potential positions. As all of the theories about how Maelzel himself might control the moves arc fatally flawed, the only reasonable conclusion is "that when the machine is first rolled into the presence of the spectators, a man is already within it." Poe explains to the reader how the deception is accomplished, with the man concealed in various partitions inside the cabinet as Maelzel opens each successive door. His reasoning, he claims, is founded on seventeen observations made during visits to the exhibition in Richmond: the dimensions of the cabinet are sufficient for a man to lie inside it; the interior of the cabinet is lined with cloth, presumably to deaden any sounds emanating from inside; the Turk's adversary does not sit at the board, but is seated some distance away; and so forth.

Little of Poe's study was new, and it did not culminate in a solution different from the one Willis had earlier proposed. Still, unlike his critique of Locke's moon story, Poe's essay on the automaton chess player was received with widespread interest; the *Charleston Courier,* for instance, called it "highly ingenious," while in Philadelphia, the *United States Gazette* said it was "the most successful attempt we have seen to explain the *modus operandi* of that wonderful production." The reason for the praise lies less in *what* Poe wrote than in *how* he wrote it. Poe had criticized earlier analyses of the automaton chess player for not providing sufficient evidence to prove their claims, and in his essay he employed a very different approach. After first stating the problem (he provides a long, vivid description of the Turk's performance), he then examines its elements, bringing the reader along step by step as he ticks off his seventeen clues, none decisive in itself but each one narrowing the field of possibilities, moving ever closer to the answer, until by the end he has demonstrated that his is the only logical solution. It was a highly effective dramatic structure, and one that Poe would later put to brilliant use in his detective fiction, the stories featuring C. Auguste Dupin, master ratiocinator, who solved crimes purely by the force of observation and deduction. The original detective, though, had been Poe himself, and the subject of the investigation not a murder but a hoax.

JOHANN Nepomuk Maelzel never responded to any theory about the Turk's operation; the true showman, he understood, prefers to cultivate an air of mystery. That was just one of the many lessons he imparted to the young promoter who had arrived in Boston in the fall of 1835 with his own curious attraction in tow. The Turk had been performing in the main ballroom of the city's Concert Hall, but the crowds coming to see the new exhibition soon grew so large that Maelzel was asked to move to a smaller room next door. Eventually, though, the crowds for the new exhibition began to fall off and the young showman—P. T. Barnum—had to find a way to revive public interest.

Soon he set into motion a plan he had devised while watching Maelzel exhibit the Turk. He surreptitiously planted stories in the local papers revealing that what appeared to be a very old woman was in fact "a curiously constructed automaton made up of whalebone, india-rubber, and numberless springs ingeniously put together, and made to move at the slightest touch, according to the whim of the operator." Joice Heth, Barnum now claimed, was not a human being at all.

CHAPTER 15

"Joice Heth
Is Not Dead"

Little by little P. T. Barnum was learning his trade. It was Barnum himself, in September 1835, who induced Johann Nepomuk Maelzel to move the Turk to a smaller room in Boston's Concert Hall (presumably he paid Maelzel to do so) because the crowds coming to see Joice Heth were too large for the room. Eventually, though, the crowds began to thin out. That was the natural ebb and flow of show business, as predictable as the tides and about as impervious to resistance; when the people stopped coming, the showman simply moved on to the next engagement. This time, however, was different.

One day a letter appeared in a Boston newspaper that put forward the astonishing claim that Joice Heth was an automaton, her motions controlled by an unseen operator, her words spoken by the ventriloquist promoter who always stood at her side. The letter was signed "A Visitor," and its authorship has never been conclusively determined, but Barnum's fingerprints are all over it. It would hardly be the only fake letter he ever planted in a newspaper, and this one—so clearly inspired by his observations of Maelzel and the Turk—suited his purposes precisely. As he remarked in his autobiography, "The consequence was, our audience again largely increased." Bostonians who had not yet attended the exhibition rushed to Concert Hall to see for themselves the workings of the ingeniously crafted automaton; those who had already attended came back again to determine if this new claim could be true, and if so, how they had been so thoroughly deceived. With careful attention they listened to the voice that might or might not be hers; felt for the beating of a pulse created either by heart or mechanical pump; watched the narrow chest rise and fall in sleep, hiding inside it lungs or bellows; stroked the rough, wrinkled brown flesh that might be nothing more than India rubber. The people pressed around Joice Heth more thickly than ever before, and as they scrutinized her Barnum eyed them just as closely, listened to them debate among themselves, noting to himself how many were coming back again to get another look.

After completing the exhibition at Concert Hall, Barnum and his assistant Levi Lyman bundled up Joice Heth and set out on the road again. They traveled west across Massachusetts, made their way down into Connecticut, and then finally, in October 1835, arrived again in New York, where Joice Heth was scheduled to reprise her engagement at Niblo's Garden. By then they had been touring for nearly two months, often staying in a town for no more than a few days before packing up and moving on. The travel was difficult and exhausting, but Joice Heth never missed a performance. When the doors opened at nine, she was there on her couch, still telling her tales of "little George," still gazed upon by a parade of strangers, some of them moved to tears by her, some laughing, others shamelessly pointing. The shows went on six hours a day, six days a week; Joice Heth had only Sundays free from public display.

Her second engagement at Niblo's overlapped with the annual fair of the American Institute of the City of New York, designed to show off the latest products being turned out by the city's factories and workshops. The eight-day fair drew as many as a hundred thousand visitors from all over the country, who wandered through the hall marveling at the more than ten thousand specimens of New York industry—plated candlesticks and embossed card racks and artificial flowers, air-spring beds and cooking stoves, steam engines and waterwheels. Drawing the largest and most enthusiastic crowds were the scores of new machines, emblems of the limitless future: washing machines, threshing machines, machines for cutting straw and grinding apples and extracting stumps, for pressing hats and knitting cotton stockings. Many of the fair's visitors, having taken in all they could, then strolled across Niblo's sculpted garden into Joice Heth's viewing room, where they encountered what might have been (they could not say for sure) the most wondrous machine of all, one that could talk and laugh and sing hymns.

At the end of October, Joice Heth began a weeklong exhibition upstate at the Albany Museum, where the evening performers included an Italian calling himself Signor Antonio. As an entertainer Antonio was something of a jack-of-all-trades—he could, for instance, hit a target with a musket shot while jumping up and down on a single stilt—but his special gift was for spinning plates and bowls; in one of his more spectacular routines he spun ten dinner plates simultaneously on sticks balanced on various parts of his body. P. T. Barnum had never seen a crockery spinner before, and he was entranced. By the end of his week in Albany he had signed Antonio to a year-long contract—having first obtained the proviso that he change his stage name to "Signor Vivalla," as Barnum did not believe that "Antonio" sounded sufficiently foreign.

So the showman and his two performers, the slave and the immigrant, returned once more to New York City. Rather than pursue another engagement at Niblo's (he probably thought he had reached a point of diminishing returns there), Barnum instead headed east, into the Bowery. The Bowery was quickly earning a reputation as the workingman's Broadway, a boisterous promenade bursting with theaters, music halls, gambling dens, brothels, and—unique among New York's avenues—not a single church. Barnum booked Joice Heth into a hall at the corner of Bowery and Division, but little is known about this exhibition, because by now he was devoting most of his attention to his newer attraction, whose extravagant routines he believed would especially appeal to Bowery audiences. He called first on the manager of the Franklin Theater, William Dinneford. Dinneford was dubious about the act of Signor Vivalla, saying that he had seen similar feats executed by others.

"Mr. Dinneford, I beg your pardon," Barnum replied, "but I must be permitted to say that you are mistaken. You have no doubt seen strange things in your life, but my dear sir, I should never have imported Signor Vivalla from Italy, unless I had authentic evidence that he was the only artist of the kind who ever left that country."

For the rest of that week and part of the next, Barnum appeared nightly onstage as Vivalla's assistant, arranging his plates, carrying his stilts, handing him his muskets, and addressing the audience on his behalf (although Signor Vivalla had spent several years living in England, Barnum thought that the overall effect would be destroyed if he were heard speaking English). The act was received so enthusiastically that when the engagement at the Franklin was completed Barnum entrusted Joice Heth to his assistant Levi Lyman, and accompanied Signor Vivalla to a booking in Washington.

Joice Heth remained on the Bowery for several more weeks, and then left with Lyman on another tour of Connecticut, making stops in several small towns before arriving in New Haven in January 1836. The rigors of touring may finally have worn her down, or maybe it was her first New England winter and the constant proximity of so many other bodies, but during the exhibition in New Haven she began to feel ill. Joice Heth, the local papers reported, was "ailing from a cold." Lyman brought her to the home of Barnum's brother Philo in Bethel, where she was cared for by her private nurse, a "faithful colored woman" Barnum had hired in Boston. On February 21, 1836, a horse-drawn sleigh pulled up at Barnum's boardinghouse in New York, and at the door the driver handed him a note from Philo. Aunt Joice, the note said, was no more. She had died peacefully in her bed, and her body was being conveyed to him to dispose of as he deemed proper. It was outside, in the sleigh.

Barnum had Joice Heth's body carried inside and placed in a small room to which he had the only key. He had already decided that she should be returned to Bethel and interred in the village burial ground there, but that trip would have to wait. The next morning he went to call on a surgeon of his acquaintance. Joice Heth still had one more show to perform.

Dr. David L. Rogers was one of New York's most eminent physicians. A resident surgeon at New York Hospital, at the age of thirty-six he had been performing surgeries for well over a decade. He had pioneered several surgical techniques that were now in wide use and was also renowned as an expert anatomist, often called upon to conduct autopsies in unusual or challenging cases.

Like so many New Yorkers, Dr. Rogers had attended the Joice Heth exhibition at Niblo's Garden, and like everyone else he had been fascinated to observe a woman said to have lived for the better part of two centuries. His, though, was an uncommonly trained eye, and by the time he exited the viewing room he was a skeptic about the longevity of Joice Heth. He noted that her pulse recorded a steady seventy-five beats per minute, while her hearing, voice, intellect, and general bodily functions appeared to be no more impaired than those of persons half as old as she claimed to be. (Joice Heth's blindness, Rogers believed, was the result of an eye disease that had likely befallen her many years earlier.) As Barnum recounted the story in his autobiography, Dr. Rogers "expressed a desire to institute a post-mortem examination if she should die in this country. I agreed that he should have the opportunity, if unfortunately it should occur while she was under my protection." On the morning of February 22, Barnum went to see Rogers, likely at his medical offices on Chambers Street, and told him that Joice Heth had died. Rogers reiterated his wish to examine her, and by the time Barnum returned home, an autopsy had been scheduled.

Two days later the *Sun* carried the news of the death of Joice Heth. "She was treated with the utmost attention and care," the story reported, "and died with perfect tranquility." Richard Adams Locke and Dr. David L. Rogers were close friends; it is possible they had first met when Rogers testified about his examination of Robert Matthews—the self-proclaimed Matthias the Prophet—at the trial Locke attended as a reporter. Locke undoubtedly knew of Rogers' desire to examine Joice Heth, and in the *Sun* report of her death he endorsed the idea of a postmortem, declaring that an opportunity such as this one, to examine the effects of extreme old age on the human body, would not soon come again. Locke did have some qualms about the propriety of such a procedure—"We felt as though the person of poor old Joice Heth should have been sacred from exposure and mutilation," he acknowledged in a story later that week—but in the end those doubts were outweighed by his abiding faith in the importance of scientific research: "The investigation, conducted by a competent hand, would doubtless form an instructive and valuable record in anatomical science." Yet even here Richard Adams Locke could not resist taking a swipe at those who would deny slaves their full complement of rights. "The old woman's soul, we trust, is quite comfortable in heaven," he wrote, "where, perhaps, distinctions of color are of less consequence than they are here."

Perhaps: but in nineteenth-century New York there was no avoiding racial discrimination, even in the care of the dead. Though autopsies had long been considered a critical tool in advancing understanding of the human body, and particularly the effects of age and disease, not many New Yorkers were willing to give up the body of a loved one for dissection. In earlier years the shortage of cadavers had led to some highly unsavory practices, and ultimately, to one of the first of New York's great riots, the "doctors' riot" of 1788, when residents of the neighborhood around New York Hospital discovered that medical students had been digging up graves—body snatching—to obtain their specimens. More than five thousand rioters stormed the hospital, destroying its laboratories and reburying every body they could find inside. The medical students at the hospital were also taken hostage; the mayor was summoned to the scene, and after obtaining the release of the students, he ordered them placed in jail for their own protection. Soon the mob had surrounded the jail, and the militia defending it fired on the crowd, killing three people and wounding many more. The experience was deeply disturbing to the city in every imaginable way, and grave robbing, which had once been, if not condoned by the medical establishment, at least not actively discouraged, all but ceased. Medical schools had to look elsewhere for their specimens—and by the early decades of the nineteenth century autopsies were primarily reserved for those who, in death as in life, had few to defend them: paupers, criminals, blacks, and especially, like Joice Heth herself, slaves.

It was not unusual for an autopsy to be conducted in front of an audience of interested spectators; indeed, by the 1830s American universities had begun to construct anatomical theaters where medical students could watch autopsies being performed. Still, there had not been anything even remotely resembling the spectacle P. T. Barnum dreamed up for Joice Heth's autopsy. Barnum had rented out the amphitheater of the City Saloon on Broadway (where one of the other viewing rooms showed Henry Hanington's peristrephic dioramas) and publicized the event with a generous application of printer's ink. "ANATOMICAL EXAMINATION," announced one of his newspaper advertisements, promising an event that would be "particularly interesting as well to the public generally as to the Faculty and Medical Students." (In his autobiography Barnum indicated that the autopsy was arranged for the day after his visit to Rogers; in fact it took place three days later, on February 25, more than enough time for him to organize the publicity.) By Thursday at noon, when the autopsy was scheduled to begin, the theater was filled with nearly fifteen hundred people, each of whom had paid an admission fee of fifty cents for the privilege of being among the first New Yorkers to discover, at last, the answer to the mystery of Joice Heth.

An excited, anticipatory buzz must have arisen from the crowd when the hour drew near, as before any long-awaited show of which there will be only a single performance, followed by a respectful hush when the mahogany coffin was carried into the hall. Joice Heth's body was removed and placed on the examination table. Barnum and Levi Lyman strode solemnly to the table, where they were joined by Dr. David L. Rogers. Behind him stood his friend Richard Adams Locke, who had been granted exclusive coverage of the autopsy for the *Sun*.

Dr. Rogers's surgical case lay open beside the table, revealing an array of instruments, their blades gleaming impressively in the light of the lamps. Rogers took a moment to explain to the audience that the surest evidence of extreme old age was the ossification—the conversion into bone—of various parts of the body. It was very common to find ossification in the major arteries; in the case of one woman he had examined in Italy, who had died at the age of 115, he had found the heart to be almost entirely ossified. With that, he took scalpel in hand and made the first incision, slicing across Joice Heth's abdomen. After some examination he pronounced her abdominal viscera to have, as Locke recorded it for the *Sun,* "a perfectly natural and healthy appearance." The liver was of proper size, and to all indications unmarked by disease. Exchanging the scalpel for a handsaw, Rogers cut through the sternum and pried apart the ribs. With great delicacy he opened the heart—surely some silent prayers were said among those watching from the seats above—only to discover a complete absence of ossification of the valves, and just the slightest trace of it at the arch of the aorta. (Rogers later told Barnum that he had "expected to have spoiled half a dozen knives" on the ossification of the chest.) Upon examining the lungs, he found many tubercles in the left lobe, which he determined to have been the immediate cause of death. Joice Heth had not been suffering from a cold after all; she had tuberculosis.

As Dr. Rogers had surely anticipated, given Joice Heth's great garrulousness and remarkable memory, he found her brain to be perfectly healthy. At last the doctor set down his knife. Based on numerous observations, he declared, he felt quite confident in his ultimate judgment (as excitedly recounted by Locke in the *Sun*): "Joice Heth could not have been more than *seventy-five,* or, at the utmost, *eighty years of age!"*

Later, when the commotion had died down and the audience had filed out of the amphitheater, P. T. Barnum took Dr. Rogers aside and assured him that he had engaged Joice Heth in good faith, relying on her appearance and the accompanying documents as evidence of the truth of her story. (It was a version of events that he would insist on to the end of his life, as in 1877, when he told an interviewer, "I believed the documents in her possession as much as I believe the declaration of independence.") Rogers graciously replied that he had no doubt Barnum had been deceived in the matter, because her outward appearance really was that of a much older woman. The encounter might have ended there, with the two men shaking hands and heading home, but Levi Lyman took the moment to step forward and suggest to Dr. Rogers that perhaps the medical profession was not able to decide with much precision in cases such as this one. In his autobiography Barnum claimed that the remark had been meant as a joke (Lyman, he explained somewhat apologetically, "was always ready for a joke, no matter what the cost or at whose expense"), but if it was a joke it was not much of one—and that is certainly not how it was taken by the man at whom it was directed. David Rogers's height would generously be described as middling, but he carried himself with an erect bearing that, in the words of his obituary writer, "gave great dignity to his whole deportment"; his only reply to Lyman's remark was to turn stiffly and, with Locke at his side, exit the hall ("I fear," Barnum wrote later, "in not very good humor").

The next day, February 26, Richard Adams Locke broke the story of Joice Heth's true age, providing the *Sun*'s readers an exclusive accounting of the autopsy, from the initial observation of the body to Dr. Rogers's determination that Joice Heth had lived no more than half the number of years claimed for her. Locke wrote, "There is therefore a moral certainty that her pretensions to the extraordinary longevity of 161 years, all her stories about her suckling George Washington, and about her fondness for the 'young master George,' have been taught her, in regular lessons, for the benefit of her exhibitors." He did not implicate Barnum himself in the deception; instead, he stated that he believed Joice Heth's current exhibitors "took her, at a high price, upon the warranty of others." Still, he could not help but note (ever mindful of the money he struggled to earn in journalism) that the exhibitors had probably earned ten thousand dollars as a consequence.

The Joice Heth affair was, concluded Locke, "the most precious humbug of modern times."

On the morning after Richard Adams Locke's account of the Joice Heth autopsy, P. T. Barnum unexpectedly showed up at the *Sun* offices on Nassau Street. He did not give a reason for his visit, but he did not often forgo an opportunity to cultivate friendly relationships with the press, and he must have been especially intrigued to talk with the man who had so impressed him—as both exposer and deceiver. Richard Adams Locke was not only the journalist who had finally revealed Joice Heth's true age, but he was also the one who created the magnificent hoax that thirty years later, in *The Humbugs of the World,* Barnum would hail as "the most stupendous scientific imposition upon the public that the generation with which we are numbered has known."

According to the *Sun* article about the visit, Barnum admitted to Locke that he now believed Joice Heth had *not* been the oldest woman in the world, as he had for months proclaimed, and in general "took our exposure of the humbug with perfect good humor." It is not known what else the two men discussed, but Locke wrote the next day that he had "heard it hinted" (undoubtedly from Barnum) that Joice Heth's exhibitors were planning to embalm the body like a mummy and ship it to England in the company of an old black man who would claim to be Joice Heth's 180-year-old husband, with letters from George Washington as proof. It was all a joke by Barnum, of course, and Locke took it that way. This latest was a fine idea, he wrote, because the audiences of England would certainly be as gullible as those of America—and he further suggested, referring to the Exodus tale of the ten plagues, "if the shrewd Yankee proprietors will only take with them a few phials containing a part of the darkness which covered the land of Egypt, they might successfully travel through all the continents of Europe."

WHILE Barnum bantered with Locke at the *Sun,* the showman's assistant Levi Lyman was paying a call on another prominent newspaper editor. James Gordon Bennett had not yet addressed the *Sun's* autopsy report, but he certainly meant to; the Joice Heth affair was the most fascinating story in the city, the one everyone was talking about, and he would not concede the field to his rival. At the *Evening Star,* Mordecai Noah was preparing an item asserting that Joice Heth was as old as advertised, since no autopsy of a person over seventy could indicate true age. That idea might suffice if nothing better presented itself, but wherever possible Bennett looked for the more sensational approach, especially when it came to hoaxes. He was still seething about *Great Astronomical Discoveries,* furious that the *Sun* had won so many readers on the basis of a public deception, and eager to expose its proprietors as the swindlers he knew them to be. So he leaped at the opportunity that was unexpectedly provided by Levi Lyman—who, after arriving at the *Herald's* basement offices on Broadway, confessed to Bennett the marvelous humbug about Joice Heth that he and Barnum had put over on Dr. David L. Rogers.

P. T. Barnum never revealed why he and Lyman decided to play this trick on James Gordon Bennett. (In his autobiography he placed the responsibility on Lyman alone, but there can be no doubting his involvement.)

Maybe, with Joice Heth's great age now exposed as a hoax, they were looking for another career-advancing bit of self-promotion; maybe they were still bitter that back in August Bennett had been the only newspaperman in town who did not accept their money in exchange for writing a puff piece about Joice Heth. Or maybe they were simply in the mood for a practical joke and Bennett—so arrogant, so pompous, so maddeningly sure of himself—provided an especially inviting target.

Whatever its motivation, their tale appeared in the next morning's *Herald*. The *Sun*'s report of the autopsy, Bennett triumphantly announced, "is nothing more or less than a complete hoax from beginning to end. *Joice Heth is not dead.*"

That had not been Joice Heth on the examining table at all, Bennett declared: Joice Heth was alive and well and living in Hebron, Connecticut. The woman on whom Dr. Rogers had performed the autopsy was actually "a respectable old negress called AUNT NELLY," who had lived the past many years up in Harlem. At the time of her recent death she was eighty years of age, just as Dr. Rogers had determined. Someone in New York (Bennett believed it was a physician who had been "hoaxed by the Lunar Discoveries") had heard of Aunt Nelly's death and arranged to have her body shipped into the city and passed off as the venerable Joice Heth. The ruse had worked perfectly: the autopsy was conducted, the *Sun* wrote the story, and the public—once again—"swallowed the pill."

"Such is the true version of the hoax," Bennett pronounced with great satisfaction. The information had been given to him on the best authority, and "for the verity of which we have names and certificates in our possession." There was, however, still one more matter to address. Before he concluded, he wanted to "put a few plain questions" to Dr. David Rogers, who had played such a large role in the Joice Heth hoax and—Bennett now astonishingly charged—in the other great one of the age as well:

Are you not, Sir, the real author of the Lunar Hoax? Did you not furnish Richard A. Locke with the most of that humbug? Did he not, at your request, undertake to pass for the author of the work? Is it not known to you that he is incapable of writing the scientific portion of that hoax?

Bennett declared that he would await Dr. Rogers's explicit denial of the charges, written and signed by him. Once it was received, "we shall then stir our stumps" (a colloquialism of the time, meaning to get oneself moving) "and see if we can't produce certificates of their truth." To put it another way: he had not yet obtained any evidence for his new moon story accusations, not even "certificates" as authentic as the ones he claimed to have for the truth of the Aunt Nelly story. David Rogers never deigned to reply to James Gordon Bennett, which may have been fortunate for Bennett; numerous libel suits had been filed against newspapers of the day for less cause. Nor did Richard Adams Locke respond to Bennett's allegations about the authorship of the moon series, although about the "Aunt Nelly" story he did compose a single, extraordinary item.

The exhibitors of Joice Heth, Locke noted in the *Sun,* were apparently not content with making ten thousand dollars from "their humbug representation of her age when alive," nor with charging fifty cents a head to exhibit her body after death; now they had been "amusing themselves with hoaxing some stupid editors with the story that the body dissected the other day at the City Saloon, was not that of Joice Heth."

> One of these editors, if the despicable and unprincipled scribbler to whom we allude can be so termed, believed this story of the non-identity of the body, and proclaimed it in his loathsome little sheet, not knowing that the persons who had deceived him came directly from his office to ours and boasted of their new exploit!

This was a highly unusual display of personal invective from Richard Adams Locke, who seems to have been inflamed by Bennett's defamation of his friend David Rogers. It is worth noting that Locke referred here to the "persons" who had perpetrated the Aunt Nelly humbug—that is, Barnum as well as Lyman—and it was to both of them that he addressed the final sentence of the item, about as close to a direct threat as he ever produced in the pages of the *Sun:* "With the agents in this infamous imposture, we have hitherto dealt very mercifully, but if they proceed further, we will make this city rather uncomfortable for them."

In the *Sun* Joice Heth was dead at eighty years old; in the *Evening Star* she was dead at twice that age, while in the *Herald* she had not died at all. All over the city New Yorkers argued vigorously for each of these mutually exclusive propositions, just as a few months earlier they had debated whether intelligent life had been discovered on the moon. In New York in the 1830s, such arguments were precisely what it meant to participate in civic life. As New Yorkers increasingly claimed the right to vote, so too were they claiming their democratic right to judgment—the right to hold and express their own opinions. "That's just the question," Barnum once replied to someone who asked if an exhibit at his museum was "real." "Persons who pay their money at the door have the right to form their own opinions after they have got up stairs."

In this democratizing age the traditional practices of the older world were fast disappearing, like the venerable hillside estates leveled to make room for new avenues. The city's mayors, who for more than a century had been appointed by the governor and for a decade chosen by the Common Council, had since 1834 been voted in by direct election. At the beginning of the 1830s, trade unions were still a rarity in New York; by 1836, the *Evening Post* was estimating that "two-thirds of the working men in the city" were union members. Cartmen now called their employers "Mister" rather than the old-fashioned "Sir," and no longer felt inclined to doff a cap and bow deeply with averted eyes, the ritual of deference that went by the name "courtesy." Shaking hands had become the preferred greeting between men, a gesture that bespoke social equality rather than superiority and subordination. In 1835 the English novelist Frederick Marryat noted that it was "invariably the custom to shake hands," and complained that in America he was no longer able to size up a man's breeding at a glance.

The act of reading was changing too, with a flood of books, journals, and especially newspapers streaming from the new generation of printing presses. Not five years earlier, a newspaper had been a luxury reserved for the elite; its content as well as its prohibitive price had made sure of that. "Such a paper," declared an early issue of the *Sun*, "is an insult to a civilized community." There was power in information, Benjamin Day knew, and pleasure as well. So Day made sure that his paper, alongside its coverage of the issues of the day, included in its police court reports a healthy measure of sin, spectacle, tragedy, and amusement. A newspaper was a like a show hall that could be carried around in the pocket, available for viewing at any free moment of the day, and just a penny covered the price of admission.

Of course Benjamin Day was a newspaperman, not a showman, but in the 1830s the differences between the two were not as marked as might be imagined. "At the outset of my career," P. T. Barnum wrote in *Struggles and Triumphs,* a late edition of his autobiography, "I saw that everything depended on getting the people to think, and talk, and become curious and excited." Were he the type of man to write his autobiography, Benjamin Day could not have better related the secret of his own success. Like his fellow Yankee Barnum (the two men had been born just three months and eighty miles apart), Day understood that the *Sun* would rise and fall on its ability to engage the attention of the public, and like Barnum he was willing to offer some attractions that might not be considered strictly legitimate; he had made this clear in the very first issue of the *Sun,* when he placed a story on the front page about a Vermont boy who whistled even as he slept.

The following year Day had published a story about a four-foot snake removed from a sailor's stomach with the aid of a bowl of warm milk. The *Evening Star* had denounced the snake story as a hoax, and maybe it was and maybe it wasn't; the *Sun*'s readers hadn't seemed to care. To them, the story was not simply a fabrication, as it would be described today, irresponsible and deserving of condemnation; it was instead—to use that proud nineteenth-century word—a *humbug.*

As P. T. Barnum explained in his book on the subject, a humbug "consists in putting on glittering appearances—outside show—novel expedients, by which to suddenly arrest public attention, and attract the public eye and ear." Superficially, at least, Barnum's humbug is similar to Edgar Allan Poe's diddle, as each is a form of hoax. The diddle, however, is carefully designed to preclude any awareness that it has taken place: the grocery store owner does not realize he has been tricked out of his whiskey, or the camp-meeting attendee out of his bridge toll. A humbug, on the other hand, noisily calls attention to itself; it also allows for the possibility of doubt, and requires consent from those who participate in it. The humbug might well turn out to be authentic (many of Barnum's attractions were just what they were advertised as being), but whether it is true or false, the customers must depart believing they have gotten their money's worth. A promoter who fails to provide his customers what Barnum called "a full equivalent for their money" will be denounced as a swindler and a fraud, while one who delivers a proper humbug will find his customers coming again and again—the first time because they believe the attraction is authentic, the second time because they are not sure, and the third time to figure out how the trick has been pulled off. The entertainment lies less in the nature of the attraction (although as Barnum pointed out, a certain amount of "glitter" is essential) than in the implicit competition between patron and promoter, each one seeking to outwit the other in a game of deception and exposure. It was a distinction on which P. T. Barnum would build a career, and it helps to explain the continuing success of the *Sun* in the aftermath of the moon series.

James Gordon Bennett had predicted that New Yorkers would turn away from the *Sun* after the moon series was revealed as a hoax, but the *Sun*'s circulation never went down. A year later, in August 1836, the *Sun* was reporting a daily circulation of 27,000—more than 5,000 copies greater than the *combined* circulation of the city's eleven six-penny dailies. Like the patrons of the Joice Heth exhibition, who passionately debated her age and even her humanity—and who would continue to give Barnum their business for decades to come—New Yorkers admired the skill and ingenuity with which the Moon Hoax had been perpetrated. In Barnum's formulation, they had gotten their money's worth. They had been thoroughly fooled, but in looking back they felt less resentment than wonder.

The general sentiment was captured by Horace Greeley in the *New-Yorker,* in an item he wrote not long after the *Journal of Commerce* had identified Richard Adams Locke as the true author of the moon series.

> For our own part—frankly admitting that we were taken in to the full amount—we can feel no uncharitableness towards the perpetrator of the hoax. On the contrary, we advise all who have not read the whole story to buy a copy of his pamphlet, which costs but a shilling. . . . We shall not trumpet his name to the general ear—our acquaintance does not warrant even a passing nod—but we can say plumply that if the operator nets a few hundreds by his ingenuity, we shall find a gratification.

He felt confident that New Yorkers would, as he did, "relish a joke," and not harden their hearts against the *Sun* over "the whole magnificent hoax." Even the skeptics (of which, he noted, there had been not one where twenty now claimed the honor) would have to admit the brilliance of the work, its "air of unquestionable plausibility and verisimilitude," and the excitement that it had created in the city. Greeley reminded his readers of the trial, in ancient times, of the Greek who had circulated a false report of a military victory. "Am I worthy of punishment, O Athenians?" the man had proclaimed in his own defense. "Am I worthy of punishment for having given you a day of happiness?"

CHAPTER 16

The Best Self-Hoaxed
Man in New York

I~~N THE FALL~~ of 1836, after fifteen months as editor of the *Sun,* Richard
Adams Locke left to begin work on a new penny paper called the *New
Era.* Financed by a consortium of prominent New Yorkers, the newspaper
was coedited by Locke and Joseph Price, a poet and fellow journalist, formerly editor of the weekly journal the *New-York Mirror.* (Price stayed as
editor for only a few months, and then left to concentrate on his literary
pursuits.) The *New Era* would be New York's fourth penny paper, but one
that proposed to be something markedly different.

By this time, Locke had been in New York for nearly half a decade. He
had spent years trolling in the city's low places as a police court reporter,
and after becoming an editor once again, he had earned renown not as an
eloquent and impassioned editorialist against slavery but as the author of
a hoax. Now, with the *New Era,* he hoped to pursue a more high-minded
variety of journalism, one more consistent with his intellectual principles;
the enterprise would be his last great attempt to realize his promise as a
journalist and man of letters.

In the premiere issue of the *New Era,* published October 3, 1836, the
editors vowed to conduct a newspaper that "gentleman can patronize,
and ladies read without a blush," free of "recklessness and brutality, indecency and exaggeration, ribaldry and scurrility." They lamented how
the "immense capability of the daily press," which might be used to foster the public good, was instead devoted to "the most trivial and unin-
structive details of unimportant incidents, or the worse than useless, the

demoralizing disclosure of scenes of low pollution, and to unprincipled political machination." Though the *New Era* would offer a police court column (for a New York penny paper, not to do so was tantamount to a death wish), its editors made a point of refusing, in their word, the "disgusting" items; they also abjured what they saw as the manipulation and duplicity of the political newspapers, which, they claimed, sacrificed "every principle of freedom" for the short-term gain of whichever party they happened to favor.

In a declaration certainly inspired by Locke's own avocation, the editors vowed that their paper would not only be the equal of any in coverage of local, national, and foreign news, but that it would also give special attention to the latest developments in the world of science. For too long, they argued, science had been seen as the exclusive province of an intellectual elite; their paper would herald a new era "in which knowledge will be empowered with ubiquity, will be equally present in the cottages of the poor as in the mansions of the rich." Within the span of a single year, the *New Era* "shall render every one of its constant readers as well read in the great cyclopædia of universal knowledge as the man of leisure who makes it his study." This was a highly ambitious—some might even say quixotic—goal for a daily newspaper to set for itself, but it is a sign of the seriousness with which Richard Adams Locke undertook it that the *New Era* was the first literary production of any sort to which he signed his own name.

In the first issue the editors promised their readers "a diversified, a piquant, an elegant, sparkling, racy, and amusing chronicle of the times," and for a while the *New Era* delivered handsomely on that promise. Early on, the paper published an exposé of barbarous conditions at the Lunatic Asylum at Bloomingdale (in what is today called Morningside Heights), which resulted in the firing of at least one asylum employee. In its first month the *New Era* launched a regular series, *New York Medical Reports,* in which unnamed "competent medical gentlemen" (presumably one of them Locke's good friend Dr. David L. Rogers) reported on recent cases of interest at various city hospitals, and analyzed the treatment provided. "The state of medical science and practice in New York is most deplorable and degrading," declared the *New Era,* "and we mean to effect a thorough reform in it."

In a crusade of a more lighthearted nature, Richard Adams Locke wrote a satirical proposal for the reform of modern poetry, which he called *Poetical Economy.* Poetical economy, he explained, was "an important branch of political economy," although it had "hitherto escaped the attention of the most acute writers on the latter science." Paper, he wrote, was a highly expensive material, and no one wasted more of it than poets, what with their reliance on wide margins and ragged lines. (Not to mention the habitual overuse of capital letters: "Why should every line begin with a capital letter," Locke wondered, "when not one out of ten has anything capital in it?") Locke offered his readers "a practical illustration of the principles which we preach," a long original poem presented in the form of a news item, fully punctuated and broken up into paragraphs. It began:

> The hills of the Sun were thronged that day with Seraph Bards in bright array; and each bore thither a diamond lyre, itself an heaven of hallowed fire. The valleys glowed with hastening crowds, of peerless form and lofty mien, whose halos sprung to the downy clouds and fused afar the living green.

The item's byline identified Richard Adams Locke as "The Author of the Moon Story." It was the first time Locke had acknowledged himself in print as the hoax's creator; as the editor of his own paper, he clearly no longer felt himself bound to silence.

The first few months of the *New Era* also brought discussions of numerous scientific topics, among them physiology and phrenology ("an enlarged development of parts of the brain," the item explained, "will produce the intellectual characteristics to which they correspond"); the latest meetings of the British Scientific Association, at which the ubiquitous Sir David Brewster revealed that he was close to attaining his long-held goal of constructing powerful lenses out of rock salt; a recently made drawing from Germany of the fossilized remains of a "pterodactytus," a flying creature armed with a mouthful of monstrously sharp teeth ("The discovery of many gigantic reptiles in the ancient strata of the globe, proving, as it does, prodigious changes in its constitution and animal economy, is one of the most exciting and instructive results of modern science"); and a recent letter (this one entirely authentic) published by "our old friend, Sir John Herschel," marveling at the extraordinary transparency of the sky over the Cape of Good Hope. "With such a sky," remarked Locke cheerfully, "and such glasses as we know he has, who shall say that he will not eventually realize all the discoveries which we made for him last year in the moon?"

Still, despite its lively writing and energetic reporting the *New Era* had trouble finding a wide readership. In part the problem was one of timing: in early 1837, only a few months after the paper's founding, the country slid into a deep recession. Banks collapsed, financial firms shuttered their doors. Real estate prices, which had been soaring for years, suddenly plunged; lots that the previous September had sold for nearly five hundred dollars an acre now brought less than fifty. In New York, at least ten thousand mechanics and another two thousand clerks had been thrown out of work, and many thousands of families—even those fortunate enough to have a wage earner—were living in destitution. "At no period of its history," the *New Era* observed about New York, "has there been as great a degree of general distress as there is at this day."

Not surprisingly, the year was disastrous for the city's newspaper business. The *Transcript* was crippled by the downturn in advertising revenue and would fold just two years later. Even the mighty *Sun* felt the pinch. In 1835 and 1836 the paper had turned a profit of twenty thousand dollars per year; by 1837 it was struggling to break even. If the hard times could so dramatically affect even the world's most widely read newspaper, it is not difficult to imagine the problems faced by an upstart, one that had not yet found its footing in the country's most competitive market against three established penny papers—and having willfully deprived itself of the racier items that had helped win readers to the penny papers in the first place.

As the months passed and the financial panic worsened, the pressure on Richard Adams Locke must have been enormous. By this time he and Esther had left their small apartment on Franklin Street and settled in the village of Tompkinsville on Staten Island, a cluster of houses peeking out amid the green hills rising steeply from the water. Beyond the village lay woods and fields and a patchwork of farms, mostly small but highly cultivated and boasting a variety of fruit orchards. Far removed from the clamor of Manhattan, it was closer in spirit to Locke's childhood home of East Brent, a rural village surrounded by the apple orchards of Somerset. From their house it was just a few minutes' walk down the hill—the breezes cool even in the summer and the air smelling delightfully of salt—to the Tompkinsville landing, where Locke boarded the morning ferry across the Narrows to the Whitehall slip in "mast-hemm'd Manhattan," as Walt Whitman would later call it. He would not return home until well past dark, after the children were already asleep. Their daughter Adelaide had now been joined by two sons, Richard and Lewis. Soon even more children would arrive; with each passing year Locke's expenses increased. He owned no share in the *New Era* and was entitled only to a portion of any "clear profits" that might be generated in the future—which, as 1837 turned into 1838, seemed as remote as ever. Not long into his editorship at the *New Era* he had written of "the pecuniary difficulties to which we are subjected, owing to non-payment by subscribers—the failure of paper-manufacturers in their contracts—the sordid altercations with a certain class of advertisers, who insist upon having their own way against every idea of right and justice—the irregularities of carriers and the consequent complaints of justly dissatisfied readers." All of these, he admitted, were "trials of temper, and harrassing [*sic*] disturbers of equanimity and composure of mind." He was putting in thirteen-hour days at work, in the office from eight in the morning until nine at night, and as he made his way exhaustedly home on the ferry moving back toward the dark shore of Staten Island, his mind was surely occupied with schemes to boost the paper's circulation. Perhaps he thought he had found one in the winter of 1838, when, in his desperation, he resorted to a stratagem that had worked once before: he attempted a hoax.

"The Lost Manuscript of Mungo Park" (as the *New Era* story was entitled) purported to present entries from the travel diary of the Scottish explorer Mungo Park, who had disappeared on an expedition along the river Niger in 1806. The *New Era* trumpeted the recent discovery of Park's diary, three decades lost, which revealed the fate that had befallen the great explorer. It was an imaginative idea that might well have provided fertile ground for one of the adventure novels popular at the time. As a hoax, however, it failed utterly. Unlike Locke's moon series, the Mungo Park story fooled no one; New Yorkers were well aware of who the *New Era* editor was, and they viewed with a gimlet eye any unexpected, astonishing revelations available only in his newspaper—particularly one that brought word of discoveries made by an illustrious Briton in Africa. As Edgar Allan Poe tartly noted, "Mr. Locke's columns were a suspected district." The city's rival papers paid no attention to the *New Era* story. Nor did the general public; no crowds swarmed the Nassau Street offices of the *New Era,* located on the very same block as the *Sun* building, where they had excitedly gathered in the late summer of 1835. The attempt to market another hoax had turned out to be a colossal miscalculation. Not only did it make the *New Era* look foolish, it also confirmed Locke's reputation as a hoaxer. Like Mungo Park himself, the series came to an abrupt end and was never seen again.

With the *New Era,* Locke was facing a bitter irony: for all its strengths, the newspaper could not compete with the brand of sensationalist mass-market penny paper that his own work had helped popularize. Before long, the grim realities of the marketplace brought a pronounced shift in the paper's editorial direction. In the first issue, Locke and Price had proudly identified themselves as "belonging to no political or religious party, partizans in nothing, and entirely free from any sectarian or party prejudice," quoting with approval Alexander Pope's dictum that "Party is the madness of many, for the gain of a few." By 1838, however, notices for meetings of the Tammany Society (the Democratic Party's political machine) had begun to appear below the paper's masthead, and the idiosyncratic articles on science and literature had all but disappeared, replaced by a relentless drumbeat of attacks against the national bank, monopolies, paper money, and Whig politicians and their supporters in the press. (Political parties, unlike medical reformers, provide a ready-made readership.)

The following April, the *New Era*'s publisher, the Ann Street printer Jared W. Bell, renamed the newspaper the *Democratic-Republican New Era*—its identification as a party paper was now complete—and removed Richard Adams Locke's name from the front page, replacing it with his own. A political journalist, Theron Rudd, was now editing the paper with Locke, whose position looked to be growing increasingly tenuous. On the first day of October, Locke ran an article that criticized the collector of the New York Custom House, Jesse Hoyt, for paying his employees in small-denomination paper money issued by local banks with whom he maintained friendly relations, rather than in guaranteed government specie. The next day Locke extended his criticism to Jonathan Coddington, the city's postmaster: "We shall have but one more favor to ask of the heads of the Custom House and Post Office departments in this city, and that is that they will have the goodness to keep their hands off the Democracy."

These articles, Locke believed, led to his ouster. On October 10, 1839, almost three years to the day since that buoyant first issue of the *New Era,* Richard Adams Locke sent a letter to the *Evening Post,* writing, "I solicit the medium of your independent journal to inform the public, and more especially the Democratic party, that I am not responsible for any articles that may hereafter appear in the New Era." According to Locke, Hoyt and Coddington had made a deal to give Jared W. Bell a much-needed loan, on the condition that they be allowed to appoint editors of their own choosing. The two men were longtime Democratic power brokers in the city; Hoyt was widely suspected of embezzling from the Custom House, and although Locke did not state this directly, he clearly implied that they were proposing to funnel public money to the *New Era* in exchange for editorial favors. Locke alleged that he had been summarily dismissed by Bell, without even being permitted to make his good-byes in the pages of the newspaper he had helped to found. In his anger and frustration, he had delivered a swift, highly uncharacteristic act of violence, directed not against the men who had stripped him of his job but against their offending words.

> Having, by a most odious and despicable act of usurpation, been prevented from announcing my disconnection with the New Era in its editions of this morning, and not choosing even to tacitly incur the responsibility of the political articles which had been introduced to it by others, I broke to pieces the type in which they were set up for publication; and I deem this an act of justice not less due to myself than the democratic party.

For his part, Jared W. Bell firmly denied all of Locke's charges. On October 11, in a long letter addressed to the readers of the *New Era*, Bell insisted, "I have never exchanged a word, or had any intercourse, either directly or indirectly, with Mr. Hoyt or Mr. Coddington on the subject of this paper; I have neither solicited nor received any assistance from them." He had assured Locke of this fact, again and again; nevertheless, according to Bell, Locke took it into his head that he was about to be dismissed, and on the day of his letter to the *Post* he had announced to many of his associates that he no longer had any connection with the paper. Bell made other arrangements for the production of the next morning's issue and went home around ten o'clock. Later that evening, he wrote, Locke came to the office to insert in the paper an item he called his "valedictory," reiterating his conviction that Hoyt and Coddington would soon be naming their own editors. But the *New Era*'s foreman, on orders from Bell himself (word of Locke's actions had been sent to his home), refused to allow the statement to be published. "Learning this," Bell wrote of Locke,

> he came again into the office, accompanied by his accomplice, after the type had all been prepared for the paper, and with many professions of

friendship for the establishment, threw my men off their guard and availed himself of the temporary absence of my foreman from the form, which was then nearly made up, to seize the chase, and in the instant he tumbled the whole inside form into pi. The moment he did this, he fled from the office as fast as he could run.

Bell was willing to concede one point: "It is true that I have requested several persons to assist, at many times, in writing articles for the paper, for it was not always that I could rely upon Mr. Locke's discharging his duty." He provided no substantiating details for this assertion (due to their absence or his kindness, it is impossible to say), but one explanation does suggest itself: that by the end of the 1830s, alcohol had begun to get the better of Richard Adams Locke.

Not long after the launch of the *New Era* in 1837, a dispute between Locke and Benjamin Day over fifty dollars that Day claimed he was owed for uncompleted work led him to pillory Locke in the *Sun* as "contemptible" and "reckless," "the farthest extreme from veracity, and decency," and, most damningly, as "a pitiable wanderer from the pale of sobriety and honesty." Alcoholism was a charge not often made, even in the bare-knuckle world of New York journalism (where rivals tended to brand each other more generically, along the lines of "villain" or "blackguard" or "lizard"), and Day's editorial attacks tended to be relatively moderate, certainly in comparison with the awe-inspiring Niagaras of invective that a James Gordon Bennett or James Watson Webb could summon forth. Day further added a distressing bit of specificity to his accusation, making reference to an incident of some months earlier when, he claimed, Locke had been revealed as "a drunkard, lying exposed in the punch room of a public theater."

Three years later, after Locke's contentious departure from the *New Era,* an item appeared in the *New-Yorker* of December 19, 1840, concerning a lecture he gave at the American Institute on "the science of Terrestrial Magnetism." The anonymous *New-Yorker* correspondent confessed to not having understood all of the evening's presentation, in part because Locke "labored under a serious indisposition, which somewhat affected his delivery." In the nineteenth century, the word *indisposition* was often used as a euphemism for drunkenness. Several months after that, Locke was hired to coedit the new Democratic paper the *Brooklyn Daily Eagle,* but his tenure there lasted only a year, when he was replaced, in the words of a modern historian of the *Eagle,* "with the more conservative and hard working William B. Marsh." Richard Adams Locke could well be accused of lacking conservatism, but his productivity over many years, for a succession of New York newspapers, belies the notion that he was averse to hard work and raises the suspicion that Locke had begun to "wander," as Day had suggested, too often from sobriety.

Locke's behavior may have been growing erratic, his work routines irregular, but to those who knew him he was, in the phrase of the day, a gentleman and a scholar, and he seems to have inspired sympathy even among those who ultimately turned against him. ("He would have been a first-rate man," Benjamin Day later remarked of his former editor, "but for the drink.") Immediately after the break with Jared W. Bell, a group of Locke's friends raised money to publish another newspaper he would edit, under the original name *New Era;* that paper, though, did not survive for long, in part because of a court order obtained by Bell enjoining Locke from the use of the name. Richard Adams Locke had friends in all corners of the city; he was, in the words of his rival James Gordon Bennett, "a fluent and a ready speaker," and in the following years he remained a presence in New York's literary salons, among them one *soirée* that took place on January 10, 1846, in the double parlor of Miss Anne Charlotte Lynch's house on Waverly Place, where the evening's guests included not just Richard Adams Locke but also Edgar Allan Poe—the only time the two men were ever known to cross paths. (In a letter, the party's hostess referred to Locke as "the man in the moon," an indication of how, more than ten years after its publication, the moon series continued to define him in the public mind.)

In May 1840, one of Locke's literary acquaintances, Park Benjamin, editor of the popular weekly paper the *New World,* sent him a brief but highly flattering letter at his home in Staten Island. For some time, Benjamin wrote, he had hoped to republish Locke's moon series in the *New World,* because it had been "a topic prolific of lively anecdote, ever since its first publication; and there are many persons who have read it but cursorily, in the disjointed parts in which it appeared in most of the public prints, who would be gratified with a reperusal of it in a connected form." (Benjamin added that even those who had been thoroughly hoaxed by the story might be interested in reading it again, if only "from that comical sort of instinctive curiosity with which we look back at the peach-stone, or piece of orange-peel, that has sent us skating on the pavement.") He hoped that Locke might furnish him with a full copy of "your far-famed Moon-story" for publication in the *New World,* and also write an introduction discussing "the circumstances that suggested its composition and the incidents attendant upon its unexampled career."

Richard Adams Locke was then unemployed, after nearly a decade of continuous work as a New York journalist. At the *Sun,* he had disclaimed authorship of the moon series; at the *New Era,* he had claimed it but made no explanation. Now, without affiliation, he felt freer still. Perhaps he already sensed that his literary talents, once so abundant, were fleeing him; perhaps he knew he did not have many years left as a working writer, and that *Great Astronomical Discoveries* would be the only literary production for which he would be remembered. Park Benjamin had unexpectedly provided him an opportunity to set the record straight at last. After five years, Locke decided that the time had come to reveal why he had written his moon story.

His letter of reply, which was published in the *New World* on May 16, 1840, might have been more than Park Benjamin had bargained for. Running across six columns of one of the *New World's* mammoth pages, the letter comprised some nine thousand words—nearly as long as the moon series itself. If the editor was interested in "so stale a joke as my moon quiz," Locke wrote, then he was happy to provide a full copy. "The fact is," he admitted, "I am unaffectedly ashamed of it, not from any casuistry about it as a hoax, but because, in this very respect, it is so bungling a production. I have feared that it might be considered vain in me, if not impudent, to flutter it anew in the faces of those who are candid enough to say they were temporarily deceived by it—vain, if I were supposed to be unconscious of its glaring faults, and impudent if aware of them." Still, he was pleased for a chance to describe how it came to be written, "since these will explain the motives of an attempt which has been gravely denounced as mischievous and immoral, and, perhaps, supply an excuse for the imperfections in its execution."

For many years, Locke explained, he had been deeply concerned by the popularity of what he referred to as "the *imaginative school of philosophy,*" and its damaging effect on the practice of modern science. Perhaps best exemplified by—though by no means limited to—the Scottish astronomer Thomas Dick (who believed that God would not create celestial bodies without intelligent beings present to appreciate them), the school practiced what Locke called *"theological and devotional* encroachments upon the legitimate province of science," taking the painstaking, dispassionate, and logical methods by which science rightfully operates and replacing them with fanciful and ultimately unprovable theories about God's design. Its studies were pursued less with scientific experimentation than with textual interpretation, were beholden not to reason but to dogma, and were grounded not in fact but in faith. For this school, truths about the world were to be found in scripture rather than nature—or, as Locke deftly summarized it, the *"word* of God" rather than the *"works* of God."

Scientific inquiry, he argued, "should be free as the mountain air and unchartered as the light of heaven," yet in the nineteenth century it was still laboring under the same sectarian fetters that had once silenced Galileo and had for too long deprived the world of the revolutionary theories of Copernicus. Locke himself knew several geologists who had abandoned valuable lines of research "because they perceived it was leading them to the awful discovery that the globe on which we live was not formed in literally six days of twenty-four hours each!" He had tried as best he could to persuade them otherwise. Three of those days, he pointed out, were said to have elapsed before the heavenly bodies that measure time had even been created—and so they could not have corresponded to the days of our own age. Perhaps those three periods, which scripture refers to as "days," were in fact incalculably long. If so, the text might comport perfectly with the discoveries that were now being made about the true age of the earth, the theological testimony thus coming into alignment with the geological one. But Locke could not induce the geologists to continue their studies. "The imaginative and devotional philosophy prevailed; the sectarian theology of the pulpit triumphed over the theological sections of the hills."

This domineering religiosity, as well as its harmful effect on intellectual life, was not a new phenomenon in the United States, nor was it noted only by Locke. In 1835, the same year Locke created his moon story, Alexis de Tocqueville published the first volume of his classic work *Democracy in America*. "Christianity reigns without obstacles, by universal consent," he observed about the country in which he had traveled so widely. "So the human spirit never sees an unlimited field before itself; however bold it is, from time to time it feels that it must halt before insurmountable barriers. Before innovating, it is forced to accept certain primary assumptions and to submit its boldest conceptions to certain formalities which retard and check it." For three decades, going back to the turn of the century, America had been in the grip of the Second Great Awakening—a nationwide religious revival meant to root out the vestiges of deism (a heresy, it was widely felt, to which far too many of the Founding Fathers had fallen prey) and replace it with a stricter, more evangelical brand of Christianity. P. T. Barnum had seen the Second Great Awakening up close in Connecticut; he had grown to adulthood fearing it, had gone to jail for opposing it, and had eventually fled from it to New York City. (As a twenty-two-year-old newspaper editor, Barnum had been jailed for incurring the wrath of a church leader; as a twenty-five-year-old newspaper editor, Locke had been fired for the same offense.) It was a time when almost all American colleges were organized and supported by churches, when the forces of rationalism and free thought were being expunged from campuses everywhere, when science courses instructed students in the precepts of "natural theology," according to which science served as the handmaiden of theology, its highest purpose to illuminate God's ultimate design. From university to laboratory to observatory, theology exerted its dominion over science and received its tribute, like a biblical king, in almost every scientific work that issued from every press.

Though Richard Adams Locke was an enthusiast of geology—he referred to it as "this grand and particularly attractive study"—he had always been especially interested in astronomy. He knew well the work of the religious astronomers; he had read the accounts of the sublime scenery to be found on the moon, the reports of lunar fortifications, the schemes to communicate with the lunarians by means of vast Siberian figures. As he explained in his letter, he was continually astonished, and horrified, at the credence given to this fairy-tale version of astronomy, this *pseudo philosophy* (as he called it) that dressed itself so extravagantly in the robes of piety and faith; furthermore, he was convinced that if its power remained unchecked, it would continue to exert its baneful influence on future generations of young minds.

And so he related to the *New World*'s readers how he had come to write the story of the late discoveries in the moon:

I, therefore, resolved to throw a pebble at this Colossus, not, certainly, with the hope of rivalling the feat of David, but merely to express my independent and utter contempt for the imaginative and canting school, by endeavoring to out-imagine it, and ape its solemn cant, under the mask of dignified and plausible science.

The religious astronomers professed their faith in the existence of life on the moon; he would give them life on the moon. They believed that life there was a paradise; he would give them a paradise, a world in which all of God's creatures—man-bat and unicorn and biped beaver alike—lived together in harmony. They insisted that the creatures of the moon must be religious, if not avowedly Christian; he would give them lunarian temples of sapphire and gold. Moreover, he would garb his own discoveries in the very language used by the religious astronomers, full of pious platitudes and scientific-sounding nonsense—and in the process, he would expose the entire philosophy for the humbug that it was.

Great Astronomical Discoveries had not been intended as a hoax at all; it had been intended as a satire.

In 1838 Thomas Dick published another popular work of religious astronomy, entitled *Celestial Scenery; or, the Wonders of the Planetary System Displayed, Illustrating the Perfections of Deity and a Plurality of Worlds*. The section of the book called "Lunar Inhabitants" contained an extraordinary footnote—it took up nearly an entire page—in which Dick replied, for the first and only time, to Richard Adams Locke's moon series. "A short time ago," he wrote, "a *hoax* was attempted to be played off on the public in relation to this subject. . . . The author of this deception, I understand, is a young man in the city of New York, who makes some pretensions to scientific acquirements, and he may perhaps be disposed to congratulate himself on the success of his experiment on the public." He continued sternly:

But it ought to be remembered that all such attempts to deceive are violations of the laws of the Creator, who is the "God of Truth," and who requires "truth in the inward parts;" and, therefore, they who wilfully and deliberately contrive such impositions ought to be ranked in the class of liars and deceivers. The "Law of *Truth*" ought never for a moment to be sported with. On the universal observance of this law depend the happiness of the whole intelligent system and the foundations of the throne of the Eternal. The greatest part of the evils which have afflicted our world have arisen from a violation of this law, and were it to be *universally* violated, the inhabitants of all worlds would be thrown into a state of confusion and misery, and creation transformed into a chaos.

The final sentence of the footnote was addressed directly to Richard Adams Locke: "It is to be hoped that the author of the deception to which I have adverted, as he advances in years and in wisdom, will perceive the folly and immorality of such conduct."

Richard Adams Locke had read *Celestial Scenery*, including that disapproving footnote, and he resented the notion of Thomas Dick lecturing him on the fundamental nature of truth. "So far from feeling that I deserve the coarse reproaches of Dr. Dick," he wrote in his letter to the *New World*, "I think it quite laudable in any man to satirize, as I did, that school of crude speculation and cant of which he is so eminent a professor." His own astronomical production had been merely a satire, not intended to be taken seriously. "But what has Dr. Dick to say in defence of his own hoaxes, which were chiefly instrumental in preparing the way for mine, and without which I cannot conceive that it could have obtained so instantaneous and extraordinary a circulation?"

In his letter Locke addressed only a single point from *Celestial Scenery*, which he believed would be sufficient to illustrate "the serious trespasses of Dr. Dick's theological school of philosophy upon the paramount jurisdiction of physical science." Thomas Dick had long insisted—in the face of substantial evidence to the contrary—that there could be no volcanoes on the moon. Volcanoes, like earthquakes and hurricanes, were evidence of God's displeasure, and God could be displeased only with sinners; because the lunarians existed in a state of innocence, their landscape would not be blemished with such agents of physical destruction. "Is not this pretty stuff to pass for philosophy," asked Locke, "and to be presented to our youth as a rule of judgment in determining questions of fact?"

The real world of nature, he pointed out, contains an astonishing multiplicity of functions, and it was the height of arrogance—not to mention pitiable scientific reasoning—to reserve to oneself the right to define certain of them, arbitrarily, as the products of "goodness" or "sin."

The fang of the viper, the claws of the tiger, the tail of the spider, the sting of the wasp, and the beak and talons of the eagle, are as "very good," for their respective purposes, as the milky foundations of the mammalia, or the curious chrysalis of the butterfly. All nature abounds

with destructive agents; in fact the whole system of nature is one of production and destruction. The leaves of autumn fall to give birth to the
buds of spring; the aged tree dies to give place to the sapling at its feet;
and so the generations of all sentient beings pass away that others may
succeed them. . . . As to man in his paradisiacal state (perhaps I should
say estate)—that is Adam, for there was only one man, and only he for
a little while, for whom volcanoes and such things were improper—it is
only necessary to say that if he had fallen into the river Pison before he
had learned to swim, it would have closed his account for him almost as
quickly as Mount Vesuvius or Etna. And without intending the least dis-
respect to our mother Eve, I can venture to affirm that if the serpent had
crawled down her pretty throat when she was asleep with her mouth
open under the tree of life, it would as certainly have been the death of
her as if she had been swallowed up by an earthquake.

The bogus science perpetrated by Dick and his colleagues in their
many best-selling books was "a trampling upon all the evidences of nature's inherent laws to elevate a familiar figment of a creed." To lampoon
it, Locke had filled the lunar "seas" with real water, built on its surface
shining temples and smoke-emitting cottages (even in the absence of a
lunar atmosphere), and supplied many of the moon's creatures with hairy
veils to shield their eyes from the great extremes of light and dark—
when, as he well knew, the side of the moon that faces the earth receives
no great changes of light at all. "Could such an outrage upon science
have deceived for a moment," Locke asked the readers of the *New
World*, "had not the canting philosophy of the Dick school prepared the
public to swallow any thing however absurd, that came to them recommended by this peculiar stamp?"

Locke had written *Great Astronomical Discoveries* as a satire—but the
religious astronomy of the time precluded satire, so credulous was the general public about the likelihood of extraterrestrial life, so well schooled
were they in the theories of Thomas Dick and his colleagues. The great
mass of the public (nine out of ten, estimated Poe; all but the most hard-
ened skeptics, agreed Barnum) hailed the story as truth, and then, when its
authorship was revealed, condemned it as a hoax. It was neither.

Richard Adams Locke understood the tremendous influence of the religious astronomers—it was what had inspired him to write the moon series
in the first place—but he could hardly have anticipated just how deeply

ingrained their ideas had become. His friend William Griggs later remarked, "So thoroughly was the popular mind, even among the best educated and most reading classes, imbued with these fanciful anticipations of
vast lunar discoveries, that, at the time Mr. Locke's 'Moon Story' was written, scarcely any thing could have been devised and announced upon the
subject too extravagant for general credulity to receive." In 1852 Griggs issued a new edition of the complete series in a book entitled *The Celebrated
"Moon Story," Its Origins and Incidents*. In the introduction to the volume
he revealed Locke's "disappointment and chagrin" at the response of the
public to *Great Astronomical Discoveries*. As the excitement over the series continued to grow, Locke confided to close friends his own sense of
failure about it—how foolish he felt about the response it had gotten. "If
the story be either received as a veritable account, or rejected as a hoax,"
he told them, "it is quite evident that it is an abortive satire.

"And in either case," he added ruefully, "I am the best self-hoaxed man
in the whole community."

Five years before Locke's letter to the *New World*, on December 5, 1835,
the six-penny paper *Evening Star* reported on South Carolina governor
George McDuffie's recent message proclaiming that slavery "is consistent
with the laws of God, and is expressly sanctioned by the Old and New
Testaments." The *Star*'s editor, Mordecai Manuel Noah, was among slavery's most visible defenders in New York, and he agreed with McDuffie's
position. Anticipating that his readers would share his views, Noah suggested, "We should like to see this point discussed and explained." Three
days later, in the *Sun*, Richard Adams Locke offered his own discussion—
facing what he acknowledged was "the certain condemnation of public
opinion"—in an item headlined "Mr. Noah's Request Complied with."

The governor's propositions were "glaringly atrocious," Locke declared, for slavery was "a monstrously unjust and iniquitous system" that
could never find absolution in the authority of scripture. "We hesitate not
to say," he wrote,

> that even if the sacred scriptures of the Old and New Testaments really
> did sanction slavery in those ages in which they were written, and
> among those people to whom they were addressed, their authority on
> such a question would be no more binding in the present age, and upon
> the nations of the world, than the Old Testament sanction of polygamy,

or the New Testament sanction of the "right divine" of kings. The Scriptures are considered, by all believers in their divine inspiration, to be of immutable authority upon matters of faith; but upon modes of government, and systems of social polity, if not, indeed, even upon religious rites and ceremonies, it is admitted by nearly every commentator, their authority was only temporary, and not designed to extend through all future periods of time.

What would have become of the Declaration of Independence, Locke wanted to know, if the colonists had obeyed St. Paul's injunction to "honor the king"? There was not much in that document of the "submission" demanded by the apostle in an earlier age. And how were the other tenets of scripture observed by believers today? The Christians rejected the Jewish doctrines and Jews the Christian ones. The Calvinists took issue with the Methodists even on the interpretation of the same texts, to say nothing of the interpretations variously preferred by the Quakers, the Dunkers, the Jumpers, the Universalists, the Swedenborgians, the Sublapsarians, and the Supralapsarians, not to mention all the other religious sects that "have so divided the sacred volume among them, that nothing short of a theological resurrection could restore its identity in the world of faith." However infallible the ancient text might be in itself, wrote Locke, fallibility was everywhere in the human *interpretation* of it. Thus the supposed biblical "authority" claimed by one faction should never be imposed on the conduct or conscience of another—least of all in an attempt to justify slavery. The Hebrew slaves had been emancipated from their bondage in Egypt, despite having been "as useful to the Pharoahs in building pyramids and cultivating fields, as the southern slaves are to their taskmasters and sovereigns." Moreover, Locke noted pointedly, the Bible abounds with examples of bloodshed "given expressly upon divine command," and which could be produced "to justify a negro insurrection against the slave proprietors of the South, and tell the slaves that unless they slew them all, with their wives and little ones, so that not one should be left alive, divine anger would rest upon them for their forbearance."

Locke's response to Mordecai Noah was more than just a repudiation of any scriptural justification for slavery; it was, in a larger sense, a warning about the dangers of a literal-minded view of the Bible and a plea to recognize the appropriate limits of religion in society. It was a line of thinking that had informed Richard Adams Locke's entire career. As a

young writer in London, he joined with the Republicans, the radicals
who daringly advocated the right of religious nonconformism. As the editor of a literary journal in Bristol, he wrote eloquently of God without
ever invoking scripture or seeking the stamp of religious authority. As the
editor of a newspaper in Somerset, he championed Catholic emancipation despite the powerful opposition of the local clergy. Across the ocean
in New York, his pamphlet about the murder trial of Matthias, which in
other hands might have been merely a sensationalistic account of a false
prophet accused of all manner of lurid acts, became instead a reflection
on the nature of faith and on the enduring conflict between science and
religion. After his journalistic successes, when he was provided the opportunity to start his own newspaper, the one he established paid special
attention to science, which he saw—perhaps too optimistically—as a liberating force, one that, given enough support, could usher in a new era
of human enlightenment.

And of course, at the *Sun,* he created his moon story—or Moon Hoax,
as it has for so long been inaccurately termed—the work for which he is
still remembered, when he is remembered at all. *Great Astronomical Discoveries, Lately Made by Sir John Herschel, L.L.D., F.R.S., &c. at the
Cape of Good Hope* was recognized in its own time as a wonderful literary production, highly imaginative, gorgeously written, its author worthy
of mention in the same sentence as Swift and Defoe. It remains all that
today, but it is something else as well. It is a call to us, from the decades
before Darwin, not to sacrifice intellectual freedom to religious beliefs,
however strongly those beliefs are held or however loudly they are proclaimed. Richard Adams Locke's great work shone for only a very brief
time, but it never died out entirely, like the light from a distant star that
still comforts though it was produced long ago, and appears ever brighter
the darker the sky.

That Tyranny Shall
Be No Longer

BENJAMIN DAY WAS only twenty-seven years old when he sold the *Sun* to Moses Yale Beach in 1837. He had left school to apprentice as a printer at the age of fourteen, had worked day and night to make a success of himself, and the forty thousand dollars he received in the sale was enough for him and his family to live comfortably for the rest of his life. It had seemed like the correct decision at the time, but Day would live for another fifty-two years, and although he later became involved in many enterprises—including the literary monthly *Brother Jonathan* and in 1843 a short-lived daily newspaper called the *True Sun*—none ever brought him the kind of personal and financial rewards he gained from the *Sun*. "I owned the whole concern till I sold it to Beach," Day told the *Sun* in 1883, on the occasion of its semicentennial. "The silliest thing I ever did in my life was to sell that paper."

Day had left the radical labor movement as a young man, but he always retained a connection with the working people of the city, and he believed they were entitled to a newspaper that was meant for them. He had imagined a penny newspaper that was lively and sensational and deeply engaged with the life of the city—and in no time that sort of newspaper was everywhere. In 1836, just three years after the *Sun* was founded, a visitor from Philadelphia reported seeing newspapers in the hands of nearly every man in New York and Brooklyn, and nearly every boy old enough to read. "These papers are to be found in every street, lane, and alley; in every hotel, tavern, counting-house, shop, etc. Almost every porter and dray-man, while not engaged in his occupation, may be seen with a paper in his hands," he observed. (The Philadelphian did not mention this, but much the same was surely true among women: the advertisements in the papers were directed at women as much as at men.)

Each year new and ever grander buildings went up in New York, and from all around them came the cries of newsboys hawking not just the *Sun* and the *Herald,* but also the *Daily News* and the *Daily Express,* the *Evening Tattler* and the *Evening Mail,* the *Corsair,* the *Bee,* the *Serpent,* the *Union,* the *Rough Hewer,* and many others with names equally obscure today. Most of the papers had all the durability (not to mention the illuminating power) of lightning bugs, but together they demonstrated the dynamism and vitality of the penny press, and the abiding public enthusiasm for the type of newspaper Benjamin Day had first put together in his little print shop on William Street.

"The consequences of the scheme," wrote Edgar Allan Poe about the founding of the *Sun,* "in their influence on the whole newspaper business of the country, and through this business on the interests of the country at large, are probably beyond all calculation." Of course, a great many factors contributed to the rapid growth of the newspaper business in America, including faster printing presses that supported far greater circulations, but there can be no mistaking the truly revolutionary impact of the penny paper on America. From New York the penny press radiated swiftly outward, to cities all around the country. Just across the East River in Brooklyn was the *Daily Eagle,* a morning paper aligned with the local Democratic Party, which for its first year was edited by Richard Adams Locke, and later by an energetic young writer named Walt Whitman. (The official history of the *Eagle,* issued for the paper's fiftieth anniversary, recalled that Whitman "occupied the editorial chair principally on stormy days; for nothing could keep him out of the sunshine, and in pleasant weather his editorial duties received scant attention.") By the 1840s nearly every large or medium-size American city had a penny paper of its own. Philadelphia had its *Public Ledger,* Boston its *Daily Times,* New Orleans its *Picayune,* Cincinnati its *Enquirer,* Cleveland its *Plain Dealer,* and Baltimore its own *Sun*—many of which continue to publish today.

At the beginning of that vitally important decade, in 1830, the United States had a population of just under 13 million; there were 852 newspapers nationwide, with a combined circulation of 68 million copies a year. Ten years later, the population had grown to 17 million, but the country now boasted 1,631 newspapers, with a combined annual circulation of 196 million copies. Though the population had increased by about one-third, the number of newspapers had nearly doubled, and total circulation nearly tripled. The United States had become, for the first time, a nation of newspaper readers.

UNLIKE Benjamin Day, James Gordon Bennett never sold the newspaper he founded. In 1866, having entered his seventies and finally feeling the pull of old age, he passed the ownership of the *Herald* on to his twenty-five-year-old son, who was also named, unsurprisingly, James Gordon Bennett. By this time the *Herald*'s reporting had a reach and immediacy never before seen, and, just as Bennett had predicted many years earlier, it had passed the *Sun* to become the most widely read newspaper in the world.

Shortly before his retirement, Bennett gathered his energies for one last major undertaking: building a new office for the *Herald,* one that would adequately reflect the grandeur of his creation. For years he had been looking for a choice plot of land on Broadway, the city's main avenue; in 1865 he found it on the corner of Broadway and Ann Street, just below City Hall Park—and then, having purchased it, found that he had been outwitted once again by P. T. Barnum.

Bennett and Barnum had maintained a contentious relationship for three decades, ever since they first tangled over Joice Heth. It would not have been apparent to anyone who met them socially, but in significant aspects the two were a good deal alike. Each was a man of outsize ambition, a religious nonconformist, a trafficker in racial stereotypes, and an incomparable judge of public taste, who had built an empire on the force of his own personality. The two men, however, neither liked nor trusted each other. ("He is like the mother mountain of gold in California," Bennett once wrote of Barnum, "with two and one-half per cent of gold dust to a mountain of primitive rock.") Though Barnum always advertised his attractions in the *Herald,* Bennett regularly criticized them in his reviews; in 1854 Barnum sent Bennett a letter complaining that he had "been in the habit of making me a kind of target for the last 18 years." For his part, Barnum was not above passing derogatory stories about Bennett's private life to his friend Moses Beach at the *Sun.* The antagonism between the two would eventually yield a truly remarkable story; and though, like so many others of Barnum's stories, it is impossible to know how much of it is true, just the fact that it may be authentic speaks volumes.

In early 1851, the story goes, Bennett and his wife boarded the same steamship bound for New Orleans on which Barnum was touring with his celebrated attraction, the opera singer Jenny Lind. A member of Barnum's staff, furious about the *Herald*'s attacks on his employer, declared one night that he would throw Bennett overboard in the darkness—"Nobody will know it," he said wildly, "and I will be doing the world a favor"— and only Barnum's intercession prevented him from carrying out his plan. (Beyond the senselessness of the crime itself, Barnum reminded him, "from the fact of the existing relations between the editor and myself, I should be the first to be accused of his murder.") After persuading his employee to return to his own stateroom, Barnum ordered that the man be watched for the next several days until he calmed down. "More than one of my party said then," reflected Barnum, clearly relishing the irony of the story, "and has often said since, what I really believe to be true, that 'James Gordon Bennett would have been drowned that night had it not been for P. T. Barnum.'"

In 1841 Barnum bought Scudder's American Museum, a five-story marble structure at the corner of Broadway and Ann Street (the deal that he secured with his five acres of Ivy Island), and immediately set to work. He flew the flags of the world from the roof, the American flag towering over them all. He hired a band to play on the roof during the day (a deliberately unmelodious one, so that onlookers would hurry to come inside, out of earshot), and installed the first limelight New York had ever seen, its brilliant blue-white glare visible at night a mile up Broadway. The inside of the building he stuffed as full as a child's toy chest. Wandering through the museum's dimly lit hallways, visitors came upon seemingly endless exhibition rooms, each one containing its own wonders: rooms with albinos, giants, dwarfs, educated dogs and industrious fleas, living statuary, and an armless man who played musical instruments and shot a bow and arrow; rooms with Indian artifacts, famous autographs, canes with carved-head handles and umbrellas that contained bayonets, trick mirrors, a working model of Niagara Falls ("With Real Water!"); rooms with collections of insects and butterflies, rocks and seashells, skeletons and stuffed animals. Somehow there were living animals inside the museum as well, lions and tigers and bears, ostriches, hippos, rhinos, and even, for a while, a giraffe—actual wild animals living in a building right on Broadway. Perhaps most amazing was the exhibition called the "Happy Family," a menagerie of more than sixty creatures, many of them natural predators and prey (cats and rats, hawks and rabbits, and so forth), that had been trained to live together peacefully in a single cage. Barnum had turned the museum into the most popular attraction in the city, and the corner of Broadway and Ann into a magnet for crowds day and night— until the night of July 13, 1865, when a fire swept through the neighborhood and the American Museum burned down.

At the time Barnum held an eleven-year lease on the property, which after the fire he shrewdly had appraised at the inflated value of $275,000. Wanting the property for the *Herald*'s new offices, James Gordon Bennett came to Barnum to ask about purchasing the lease. Barnum explained that his experts had assured him it was worth no less than $275,000, though the bank listed it for only $225,000, but he would further deduct $25,000, thus offering Bennett the doubly reduced price of $200,000.

A few days later Bennett gave Barnum a check for the money, by which time he had purchased the land itself for $500,000, the value at which his advisers had assessed it. Those advisers, however, had not known about Barnum's lease; if they had, they would have subtracted its price from their assessment. In paying for both the land *and* the lease, Bennett had laid out $700,000 for a single plot measuring fifty-six by one hundred feet—more than had ever been paid for a comparably sized property in the history of New York.

Bennett was incensed when he discovered that he had overpaid by $200,000, and he ordered his attorney to rescind the deal. The attorney summoned Barnum to his office and informed him that Mr. Bennett had decided not to purchase the museum lot. Mr. Barnum should therefore take back the lease and return the $200,000 that had been paid for it.

"Are you in earnest?" asked Barnum.

"Certainly, quite so."

Barnum smiled. "Really," he said, "I am sorry I can't accommodate Mr. Bennett. I have not got the little sum about me; in fact, I have spent the money."

"It will be better for you to take back the lease," the attorney warned.

"Nonsense, I shall do nothing of the sort," replied Barnum. "I don't make child's bargains."

Exactly thirty years after his "exposé" of the faked death of Joice Heth, James Gordon Bennett had been gulled once more by P. T. Barnum, and for all his sputtering there was nothing he could do about it. So Bennett was forced to keep the property at Broadway and Ann, and on it he built a white-marble palace with massive black walnut doors flanked by six richly ornamented Corinthian columns. Bennett had always been a great admirer of beauty, and this was the lovely face that the *Herald* showed the city. But on the inside, where the work was actually performed, the rooms were small and the stairs made of metal, modest surroundings more in keeping with the owner's ascetic Scottish origins. There the *Herald* remained for a quarter-century, until his son moved it to a new office building far uptown, where Broadway meets Sixth Avenue at Thirty-fourth Street; and though that building is long gone, the intersection is still known as Herald Square.

As the years passed and the moon series faded from memory, its history became ever more encrusted with myth and misinformation, much of which challenged the authorship of Richard Adams Locke. In 1872, for instance, the British mathematician Augustus De Morgan produced a two-volume work entitled *A Budget of Paradoxes,* a history of ideas running contrary to conventional scientific opinion. In the first volume De Morgan devoted a brief section to "The Herschel Hoax," which he called "a curious hoax, evidently written by a person versed in astronomy and clever at introducing probable circumstances and undesigned coincidences." De Morgan was not sure about its original place of publication, but he had "no doubt that it was produced in the United States, by M. Nicollet, an astronomer, once of Paris, and a fugitive of some kind."

Born in Savoy, France, Jean-Nicolas Nicollet was a respected mathematician and astronomer, at one time an assistant to the great Pierre Simon Laplace at the Paris Observatory. Financially ruined after the revolution of 1830 (he had speculated too heavily in stocks), Nicollet sailed for the United States, eventually settling in St. Louis, where he was living when the moon series appeared in the *Sun.* According to Augustus De Morgan, Nicollet composed the moon story in order to deceive—and thus exact his revenge on—his old rival François Arago, director of the Paris Observatory; in this effort he succeeded magnificently, for upon reading of Herschel's discoveries Arago "circulated the wonders through Paris," at least until Nicollet wrote a letter to his fellow astronomer Alexis Bouvard informing him of the hoax. "R. A. Locke," De Morgan added for good measure, was the pseudonym Nicollet had adopted in writing the story.

Even De Morgan's editor conceded in a footnote about Nicollet that "there does not seem to be any very tangible evidence to connect him with the story." Nevertheless, in the second volume of *A Budget of Paradoxes* De Morgan again insisted that "I have no doubt that M. Nicollet was the author of the Moon hoax," and further noted that the hoax had appeared shortly after Edgar Allan Poe's "Hans Phaall—A Tale" was published in a Southern literary magazine. "I suspect," wrote De Morgan, "that he took Poe's story, and made it a basis for his own."

The Nicollet theory was taken up in an 1878 book by the British astronomer Richard A. Proctor, entitled, ironically enough, *Myths and Marvels of Astronomy*. Proctor pointed out that the great astronomer Arago would not have been deceived by the moon story (as indeed he was not), but he did give credence to De Morgan's notion that the original work had been in French and may have been written by Nicollet. However, Proctor recognized that the French-speaking Nicollet would not have been capable of the kind of prose exhibited in the *Sun* series, and a translator would thus have been required to convert the story into English. In the United States the credit for the moon series was popularly attributed to that translator— a man, Proctor explained, named "Richard Alton Locke."

A somewhat more plausible origin story concerns Lewis Gaylord Clark, editor of the *Knickerbocker*, the most popular and influential literary magazine of its time. Clark himself was not a major literary talent, but he was a lively and witty writer, and his gossipy column "The Editor's Table" was one of the most eagerly read features in the magazine. According to his entry in the 1924 edition of the *National Cyclopædia of American Biography*, he was also the creator and coauthor of the moon series. (The entry cites the series, oddly, as "one of Clark's most successful achievements in humorous literature.") Lewis Gaylord Clark, the *Cyclopædia* claimed, had furnished "the incidents and imaginative part" of the series, while Richard Adams Locke was responsible for "the purely 'scientific' parts." No source is provided for this statement, but it is clearly traceable to an earlier book, *History of New York City, Embracing an Outline of Events from 1609 to 1830, and a Full Account of Its Development from 1830 to 1884*, in which the historian Benson J. Lossing put forward what he called "the secret history of the 'Moon Hoax'":

Mr. Moses Y. Beach had recently become sole proprietor of the *Sun*, and Richard Adams Locke was the editor. It was desirable to have some new and startling features to increase its popularity, and Locke, for a consideration, proposed to prepare for it a work of fiction. To this proposal Mr. Beach agreed. Locke consulted Lewis Gaylord Clark, the editor of the *Knickerbocker Magazine*, as to the subject. The Edinburgh *Scientific Journal* was then busied with Herschel's astronomical explorations at the Cape of Good Hope, and Clark proposed to make these the basis of the story. It was done. Clark was the real inventor of the incidents, the imaginative part, while to Locke was intrusted the ingenious task of unfolding the discoveries. Messrs. Beach, Clark, and Locke were in daily consultation while the hoax was in preparation. It was thus a joint product.

Unfortunately for Lossing's "secret history," it was Benjamin Day, not Moses Yale Beach, who owned the *Sun* in 1835; Beach did not buy the paper until two years later. Moreover, Lewis Gaylord Clark could not have been reading about John Herschel in the Edinburgh *Scientific Journal*, because such a journal did not exist; *Edinburgh Journal of Science* was Locke's incorrect rendering of the title of the *Edinburgh New Philosophical Journal*. Nor was that journal, or any other, "busied with Herschel's astronomical explanations," for Sir John had not yet revealed any of the findings made at his observatory in Cape Town—a silence that had allowed the *Sun* to reveal the fictitious "discoveries" in the first place.

Thus there were three notable errors in Benson Lossing's paragraph-long history of the Moon Hoax—a history that had somehow remained "secret" for fifty years until he revealed it. Lossing presented no evidence for his claims other than his own assertion of them, nor did any hint of his thesis about Clark's involvement in the hoax ever surface anywhere else. For what it is worth, Lewis Gaylord Clark himself never claimed authorship of the moon series, nor did Richard Adams Locke ever mention him in his own discussion of its creation. Any connection between Clark and the series is purely speculative; but what link there is can be traced, fittingly enough, to Edgar Allan Poe.

Poe and Lewis Gaylord Clark detested one another (each man saw the other as everything that was wrong with American literature), and for years they carried on an astonishingly vicious feud in the pages of the country's literary magazines. (To Clark, Poe was "a mortified but impotent littérateur . . . an ambitious 'authorling' perhaps of a small volume of effete and lamentable trash," while Poe pronounced Clark "noticeable for nothing in the world except for the markedness by which he is noticeable for nothing.") Nearly a century later, in his introduction to *The Letters of Willis Gaylord Clark and Lewis Gaylord Clark*, Leslie W. Dunlap noted that Lewis Gaylord Clark "took an active part in the perpetration of the famous New York *Sun* 'Moon Hoax' in 1835," and further observed that this might have been a contributing factor in the enmity between the two: for Poe, presumably, because he suspected plagiarism in the *Sun* series, and for Clark, because Poe suggested as much. It is an intriguing proposition, but as evidence of Clark's role in the hoax Dunlap provided only a single source—Benson J. Lossing.

If Poe actually believed that Lewis Gaylord Clark had anything to do with the moon series, he kept that idea to himself. In all of his writings about the series he referred solely to Richard Adams Locke as its author. His last word on the subject appeared in the October 1846 issue of *Godey's Lady's Book*, in his *Literati of New York City* essay "Richard Adams Locke." In that essay, Poe again presented the striking similarities that he saw between the two hoaxes, "the one of which," he did not fail to point out, "followed immediately upon the heels of the other." It was a subject that had long bedeviled him. This time, though, there was a crucial difference, stemming from what seems to have been a discussion between Poe and Richard Adams Locke—perhaps one that took place at the literary salon in Anne Charlotte Lynch's home on Waverly Place two years earlier.

> Having stated the case, however, in this form, I am bound to do Mr. Locke the justice to say that he denies having seen my article prior to the publication of his own; I am bound to add, also, that I believe him.

By this time Poe had reason to feel magnanimous, because he had at last achieved literary fame. In January 1845, the *New-York Mirror* had published his poem "The Raven" to enormous critical and popular acclaim. Almost overnight Poe vaulted from obscurity to celebrity—as was demonstrated one evening when he attended the theater and one of the actors slyly inserted the word *nevermore* into the script, to the amusement of the audience and the great pleasure of the poem's creator. Poe himself was immensely proud of the poem. (A friend once told him that he had read "The Raven" and found it to be "uncommonly fine." "Fine!" cried Poe. "Is that all you can say of it? It is the greatest poem ever written, sir—the greatest poem in the world!") He was deluged with invitations to read his famous poem, which he did in grand style. Slim and elegant, he stood in the flickering candlelight and intoned the carefully wrought cadences in a low, rhythmic voice like the tolling of a bell—it was, remarked a guest at one of the readings, "an event in one's life."

Still, success proved to be an unexpectedly weak tonic: it could not forestall the death and despair that continued to stalk him. Virginia succumbed to tuberculosis in January 1847 at the age of twenty-four, the very age his mother had been when she died of the disease. Poe's great friend William Gowans—the New York bookseller who in 1859 would publish a new edition of the moon series as *The Moon Hoax; or, A Discovery that the Moon Has a Vast Population of Human Beings*—described Virginia as "a wife of matchless beauty and loveliness," who had been "as much devoted to him as a young mother is to her first-born." In the wake of her death Poe entered a new period of dissipation and ill health. He was then living in a small cottage in the village of Fordham at the top of a hill surrounded by cherry trees, overlooking the Bronx River. (The sweeping view of fruit trees and water might have reminded him of the vista seen from John Allan's house in Richmond.) Poe took long walks through the countryside, carried on flirtations with female admirers, and raged against his critics. Amid his grief he managed to finish some writing—including his hoax story "Von Kempelen and His Discovery," about the discovery of an alchemical method for producing gold—but none of it approached the quality of his earlier work or was received with the kind of enthusiasm that had greeted "The Raven."

By 1849, just four years after his great success, Poe had thoroughly alienated himself from the New York literary world. His enduring feud with Lewis Gaylord Clark had turned many of the city's most important writers against him, and his *Literati of New York City* sketches, a good number of them withering in their criticism, had not helped matters any. In June of that year he decided it was time to move back to the South. He embarked on a trip to his native Richmond, where he spent the summer reacquainting himself with old friends and endlessly revising his poems. In the fall he headed north again, intending to close the cottage at Fordham, but he did not get far. He arrived by steamship in Baltimore at the end of September, and sometime during the following week he began to drink. A local physician, alerted to Poe's condition, found him, "bloated and unwashed," sitting in a tavern on a cold, rain-swept night as if in a scene from one of his poems. He was shivering, drenched in perspiration, and seemingly insensible. A carriage was sent for, and he was taken to a nearby hospital, where he held on, trembling and delirious, for four more days. Edgar Allan Poe died on October 7, 1849, in Baltimore, the city where he had enjoyed his first literary success. He was forty years old.

In the early 1840s, after his departure from the *New Era*, Richard Adams Locke developed an interest in the controversial electromagnetic theories of Dr. Henry Hall Sherwood of New York. (In later years Sherwood would become known for his "savage rotary magnetic machine," which he claimed could cure all manner of diseases from rheumatism to herpes and tuberculosis.) Like Sherwood, Locke had come to believe that the earth in its orbit gradually moved from a tilted position to a perpendicular one and then back again; over eons, this movement had a profound impact on the world's climate. When the angle was greatest came a dreadful period of darkness and ice, but when the earth stood perpendicular to the sun, as Locke asserted in a lecture called "Magnetism and Astronomy," "the sun will shine from pole to pole in every part of the Earth's annual orbit, and perennial spring will load its valleys with fertility, clothe its hills with verdure, even to the tops of its mountains." The earth becomes, everywhere, a paradise—and from this observation Locke had developed a theory of his own.

Such a beneficent age, he believed, occurs every several thousand years. The earth had last experienced one in the centuries before Christ, and while its effects were unknown to modern science, among the ancients they were "the great theme of their poets and philosophers—the subject of their sacred mysteries—depicted in the spiral circles of their temples, and taught to the initiated in their noble orreries and zodiacs." The Bible spoke eloquently of this period, through the allegorical language that Locke had always seen there. Eden's tree of life stood for the magnetic axis of the earth, and the tree of knowledge of good and evil for the axis of rotation; the serpent circling the tree was not an actual snake, but rather "the serpentine or spiral motion of the earth's axis." While the Bible, then, could not be taken as literal history, it did preserve important historical information that would otherwise be lost. The magnetic theory was thus another effort by Locke—the most ambitious of all, if also the most wrongheaded—to reconcile the worlds of science and scripture.

Edgar Allan Poe reported in 1846 that "Mr. Locke is now engaged in carefully revising" his ideas about magnetism—adding, in his typical manner of backhanded praise, "My own opinion is that his theory (which he has reached more by dint of imagination than anything else) will finally be established, although, perhaps, never thoroughly by *him*." That revision never appeared; it was just one of several scientific projects on which Richard Adams Locke was said to be working, none of which ever came to light. As early as November 1835, just three months after the publication of the moon series, the *Sun* had reported that Locke ("whom our cotemporaries accuse of being the author of the celebrated 'Astronomical Discoveries'") was preparing a series of public lectures on astronomy, an abstract of which would soon be published in the *Sun*. That abstract, however, never came, and neither did the lectures. Likewise, in November 1850, the magazine *International Miscellany of Literature, Art, and Science* ran an item that remarked on how "theories of light seem now in an unusual degree to occupy the attention of men of science"; Lord Brougham would shortly be publishing an essay on the topic, while "Mr. Richard Adams Locke (who saw through it so well when he made his discoveries in the moon) has been for some years engaged upon an elaborate and we have no doubt very learned and ingenious book in the same regard." That book too never appeared. In fact, no work of any kind by Richard Adams Locke ever appeared again in his lifetime. Once he had been numbered among the most prolific and highly regarded journalists in New York, but after 1842 (when he published the last of his occasional essays on science and art in the *New-York Mirror*) there was only silence.

Not coincidentally, 1842 was also the year Locke gave up journalism for good, taking a job as an inspector for the Customs Service in New York. Employment in the Customs Service was open only to citizens of the United States. Locke, of course, had been born in Great Britain, and, according to the National Archives and Records Administration, he was never naturalized as a U.S. citizen. His nationality would seem to have been an insurmountable obstacle to his employment, but the New York Custom House was a hotbed of Democratic Party patronage—a reform commission later observed that "partisan zeal and work, the payment of partisan assessments, and the exertion of official influence for partisan purposes, have, as a rule, been essential conditions for securing appointments or promotion"— and it is not difficult to imagine that Locke, who was intimate enough with the local Democratic Party to have edited two of its newspapers (the *Democratic-Republican New Era* and the *Brooklyn Daily Eagle*), would have been able to circumvent the citizenship requirement. Presumably this requirement was why New York was listed as his birthplace in all Custom House registers of employees, and why Locke told U.S. census inspectors in both 1850 and 1860 that he had been born in New York—a falsehood that later made its way into several histories.

New York's Custom House had long been a sink of not only patronage but also graft, where inspectors were known to receive bribes from merchants whose ships' cargo they oversaw. This was a tradition, however, in which Richard Adams Locke seems not to have partaken, since he never had much money. (The writer Herman Melville, who began work at the Custom House shortly after Locke retired, also refused to accept bribes. His brother-in-law wrote of him "quietly returning money which has been thrust into his pockets behind his back, quietly avoiding offence alike to the corrupting merchants and their clerks and runners, who think that all men can be bought.") The 1860 census, for instance, shows that Locke did not own his own home, and at the end of his working life had amassed a personal estate valued at one thousand dollars, less than that of nearly all his neighbors. By 1850 Richard Adams and Esther Bowring Locke had six children, all of whom continued to live at home. The only one old enough to work was their twenty-year-old daughter Adelaide, but she could not have been bringing in much money; ten years later, the 1860 census would list her profession as "Servant."

The difficulties the family faced in those years, even after Locke took his job at the Custom House, were perhaps most vividly expressed in a brief, poignant letter that he wrote on June 7, 1850, to the *Sun*'s publisher Moses Sperry Beach (one of Moses Yale Beach's sons, who had taken over the paper two years earlier). "Dear Sir," he wrote,

> Have you any thing for me to do? My family is in a state of great exigency. If you have, you may depend upon it that, in anything I undertake I can render you effective service. Afford me a chance and you will scc.

If the younger Beach ever replied to him, there is no record of it. In any case Locke's plea went unheeded, for he never worked again for the *Sun*.

The same year he wrote to Beach, Locke became the chief boarding officer for the Customs Service on Staten Island, the position he would hold for the rest of his working life. In 1858 he was again briefly in the news when a mob, angered that Staten Island was being used as a quarantine site for yellow fever victims, burned down a government hospital that Locke had been assigned to help protect. At the subsequent trial, Locke testified that he had seen two clergymen among the crowd, looking on, as he put it, with "complacency and satisfaction." The *New York Times*, in its coverage of the trial, took umbrage at Locke's implication of the ministers. "Mr. Locke has in great perfection the gift of seeing what does not exist," the *Times* commented. "Sometimes his fictions are lunar, at other times terrestrial."

He still participated in local Democratic politics, at a certain remove; an item in a Staten Island newspaper reported that he was scheduled to present a lecture before the Richmond County Democratic Union Club "on the principles and objects of the Democratic party." A far more important invitation came in December 1851, when he was asked to deliver the welcoming address for the Hungarian patriot Louis Kossuth, a former journalist who had recently become the president of his country's first parliamentary government. This was Kossuth's first trip to America since assuming the presidency, and his first landing was in Staten Island, where he stayed overnight before departing the next morning for Manhattan. A celebration was arranged to see Kossuth off. A large tent, flying twinned American and Hungarian flags, was set up on a hill overlooking the bay. With Locke sitting beside him, Kossuth was driven by horse-drawn carriage to a tent where a crowd of three thousand had assembled. A chronicler of the day's events reported that Locke rose to the podium, "handsome, bearded, and self-possessed," where he read his prepared address.

"No impulse of the human heart is so contagious as valor in the cause of liberty," Locke proclaimed, and "no principles are so imperishable and prolific as those of freedom." He drew cheers with the rousing finish, adorned with the rhetorical flourishes so popular at the time, in which he compared the honored guest with that most revered of American patriots, George Washington:

> Go on then, Great Kossuth, his worthiest successor upon this earth, and fulfil your mission. Stand forth like the Angel of the Apocalypse, with one foot upon the land and the other upon the sea, and swear ye the Western continent to the Eastern, that tyranny shall be no longer!

The Kossuth address, Richard Adams Locke's most important public appearance, provided a fitting coda to a political life in New York that had begun seventeen years earlier, with an anonymous pamphlet written in support of the Polish uprising against the Russian invaders. *That tyranny shall be no longer*: it was a sentiment that had motivated Locke for the whole of his career, whether that tyranny was religious, racial, or economic. In nearly every case, the stance he took had been highly unpopular, so it must have been especially gratifying, that bright December morning, to stand before a crowd and receive its acclaim.

In January 1862, at the age of sixty-one, he retired from the Customs Service, having worked there nearly twenty years. After that he was rarely seen outside his house. According to every account he lived quietly, almost reclusively, for his remaining years, devoting his attention to problems in math and science.

He died on February 16, 1871, and was buried at the Silver Mount Cemetery on Staten Island, not far from his home, where in later years Esther and three of their children would be buried alongside him. His death was met with no obituaries in any of the New York papers, not even the *Sun*, whose success he had done so much to nurture. About the only notice of his death came in the weekly magazine *Every Saturday*, which used the occasion to reflect less on the life of Richard Adams Locke than on the vagaries of fame:

"Are we so soon forgotten?" asks Rip Van Winkle, in the play, with indescribable pathos. It seems to be a fact that we are forgotten very soon indeed. Twenty-five or thirty years ago the name of the author of the "Moon Hoax" was on everybody's lip. His brilliant essay made the fortune of the Sun newspaper; cravats and soaps and hair-brushes were named after him. He was a perfume in a shop-window and the winning horse on the race-course. Since then his popularity has so completely died away that when the death of Richard Adams Locke was announced last week it affected the general public very much as if some one had said, "Noah is dead." How very, very quietly a popular idol sometimes slips off his pedestal! Twenty years ago who would have dared to question the fame of this ingenious author? Popularity looks so much like fame that one is constantly mistaken for the other, as if they were twins. But they are not twins; they are not even brothers, yet it is difficult to determine at that time "which is which." Fame is frequently an undemonstrative lad with a wonderful amount of latent vitality. Popularity might be described as a precocious child who never lives to grow up.

At one time Locke's name had been known to everyone in New York, the center, for a while, of a great hubbub; thirty-five years later his death occasioned barely a whisper. There had been one moment, though, not long after the appearance of his moon series, when he had wryly imagined for himself a kind of immortality. He recalled it in 1840 at the end of his letter of reply to Park Benjamin of the *New World*, as "the incident of all others, which I considered the most complimentary to the author," one that had recently occurred aboard a ferry crossing the Long Island Sound.

So much of his life had been spent around water, ever since his summers at his grandfather's house in Burnham, just a few paces from the beach, where he could stand by the docks and watch the cargo ships coming in from all over the world, trying to decipher the strange letters burned into the wooden crates unladen by the crewmen—little suspecting, of course, that he would spend nearly twenty years of his life inspecting the cargo of just such ships, when they would no longer seem quite so romantic. Not far from there, up the Bristol Channel, was where he and Esther, carrying their baby daughter, had embarked on the ocean voyage that would take them to a new life in America. A decade after that, when they had finally arrived at their own house by the water, it was a ferry that brought him to work each morning in Lower Manhattan, first at the *New Era* and then at the Custom House.

But the ferry ride Locke recalled in his 1840 letter had been a pleasure excursion on a warm summer afternoon, sailing down the Long Island Sound from Connecticut. Up on deck, he had noticed a lovely young woman, a milliner by trade. On her lap she held a brand-new bandbox, on which were pinned a dazzling array of pink, green, and blue devices, as shiny as a fisherman's lures, and glistening now in the sun and spray. Intrigued, Locke pulled out his spyglass to get a better look. He peered at the objects more closely through the glass, like an astronomer he had once conjured up, and to his wonderment recognized there his old friends from the Ruby Colosseum, the man-bats, his very own creations: gathered together into groups of three, as if they were the Graces themselves, with wings uplifted like angels.

ACKNOWLEDGMENTS

Like all who love New York, I am indebted to the magisterial *Encyclopedia of New York City*, assembled by Kenneth T. Jackson and innumerable writers—though perhaps a bit more than most, as it was in the *Encyclopedia* that I first stumbled across a mention of something called the Moon Hoax. That book was just one of many sources in which I happily lost myself during the research for this book, in libraries and archives that included, in New York, the New-York Historical Society (the librarians of which are themselves a treasure of the city), the New York Public Library, the Staten Island Institute of Arts and Sciences, the Bobst Library of New York University, and the Butler Library of Columbia University; in Washington, the Library of Congress; and in England, the British Library and the Somerset Record Office.

Along the way I received invaluable assistance from a host of others. Lockwood Rianhard, a descendant of Richard Adams Locke, provided genealogical information about the Locke family. In Somerset, my family and I spent a lovely afternoon with John and Pat Coombes (John is chairman of the Burnham Philosophical Society, an outgrowth of the society founded by Richard Locke in 1762), who gave us a tour of various Locke-related sites in the area; also in Somerset, Chris Richards of the North Somerset Museum located various pieces of Richard Adams Locke information, including an 1871 newspaper article the existence of which I had only surmised. In London, Holly Hudson provided exemplary research assistance. James Secord of the University of Cambridge directed me to the issue of the *New World* in which Richard Adams Locke's letter appeared, and Alex Boese, curator of the online Museum of Hoaxes, generously provided me a bibliography he had compiled of Moon Hoax literature.

Caitlin Tunney, Joan Dempsey, and Deborah Schupack—dear friends and fine writers all—read the manuscript in various stages and offered thoughtful criticism and cheerful encouragement; I look forward to future opportunities to impose on their goodwill. Michael Crowe of the University of Notre Dame and Thorin Tritter of Columbia University read and commented on various chapters; this book benefited enormously from their close attention, and any errors in it that remain are mine alone.

My deepest thanks to Henry Dunow, who from the very beginning helped me to find the proper shape and best story for this book, and was its tireless advocate throughout; he manages to be at once an exceptional literary agent and a total mensch—a rare and unbeatable combination. Likewise, I am grateful for the unwavering support this book has received from everyone at Basic Books, including, though by no means limited to, Lara Heimert, Brandon Proia, and Chris Greenberg. David Groff was an editor nonpareil, who went over the book again and again, bringing to it his admirable scrupulousness, intelligence, and fine literary sensibility; it has been my good fortune to work with him.

Finally, I offer this book with love to my children, Ezra and Vivian (who now know more about nineteenth-century newspaper editors than anyone their age has any reason to), and to my wife Cassie Schwerner, who first encouraged me to write it, who listened to its every word, and who all along has been my best reader and wisest counsel, and to whom, and for whom, I am grateful far beyond the measure of this book.

NOTES

PROLOGUE: THE MAN ON THE MOON

2   *"To have a graceless child"*: The quotation from *King Lear,* as Locke had it, was somewhat in error; it should have read, "How sharper than a serpent's tooth it is to have a thankless child."

4   *"Ugly brutes"*: Dickens, 97.

5   *More than a quarter-million people*: In 1835 New York's population was 270,089. Greene, 15.

5   *Privy vaults*: See the excellent discussion in Burrows and Wallace, 588.

5   *"A person coming into the city"*: Ellis, 249.

6   *Not disease but riot*: In his *History of New York City from the Discovery to the Present Day,* William Leete Stone (the son of the newspaper editor) observed, "The year 1834 may with propriety be called the Year of Riots." Stone, 457.

6   *First direct mayoral election*: New York's earliest mayors were appointed by the governor; from 1820 to 1834, mayors were elected annually by the Common Council.

6   *"Damned Irishmen"*: Anbinder, 27.

6   *Adopting black children*: Richards, 114–115.

7   *The mayor of Brooklyn*: Brooklyn was an independent municipality until 1898, when it was incorporated into the city of New York.

7   *"I have not ventured"*: Wyatt-Brown, 231.

10   *"Organ of acquisitiveness"*: Barnum (1855), 20.

10   *"My disposition is"*: Barnum (1855), 107.

11   *"Having read the Moon story"*: Harrison (1902), 15:134.

11   *The eleven-thousand-word account*: For comparison, this prologue runs about fifty-five hundred words.

12   *"Decidedly the greatest* hit": Harrison (1902), 15:134.

12   *"The sensation created"*: Barnum (1866), 193.

CHAPTER 1: BENJAMIN DAY'S WHISTLING BOY

17   *At the north end of William Street*: The exact site of the original *Sun* office, 222 William Street, is no longer there; today it would be in the shadow of the approach to the Brooklyn Bridge.

18   *The job would require at least ten hours of printing:* Thompson (2004), 220.

20   *A set of loaded pistols:* Thompson (2004), 74.

20   *In front of the American Hotel:* Today it is the site of the Woolworth building.

20   *A circulation of some 4,500:* For circulation figures, see O'Brien, 11.

21   *"English, German, French, and Spanish":* Lieber, 80.

21   *"Human patch-work":* Greene, 12.

21   *The population of each of New York's wards:* Burrows and Wallace, 576.

22   *The area was known as the Five Points:* In his book *Five Points,* Tyler Anbinder states that the first reference in the newspapers to a neighborhood called "Five Points" was in 1829. Anbinder, 21. It was so called because of the intersection of five streets there: Mulberry, Anthony (now Worth), Cross (now Park), Orange (now Baxter), and Little Water (now gone). Burrows and Wallace, 392. Today the area is part of Chinatown.

23   *Never particularly interested in the trappings of wealth:* A thoughtful, fond reminiscence of Benjamin Day, "Mr. Day Viewed by a Grandson," by Clarence Day, appeared in the centennial edition of the *New York Sun,* September 2, 1933.

23   *His grandson Clarence:* In the 1930s Clarence Day would write a book about his comically blustering stockbroker father, also named Clarence—Ben and Eveline's fourth child—the best-selling *Life with Father.*

24   *The full text of their manifesto:* Saxton, 225.

24   *"All practical printers":* Saxton, 215.

25   *In May 1833:* There is no historical record of the move, but at that time in New York May 1 was "Moving Day," the day that leases were traditionally begun and ended. As a result, the city was always a pandemonium on that day, as thousands of people tried to move in and out of apartments at the same time. As a newspaper editor described the scene, "There scarcely could have been greater confusion had the news suddenly been circulated that the British had landed on Coney Island." Blackmar, 213.

25   *Chestnut Street:* Today it is known as Howard Street, running between Centre and Mercer streets, just above Canal.

25   *Duane Street: Longworth's American Almanac, New-York Register, and City Directory, for the Fifty-Ninth Year of American Independence* (1834), 234.

25   *A young man named Horatio Sheppard:* The story of Horatio Sheppard and his ill-fated *Morning Post* is beautifully described in James Parton's 1872 biography, *The Life of Horace Greeley,* pages 105–110. In his autobiography, *Recollections of a Busy Life,* Horace Greeley spells the name Horatio Shepard.

26   *Presidential candidate:* Ulysses S. Grant, a Republican, was reelected in a landslide; Greeley carried only six states.

27   *About three feet long by two feet wide:* The newspaper editors of the time saw large pages as evidence of prosperity, and as the years went on they engaged in a kind of war of expansion, making their pages larger and larger, until eventually a page of the *Journal of Commerce* would measure an as-

tonishing fifty-eight inches by thirty-five inches—nearly five feet long, and, when spread out on a desk, more than six feet wide.

28   *They were strikingly literate:* Literacy rates are notoriously difficult to calculate, but it is instructive to note that the 1840 state census put New York's literacy rate at 96 percent. Henkin, 21.

28   *Adventure stories and gallows confessions and broadsheet ballads:* See Burrows and Wallace, 522.

28   *Reports from the police office:* Reporting on the cases before the police court had originated with London's *Morning Herald* newspaper. In 1826 an American publisher brought out a collection of the *Morning Herald's* police court reports, entitled *Mornings at Bow Street.* It proved so popular that a second volume was issued, *More Mornings at Bow Street.* Mott (1942), 36.

30   *"Suddenly arrest public attention":* Barnum (1866), 49.

31   *After several hours of hawking:* There is no historical record of how Day sold the first day's papers, but as Susan Thompson has pointed out, "It seems likely that after gathering information, writing, editing, typesetting, and printing the first issue himself, he probably would have helped distribute the papers as well." Thompson, 220.

31   *They had more than three dollars:* Thompson, 12.

CHAPTER 2: THE NEWS OF THE CITY

34   *Under the stage name Barney Williams:* O'Brien, 18.

34   *Printers who poured water on them:* Brace, 17.

35   *The boys mostly dispensed with their given names:* Brace, 38.

35   *Sixty-seven cents cash for a hundred papers:* O'Brien, 19.

35   *"The King of the Newsboys":* Foster (1850), 47.

36   *To apprentice as a printer:* Sloan, 113.

37   *Partner on a new literary magazine:* O'Brien, 87.

37   *Four dollars a week:* O'Brien, 17.

37   *"It is a fashion which does not meet with our approbation":* Bleyer, 157.

38   *"The Balzac of the daybreak court":* O'Brien, 17.

39   *Retained the title of senior editor:* Bradshaw (1979–1980), 118.

40   *Left the editorial duties almost entirely to Wisner:* In his 1883 interview with the *Sun,* Day recalled, "When I got the printing of the American Museum to do I thought myself so lucky that I rather neglected the newspaper."

42   *A printer's salary of nine dollars a week:* Pray, 182.

42   *Wisner's share of the* Sun's *profits:* O'Brien, 23.

42   *Itching feet and a parched throat:* Mott (1962), 204.

42   *"Shrewd, active and unprincipled":* Jaffee, 110.

42   *"Facile with his pen":* Pray, 182.

42   *"Oily Attree":* Cohen, 367.

43   *Amusing descriptions of city life:* In 1837 Greene would publish a popular guidebook called *A Glance at New York.*

43 *Four-fifths of a cent per sheet:* O'Brien, 32.

44 *The black snake of slavery:* This interpretation of the snake story comes from Gary L. Whitby, in his essay "Horns of a Dilemma: The *Sun,* Abolition, and the 1833–34 New York Riots," 416–417.

44 *A man named Robert Matthews:* The best account of the Matthews case can be found in Paul E. Johnson and Sean Wilentz's book *The Kingdom of Matthias.*

44 *Clergymen, doctors, disobedient women, and men who wore spectacles:* Johnson and Wilentz, 94.

45 *Not yet grown the beard:* "Those few men daring enough to wear beards . . . two or three decades before their widespread adoption in the 1850s, actually suffered abuse and persecution." Larkin, 184.

45 *The only known image:* Print Collection, New York Public Library, EM11499.

45 *The engraving is undated:* Robin's career at the prominent New York firm of John Chester Buttre did not begin until 1846, so the engraving must have been commissioned sometime after that.

46 *"The forehead is truly beautiful":* Harrison (1902), 15:137.

47 *Did not own his own home:* National Archives and Records Administration, 1860 Census Records, Film Series M653, Roll 850, page 22.

CHAPTER 3: BEARER OF THE FALCON CREST

49 *Born on September 22, 1800:* East Brent Baptismal Register, Somerset Archive and Record Service, Taunton, U.K.

49 *Several reference works:* See, for instance, *A Dictionary of North American Authors,* 272, and *A Dictionary of American Authors,* 232; also Crowe, 213.

49 *"Of English parentage and education":* Griggs, 41.

49 *"The Locke family in this neighborhood":* Locke (1853), 342.

49 *Its own coat of arms: The Gentleman's Magazine,* September 1792, 800.

50 *Related to John Locke:* Locke (1853), 359. It should be noted that Lockwood Rianhard, who is a great-great-grandson of Richard Adams Locke, has done extensive genealogical work on the family and asserts that he has found no common ancestor between John Locke and Richard Adams Locke. Letter to the author, January 25, 2005.

50 *A direct descendant:* This story served to confuse, among others, Edgar Allan Poe, who wrote in his essay on Locke in *The Literati of New York City,* "He is a lineal descendant from the immortal author of the 'Essay on the Human Understanding.'" Harrison (1902), 15:137. John Locke was in fact a childless bachelor, and thus his line stopped with him.

50 *"The Hundreds":* Locke (1939), 20.

50 *"I never published a pamphlet":* Locke (1939), 20.

50 *A twenty-acre farm:* Locke (1939), 11.

51 *By . . . 1800 he owned 146 acres:* Ridler, 7.

51 *"Burnham's most distinguished native inhabitant"*: Wrigley, 23.
51 *Left the bulk of his estate*: Somerset Archive and Record Service, *Will of Richard Locke the elder of Burnham, gent, 6 October 1806*, DD/ALN 4.
51 *Mill Batch Farm*: Mill Batch Farm had been left to Richard Locke's third wife, Parnel Adams, by her mother, Ann Day. It remained in the family until 1920. Ridler, 7.
51 *His choice of wife*: Somerset Marriage Index, Somerset Archive and Record Service.
52 *In operation at Mill Batch Farm*: Coulthard, 47. The windmill is marked on a local road map from 1675. Apparently it was being worked as late as 1880. Mill Batch Farm was demolished in the early 1960s; today there is a bungalow (still called Mill Batch Farm) on the site of the original farmhouse, and an industrial estate on the surrounding property.
52 *"Served in Canada"*: Griggs, 41.
53 *A search conducted by the National Archives*: The National Archives of the United Kingdom, search reference number F0002667. Among the indexes consulted were the Royal Hospital Chelsea: soldiers service documents 1760–1913; Records of Service, Officers–Royal Engineers, 1796–1880; the *Roll of Officers of the Corps of Engineers from 1660 to 1898 compiled from the MS. rolls of the late Captain T. W. J. Connolly;* and the Army List of Officers for 1800–1815.
53 *Inherited his grandfather's genius*: Bailey (1955), 3.
53 *The historical citations of Richard Adams Locke*: See, for instance, *Who Was Who in America* (1963), 319; *Biographical Dictionary of American Journalism,* 424; *Encyclopedia of the British Press,* 378; O'Brien, 39; Seavey, xxxi; Collins, 262; Griggs, 41. Michael J. Crowe did note in a footnote to his discussion of Locke, "I have been unable to confirm that he studied in Cambridge." Crowe, 592.
53 *Richard Adams Locke is not among them*: Alumni Cantabrigienses, 2:4, 195–196.
53 *A student had only to matriculate*: This was confirmed by the current deputy keeper of the University Archives at Cambridge, who noted, "By the period of your interest, formal membership of the University of Cambridge, and hence appearance in the 'Alumni Cantabrigienses,' was predicated on 'matriculation.' In order to attend University lectures, sit for examinations and take a degree, students had to be matriculated." Email from Jacqueline Cox to the author, February 9, 2005.
54 *The* Republican: See Griggs, 42; O'Brien, 39.
54 *"Unsuccessful effort to indoctrinate"*: Griggs, 42.
54 *"Theories of American democracy"*: O'Brien, 39.
55 *Much as the Soviet Union did*: Crook, 3.
55 *"Courage and firmness"*: Gilmartin, 34.
55 *"Libellous caricatures adorn'd the walls"*: Gilmartin, 69.
56 *At least two literary journals*: Griggs, 42.

56 *Returning to England's southwest:* Bristol is not in Somerset proper but just across the border on the other side of the Avon River.

58 *"Remarkable individual":* Dare, 4.

59 *"The most ultra doctrines":* Griggs, 42.

59 *"Unconscionably impudent and dogmatical":* "Defender," 25.

59 *"May have been better entitled":* "Defender," 21.

60 *Chosen not to provide for him:* This is surmise, as Richard Locke's will, unlike his father's, is not held by the Somerset Archive and Record Service. However, there is no indication that Richard Adams Locke ever received any of the family estate, and much circumstantial evidence that he did not, including the cheap housing in which the family lived in New York City; an extant letter from 1850 in which he bemoans his financial circumstances; his small savings and lack of home ownership later in life; and his son's unsuccessful efforts to claim the eight tenement houses built by Richard Locke for the officers of the Burnham Society, that should have reverted to the family when the Burnham Society ceased to exist. Ridler, 10.

60 *Died the next year:* Somerset Archive and Record Service, East Brent register of burials, d/p/brnt.e 2/1/18, 23.

60 *"The apostle of the hill country":* Ridler, 10.

61 *"One seemed to look down upon Dante's Inferno":* Latimer, 167.

62 *"Most disastrous outbreak of popular violence":* Latimer, 146. Most of Latimer's annals (in his *Annals of Bristol in the Nineteenth Century*) consist of single-paragraph entries; the discussion of the 1831 Bristol riots runs thirty-five pages.

62 *Into five bags:* National Archives and Records Administration, *Passenger Lists of Vessels Arriving at New York,* Film Series M237, Roll 15.

62 *Booked passage on the* James Cropper: Launched as a Black Ball packet ship in 1821, the *James Cropper* was retired from packet service in 1828 and sold to a Virginia ship owner, and by 1831 was serving as a tramp steamer. On December 15, 1832, less than a year after the Lockes' cross-Atlantic voyage, the *James Cropper* "pounded her bottom out near Cape Henlopen at the mouth of the Delaware, while loaded with some of the first rails for the pioneer Camden & Amboy Railroad." Albion, 102.

62 *Nights were always worst:* See, for instance, Fox, 11–12; and Albion, 9–10.

64 *Orion stalking the east:* My thanks to William Jacobs of the American Museum of Natural History Library for providing me a star chart for the North Atlantic for November 1831.

CHAPTER 4: THE ATROCIOUS IMPOSITIONS OF MATTHIAS

65 *Arrived in New York on January 13, 1832:* National Archives and Records Administration, *Passenger Lists of Vessels Arriving at New York,* Film Series M237, Roll 15.

67 *"Without a pot to piss in":* Burrows and Wallace, 476.

67 *"Rookeries":* Jackson (1995), 1161.

67 *Sometime between May 1833 and May 1834:* Richard Adams Locke does not appear in *Longworth's American Almanac, New-York Register, and City Directory* until the 1834 edition.

67 *18 Duane Street:* Longworth's American Almanac, New-York Register, and City Directory, for the Fifty-Ninth Year of American Independence (1834), 436.

67 *Tidy whitewashed farmhouse:* My thanks to John Coombes of Burnham, England, for providing me a photograph of Mill Batch Farm.

68 *Set himself the task of learning shorthand:* It is not known precisely when Locke learned shorthand. But there is no indication of his having known shorthand in England, and he was a practicing stenographer no later than the year following his arrival in New York. Additionally, P. T. Barnum wrote that Locke "was the only shorthand reporter in the city, where he laid the basis for a competency he now enjoys." Barnum (1866), 202.

68 *"The only shorthand reporter in the city":* Barnum (1866), 202.

68 *A pamphlet for a Cortland Street bookseller:* The pamphlet is not dated, but it very likely came out in 1833, as the seller would have wanted to hurry the transcript into print to capitalize on the publicity surrounding the case.

68 *"Shortly after the Judges":* Report of the Trial of the Rev. Ephraim K. Avery . . . , 3.

69 *Published anonymously:* Reference to Locke's authorship of the pamphlet can be found in Griggs, 43.

70 *"The Apollo of the press":* Crouthamel (1969), 81.

70 *"What benefit can it be":* Crouthamel (1969), 57.

70 *Fought his own duel:* Crouthamel (1969), 75–76.

72 *"He was a little too gorgeous and florid":* Seavey, xv.

72 *The first feature articles:* O'Brien, 37.

73 *Sojourner Truth:* Johnson and Wilentz, 179.

74 *The trial became something greater:* For a full discussion of the various meanings read into the Matthias trial, from which I have drawn here, see Johnson and Wilentz, pp. 150–153.

75 *Sold more than six thousand:* An item in the May 16, 1835, edition of the *Sun* reads: "We yesterday printed an edition of 10,000 of this pamphlet, more than 6,000 of which were disposed of."

76 *Day paid him $150:* Griggs, 4.

76 *"There must come a change":* Hone, 156.

77 *Not far from the ferry terminal:* See Theodore S. Fay's description of the Elysian Fields in Dakin, 20–21.

77 *Sybil's Cave:* For some reason it was spelled *Sybil,* as opposed to the *Sibyl* of classical tradition.

77 *Bludgeoned Attree:* Extensive accounts of the attack on Attree were provided in the *Sun* and the *Transcript* of June 8, 1835, with several follow-up reports in the ensuing days.

78 *An assault charge made against Boyd:* Cohen, 85–86. The prostitute's name was Helen Jewett. The following year Jewett was murdered, and one of her clients, Richard Robinson, was arrested for the crime. The trial—and Robinson's eventual acquittal—made sensational fodder for New York's penny papers.

79 *Roach Guards, Shirt Tails, and Plug Uglies:* Sante, 199.

79 *Had a wife and a young son:* Bradshaw (1983), 3.

79 *His habit of chewing tobacco:* James Stanford Bradshaw has referred to his "excessive tobacco chewing." Bradshaw (1983), 8.

79 *"The odious practice of chewing and expectorating":* Larkin, 166.

79 *"He was a pretty smart fellow":* This is from the interview Day gave for the *Sun*'s fiftieth anniversary issue, "Benjamin Day's Own Sun Story," published on September 2, 1883.

79 *By the last week of June:* The *Sun* of June 26, 1835, is the last issue to include Wisner's name on the masthead.

79 *Five thousand dollars:* O'Brien, 37.

80 *Yet another account:* See Seavey, 15.

81 *Windust's restaurant on Park Row:* Turner, xv–xvi.

81 *Locke had wanted to write editorials:* See James Gordon Bennett's item "The Astronomical Hoax Explained" in the August 31, 1835, issue of the *Herald*.

82 *Twelve dollars a week:* O'Brien, 38.

CHAPTER 5: "THE EVIL SPIRIT OF THE TIMES"

84 *"A reptile marking his path with slime":* Reynolds, 174.

85 *Slump-shouldered posture:* Thompson, 31.

85 *"It would be worth my while":* Fermer, 24.

86 *First to put the news on the front page:* Stevens, 33.

86 *A tenement building on Nassau Street:* Carlson, 124.

86 *He was the* Herald's *publisher:* Carlson, 124.

86 New-York Enquirer: By the late 1820s, the hyphenation of "New-York" was a matter of personal preference on the part of a newspaper owner; some papers had begun to drop the hyphen, while others retained it well into the 1850s. Fox (1928), 1–2.

86 *Made it known:* Fox (1928), 95.

87 *To engineer the merger:* Tucher, 18.

87 *Seeking a consulship:* Fermer, 16.

91 *Runners passing information:* Headley, 61.

91 *A full-scale campaign:* Much of this discussion is based on Bertram Wyatt-Brown's essay, "The Abolitionists' Postal Campaign of 1835," published in the *Journal of Negro History*, October 1965.

91 *Passed through the New York post office:* Wyatt-Brown, 230.

92 *"If that sum is placed":* Wyatt-Brown, 231.

92 *"The least spark would create a flame":* Richards, 17.

94 *More than one hundred riots:* Reiss (2001), 7.

94 *"We have complied"*: The letter, and Locke's response to it, can be found in the *Sun*'s issue of August 20, 1835.

CHAPTER 6: THE PRINCE OF IVY ISLAND

97 *The village of Bethel*: Bethel was actually a parish of Danbury until 1855, when it was incorporated as its own town.

97 *"The smoke had all cleared away"*: Barnum (1855), 12.

97 *Children ate their meals with lead spoons*: Werner, 11.

97 *Calomel, jalap, and Epsom salts*: Werner, 13.

98 *"A pretty pass, indeed"*: Barnum (1855), 50.

98 *The presiding spirit of the town was Calvinist*: See the excellent discussion in Saxon, pp. 47–48.

98 *"Almost smelling, feeling and tasting"*: Saxon, 48.

99 Love God and Be Merry: Saxon, 158.

99 *Ivy Island*: The story of Ivy Island is found in Barnum (1855), pp. 30–35.

101 *"One seldom hears"*: Brooks, 258.

102 *Like all tribal initiations*: Van Wyck Brooks called Ivy Island "a clear case of tribal initiation, as the anthropologists know it" (259).

102 *Barnum's inheritance*: The outrageous practical joke of Ivy Island would seem to be one of Barnum's own inventions. But Barnum biographer A. H. Saxon, who has been there, reports that "Ivy Island does indeed exist, and is nearly every bit as awful as Barnum makes it out to be." And Barnum did in fact own the property as a boy; his grandfather deeded it to him when he was nearly two years old. Saxon, 29–30.

102 *"I have drawn and bottled more rum"*: Roarke, 374.

105 *Tens of thousands of items*: For a detailed listing of the museum's remarkable collections, see its 1823 catalogue, *A Companion to the American Museum: Being a Catalogue of Upwards of Fifty Thousand Natural and Foreign Curiosities, Antiquities, and Productions of the Fine Arts,* compiled by the son of the museum's founder, John Scudder.

105 *On the corner of Ann Street*: In 1830 John Scudder, the proprietor, moved his museum from the former almshouse in City Hall Park to a five-story building on the corner of Broadway and Ann.

105 *"Advertising is like learning"*: Saxon, 77.

106 *"People would gamble in lotteries"*: Barnum (1855), 75.

106 *Not disestablished until 1818*: Saxon, 41.

107 "Hireling Priests": Saxon, 51.

107 *Two of his sons*: Saxon, 43.

108 *"The same spirit governs my enemies"*: Werner, 20.

108 *"The fearless advocate"*: Saxon, 44.

109 *"By friendship"*: Saxon, 41.

109 *His last issue*: After issue number 160, Barnum's brother-in-law, John W. Amerman, moved the *Herald of Freedom*'s offices to Norwalk and continued

to publish for another year before finally selling the paper to another publisher, George W. Taylor.

110 *"Fortunes equalling that of Croesus"*: Barnum (1855), 143.

111 *"CURIOSITY"*: Barnum included a transcription of the *Inquirer* article in his autobiography. Barnum (1855), 148.

112 *"The least deserving of all my efforts"*: Barnum (1888), 37.

112 *It was the fall of 1841*: For Barnum's account of the sale of the American Museum, see Barnum (1855), 216–223.

112 *The problem of money*: When a friend, knowing his lack of funds, asked him what he would use to buy the museum, Barnum says that he replied, "*Brass*, for silver and gold I have none." Barnum (1855), 216.

114 *Recently bought the paper*: Benjamin Day sold the *Sun* to his brother-in-law Moses Beach in 1838 for $40,000.

114 *"Five acres of land in Connecticut"*: A. H. Saxon has pointed out that when the deal for the American Museum was finally completed, Barnum had pledged as security two other parcels of land in Bethel in addition to Ivy Island. Saxon, 32.

CHAPTER 7: STRANGE ATTRACTIONS

115 *A thousand years old*: Barnum wrote in his autobiography, "So far as outward indications were concerned, she might almost as well have been called a thousand years old as any other age." Barnum (1855), 148.

115 *She was reclining on a high lounge*: For Barnum's account of his first encounter with Joice Heth and how he purchased her contract, see Barnum (1855), 148–152.

115 *Barnum was examining this woman*: See Reiss (2001), 19–20.

117 *"This whole account"*: Barnum (1855), 150.

117 *He always denied this*: In an article entitled "A Go-A-Head Day with Barnum," published in *Bentley's Miscellany* in 1847, an associate of Barnum's named Albert Smith wrote that Barnum had told him in 1844 that he had created the Joice Heth hoax himself, teaching her the George Washington stories and faking her documents. Smith (1847), 627. However, Barnum's claims here (which he never repeated and later often contradicted) can be dismissed as the idle boasting of a young showman who preferred to be seen as the "humbugger" rather than the "humbugged"; see Saxon, 73. Moreover, the historical record clearly indicates that Joice Heth was being advertised as "George Washington's nursemaid" well before Barnum became acquainted with her in the summer of 1835.

117 *First consulted with Charity*: Wallace, 9.

118 *"Golden harvest"*: Barnum (1855), 150.

118 *"Became Joice Heth's sole owner"*: Harris, 21.

118 *"Overnight became showman and slaveholder"*: Wallace, 9.

118 *Purchasing the right to exhibit Joice Heth*: See also the discussions in Reiss (2001), 23–27; and Saxon, 21.

118 *William Henry Johnson:* Johnson was actually the last of a series of What Is It?'s employed by Barnum. The first one was a disabled actor from New York named Harvey Leetch, who played the What Is It? for Barnum in London in 1846. Cook, 126.

118 *Born in New Jersey:* Cook, 128.

118 *A heated debate:* See Saxon, 83.

119 *"If the blacks were unceremoniously set free":* Saxon, 83.

119 *"I am no apologist for slavery":* Saxon, 83.

119 *An unsigned article published in the* Atlas: Saxon, 84.

119 *Mentioned the* Ceres *in his autobiography:* Barnum (1855), 205.

119 *Cited the* Atlas *article:* "The proprietors of the Atlas had published my portrait with a brief sketch of my life, interspersed with numerous anecdotes." Barnum (1855), 356.

120 *"Gazed, wondered, looked":* This description is from a front-page article, "The Joice Heth Hoax," published in the *Herald,* September 24, 1836.

120 *A former stud farm:* The widespread notion that Niblo built on the former site of the open-air venue called the Columbia Garden is mistaken; the Columbia Garden was across the street. See Garrett, 9.

120 *A full city block:* The block bounded by Prince, Houston, Broadway, and Crosby streets, in what is today Soho.

120 *Pleasure garden:* Thomas Garrett has defined a pleasure garden as "a privately owned (as opposed to a governmentally owned) enclosed ornamental ground or piece of land, open to the public as a resort or amusement area, and operated as a business." Garrett, 4. Pleasure gardens were enormously popular in New York from the early eighteenth century well into the twentieth century.

120 *Niblo's Suburban Pleasure Garden:* Dayton, 227.

121 *A white apron and a blue sash:* Lines, 3.

121 *Carried in a sedan chair:* Reiss (2001), 32.

121 *"Newspapers friendly":* Saxon, 75.

121 *"I am indebted to the press":* Saxon, 76.

122 *"The expense of making these sudden conversions":* Lyman recounted the story of Barnum's dealings with the newspaper editors in a front-page article, "The Joice Heth Hoax," published in the *Herald* on September 24, 1836.

123 *"Victoria herself":* Reiss (2001), 37.

123 *Fourteen hours a day:* Reiss (2001), 38.

124 *Gross receipts of fifteen hundred dollars:* Barnum (1855), 152.

124 *The differences between the races:* See the discussion in Reiss (2001), 42–45.

125 *He whose portrait hung in almost every house:* In 1858, Walt Whitman wrote of Washington, "His portrait hangs on every wall, and he is almost canonized in the affections of our people." Reiss (2001), 56.

125 *On August 8:* In his history of the *Sun,* Frank O'Brien gives the date of the move as August 3 (O'Brien, 49), but issues of the newspaper from the period clearly indicate that the move took place on Saturday, August 8.

125　*One of the most destructive fires:* An even more destructive fire would strike the following December 16. Though only two lives were lost, more than six hundred buildings would be destroyed and many thousands of people thrown out of work. See, for example, Burrows and Wallace, 596–598.

127　*Its circulation spiked:* On August 13 the *Sun* proclaimed, "We may safely assert that no other one paper in the Union, nor in the world, ever sold as many papers in one day, as we did yesterday." See Thompson, 24.

127　*Afong Moy, "the Chinese Lady":* Caldwell, 86.

CHAPTER 8: CELESTIAL DISCOVERIES

131　*Guessed Locke to be an inch shorter:* Harrison (1902), 15:136.

131　*"A calm, clear luminousness":* Harrison (1902), 15:136.

131　*"Strongly pitted by the smallpox":* Harrison (1902), 15:136.

132　*Two years later a son would arrive:* National Archives and Records Administration, 1860 Census Records, Film Series M653, Roll 850, page 22.

132　*Manor house:* My thanks to Anna and Robert Orledge, its present-day owners, for graciously allowing me to visit their home.

133　*"The Universe Restored":* Griggs, 42.

133　*"The Moon and its Inhabitants": Edinburgh New Philosophical Journal* 1 (April–October 1826), 389–390. William Griggs mistakenly claimed that this article was written by Thomas Dick. However, Dick's article was earlier in the issue and concerned a new type of telescope, not the possibility of life on the moon. Griggs, 5.

134　*A longer article:* Thomas Dick, "Description of a New Reflecting Telescope, Denominated the Aërial Reflector," 41–51.

134　*"The operations of intelligent agents":* Dick (1828), 371.

134　*"There can be little doubt":* Dick (1828), 372.

135　*Locke asked three hundred dollars:* In his interview with the *Sun* published on September 1, 1883, entitled "Benjamin Day's Own Story," Day recalled, "I paid between $500 and $600. That was more than the sum first agreed upon, which was $300."

135　*A penny paper they called the* True Sun: O'Brien, 33.

139　*"It can, in truth represent objects":* This item from the *Times* of London was reprinted in the Richmond *Enquirer* of April 12, 1833.

140　*An estimated $70,000:* The following day the *Sun* noted in an Erratum item that this should have been printed as £70,000. Locke had been living in the United States too long.

141　*Astronomers had not even tried:* Buttman, 5.

142　*John joined his father:* Buttman, 19–20.

142　*Seventy-two hours straight:* Clerke, 35.

143　*"Not as a matter of choice":* Moore, 6.

143　*"Tranquility of the retina":* Clerke, 101.

143　*"Sick of star-gazing":* Fernie, 77.

143   *Never again sit behind a telescope:* Clerke, 183.
143   *Has been compared to Einstein's:* Fernie, 104.
145   *Making observations of everything:* Fernie, 79.

CHAPTER 9: A PASSAGE TO THE MOON

147   *"Excited my fancy":* Harrison (1902), 15:127.
148   *"Conspicuous, as well":* Varle, 9.
149   *E. J. Coale's bookstore:* Allen, 267.
149   *"The Bard":* Allen, 267.
149   *Fig trees and raspberry bushes:* Allen, 105.
149   *Eight houses and an estate:* Silverman, 99.
150   *"I think I have already had":* Ostrum, 1:24.
150   *"My determination is at length taken":* Ostrum, 1:7.
150   *"After such a list":* Silverman, 37.
150   *"I am in the greatest necessity":* Ostrum, 1:9.
150   *"Pretty Letter":* Ostrum, 1:9.
151   *"For my little son Edgar":* Silverman, 38.
151   *"I have no energy left":* Ostrum, 1:42.
152   *Sixty-six misconduct citations:* Silverman, 66.
152   *"He did not drink as an epicure":* Baudelaire, 63.
153   *Agate lamp:* Allen, 105.
153   *Installed a powerful telescope:* Woodberry, 25.
153   *"Old wine and good cigars":* Latrobe, 58.
154   *"Capital!":* Latrobe, 58.
155   *Recent scholarship has decisively shown:* See, for example, William H. Gravely Jr., "A Note on the Composition of Poe's 'Hans Pfaal,'" which addresses this question directly. As Gravely points out, Latrobe indicated elsewhere that he and Poe actually met several times while Poe was living in Baltimore. Gravely, 3.
155   *He avidly read the literary journals:* Campbell, 168.
155   *Use of a test pigeon:* See the discussion of "Hans Phaall" and "Leaves from an Aeronaut" in Pollin, 370–371.
155   *"The focus of ten thousand eyes":* "Leaves," 64.
156   *Latin word for bellows:* Reiss (1957), 307.
156   *"Unparalleled adventure":* In the manuscript Poe prepared in 1842 for the second edition of *Tales of the Grotesque and Arabesque,* the story is entitled "The Unparalleled Adventure of One Hans Pfaall." In fact, Poe spelled the character's surname three different ways: Phaall (in the magazine version of the tale and its first book publication), Phaal (in several written references to it), and Pfaall (in the later book publications). Pollin, 457.
158   *A lengthy appendix:* This appeared at the end of volume 2 of the 1839 *Tales of the Grotesque and Arabesque.* Poe would enlarge the appendix slightly for a subsequent edition of *Tales,* adding two paragraphs at the end. His

comments on Cyrano and Tucker, and his assertion of the originality of his story's "design," come from that version.

158 *"Somewhat ingenious"*: This and Poe's other comments on the earlier lunar voyages can be found in Pollin, 430–432.

158 *"The Flight of Thomas O'Rourke"*: Poe does not cite an author; it was the Irish writer William Maginn. Pollin, 502.

159 *"Verisimilitude, in the application"*: Pollin, 433.

159 *One of the important sources*: See Pollin, 502; Posey, 501. In an earlier essay, J. O. Bailey had suggested that Poe used Tucker's book itself, not merely the review of it. See Bailey (1942), 522–525.

159 *"Much interested in what is there said"*: Harrison (1902), 15:127.

160 *"Cotopaxi"*: Cotopaxi is a volcano in Ecuador with an elevation of 19,347 feet.

161 *As many as a dozen passages*: Posey, 502.

161 *"The two cusps"*: Posey, 505.

161 *"Design is original"*: Pollin, 433.

161 *Important elements of his critique*: Burton Pollin has pointed out that in his 1839 critique of Locke's moon series, "Poe directly paraphrased or incorporated material, unacknowledged, from Dr. Dick's works." Pollin, 494.

162 *"Extraordinary production"*: Pollin, 372.

162 *"I will take care"*: Pollin, 375.

162 *"Hairbreadth 'scapes and stirring incidents"*: Pollin, 372.

162 *"The chief design"*: Harrison (1902), 15:134.

163 *He discussed his idea*: Harrison (1902), 15:128.

163 *"To give what interest I could"*: Harrison (1902), 15:128.

CHAPTER 10: "IF THIS ACCOUNT IS TRUE, IT IS MOST ENORMOUSLY WONDERFUL"

167 *It was a rainy day*: The August 26, 1835, diary entry of Michael Floy, a nurseryman living on Broadway at Eleventh Street, contains this notation: "Rainy." Floy, 177.

168 *He worked furiously*: Locke's friend William Griggs later noted, "The author was compelled to write the greater number of the successive portions as a daily task, amid the distracting avocations and interruptions of an editorial office." Griggs, 21.

168 *The Peterloo Massacre*: The political journal Locke had contributed to in London—the *Republican*—had taken its name from the one founded by radical printer Richard Carlile in the wake of the massacre.

168 *"Clear, bold, and forcible"*: Harrison (1902), 15:260.

169 *The crater called Endymion*: In fact, Endymion is located on the northeastern limb of the moon, not the western. As Edgar Allan Poe pointed out in his critique of Locke's moon series, Locke had apparently been misreading Blunt's lunar map, reversing east and west. Pollin, 429. Burton Pollin, by the way, misidentifies Charles Blunt as Edmund March Blunt, the prominent

New England mapmaker, and as a result characterizes the Blunt lunar map as "Locke's joke." Pollin, 495.

170   *The Cleomedes crater:* Like Endymion, the Cleomedes crater is on the moon's northeastern, not western, limb.

173   *"Ice! Rockland ice!":* For descriptions of this and other street cries, see the 1834 volume *The New-York Cries in Rhyme*, published anonymously; and Francis S. Osgood's *The Cries of New-York* (1845).

174   *"Besieged by thousands of applicants":* Griggs, 23.

174   *"A fine broadcloth Quaker suit":* Griggs, 23.

174   *"A look of mingled astonishment and contempt":* Griggs, 23.

175   *Twenty thousand copies sold almost instantly:* Griggs, 26.

175   *More than forty thousand copies:* Griggs, 4.

175   *Sixty thousand:* Benjamin Day gave that figure in his 1883 interview with the *Sun.* This was also the number cited by P. T. Barnum in his earlier *Humbugs of the World.* Barnum (1866), 202.

175   *Looking glasses and mourning pictures:* See Larkin, 144.

175   *Day himself was occupied:* O'Brien, 53.

175   *"The most talented lithographic artist":* The *Sun*'s praise notwithstanding, Mr. Baker's first name is no longer known. In *America on Stone,* the definitive history of American lithography, Harry Twyford Peters was unable to establish the identity of either Norris or Baker, though he did cite their Wall Street firm as the producer of the *Lunar Temples* lithograph.

177   *No less than fifty thousand dollars:* Barnum (1866), 202.

177   *A circulation of more than a few thousand:* For circulation figures of the time, see O'Brien, 11.

177   *A daily circulation no greater than 17,000:* Thompson, 26.

178   *"As these discoveries were gradually spread":* Harrison (1902), 15:127.

178   *"Not one person in ten":* Harrison (1902), 15:134.

178   *"The construction of the telescope":* Lossing, 361.

178   *"Unquestionable plausibility and verisimilitude":* Greeley wrote a long, thoughtful reflection on the moon series on the front page of the September 2, 1835, issue of the *New Yorker.*

178   *"The majestic, yet subdued, dignity":* Barnum (1866), 195.

179   *"A great talk":* Floy, 179.

179   *"An exceedingly well written article":* The *Diary of Philip Hone,* collection of the New-York Historical Society, microfilm reel 3.

180   *"Ferdinand Mendez Pinto":* Mendez Pinto was a sixteenth-century Portuguese explorer; the veracity of his adventures, as recounted in his memoirs, was widely questioned.

180   *To the* Edinburgh Journal of Science: On the front page of its issue of August 29, 1835, the New Haven *Daily Herald* stated: "According to the Edinburgh Journal of Science, we are likely soon to be made familiarly acquainted with the Man in the Moon, his habits and character, as well as with the Geography and Natural History of the beautiful place of his residence."

180   *"Yale College was alive"*: "Locke Among the Moonlings," 502.

181   *The tower of its Atheneum*: Musto, 8.

181   *"I suppose the magazine is somewhere upstairs"*: Day recalled the incident in the interview he gave to the *Sun* on the occasion of its fiftieth anniversary, September 1, 1883.

181   *He directed them to his editor*: This portion of the story was recounted by Frank O'Brien in his article "The Story of 'The Sun,' 1833 to 1918," which appeared in the *Sun* on March 10, 1918.

181   *Olmsted and Loomis did claim that honor*: In a letter to the New Haven *Daily Herald,* published September 12, 1835, Olmsted and Loomis wrote about Halley's Comet: "Yesterday morning, August 31st, we had the satisfaction of first observing this interesting body, in the field of Clark's great telescope."

182   *A letter sent to the New Haven* Daily Herald: The letter appeared on September 21, 1835.

182   *Authorship has been attributed*: Musto, 9.

182   *Not since ancient Greece*: Thomson, 21.

182   *A virus found on cows' udders*: Smith (1987), 92.

182   *No more than six months earlier*: See the *Sun* for February 23, 1835.

183   *Sir Francis Beaufort*: This anecdote was recounted by the Irish theologian and astronomer Josiah Crampton in his 1863 book *The Lunar World.* Crampton, 84. Crampton referred to Herschel's correspondent as "Sir Frederick Beaufort," but in this he was likely mistaken, for Sir Francis Beaufort was a friend of John Herschel's and corresponded with him while he was working at the Cape of Good Hope. Evans, 5.

183   *Purchase Bibles for the unenlightened inhabitants*: This story would subsequently be expanded in the account, much repeated, of the British journalist Harriet Martineau, who wrote that friends of Herschel were claiming that "the astronomer has received at the Cape, a letter from a large number of Baptist clergymen of the United States, congratulating him on his discovery, informing him that it had been the occasion of much edifying preaching, and of prayer-meetings for the benefit of brethren in the newly explored regions; and beseeching him to inform his correspondents whether science affords any prospects of a method of conveying the Gospel to residents in the moon." Martineau, 3:22–23.

CHAPTER 11: THE PICTURESQUE BEAUTY OF THE MOON

185   *"Now, for what purpose are we to suppose"*: See Crowe, 217. Michael Crowe's book, *The Extraterrestrial Life Debate, 1750–1900,* is the most thorough and valuable work on the subject, and my discussion of it in this chapter is indebted to it.

185   *"If there be inhabitants on the moon"*: Herschel (1833), 231.

186   *"Nature has ceased to rage"*: Crowe, 71.

186   *"Great artificial works on the moon"*: Guiley, 33.

187   *Its origin is actually rather murky:* See the excellent investigation of the issue in Crowe, 205–207.

187   *"With 100 separate mirrors":* Crowe, 207.

187   *"I hold it to be very probable":* Crowe, 206.

187   *"An English journal article":* Crowe, 207.

188   *"In all worlds there are living creatures":* Crowe, 3.

188   *An agnostic on the question:* "While belief in lunar life was often attributed to Galileo by the seventeenth century, he himself was one of the few of his period to deny the possibility, though he refused to commit himself on the possibility of life on other planets." Nicolson (1936), 37.

189   *"There is a great chasm":* Crowe, 13.

189   *If these creatures were not human:* See the discussion in Brooke, 255.

189   *"Thousands of thousands of Suns":* Crowe, 60.

189   *"A bason of milk or a glass of water":* Crowe, 62.

189   *"Large and lucid planet":* Crowe, 67.

190   *"Its similarity to the other globes":* Crowe, 67.

190   *"A system in every star":* Crowe, 186.

190   *"Magnitude does not overpower him":* Crowe, 186.

190   *"Ran like wild-fire":* Crowe, 184.

190   *"All the world":* Crowe, 182.

191   *Sometime in the midafternoon:* Nine o'clock in the morning is the hour usually attributed to Ussher, but that time was actually determined by Sir John Lightfoot, the vice chancellor of the University of Cambridge; Ussher had dated the creation to several hours later. Thomson, 115.

191   *"Raises to sublimer views":* Paley, 212.

192   *"The most varied and comprehensive":* Dick (1828), 131.

192   *Useless splendor:* "They were not intended merely to diversify the void of infinite space with a useless splendor which has no relation to intellectual natures." Dick (1828), 70.

192   *Sixty quadrillion in the visible universe:* The exact number was 60,573,000,000,000,000. Dick (1840), 318.

193   *"Our terrestrial sovereigns":* Dick (1838), 247.

193   *"May contain a population of intelligent beings":* Dick (1838), 243.

193   *No fewer than 4.2 billion inhabitants:* Dick (1838), 243.

193   *"Beautiful diversity":* Dick (1840), 289.

193   *"All the parts uniformly present":* Dick (1838), 243.

194   *A representation of man's sinful nature:* An article in the *Edinburgh New Philosophical Journal* from 1826 is entitled "The Destruction of Sodom and Gomorrah, occasioned by Volcanic Agency."

194   *"That such destructive agents exist in the moon":* Dick (1838), 238.

194   *"It is not improbable":* Dick (1840), 299.

194   *"Certain relations, sentiments, dispositions, and virtues":* Dick (1840), 299.

195   *"Beings not much unlike ourselves":* Dick (1840), 299.

195   *"Read with the utmost avidity":* Barnum (1866), 194.

195 *"Where the Christian religion"*: Tocqueville, 291. Tocqueville saw both strength and weakness in the thoroughgoing nature of American Christianity. One the one hand it tended to maintain a free and democratic republic, and maintain social order and happiness; on the other, it tended to stifle free thought and innovation.

195 *"Spiritual necessities"*: Tewksbury, 55.

196 *"The forces of irreligion"*: Tewksbury, 66.

196 *"A perennial fountain of orthodoxy"*: Tewksbury, 67.

196 *"It is most rationally concluded"*: Crowe, 176.

196 *"The history of the works of the Deity"*: Daniels, 49.

196 *"Receives with gratitude and joy"*: Daniels, 52.

196 *"Well adapted to arrest the attention"*: Miller, 278.

196 *"More calculated to exalt the soul"*: Miller, 278.

197 *"Peculiar mania of the time"*: Barnum (1866), 194.

CHAPTER 12: "THE ASTRONOMICAL HOAX EXPLAINED"

199 *Encouraging blacks to dress as dandies*: Richards, 114.

199 *Shillings*: In the first half of the nineteenth century in New York, the English term "shilling" was used to express a value of twelve and a half cents.

201 *From 123,000 to 270,000*: Greene, 15.

202 *Reprint the moon series*: For a newspaper to reprint a story that had appeared in another paper was legal and commonplace at the time.

202 *"We did not dream"*: *New-Yorker,* September 2, 1835.

203 *"Penny trash"*: O'Brien, 28.

203 *A wager of one thousand dollars*: O'Brien, 35.

203 *The Native American Democratic Association*: Crouthamel (1969), 59.

208 *James Gordon Bennett awoke early*: A description of Bennett's typical working day can be found in James Parton's excellent essay, "James Gordon Bennett and the New York Herald." Parton, 282–283.

208 *His birthday had come a day early*: Bennett was born September 1, 1795.

209 *A former coal cellar*: Thompson, 33.

212 *Bennett had a dilemma*: See the discussion in Seavey, xvii.

213 *"Sir John J. H. Herschell"*: This was another error by Bennett. The astronomer's name was actually John F. W. Herschel—Frederick William, after his father.

213 *"Turkey buzzard"*: Carlson, 186.

213 *"Moral pestilence"*: Crouthamel (1964), 96.

213 *"Lizard looking animal"*: Turner, 14.

214 *Day's brother-in-law Moses Yale Beach*: Beach was married to Day's sister Nancy.

215 *Bound to silence by contract*: Years later Locke's friend William Griggs wrote that he "must inevitably have been embarrassed in the dilemma of either sustaining a literary fiction by personal assurances amounting to a conscious

falsehood, or of violating a business contract by exposing a secret no longer, in honor, at his own disposal." Griggs, 26.

215 *"An if is your only peacemaker"*: The quotation is from *As You Like It*, Act V, Scene 4.

215 *The mails would soon arrive from Europe*: Griggs, 26.

216 *No one had even noticed it*: The flaw remained unnoticed for more than forty years, until the British astronomer Richard A. Proctor pointed it out in his 1878 book *Myths and Marvels of Astronomy*. Proctor, 251. Proctor, it must be said, got many other details wrong, including misidentifying the author of the series as "Richard Alton Locke."

216 *"Suffered severely"*: Griggs, 26.

216 *The taproom of the Washington Hotel*: In his book *The Story of the Sun*, Frank O'Brien wrote that the conversation took place either in the taproom of the Washington Hotel or in the *Sun* office. O'Brien, 55. Locke's admission would more likely have come away from the office.

216 *A reporter friend of his named Finn*: Finn's first name is no longer known.

216 *"Don't print it right away"*: O'Brien, 55.

CHAPTER 13: MOONSHINE

217 *"The name of the author"*: *Every Saturday*, March 11, 1871, 235.

218 *"The Great Hoax"*: For the titles of many newspaper stories, see Bjork, 24.

218 *Most widely circulated newspaper story*: Hughes, 184.

218 *"As if their appetite had increased"*: "Why, she would hang on him / As if increase of appetite had grown / by what it fed on." *Hamlet*, 1.2.

219 *A recently published paper*: Proctor, 260.

220 *"The British government at Botany-bay"*: At the time, the term "Botany Bay" denoted an Australian penal colony.

221 *A stage lit entirely by gas*: O'Brien, 73.

222 *Painted gold in the front*: Burrows and Wallace, 486.

222 Moonshine, or Lunar Discoveries: There is a brief discussion of the play in Odell, 4:72.

222 *Henry Hanington*: His last name was often misspelled "Hannington," by the *Sun*, among others.

224 *Sixteen traveling menageries*: Information about the menageries of the 1830s can be found in the circus magazine *Bandwagon* 35, no. 6 (November–December 1991), 64–71; and 36, no. 1 (January–February 1992), 31–36.

224 *First to exhibit a giraffe*: *Brooklyn Daily Eagle*, June 22, 1857, 2.

224 *Where he might find Sir John Herschel*: The story of the meeting between Weeks and Herschel is recounted in some detail in Griggs, 37–39.

224 *His observatory was some five miles away*: Evans, 40.

224 *"A person possessed of a fund of humor"*: *Brooklyn Daily Eagle*, June 22, 1857, 2.

226 *"As I perceive by an Advertisement"*: Ruskin, 97.

227   *"I have been pestered from all quarters"*: Evans, 282.

227   *Received copies of the* Sun's *pamphlet*: William Griggs claimed that the pamphlets had been sent by "the shrewd proprietors of the Sun," in the hopes, presumably, that the European papers would reprint the story and thus buttress the *Sun*'s claims. Griggs does not cite the proprietors by name, but they undoubtedly included Benjamin Day, as shrewd a businessman as there was in New York's newspaper district. Griggs, 34.

227   *"With all the gravity and reserve"*: Griggs, 35.

227   *Some of the interior parts of Germany*: Griggs, 35.

229   *No fewer than four editions*: References to the four French-language editions can be found in Sohncke, 258.

229   *His friend John Herschel*: The two had first met in 1821, when Herschel was traveling in France. Clerke, 150.

230   *"If one asked me"*: Crowe, 246.

230   *"Repeated interruptions"*: Griggs, 33.

230   *"Utterly incredible"*: After the passage of the resolution Arago received a letter from John Herschel. "I beg you to accept my sincere thanks for your good offices," he wrote, "although in truth I must regret that time as precious as yours should be thus employed. Since there are some people silly enough to believe any wild story anyone sells them, we must wish that the stories should always be as harmless as this; in any case, I am not disposed to complain seriously about an event which has reminded me of you and which has established you as my defender." Seavey, xxii.

231   *History would more often accord*: In his study of nineteenth-century science fiction, H. Bruce Franklin observed, "Poe has continually been called, both in America and Europe, the father of the genre." Franklin, 93.

232   *"Have you seen the 'Discoveries in the Moon'?"*: Ostrum, 1:73.

CHAPTER 14: MONCK MASON'S FLYING MACHINE

233   *A salary of $520 a year*: Ostrum, 1:73.

233   *"In a state of starvation"*: Woodberry, 66.

234   *"My feelings at this moment"*: Ostrum, 1:73.

234   *Biting his nails to the quick*: Pope-Hennessy, 153.

234   *"Miserable"* and *"wretched"*: Ostrum, 1:73.

234   *"More than yourself have remarked"*: Thomas and Jackson, 170.

235   *"Philosophical blunders"*: Spannuth and Mabbott, 54.

235   *"No sooner had I seen the paper"*: Harrison (1902), 15:128.

235   *A comic scene*: For instance, the president and vice president of the Rotterdam College of Astronomy, to whom Hans Phaall addresses his letter, are named Von Underduk and Rubadub.

235   *"Half plausible, half bantering"*: Harrison (1902), 15:128.

236   *Encyclopedias and earlier travel narratives*: See the discussion in Pollin, 17–19, 286–299.

236   *One-fifth of the entire book:* Pollin, 17.

236   *"Bare-faced and barbarous plagiarism":* Silverman, 146.

236   *"Nothing yet appears":* Jackson (1974), 47. Remarkably enough, the report's author, Robert Greenhow, was a native of Richmond, Virginia, who contributed various travel sketches to the *Southern Literary Messenger* from 1834 to 1836; during that time he must have either met Edgar Allan Poe or corresponded with him. Greenhow's error would eventually be corrected: when his Senate report was published in book form four years later, it did not contain references to Julius Rodman or his ill-fated expedition.

236   *Gold fever then gripping the country:* Gold was discovered in California in 1848, the year before the publication of Poe's story "Von Kempelen and His Discovery."

237   *"Last night, for supper":* Ostrum, 1:251–252.

238   *Romantic fiction:* Burrows and Wallace, 640.

238   *Fifty dollars:* Nichols, 1:348.

239   *The story itself:* The complete Balloon Hoax can be found in Harrison (1902), 5:224–240.

241   *A balloon trip across the English Channel:* Scudder (1949), 181–182.

241   *Taken place in 1837:* Scudder (1949), 226.

241   *Pamphlet that accompanied the exhibition:* The pamphlet was published anonymously but was likely written by Monck Mason. Wilkinson, 313.

241   *"An ellipsoid or solid oval":* This quote, and the others that follow, are from Wilkinson, 314–317.

241   *More than one-quarter of Poe's balloon story:* Franklin, 94.

242   *"Made a far more intense sensation":* Spannuth and Mabbott, 33.

243   *"Water cure":* This involved the use of cold water (for drinking and bathing) in a spa-like clinic for the treatment of various illnesses.

243   *"A man of much talent":* Spannuth and Mabbott, 32.

243   *"A man of rare genius":* Nichols, 1:348.

244   *"The publisher, as is the American custom":* Ibid.

244   *"I love fame":* Allen, 571.

244   *Nichols's version is the more likely one:* This is the argument advanced by Doris V. Falk in her brief article "Thomas Low Nichols, Poe, and the 'Balloon Hoax,'" *Poe Studies* 5, no. 2 (December 1972).

245   *"Poe's account of the publication":* Spannuth and Mabbott, 36.

245   *"Diddling Considered as One of the Exact Sciences":* The quotes from the essay can be found in Harrison (1902) 5:210–223.

245   *"Childish and almost unbalanced delight":* Allen, 463.

246   *"The rabble":* Spannuth and Mabbott, 34.

246   *"Nothing intelligible can be written":* Silverman, 164.

247   *Maelzel's automaton chess player:* Tom Standage wrote an insightful book-length history of the automaton chess player, *The Turk.* See also W. K. Wimsatt Jr.'s essay; and Cook, 30–72.

247 *Baron Wolfgang von Kempelen:* In tribute to him, Poe named the protagonist of his lead-into-gold hoax Baron von Kempelen.

248 *"Maelzel's Chess-Player":* The entire essay can be found in Harrison (1902), 14:6–37.

249 *Little more than a gloss:* This similarity Brewster freely admitted: "There can be little doubt, however," he remarked about Willis's earlier pamphlet, "that the secret has been discovered." Brewster, 248.

249 *So did Poe rely heavily on Brewster:* In his essay "Poe and the Chess Automaton," W. K. Wimsatt Jr. considers the question of how much of his analysis Poe owed to Brewster, and concluded that "the answer is: almost everything, all that was correct, as well as much that was incorrect. As far as Brewster is right, Poe is right. Where Brewster is wrong, Poe is wrong." Wimsatt, 147.

249 *Poe acknowledged his debt by disparagement:* Wimsatt, 149.

249 *"Highly ingenious":* Thomas and Jackson, 205.

249 *"The most successful attempt":* Thomas and Jackson, 216.

249 *His detective fiction:* See Standage, 181.

249 *"A curiously constructed automaton":* Cook, 8.

CHAPTER 15: "JOICE HETH IS NOT DEAD"

251 *"Our audience again largely increased":* Barnum (1855), 157.

252 *More than ten thousand specimens:* See the report of the fair in the *Journal of the American Institute* 1, no. 2 (November 1835).

253 *Not a single church:* Sante, 12.

253 *"Mr. Dinneford, I beg your pardon":* Barnum (1855), 161.

254 *"Ailing from a cold":* Reiss (2001), 126.

254 *"Faithful colored woman":* Barnum (1855), 171.

254 *Aunt Joice . . . was no more:* This is how Barnum characterized the note's description of her death. Barnum (1855), 171.

254 *Pioneered several surgical techniques: Medical Register of New York, New Jersey, and Connecticut* 16 (1878): 189.

254 *"Expressed a desire to institute a post-mortem":* Barnum (1855), 171.

255 *Medical offices on Chambers Street: Medical Register,* 189.

255 *"Doctors' riot":* See, for example, Headley, 31–39.

257 *Exchanging the scalpel for a handsaw:* Reiss (2001), 138.

257 *"Spoiled half a dozen knives":* Barnum (1855), 173.

257 *"I believed the documents in her possession":* Reiss (2001), 21.

258 *"Always ready for a joke":* Barnum (1855), 172.

258 *"Gave great dignity to his whole deportment": Medical Register,* 189.

258 *"In not very good humor":* Barnum (1855), 172.

258 *"The most stupendous scientific imposition":* Barnum (1866), 193.

259 *He placed the responsibility on Lyman:* "Lyman determined to put a joke upon James Gordon Bennett, of the Herald." Barnum (1855), 173.

262 *Increasingly claimed the right to vote:* Property qualifications for voting had been removed in 1821 for white males, and starting in 1834 the mayor was elected by direct vote rather than appointed by the Common Council.

262 *Their democratic right to judgment:* See the excellent discussion in Tucher, 57.

262 *"That's just the question":* Harris, 77.

262 *"Two-thirds of the working men":* Wilentz, 220.

262 *Cartmen now called their employers "Mister":* Lyon, ix.

262 *Doff a cap and bow deeply with averted eyes:* Larkin, 155.

262 *"Invariably the custom to shake hands":* Larkin, 155.

262 *"At the outset of my career":* Tucher, 48.

263 *"Putting on glittering appearances":* Barnum (1866), 8.

263 *Requires consent from those who participate:* Tucher, 56.

263 *"A full equivalent for their money":* Barnum (1866), 9.

263 *Competition between patron and promoter:* Harris, 77.

264 *A daily circulation of 27,000:* O'Brien, 69.

CHAPTER 16: THE BEST SELF-HOAXED MAN IN NEW YORK

268 *Nearly five hundred dollars an acre:* Burrows and Wallace, 612.

268 *Ten thousand mechanics:* Schlesinger, 220.

268 *"At no period of its history":* Schlesinger, 220.

268 *A profit of twenty thousand dollars:* O'Brien, 79.

268 *On Staten Island:* Richard Adams Locke can be found in the 1840 Census Records for Staten Island, Richmond County, where he is identified as belonging to the occupational category "Learned professionals and engineers."

268 *Woods and fields and a patchwork of farms:* Smith (1970), 103.

268 *Joined by two sons:* National Archives and Records Administration, 1850 Census Records, Film Series M432, Roll 587, page 24.

269 *"Clear profits":* This was the phrase used by Locke in his discussion of his own economic arrangements with the proprietors of the *New Era*, published in the issue of January 5, 1837.

269 *"Mr. Locke's columns":* Harrison (1902), 15:135.

272 *A euphemism for drunkenness:* Silverman, 7.

273 *"More conservative and hard working":* Schroth, 39.

273 *"He would have been a first-rate man":* This remark can be found in the interview Day gave to the *Sun* for its fiftieth-anniversary issue, September 3, 1883.

273 *A court order obtained by Bell:* New York Chancery Court, October 26, 1839, Reference No. BM 865-B.

273 *Double parlor:* Allen, 542.

273 *The evening's guests :* Thomas and Jackson, 619–620.

273 *"The man in the moon":* Thomas and Jackson, 619–620.

274 *His letter of reply:* The letter was published in the *New World* as "Mr. Locke's Moon Story," on page 1. All of the quotes that follow are contained therein.

275   *"Christianity reigns without obstacles"*: Tocqueville, 292.

277   *"A short time ago"*: Tocqueville. The footnote runs from page 245 through page 246.

280   *"So thoroughly was the popular mind"*: Griggs, 16.

280   *"Disappointment and chagrin"*: Griggs, 30.

280   *"If the story be either received"*: Griggs, 30.

EPILOGUE: THAT TYRANNY SHALL BE NO LONGER

283   *Forty thousand dollars*: O'Brien, 79.

283   *Another fifty-two years*: Day died at his home at 55 East Twenty-fifth Street on December 21, 1889.

283   *"I owned the whole concern"*: O'Brien, 79.

283   *"These papers"*: Mott (1962), 241.

284   *The* Daily News *and the* Daily Express: For newspapers' names, see Payne, 245; Jackson (1995), 814; O'Brien, 85.

284   *"The consequences of the scheme"*: Harrison (1902), 15:126.

284   *"Occupied the editorial chair"*: Brooklyn Daily Eagle, 95.

284   *A population of just under 13 million*: These statistics are from O'Brien, 86.

285   *His twenty-five-year-old son*: The younger Bennett, familiarly known as "Jamie," was even more eccentric than his father, and more generally disliked. He was headstrong, erratic in his decision making, and he led the extravagant life of a millionaire playboy. Eleven years after taking over as proprietor of the *Herald* Jamie moved from New York to Paris, after fighting a duel of honor with the brother of his fiancée, in whose fireplace he had urinated during a New Year's celebration.

285   *The most widely read newspaper in the world*: Carlson, 300.

285   *"He is like the mother mountain of gold"*: Seitz, 144.

285   *"Been in the habit"*: Seitz, 148.

285   *Passing derogatory stories*: See Saxon, 178.

286   *In early 1851*: The story can be found in Seitz, 145–146.

286   *A mile up Broadway*: Caldwell, 80.

287   *"Are you in earnest?"*: Barnum (1888), 254.

288   *Black walnut doors*: Carlson, 380.

288   *"The Herschel Hoax"*: See De Morgan, 1:326–327.

288   *Born in Savoy, France*: Nicollet was born in 1796; unaccountably, De Morgan dates the birth to thirty years earlier. De Morgan, 1:326.

289   *"Any very tangible evidence"*: De Morgan, 1:326.

289   *"I have no doubt"*: De Morgan, 2:132.

289   *"Richard Alton Locke"*: Proctor, 242.

289   *"One of Clark's most successful achievements"*: National Cyclopædia, 8:455.

289   *"The secret history of the 'Moon Hoax'"*: Lossing, 361.

289   *"Mr. Moses Y. Beach"*: Lossing, 361–362.

290   *"A mortified but impotent littérateur"*: Moss, 95.

290   *"Noticeable for nothing in the world"*: Harrison (1902), 15:115.

291   The Letters of Willis Gaylord Clark: Willis Gaylord Clark, a poet, was Lewis Gaylord Clark's twin brother.

291   *"Took an active part"*: Dunlap, 16.

291   *Further observed:* According to Dunlap, the suggestion was first made to him by the Poe scholar Thomas O. Mabbott. Dunlap, 16.

291   *"The one of which"*: Harrison (1902), 15:129.

291   *"Having stated the case"*: Harrison, 15:129.

291   *Attended the theater:* Silverman, 238.

291   *"Uncommonly fine"*: Wilson, 343.

292   *"An event in one's life"*: Silverman, 279.

292   *"A wife of matchless beauty"*: Allen, 332.

292   *The village of Fordham:* Today it is part of the Bronx.

292   *"Bloated and unwashed"*: Allen, 672.

293   *"The sun will shine"*: Locke (1842), 6.

293   *"The great theme of their poets"*: Locke, 5.

294   *"Mr. Locke is now engaged"*: Harrison (1902), 15:136.

294   *In his lifetime:* A posthumously published poem entitled "The Scythe and the Sylphids" appeared in the art journal *Aldine* in February 1874.

294   *An inspector for the Customs Service:* Locke began work on August 1, 1842. U.S. Customs Service, New York, *Register of Employees, 1843–1854*, National Archives and Records Administration, Northeast Office.

294   *"Partisan zeal and work"*: Eaton, 1.

295   *"Quietly returning money"*: See the discussion of Melville at the Custom House in Delbanco, 291–292.

295   *Did not own his own home:* Ownership of the house was listed under the name of his son Richard. National Archives and Records Administration, 1860 Census Records, Film Series M653, Roll 850, page 22.

295   *"Have you any thing for me"*: Beach Family Papers, Library of Congress, Manuscript Collection, LC 820561812.

295   *The same year:* Locke began work at the Staten Island office on January 31, 1850. U.S. Customs Service, New York, *Register of Employees, 1853–1864*, National Archives and Records Administration, Northeast Office.

296   *"Complacency and satisfaction"*: "Richard A. Locke and the Clergymen," *New York Times*, October 2, 1858, 4.

296   *"Mr. Locke has in great perfection"*: "Richard A. Locke and the Clergymen," 4.

296   *"Handsome, bearded, and self-possessed"*: Abbott, 40.

296   *"No impulse of the human heart"*: "Kossuth," *New York Evangelist*, December 11, 1851, 199.

296   *"Go on then, Great Kossuth"*: Abbott, 40.

297 *Retired from the Customs Service:* U.S. Customs Service, New York, *Register of Employees, 1853–1864,* National Archives and Records Administration, Northeast Office.

297 *Silver Mount Cemetery:* When I visited the Silver Mount Cemetery, Locke's marble tombstone was lying facedown on the ground, apparently toppled by the root of a large tree growing nearby. The cemetery's director, Dora Arslanian, very kindly commissioned a work crew that lifted the stone and set it upright, and cleaned it until it shone.

297 *Three of their children:* According to Lockwood Rianhard, who is a great-great-grandson of Richard Adams Locke, Locke's eldest son Richard was court-martialed, while his third son, John, died in January 1865 in the Southern prison camp at Andersonville. His two other sons, Lewis and Walter, moved to Colorado and never returned. Lockwood Rianhard notes as well that Locke's youngest daughter Emma never married. Letter to the author, October 19, 2004.

298 *"The incident of all others":* Locke (1840), 1.

SELECTED BIBLIOGRAPHY

Abbott, Mabel. "An Old Manuscript: Locke's Address to Kossuth." *Proceedings of the Staten Island Institute of Arts and Sciences* 12, no. 2 (January 1950): 37–41.

Albion, Robert Greenhalgh. *Square-Riggers on Schedule: The New York Sailing Packets to England, France, and the Cotton Ports.* Princeton: Princeton University Press, 1938.

Allen, Hervey. *Israfel: The Life and Times of Edgar Allan Poe.* New York: Farrar & Rinehart, 1934.

Anbinder, Tyler. *Five Points.* New York: Plume, 2002.

Bailey, J. O. "Sources for Poe's Arthur Gordon Pym, 'Hans Pfaal,' and Other Pieces." *PMLA* 57, no. 2 (June 1942): 513–535.

Bailey, Ronald. "East Brent Boy Who Became a Famous American Journalist." *Weston Mercury and Somersetshire Herald,* January 7, 1955, 3.

Barnum, P. T. *The Humbugs of the World.* London: John Camden Hotten, 1866.

———. *The Life of P. T. Barnum, Written by Himself.* 1855. Urbana: University of Illinois Press, 2000.

———. *The Life of P. T. Barnum, Written by Himself.* Buffalo, New York: Courier, 1888.

Baudelaire, Charles. *Baudelaire on Poe.* Translated and edited by Lois and Francis E. Hyslop Jr. State College, Pennsylvania: Bald Eagle Press, 1952.

Bittner, William. *Poe: A Biography.* Boston: Little, Brown, 1962.

Bjork, Ulf Jonas. "'Sweet Is the Tale': A Context for the *New York Sun*'s Moon Hoax." *American Journalism* 18, no. 4 (Fall 2001): 13–27.

Blackmar, Elizabeth. *Manhattan for Rent, 1785–1850.* Ithaca, New York: Cornell University Press, 1989.

Bleyer, Willard Grosvenor. *Main Currents in the History of American Journalism.* Boston: Houghton Mifflin, 1927.

Bondurant, Agnes M. *Poe's Richmond.* Richmond, Virginia: Garrett & Massie, 1942.

Booth, Mary L. *History of the City of New York.* New York: E. P. Dutton, 1880.

Brace, Charles Loring. *Short Sermons to News Boys.* New York: Charles Scribner, 1866.

Bradshaw, James Stanford. "A Forgotten Firebrand, George W. Wisner." *Quarterly* (Historical Society of Michigan) 19, no. 3 (Fall 1983): 2–11.

———. "George W. Wisner and the New York *Sun.*" *Journalism History* 6, no. 4 (Winter 1979–1980): 112–121.

Brewster, David. *Letters on Natural Magic.* New York: Harper & Brothers, 1839.

Brooke, John Hedley. "Natural Theology and the Plurality of Worlds: Observations on the Brewster-Whewell Debate." *Annals of Science* 34, no. 3 (May 1977): 221–286.

Brooks, Van Wyck. *Sketches in Criticism.* New York: E. P. Dutton, 1932.

Bryant, William Cullen. *Reminiscences of the Evening Post.* New York: Wm. C. Bryant, 1851.

Burrows, Edwin G., and Mike Wallace. *Gotham: A History of New York City to 1898.* New York: Oxford University Press, 1999.

Buttman, Günther. *The Shadow of the Telescope: A Biography of John Herschel.* New York: Charles Scribner's Sons, 1970.

Caldwell, Mark. *New York Night: The Mystique and Its History.* New York: Scribner's, 2005.

Campbell, Killis. "Poe's Reading." *Studies in English* 5 (October 8, 1925): 166–193.

Carlson, Oliver. *The Man Who Made News: James Gordon Bennett.* New York: Duell, Sloan & Pearce, 1942.

Clark, John. "A Defender of the Faith." In *A Defence of a Sermon, Entitled "The Necessity of Philosophy to the Divine."* Bridgwater, U.K.: J. Clark, 1826.

Clerke, Agnes M. *The Herschels and Modern Astronomy.* New York: Macmillan, 1895.

Cohen, Patricia Cline. *The Murder of Helen Jewett: The Life and Death of a Prostitute in Nineteenth-Century New York.* New York: Alfred A. Knopf, 1998.

Collins, Paul. *Banvard's Folly.* New York: Picador, 2001.

Cook, James W. *The Arts of Deception: Playing with Fraud in the Age of Barnum.* Cambridge: Harvard University Press, 2001.

Coombes, John. *A Short History of Richard Locke and the Burnham Society.* Burnham, U.K.: Burnham Philosophical Society, 2001.

Coulthard, Alfred J. *Windmills of Somerset.* London: Research Publishing, 1978.

Crampton, Josiah. *The Lunar World.* Edinburgh: Adam and Charles Black, 1863.

Crook, David Paul. *American Democracy in English Politics, 1815–1850.* Oxford: Clarendon, 1965.

Crouthamel, James L. *James Watson Webb: A Biography.* Middletown, Connecticut: Wesleyan University Press, 1969.

———. "The Newspaper Revolution in New York 1830–1860." *New York History* 45, no. 2 (April 1964): 91–113.

Crowe, Michael J. *The Extraterrestrial Life Debate, 1750–1900.* Mineola, New York: Dover, 1999.

Dakin, James H. *Views in New-York and Its Environs.* New York: Peabody, 1834.

Daniels, George. *American Science in the Age of Jackson.* New York: Columbia University Press, 1968.

Dare, James. "A Lost Somersetshire Worthy." *Weston Mercury and Somersetshire Herald,* March 25, 1871, 4.

Dayton, Abram C. *Last Days of Knickerbocker Life in New York.* New York: George W. Harlan, 1882.

Delbanco, Andrew. *Melville: His World and Work.* New York: Alfred A. Knopf, 2005.

De Morgan, Augustus. *A Budget of Paradoxes.* 1872. Edited by David Eugene Smith. 2d ed. 2 vols. London: Open Court, 1915.

Dick, Thomas. *Celestial Scenery; or, the Wonders of the Planetary System Displayed.* Philadelphia: Edward C. Biddle, 1838.

_____. *The Christian Philosopher; or, the Connection of Science and Philosophy with Religion.* Brookfield, Massachusetts: E. & G. Merriam, 1828.

_____. *The Sidereal Heavens.* New York: Harper & Brothers, 1840.

Dickens, Charles. *American Notes.* 1842. London: Penguin, 2000.

Dunlap, Leslie W., ed. *The Letters of Willis Gaylord Clark and Lewis Gaylord Clark.* New York: New York Public Library, 1940.

The Eagle and Brooklyn. Brooklyn: Brooklyn Daily Eagle, 1893.

Eaton, Dorman B. *The "Spoils" System and Civil Service Reform in the Custom-House and Post-Office at New York.* New York: G. P. Putnam's Sons, 1882.

Ellis, Edward Robb. *The Epic of New York City.* New York: Coward-McCann, 1966.

Evans, David S., et al., eds. *Herschel at the Cape: Diaries & Correspondence of Sir John Herschel, 1834–1838.* Cape Town: A. A. Balkema, 1969.

Fermer, Douglas. *James Gordon Bennett and the New York Herald.* New York: St. Martin's, 1986.

Fernie, Donald. *The Whisper and the Vision: The Voyages of the Astronomers.* Toronto: Clarke, Irwin, 1976.

Floy, Michael. *The Diary of Michael Floy, Jr., Bowery Village, 1833–1837.* Edited by Richard Albert Edward Brooks. New Haven: Yale University Press, 1941.

Foster, George G. *New York by Gas-Light.* New York: Dewitt & Davenport, 1850.

_____. *New York in Slices.* New York: William H. Graham, 1849.

Fox, Louis H. "New York City Newspapers, 1820–1850." *The Papers of the Bibliographical Society of America.* Vol. 21. Chicago: University of Chicago Press, 1928.

Fox, Stephen. *Transatlantic: Samuel Cunard, Isambard Brunel, and the Great Atlantic Steamships.* New York: HarperCollins, 2003.

Francis, John W. *Old New York: Or, Reminiscences of the Past Sixty Years.* New York: W. J. Widdleton, 1865.

Franklin, H. Bruce. *Future Perfect: American Science Fiction of the Nineteenth Century.* New York: Oxford University Press, 1966.

Garrett, Thomas M. "A History of Pleasure Gardens in New York City, 1700–1865." Ph.D. diss., New York University, 1978.

Giddings, T. H. "Rushing the Transatlantic News in the 1830s and 1840s." *New-York Historical Society Quarterly* 42 (1958): 47–59.

Gilje, Paul A. *The Road to Mobocracy: Popular Disorder in New York City, 1763–1834.* Chapel Hill: University of North Carolina Press, 1987.

Gilmartin, Kevin. *Print Politics: The Press and Radical Opposition in Early Nineteenth-century England.* Cambridge: Cambridge University Press, 1996.

Gravely, William H., Jr. "A Note on the Composition of Poe's 'Hans Pfaal.'" *Poe Newsletter* 3, no. 1 (June 1970): 2–5.

Greene, Asa. *A Glance at New York.* New York: A. Greene, 1837.

Griggs, William N. *The Celebrated "Moon Story," Its Origins and Incidents.* New York: Bunnell & Price, 1852.

Guiley, Rosemary Ellen. *The Lunar Almanac.* London: Piatkus, 1991.

Hamill, Pete. *Downtown: My Manhattan.* New York: Little, Brown, 2004.

Hamilton, Thomas. *Men and Manners in America.* Edinburgh: William Blackwood, 1834.

Harris, Neil. *Humbug: The Art of P. T. Barnum.* Boston: Little, Brown, 1973.

Harrison, James A., ed. *The Complete Works of Edgar Allan Poe.* 1902. New York: AMS Press, 1965.

_____. *Life of Edgar Allan Poe.* 1903. New York: Haskell House, 1970.

Haswell, Chas. H. *Reminiscences of an Octogenarian of the City of New York (1816 to 1860).* New York: Harper & Brothers, 1896.

Headley, Joel Tyler. *The Great Riots of New York, 1712–1873.* 1873. New York: Thunder's Mouth Press, 2004.

Herschel, John. *Outlines of Astronomy.* 8th ed. London: Longmans, Green, 1865.

_____. *A Treatise on Astronomy.* London: Longman, Rees, Orme, Brown, Green & Longman, 1833.

Henkin, David M. *City Reading: Written Words and Public Spaces in Antebellum New York.* New York: Columbia University Press, 1998.

Hershkowitz, Leo. *New York City, 1834–1840: A Study in Local Politics.* 1960. Ann Arbor: University Microfilms International, 1981.

Hewitt, John Hill. *Recollections of Poe.* Atlanta: Emory University, 1949.

History of the Polish Revolution, with the Latest Atrocities of the Russian Conquerors, Compiled upon the Authority of Personal Sufferers. New York: J. & W. Day, 1834.

Hone, Philip. *The Diary of Philip Hone, 1828–1851.* Edited by Allan Nevins. New York: Dodd, Mead, 1936.

Hudson, Frederic. *Journalism in the United States, from 1690 to 1872.* 1873. New York: Haskell House, 1968.

Hughes, Helen MacGill. *News and the Human Interest Story.* New York: Greenwood, 1968.

Jackson, David J. "A Poe Hoax Comes Before the U. S. Senate." *Poe Studies* 7, no. 2 (December 1974): 47–48.

Jackson, Kenneth T., ed. *The Encyclopedia of New York City.* New Haven: Yale University Press, 1995.

Jaffe, Steven Harold. *Unmasking the City: The Rise of the Urban Newspaper Reporter in New York City, 1800–1850.* Ann Arbor: UMI Dissertation Information Services, 1995.

Johnson, Paul E., and Sean Wilentz. *The Kingdom of Matthias.* New York: Oxford University Press, 1994.

Lankevich, George J. *American Metropolis: A History of New York City.* New York: New York University Press, 1998.

Larkin, Jack. *The Reshaping of American Life, 1790–1840.* New York: Harper & Row, 1988.

Latimer, John. *The Annals of Bristol in the Nineteenth Century.* Bristol, U.K.: W. & F. Morgan, 1887.

Latrobe, John H. B. "Reminiscences of Poe." *Edgar Allan Poe: A Memorial Volume,* 57–62. Edited by Sara Sigourney Rice. Baltimore: Turnbull Brothers, 1877.

"Leaves from an Aeronaut." *Knickerbocker* 5, no. 1 (January 1835): 57–68.

Ley, Willy. *Watchers of the Skies: An Informal History of Astronomy from Babylon to the Space Age.* New York: Viking, 1963.

Lieber, Francis. *The Stranger in America: Comprising Sketches of the Manners, Society, and National Peculiarities of the United States.* London: Richard Bentley, 1835.

Lines, Harry. "Niblo's Garden." *Marquee* 13, no. 3 (Fall 1981): 3–9.

"Locke Among the Moonlings." *Southern Quarterly Review* 8, no. 16 (October 1853): 501–514.

Locke, John Goodwin. *Book of the Lockes.* Boston: James Munroe, 1853.

Locke, Richard. *Supplement to Collinson's History of Somerset.* Taunton, U.K.: Barnicotts, 1939.

Locke, Richard Adams. *Magnetism and Astronomy: A Lecture.* New York [1842].

––––––. *The Moon Hoax; or, A Discovery That the Moon Has a Vast Population of Human Beings.* New York: William Gowans, 1859.

––––––. "Mr. Locke's Moon Story." *New World* 1, no. 30 (May 16, 1840): 1.

Longworth, David. *Longworth's American Almanac, New-York Register, and City Directory.* New York: David Longworth, various dates.

Lossing, Benson J. *History of New York City, Embracing an Outline of Events from 1609 to 1830, and a Full Account of Its Development from 1830 to 1884.* New York: George E. Perine, 1884.

Lyon, Isaac S. *Recollections of an Old Cartman.* 1872. New York: New York Bound, 1984.

Martineau, Harriet. *Retrospect of Western Travel.* 3 vols. London: Saunders & Otley, 1838.

Matthew, Marie-Louise Nickerson. *Forms of Hoax in the Tales of Edgar Allan Poe.* New York: Columbia University, 1974.

Memoirs of Matthias the Prophet, With a Full Exposure of His Atrocious Impositions, and of the Degrading Delusions of His Followers. New York: New York Sun, 1835.

Miller, Perry. *The Life of the Mind in America, from the Revolution to the Civil War.* New York: Harcourt, Brace & World, 1965.

Moore, Patrick. *Sir John Herschel. Explorer of the Southern Sky.* Bath, U.K.: William Herschel Society, 1992.

Moss, Sidney P. *Poe's Literary Battles.* Durham, North Carolina: Duke University Press, 1963.

Mott, Frank Luther. *American Journalism: A History, 1690–1960.* 3rd ed. New York: Macmillan, 1962.

––––––. "Facetious News Writing, 1833–1833." *Mississippi Valley Historical Review* 29, no. 9 (June 1942): 35–54.

Musto, David F. "Yale Astronomy in the Nineteenth Century." *Ventures* 8, no. 1 (Spring 1968): 7–17.

National Cyclopædia of American Biography. New York: James T. White, 1924.

New-York As It Is, in 1835. New York: J. Disturnell, 1835.

The New-York Cries in Rhyme. New York: Mahlon Day, 1834.

Nichols, Thomas Low. *Forty Years of American Life.* 1864. 3 vols. New York: Johnson Reprint, 1969.

Nicolson, Marjorie Hope. *Voyages to the Moon.* New York: Macmillan, 1960.

––––––. "A World in the Moon: A Study of the Changing Attitude Toward the Moon in the Seventeenth and Eighteenth Centuries." *Smith College Studies in Modern Languages* 17, no. 2 (January 1936): 1–72.

O'Brien, Frank M. *The Story of "The Sun."* New York: D. Appleton, 1928.

Odell, George C. D. *Annals of the New York Stage.* New York: Columbia University Press, 1928.

Osgood, Frances S. *The Cries of New-York.* New York: John Doggett, Jr. 1846.

Ostrum, John Ward, ed. *The Letters of Edgar Allan Poe.* 15 vols. Cambridge: Harvard University Press, 1948.

Paley, William. *Natural Theology: Or, Evidences of the Existence and Attributes of the Deity, Collected From the Appearances of Nature.* 1802. Boston: Gould & Lincoln, 1854.

Parton, James. *Famous Americans of Recent Times.* Boston: Ticknor & Fields, 1867.

Payne, George Henry. *History of Journalism in the United States.* New York: D. Appleton-Century, 1940.

Pollin, Burton R., ed. *The Imaginary Voyages / Edgar Allan Poe.* New York: Gordian, 1994.

Pope-Hennessy, Una. *Edgar Allan Poe, 1809–1842: A Critical Biography.* London: Macmillan, 1934.

Posey, Meredith Neill. "Notes on Poe's *Hans Pfaall.*" *Modern Language Notes* 45, no. 8 (December 1930): 501–507.

Pray, Isaac Clark. *Memoirs of James Gordon Bennett and His Times.* New York: Stringer & Townsend, 1855.

Proctor, Richard A. *Myths and Marvels of Astronomy.* London: Chatto & Windus, 1878.

Reiss, Benjamin. *The Showman and the Slave: Race, Death, and Memory in Barnum's America.* Cambridge: Harvard University Press, 2001.

Reiss, Edmund. "The Comic Setting of 'Hans Pfaall.'" *American Literature* 29, no. 3 (November 1957): 306–309.

Report of the Trial of the Rev. Ephraim K. Avery, Methodist Minister, for the Murder of Sarah Maria Cornell, at Tiverton, in the County of Newport, Rhode Island, Before the Supreme Judicial Court of that State, May 6th, 1833. New York: William Stodart [1833].

Reynolds, David S. *Beneath the American Renaissance: The Subversive Imagination in the Age of Emerson and Melville.* New York: Alfred A. Knopf, 1988.

Richards, Leonard L. *"Gentlemen of Property and Standing": Anti-Abolition Mobs in Jacksonian America.* New York: Oxford University Press, 1970.

Ridler, J. K. "Richard Locke—Man of Many Works." *Four Men of Somerset.* Washford, U.K.: G. Court, 1984.

Riis, Jacob. "The New York Newsboy." *Century Magazine,* November 1912, 247–255.

Roarke, Constance Mayfield. *Trumpets of Jubilee: Henry Ward Beecher, Harriet Beecher Stowe, Lyman Beecher, Horace Greeley, P. T. Barnum.* New York: Harcourt, Brace, 1927.

Ruskin, Steven. *John Herschel's Cape Voyage: Private Science, Public Imagination, and the Ambitions of Empire.* Burlington, Vermont: Ashgate, 2004.

Sante, Luc. *Low Life: Lures and Snares of Old New York.* New York: Vintage, 1992.

Saxon, A. H. *P. T. Barnum: The Legend and the Man.* New York: Columbia University Press, 1989.

Saxton, Alexander. "Problems of Race and Class in the Origins of the Mass Circulation Press." *American Quarterly* 36, no. 2 (Summer 1984): 211–234.

Schlesinger, Arthur M., Jr. *The Age of Jackson.* Boston: Little, Brown, 1945.

Schroth, Raymond A. *The* Eagle *and Brooklyn.* Westport, Connecticut: Greenwood, 1974.

Scudder, Harold H. "Poe's 'Balloon Hoax.'" *American Literature* 21, no. 2 (May 1949): 179–190.

Scudder, John. *A Companion to the American Museum: Being a Catalogue of Upwards of Fifty Thousand Natural and Foreign Curiosities, Antiquities, and Productions of the Fine Arts.* New York: G. F. Hopkins, 1823.

Seavey, Ormond, ed. *The Moon Hoax: Or, A Discovery that the Moon Has a Vast Population of Human Beings.* Boston: Gregg, 1975.

Seitz, Don C. *The James Gordon Bennetts.* Indianapolis: Bobbs-Merrill, 1928.

Sherwood, Henry Hall. *The Magnetic Organization of the Human System, and Its Application to the Cure of Chronic Diseases.* New York: Tribune Steam Printing Office, 1849.

_____. *Manual for Magnetizing, with the Rotary and Vibrating Magnetic Machine, in the Duodynamic Treatment of Diseases.* New York: Wiley & Putnam, 1845.

Silverman, Kenneth. *Edgar A. Poe: Mournful and Never-ending Remembrance.* New York: Harper Perennial, 1991.

Sloan, Wm. David. "George W. Wisner: Michigan Editor and Politician." *Journalism History* 6, no. 4 (Winter 1979–1980): 113–116.

Smith, Albert. "A Go-Ahead Day with Barnum." *Bentley's Miscellany* 21 (1847): 522–527, 623–628.

Smith, Dorothy Valentine. *Staten Island: Gateway to New York.* New York: Chilton, 1970.

Smith, Elizabeth Oakes. *The Newsboy.* Boston: Phillips, Sampson, 1854.

Smith, J. R. *The Speckled Monster: Smallpox in England, 1670–1970, with Particular Reference to Essex.* Chelmsford, U.K.: Essex Record Office, 1987.

Sohncke, L. A. *Bibliotheca Mathematica.* Leipzig: Wilhelm Engelmann, 1854.

Spannuth, Jacob, and Thomas Ollive Mabbott, eds. *Doings of Gotham, by Edgar Allan Poe.* Pottsville, Pennsylvania: Jacob E. Spannuth, 1929.

Standage, Tom. *The Turk: The Life and Times of the Famous Eighteenth-Century Chess-Playing Machine.* New York: Walker, 2002.

Stevens, John D. *Sensationalism and the New York Press.* New York: Columbia University Press, 1991.

Stone, William Leete. *History of New York City from the Discovery to the Present Day.* New York: Virtue & Yorston, 1872.

Stovall, James Glen. "Richard Adams Locke." In *American Newspaper Journalists, 1690–1872,* 309–312. Edited by Perry J. Ashley. Detroit: Gale, 1985.

Tappan, Lewis. *The Life of Arthur Tappan.* London: Sampson, Low, Son, & Marston, 1870.

Taylor, Henry. *New York As It Was Sixty Years Ago.* Brooklyn: Nolan Bro's Print, 1894.

Tebbel, John. *The Compact History of the American Newspaper.* New and rev. ed. New York: Hawthorn, 1969.

"Thomas Dick, LL.D." *Living Age* 16 (April 16, 1859): 131–136.

Thomas, Dwight, and David K. Jackson. *The Poe Log: A Documentary Life of Edgar Allan Poe.* 1809–1849. Boston: G. K. Hall, 1987.

Thompson, Susan. *The Penny Press: The Origins of the Modern News Media, 1833–1861*. Northport, Alabama: Vision, 2004.

Thomson, Keith. *Before Darwin: Reconciling God and Nature*. New Haven: Yale University Press, 2005.

Tocqueville, Alexis de. *Democracy in America*. 1835. Garden City, New York: Anchor, 1969.

Trial of Henry B. Hagerman, Esq., on an Indictment for an Assault and Battery, with Intent to Murder, Committed on William Coleman, Esq., Editor of the N. Y. Evening Post. New York: Oram & Mott, 1818.

Trollope, Francis (Mrs.). *Domestic Manners of the Americans*. London: Whittaker, Treacher, 1832.

Tucher, Andie. *Froth & Scum: Truth, Beauty, Goodness, and the Ax Murder in America's First Mass Medium*. Chapel Hill: University of North Carolina Press, 1994.

Turner, Hy B. *When Giants Ruled: The Story of Park Row, New York's Great Newspaper Street*. New York: Fordham University Press, 1999.

University of Cambridge. *Alumni Cantabrigienses*. Cambridge: Cambridge University Press, 1951.

Varle, Charles. *A Complete View of Baltimore*. Baltimore: S. Young, 1833.

Wallace, Irving. *The Fabulous Showman: The Life and Times of P. T. Barnum*. New York: Alfred A. Knopf, 1959.

Ward, Phyllis. *Somerset*. London: Alfred A. Knopf, 1928.

Weissbuch, Ted N. "Edgar Allan Poe: Hoaxer in the American Tradition." *New York Historical Society Quarterly* 45 (1961): 291–309.

Werner, M. R. *Barnum*. New York: Harcourt, Brace, 1923.

Whitby, Gary L. "Horns of a Dilemma: The *Sun*, Abolition, and the 1833–34 New York Riots." *Journalism Quarterly* 67, no. 2 (Summer 1990): 410–419.

Wilentz, Sean. *Chants Democratic: New York City and the Rise of the American Working Class, 1788–1850*. 1984. New York: Oxford University Press, 2004.

Wilkinson, Ronald Sterne. "Poe's 'Balloon-Hoax' Once More." *American Literature* 32, no. 3 (November 1960): 313–317.

Williams, Michael. *The Draining of the Somerset Levels*. Cambridge: Cambridge University Press, 1970.

Wilson, James Grant. *Bryant and His Friends: Some Reminiscences of the* Knickerbocker *Writers*. New York: Fords, Howard, Hulbert, 1886.

Wimsatt, W. K., Jr. "Poe and the Chess Automaton." *American Literature* 11, no. 2 (May 1939): 138–151.

Woodberry, George E. *Edgar Allan Poe*. 1885. Boston: Houghton Mifflin, 1913.

Wyatt-Brown, Bertram. "The Abolitionists' Postal Campaign of 1835." *Journal of Negro History* 50, no. 4 (October 1965): 227–238.

INDEX